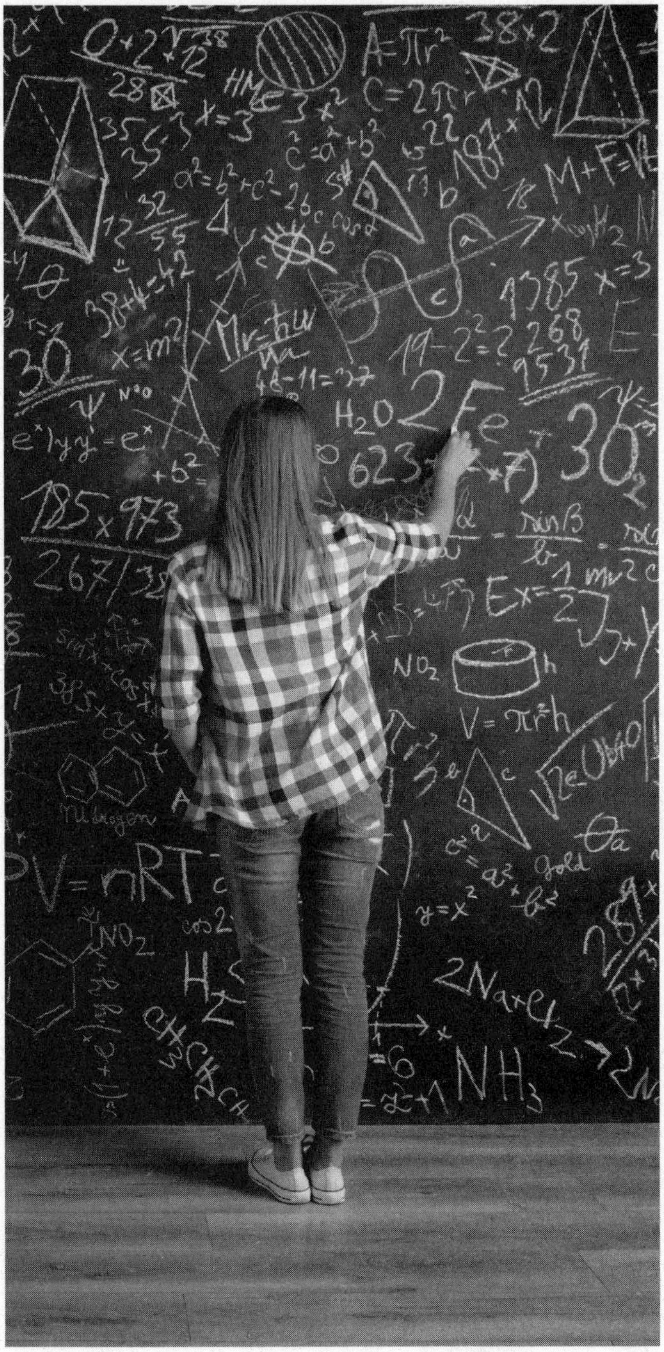

ACE THE ACT®

Kelly C. Roell, M.A.

America's Top ACT Expert

Research & Education Association

www.rea.com

Research & Education Association
61 Ethel Road West
Piscataway, New Jersey 08854
Email: info@rea.com

Ace the ACT®

Printed in the United States of America

Library of Congress Control Number 2017932504

ISBN-13: 978-0-7386-1223-2
ISBN-10: 0-7386-1223-5

E17

Contents

Week 4: Science Reasoning 191

Week 5: Writing 257

About Our Author

As a test prep contributor for both Scholastic and MSN, **Kelly C. Roell** has written thousands of articles on standardized testing that teach and inspire students all over the world to reach their highest marks on the ACT, SAT, GRE, and LSAT. A certified teacher with her master's degree in education, Kelly has designed SAT and ACT curriculum while developing individualized strategies for her students in Florida's Hillsborough County School District. She has also worked as a private ACT tutor, helping her students bump up their scores an average of 6 points on the ACT test's 36-point composite scale.

About REA

Founded in 1959, Research & Education Association (REA) is dedicated to publishing the finest and most effective educational materials—including study guides and test preps—for students of all ages.

Today, REA's wide-ranging catalog is a leading resource for students, teachers, and other professionals. Visit *www.rea.com* to see a complete listing of all our titles.

Acknowledgments

Pam Weston, Publisher

Larry Kling, Vice President, Editorial

John Cording, Vice President, Technology

Diane Goldschmidt, Managing Editor

Jennifer Calhoun, Page Design and File Preparation

Karen Lamoreux, Copyediting

Ellen Gong, Proofreading

Kathy Caratozzolo of Caragraphics, Typesetting

Welcome to REA's *Ace the ACT*!

The smart way to prepare for the ACT!

You're hoping to secure a spot at a *great* college. Funny how I know all about you, right? You're excited about what the future—college, specifically—has in store for you. The dorms, the dates, the drama, the drudgery, the degree; the classes, the credits, the community—all of it.

You're rushing full speed ahead, but stop and think for a minute. . . . How do you get into this great college? How do you score a spot in the university that is supposed to shape the rest of your life?

Your first step in the race to get in the door is to take an exam like the ACT. (But since you're reading this book, you already know that.)

Your second step is acing the ACT, which is where your purchase comes in *really* handy. This book, and the online tools that come with it, will help you maneuver your way through the ins and outs of the ACT test in just four or five weeks (the fifth week being reserved exclusively for students who *really* want to get into the colleges of their dreams).

Inside, you'll find a complete week-by-week study program with key test-taking strategies, practice questions, and a review of the skills you absolutely must have before you take the ACT. (All of this will help you get a high score on the ACT so you're accepted into that great college.)

Ace the ACT gives you everything you need to get a great ACT score, and nothing more. I don't waste your valuable study time talking about non-essential material—I give you the important stuff in an easy-to-follow, organized test prep.

Kelly Roell

How to Use REA's *Ace the ACT*

This book and the online tools that come with it are organized into weekly study sections that align with the four subtests that make up the ACT: English, Math, Reading, and Science Reasoning. We've also included a section for the optional ACT Writing Test.

Ace the ACT puts you on the path to success and gets you ready for the exam. Here's how:

Review the Book: Each week, study the material related to a single section of the ACT. The proven strategies will help you tackle any question you may see on test day.

Test Yourself & Get Feedback: After you finish reviewing for the week, go to the online REA Study Center and test yourself with a full-length practice test for that week's subject. Score reports from your online test give you a fast way to pinpoint what you really know and what you should spend more time studying.

Improve Your Score: Armed with your score reports, go back and review the parts of the book where you are the weakest, or, if you've mastered the material, simply move on to the next week's study section.

The REA Study Center

The best way to improve your score is to get frequent feedback on what you know and what you don't. At the online REA Study Center (*www.rea.com/studycenter*) you have access to two types of assessment tools: practice tests for each section of the ACT and a full-length practice test covering all five test sections. Each of these tools provides true-to-format questions and delivers a detailed score report that pinpoints your strengths and weaknesses and shows you where to focus your study.

The ACT Test Basics

The ACT Test Has 4 Required Multiple-Choice Sections

- **English**
    - 75 questions
    - 45 minutes
    - Reporting categories: Production of Writing, Knowledge of Language, and Conventions of Standard English

- **Math**
  - 60 questions
  - 60 minutes
  - Reporting categories: Preparing for Higher Math, Integrating Essential Skills, and Modeling
- **Reading**
  - 40 questions
  - 35 minutes
  - Reporting categories: Key Ideas and Details, Craft and Structure, Integration of Knowledge and Ideas
- **Science Reasoning**
  - 40 questions
  - 35 minutes
  - Reporting categories: Interpretation of Data, Scientific Investigation, Evaluation of Models, Inferences, and Experimental Results

The ACT Test Has 1 Optional Essay

Although the essay is technically optional, there are three phenomenal reasons you should just go ahead and register for the Enhanced ACT Writing Test, too.

1. **It's short:** The essay is only 40 minutes long. That means it's less time than a typical class period. So why sweat 40 minutes?
2. **It could be required:** Many universities that you'd like to attend actually require the ACT essay. So, although it's "optional," it isn't always. You'll have to check with each school to which you want to apply. Why hesitate? Just take it so you're covered. For the record, I searched 20 different schools randomly—everything from Harvard to Wichita State University—and every single one of them either required or recommended that you take ACT Plus Writing. So, your chances of getting out of this thing are slim.
3. **It'll reduce later stress:** If you end up deciding to attend a school where the Writing test is required, then you don't have to schedule another day of testing

to go back and take the *whole* ACT over again just for the essay. Yes, you read that right. The Writing test only comes as an attachment to the *entire ACT test,* so if you need the essay, you'll have to take each multiple-choice section again!

"I'm Not Taking ACT Writing Test"

Did I just hear you say you're still not taking the ACT Writing Test? First of all, why not? You should be, and will probably have to. Regardless, if you're 100% sure you don't have to take the ACT Writing Test, you can still follow the program in this book. Just be sure NOT to complete the optional Week 5. There, fixed.

Taking the ACT Online

The online version of the ACT is available only to schools, districts, and states that administer the ACT to all students on a school day as part of their assessment programs. It is not available on the national test dates, so if you were hoping to sign up for the online ACT and forego bubbling in all of those little ovals, sorry! You can't sign up for it.

The good news? The only difference between the online version of the ACT and the paper-and-pencil version is the delivery format itself. Instead of filling in bubbles next to the answers with a pencil, you will select the answers on a computer screen. Other than that, the tests are the same. So, the preparation is the same, regardless of the test format.

ACT Scores

As of 2016, the ACT changed how it reports scoring. Instead of receiving subscores based on the subcategories under each section, students now receive percentages on a comprehensive set of reporting categories. These reporting categories make it easier for parents and students to determine exactly what types of skills testers need to brush up on the most. Here's what your current score report will contain:

- **Composite Score:** Your composite score will be between a 1 (really low) and 36 (genius). This is an average of each multiple-choice section.

- **Section Scores:** Each multiple-choice test section (English, Math, Reading, and Science) will get a raw score, based on the total number of questions you answer correctly. That score will then be converted to a scaled score, between 1 and 36.
- **STEM Score:** The ACT reports a STEM score that is the rounded average of Math and Science.
- **ELA Score:** The ACT reports the rounded average of English, Reading, and Writing scores as a general English Language Arts score.
- **Reporting Categories:** Although you will not get scores for these specific reporting categories per se, you will receive percentages correct out of the categories along with the total possible and total correct.
- **ACT Plus Writing:** If you take the Writing test, you'll get an overall score between 2 and 12, along with four writing competency scores on a scale of 2 to 12 in these areas: Ideas and Analysis, Development and Support, Organization, and Language Use and Conventions.

Good Scores: The national average for composite scores tends to hover around a 21 (ACT.org). Many scholarships require at least a 27 composite score, depending on the school and program. If you care to see a sample score report for the ACT test, search "score report" at *www.act.org.*

ACT Registration

- Registering for the ACT is a piece of cake. If you are not testing internationally, you can do it right online at *http://ACTstudent.org.* Or, you can register with a "Register by Mail" packet, which you *must do* if you cannot pay by credit card or are testing under the age of 13.
- The ACT Test fee changes yearly, so it's best to check the website for the most up-to-date fees. Speaking of fees, the ACT also has a slew of other costs for things like changing your test center or test date, testing on a standby basis, or registering late.

Test Day

Test Day Schedule

8:00 AM	Check-in deadline. Don't be late! The test will start shortly after 8:00 AM, as soon as everyone is checked in and seated.
45 min.	ACT English Test
60 min.	ACT Mathematics Test
10 min.	Short Break
35 min.	ACT Reading Test
35 min.	ACT Science Reasoning
12:15 PM	Students taking the ACT Test without Writing are dismissed.
5 min.	Short Break
40 min.	ACT Writing Test
1:00 PM	Students taking ACT Plus Writing are dismissed.

Bring This Stuff to the Test Center

- **Your admission ticket.** You get this when you register. It must be a printed copy; the test center will NOT allow you to show you the ticket from your phone, nor will they print it for you.
- **Photo ID.** Your driver's license, a passport, student photo ID, etc. Check the official ACT website at *ACTstudent.org* if you don't have any of those things for other appropriate photo IDs.
- **Pencils.** If you're taking the paper-and-pencil ACT, be sure to have a handful of No. 2 sharpened pencils. If you're taking the Writing tests, you'll be writing your essay in pencil.
- **Eraser.** Make it a big one, in case things go wrong and you have to erase a whole page of ovals at a time.
- **Calculator.** This must be an ACT-approved one.

- **A silent watch.** If your watch's alarm goes off, you automatically have to turn in your test without it being scored and leave. I'm not kidding. You won't be allowed to have your cell phone with you either, so make sure to have a noiseless watch—there's no guarantee your testing site will have a working clock on the wall.

General Strategies for the ACT Test

- Answer Easy Questions First: Although the ACT doesn't arrange the test questions in order of difficulty, you should always answer the easy questions first—tough questions aren't worth any more points, so don't waste your time if you can solve two easy questions in the time it takes you to solve one toughie.
- If It's Half Right, It's All the Way Wrong. The ACT is tricky in that it will provide answer choices that are *almost* correct. If part of the answer choice is wrong, the whole thing is wrong. Cross it off, and choose another letter.
- Answer Every Question. Always. You aren't penalized for guessing, so always give it a shot. You have a 25 percent chance of answering correctly on English, Science, and Reading, and a 20 percent chance of answering correctly on Math. You never know—you may just get it right by dumb luck. But first, be sure to follow my next strategy.
- Eliminate Answer Choices Before Guessing: You've learned this skill throughout high school; now is a great time to use it. When taking a multiple-choice test, there will be at least one answer choice that will be obviously incorrect. Scratch it off and guess from there to increase your odds of getting the answer right.
- Use Your Pencil: When you get rid of answer choices, cross them off with your pencil so you're not tempted to choose them again. Underline anything you think is important as you read. Make diagrams to work out problems. Use that pencil in your hand to help you. If your hand is engaged, your mind will stay more focused.
- Pick a Guessing Letter if You Only Have a Minute Left: If you run out of time, and you need to go through the test and fill in ovals in the last minute (remember, no penalty), choose the *same letter* to use on every guess. Statistically, you'll guarantee yourself more points if you choose the same letter every time, whereas if you oval in different letters, you could miss every one of the questions. Because the ACT switches back and forth between A, B, C, D, F, G, H, and J for answer choices, be

sure to keep the letter position the same. (Choose B and G for example). Only do this if you can't narrow down an answer!

- **Answer Questions in Your Test Booklet.** Instead of going back and forth between the test and your answer sheet, just circle the letters of the correct answers in the test booklet while you're working, and then, every ten questions or so, fill them in on the answer sheet. You'll save time!
- **Don't Stress Out.** You have already learned all the skills you need to know to smash the ACT test into the next century. Relax. You can do this.

Get Started!

Now let's jump into Week 1 and get ready to master the strategies that will lead you to an excellent ACT score!

Week 1: English

1

ACT English Test Basics

The ACT English test has:

- 5 passages of text 30–40 lines long or approximately 325 words on average.
- 15 questions per passage.
- 5 passages × 15 questions = 75 questions total.
- 4 answer choices per question.

You'll be tested:

- for 45 minutes.
- with questions related to a single word, a single sentence, a paragraph, or the entire passage as a whole.

You'll receive:

- a single subject ACT English score on a scale of 1–36.
- three competency scores in these subareas: Production of Writing, Knowledge of Language, and Conventions of Standard English.

In order to score well:

- you must master ACT test-taking strategies.
- you must master ACT English content strategies.

General Strategies for the English Section

- **Pace Yourself.** To answer all 75 questions in 45 minutes, you'll have to spend 36 seconds or less per question, so don't spend all day on a question that's stumping you.
- **Don't Change Every Answer.** Nearly one in five of the ACT English error-correction questions are correct as written. The first answer choice on many of the questions will be "NO CHANGE." Consider it every single time.
- **Use "DELETE."** Once in a while, "DELETE the underlined portion" (take it out of the sentence altogether) will be one of your answer choices. Twenty-five percent of the time, this will be the correct choice when it's offered.
- **Speak.** As a last-ditch effort if you truly have no idea, try mouthing the sentence to yourself. The test proctor will probably shush you, but he or she isn't the one with an ACT score at stake.
- **Don't Make a New Error:** Many of the questions on the ACT will test more than one aspect of English (i.e., comma usage and sentence parallelism). Check out each answer choice carefully! Be careful not to choose an answer that creates a new, different error.
- **Pay Attention to Paragraphs:** The ACT English section looks funny. The paragraphs have big spaces in between them to keep the text in line with the questions. Do not mistake these spaces for paragraph breaks! Just pay attention to the indents of the first sentences, so you'll know where one paragraph starts and another ends. If you don't know what this looks like, check out the practice test on p. 293.
- **Answer Easy Questions First.** Tough ACT English questions are easy to spot—they'll actually ask you a question. The easy ones will not. Answer all of the easy questions first. Why? Since they dive right into the answer choices without asking you a question first, they take up less time and are worth the same number of points as the difficult questions.

Here is how some of them look:

- Easy Question

  1. The next day, using old thread, for weaving she sets the loom and begins the quilt that will become her baby's only source of nightly warmth during the upcoming winter.

     A. NO CHANGE

     B. day, using old thread for weaving,

     C. day, using old thread for weaving;

     D. day using old thread, for weaving,

- Tougher Question

  2. Which of the following sentences would best continue the personal theme expressed here?

     A. As I grew older, I found I had a talent for numbers, and studied accountancy.

     B. Twenty years later, I had gone into engineering, and soon went to work for NASA.

     C. Throughout high school, I studied acting and drama, and began working with dinner theatre after graduation.

     D. It took me several years, but by the time I was 20, I had graduated from Clown College and begun working with a small family-run operation.

Take a peek at the following steps for solving an easy ACT English question.

Steps for Solving an Easy ACT English Question:

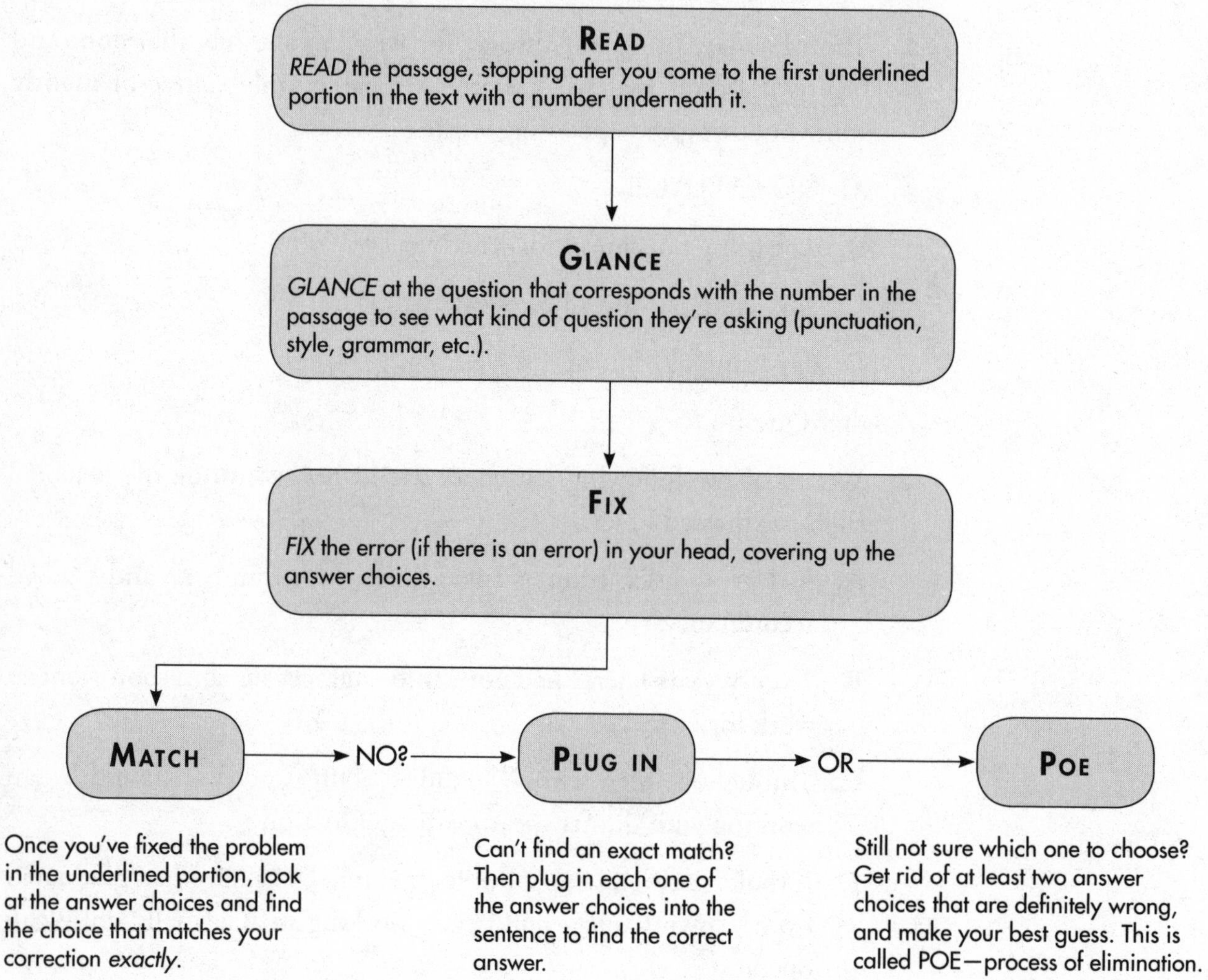
READ
READ the passage, stopping after you come to the first underlined portion in the text with a number underneath it.
GLANCE
GLANCE at the question that corresponds with the number in the passage to see what kind of question they're asking (punctuation, style, grammar, etc.).
FIX
FIX the error (if there is an error) in your head, covering up the answer choices.
MATCH
NO?
PLUG IN
OR
POE
Once you've fixed the problem in the underlined portion, look at the answer choices and find the choice that matches your correction *exactly*.
Can't find an exact match? Then plug in each one of the answer choices into the sentence to find the correct answer.
Still not sure which one to choose? Get rid of at least two answer choices that are definitely wrong, and make your best guess. This is called POE—process of elimination.

You'll use this **RGFM**, **No**, and **PorP** strategy often when answering easy questions.

Once you've mastered the easy ACT English questions, I'll introduce you to the steps for solving a tough ACT English question.

Conventions of Standard English: 38–42 questions

Remember when I said that you will be tested in three different areas on the ACT English section? Well, one of them is Conventions of Standard English, which sounds scary and downright mean, but it isn't. Basically, you will see questions about this kind of stuff:

- Punctuation
- Sentence Structure and Formation
- Grammar and Usage

These questions typically fall into the "easy" category, so I'll show you how to solve them using the easy method.

Punctuation

For most of these punctuation questions, you'll have little difficulty determining which answer selection to choose. But just in case you're unsure of a skill, we'll review the areas most commonly tested.

Let's start by figuring out the difference between a sentence and something not so sentency. Why? There's no use explaining where a comma goes if you're stuck on a basic skill.

Complete Sentences

Complete sentences will always have a subject, a main verb, and a complete idea:

Despite Blake's continued efforts to get Stacy to notice him, Stacy chose to date Matt.

Subject: Stacy

Main Verb: chose

Complete idea? Yes. We know exactly what's going on here.

Everything changed, however, once Stacy realized that Matt was in love with someone else.

Subject: Everything

Main Verb: changed

Complete idea? Yes. Again, we know the intended meaning of the sentence. Things are clear.

Stop.

Subject: You (the understood "you")

Main Verb: stop

Complete idea? Yes. When someone says "stop," we know exactly what to do.

Incomplete Sentences

Incomplete sentences may or may not have a subject/verb combo, but they NEVER have a complete idea.

After Stacy realized that Matt wasn't worth her time, and decided to focus on school, anyway.

Subject: We're still waiting for that. We'll have to assume it's Stacy, but we could be wrong.

Verb: Again, we're still waiting for it.

Complete idea? No. We're left with questions. After she decided to focus on school, did she dump him? Did she start dating Blake? Did she get that 4.0 she'd been chasing? We'll never know. It would be complete if the "After" were removed, but it isn't.

Commas

Commas have a multitude of jobs in a sentence. They set off appositives and nonrestrictive clauses; they separate lists; they follow introductory material in a sentence; they connect independent clauses when used with a conjunction, and perform many other tasks.

HEADS UP

Make sure the words and phrases in between commas in a list are parallel:

> *Dogs and cats, lizards, and fish make great pets* = bad.
>
> *Dogs, cats, lizards, and fish make great pets* = good.

Although you should be somewhat familiar with what a comma does in a sentence, you don't need to know all of those technical terms. Why? The only job you'll have on ACT English is determining if comma placement is correct or incorrect.

STRATEGY ALERT

How to Figure Out if a Comma Is Right or Wrong

Do the Comma Pause Test. Commas are most often used for pause in a sentence. And yes, I realize that "pausing" is not an official comma job, but figuring out if the commas match where you'd naturally breathe in a sentence is the best way for you to determine where they should go.

Let's try it. Take a look at this sentence, similar to something you'd find on the ACT:

> The next day, using old thread, for weaving she sets the loom and begins the quilt that will become her baby's only source of nightly warmth during the upcoming winter.

A. NO CHANGE

B. day, using old thread for weaving,

C. day, using old thread for weaving;

D. day using old thread, for weaving,

HEADS UP

Make sure there are commas on either side of a word or group of words you can pull right out of a sentence and still have a sentence, like "**using old thread for weaving**." Totally yankable.

So, to determine if the commas work in this sentence, do the **Comma Pause Test**. Read the sentence from above, pausing or taking a breath where the commas are in the text to see if they make sense to you.

The next day (pause) using old thread (pause) for weaving she sets the loom . . .

Err??? That sentence does not compute with the commas where they are, which is one reason you should always use **RGFM No? P or P** for easy questions. Step four tells you to fix the problem (if there is one) yourself before reading the answer choices.

Try it with the sentence above. Read the sentence with the commas removed to see where you naturally pause.

The next day using old thread for weaving she sets the loom . . .

Did it sound something like this?

The next day (pause) using old thread for weaving (pause) she sets the loom . . .

If so, you'd be correct. If you replace those pauses with commas, you have the correct comma locations. Match it against the answer choices. See a choice that fits the pauses you put in? Answer Choice B! It's the best answer. Choice C includes a semicolon instead of a comma. Why isn't that correct? Read on.

Semicolons

Semicolons come at the end of a complete idea. The only difference between semicolons and end marks is that semicolons have to have words behind them that relate to the complete idea, whereas end marks like periods, exclamation points, and question marks do not.

> **HEADS UP**
>
> Semicolons should never come before a coordinating conjunction such as *and, but, for, nor, or, so, yet.*
>
> *I love the banjo; and Jimmy likes polka.* = bad.

Natalie, a muenster cheese aficionado, often has noxious breath.

Natalie, a muenster cheese aficionado, often has noxious breath; since she's my best friend, I always give her a mint when she has indulged too much.

Think of the semicolon as a yield sign; you definitely need to slow down, but unlike the full stop provided by an end mark, you can resume driving a little sooner.

STRATEGY ALERT

How to Figure Out if a Semicolon Is Right or Wrong

Replace it with an end mark: Since a semicolon functions almost identically to an end mark, and you will never be forced to choose between a properly used end mark and a semicolon on the ACT, just take the semicolon out and see if a period would work in its place. If it does, you're right on the money.

Choosing correctly will become even clearer when we get to sentence structure!

Colons

Colons are used after a statement (an independent clause, a complete idea) to let you know that a quotation, example, list, or explanation is coming up.

Teenagers have three choices: be good, be bad, or be good at being bad.

Colons basically function like an equal sign in a math equation. The complete idea in front of the colon should be equal to the stuff behind it. In fact, if you think about it visually, a colon can be extended to form an equal sign. Take the two dots of the colon and draw them out to the right. What do you get? : = Exactly.

STRATEGY ALERT

How to Figure Out if a Colon Is Right or Wrong

Check for independence and equality. In order for a colon to be correct, two things have to happen:

1. **Independence:** The statement in front of the colon has to be able to stand alone as a sentence.
2. **Equality:** The words behind the colon need to equal the statement in front of the colon.

Teenagers have three choices = be good, be bad, or be good at being bad.

See? The three choices = being good, being bad, and being good at being bad. Each side of the equation is equal to the other (**equality!**), and the statement in front of the colon could stand alone as a sentence (**independence!**).

Let's try it. Take a look at this easy question, similar to something you'd find on the ACT:

> Being indebted to my family, especially <u>my aunts: Alexa Perez,</u> my first teacher, and Isabel Caminero, the woman who taught me how to sing—only makes me work harder to please them.
>
> **A.** NO CHANGE
>
> **B.** my aunts, Alexa Perez,
>
> **C.** my aunts. Alexa Perez,
>
> **D.** my aunts—Alexa Perez,

First, follow the first part of the **RGFM No? P or P** strategy for easy questions: read, glance, fix, and match. The first three are already done for you. So, try to fix the problem (if you think there is one) yourself before looking at the answers. Are "my aunts" = Alexa Perez and Isabel Caminero? Yes! The equal-sign test works. Is the statement in front of the colon a complete idea? It isn't! It couldn't stand alone as a sentence. So, can you fix it by yourself? It might be hard, what with all the dashes, commas, and strange sentence parts hanging around.

So, move on to **P or P. Plug In or POE**. Start by taking a look at the answer choices and plug them in to see if one would work. We only have two to choose from because we know Choice A is wrong as is, so we can automatically knock out Choice C, because just like a colon, you can't put a period in there unless the statement is complete.

That leaves B and D. Does B work? No! That comma would need a second one, right after the word *sing*. Choice D is the correct one, because of that dash. The dash mirrors the one later in the sentence, and if you take out all of the info in between those two dashes, the sentence would still make sense. Not familiar with dashes? Read on.

Dashes

Dashes can be used exactly like the colon when only one shows up in a sentence.

> *Teenagers have three choices—be good, be bad, or be good at being bad.*

Dashes can function like commas, by sitting on either side of some sort of interruption in a sentence. In this scenario, two of them must be in the sentence.

> *My English teacher, the one who tucks in her sweaters, is really smart, but socially awkward.*

> *My English teacher—the one who tucks in her sweaters—is really smart, but socially awkward.*

HEADS UP

On the ACT, dashes and colons will often follow an incomplete idea. They'll also come in front of a clause beginning with the word "that." Those are the two most popular ways the ACT writers will trip you up.

> *After I bought this stuff at the mall: sweaters, hats, and scarves.* (BAD)

> *I bought this stuff at the mall: sweaters, hats and scarves.* (GOOD)

> *I have to tell you something: that you are cool.* (BAD)

> *I have to tell you something: you are cool.* (GOOD)

STRATEGY ALERT

How to Figure Out if a Dash Is Right or Wrong

For one dash, use the Independence and Equality Test. If there is just one dash, make sure that there is a complete sentence before the dash, and an equal statement following it.

> My English teacher has some strange quirks—she tucks her sweaters into her skirt and mutters prepositions to herself when she grades in class.

> My English teacher has some strange quirks = she tucks her sweaters into her skirt and mutters prepositions to herself when she grades in class.

For two dashes, take out the interruption. If the interrupting material in the sentence can be taken out with the meaning intact, then the dashes are correct in the sentence.

> My English teacher—the one who tucks in her sweaters—is really smart, but socially awkward.

> My English teacher is really smart, but socially awkward.

Apostrophes

Apostrophes show possession.

Mark's new helmet sure is shiny.

Bess's elliptical machine is really dusty.

Apostrophes take the place of missing letters.

I cannot begin to express my irritation.

I can't begin to express my irritation.

Sounds easy, right? It is! However, there are a couple of instances of apostrophe usage that can be confusing.

HEADS UP

Add 's to the end of a singular word, even if it ends in *s*:

Bess's homework

Add ' to the end of plural words to show possession:

cats' snack

philanthropists' contributions

Tricky Apostrophe Usages

1. The difference between "its" and "it's"
2. The difference between "whose" and "who's"

It's: The apostrophe takes the place of letters here. "It's" means "It has" or "It is."

***It's** rained for seven days straight.*

*I'd love to go with you tonight, but **it's** crazy at band practice right now.*

Its: This word shows possession of the pronoun "it."

*Those little pointy things on the front of the beetle are **its** pincers.*

*Even though the show ended tragically, I wasn't sad because of **its** theme.*

Who's: This word is the contraction between "who" and "is" or "who" and "has."

***Who's** already signed up for the Irish dancing class?*

*I'd love to know **who's** going to be fortunate enough to take me to prom.*

Whose: This word shows possession of the word "who."

Whose *shoes are out in the rain?*

Brady wonders about those people ***whose*** *lives revolve around Sasquatch sightings.*

STRATEGY ALERT

How to Figure Out if an Apostrophe Is Right or Wrong

Make it a Movie Title. To determine if something is possessive, turn the words into a movie title by switching the order and putting "of" or "of the" in the middle. "The dog's day," becomes "The Day of the Dog." "Its pincers" becomes "The Pincers of It."

If you can turn it into a movie title, the apostrophe is showing possession. If you can't, the apostrophe is either showing a contraction, or is misplaced. Practice your new movie title skills in question two on page 22.

Practice Punctuation

Here is your first real chance to use the entire **RGFM No? P or P** strategy. So, **R**ead the text until the first underlined section, **G**lance at the question for that underline to see what's being tested, **F**ix the problem (if there is one and it's easy) yourself, and **M**atch your answer to the choices.

If you can't find your match, then **P**lug in the answer choices. Still not sure? Use the **P**rocess of **E**limination and get rid of at least two answers that are definitely incorrect.

Anyone who has been an American citizen for any length of time has been acquainted with the "I have a dream" speech given by Dr. Martin Luther King. He speaks of a place where people of all races, nationalities [1] and colors can live together peaceably, as brothers. Apparently, Spike Lee was feeling ambitious in much the same way when he directed the movie *Do the Right Thing*. This film stresses the disharmony between the races, and it's effect [2] on the American Dream.

Do the Right Thing, set in Brooklyn, New York, is the epitome of the American Dream gone awry. Sal, after working hard to save money, follows his dreams of success, he opens [3] a pizzeria, and hangs pictures of famous Italian-Americans on the wall. He "built the place with his own two hands," he later told Mookie, his best friend. His American Dream was taking place before his own eyes, although his son, Pino—racist by anyone's standard—hates [4] the shop and the African-Americans that move in after the Italians move away.

The racial stresses in the movie are incredibly obvious the message [5] that Spike Lee tries to get across is not. He furtively instructs the audience to make up its own mind about racism, violence, and the American Dream.

1.
- A. NO CHANGE
- B. races and nationalities,
- C. races; nationalities
- D. races, nationalities,

2.
- F. NO CHANGE
- G. its effect
- H. its' effect
- J. it's, effect

3.
- A. NO CHANGE
- B. success he opens
- C. success: by opening
- D. success; he opens

4.
- F. NO CHANGE
- G. Pino—racist by anyone's standard, hates
- H. Pino racist by anyone's standard; hates
- J. Pino, racist by anyone's standard hates,

5.
- A. NO CHANGE
- B. obvious, however the message
- C. obvious, the message
- D. obvious; the message

Answers on page 58.

Sentence Structure and Formation

Sentence structure is associated closely with punctuation; now that you have punctuation firmly in your grasp, we can move forward.

Today, you'll be figuring out how to identify structure errors like run-ons, comma splices, parallelism shifts, and a few other awesome issues with which the ACT likes to test your skills.

These types of ACT questions are almost always easy, which means that the answer choices usually will not be preceded by a question. So for the most part, you'll again use your RGFM No? P or P method for answering easy questions.

SENTENCE STRUCTURE ERRORS

FRAGMENTS

The sentence is missing a major piece—subject, main verb, or complete idea.

I. Use. Fragments. All. The. Time. Because they're cute. And Because they're fun.

Even though she told him she'd be there by 9:00.

RUN-ONS

Two or more sentences are smooshed together without punctuation.

Bill decided to just go home he was tired after basketball practice, and the party was lame, anyway.

Aristotle was a genius he invented the light bulb, right?

COMMA SPLICES

A comma joins two complete sentences.

Kaden could think of two reasons to join the chess club, he was smart, and Lily, his crush since preschool, was president.

Joanna tried on shirts and shorts, dresses and overalls, she found nothing to wear to the barn dance.

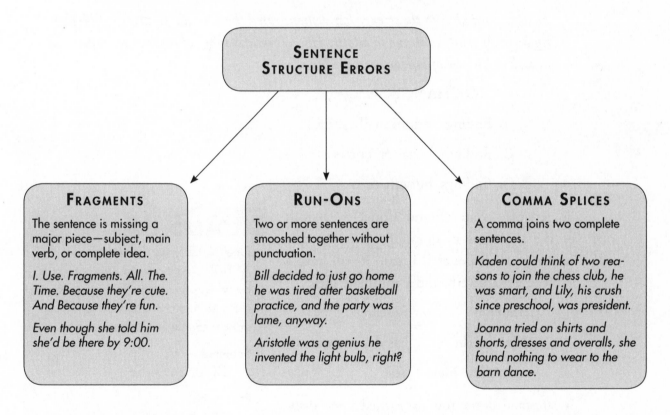

STRATEGY ALERT

How to Figure Out if a Sentence Contains Structural Errors

Play the "Can It Stand Alone?" Game Show: Make like Pat Sajak and host your own fabulous new game show—"Can It Stand Alone?" Look at both sentences on either side of the underlined word, and decide if each can stand alone as complete sentences with a subject, a main verb, and a complete idea. Do this, and win a fabulous prize: a higher score on the ACT.

Let's try playing the sentence parts game show with a few questions similar to those you'd see on the ACT:

> *Further research into the science has demonstrated the absolute certainty of Horace's <u>findings. As critics</u> continue to admire Horace's skillful usage of modern scientific tools as well as his ease of language in the lab reports.*

A. NO CHANGE

B. findings. Additionally, critics

C. findings; however, critics

D. findings, but critics

So, let's play "**Can It Stand Alone?**" with both of the sentences in question. Can the first sentence stand alone? If it can, it will have a subject, a main verb, and a complete idea:

Subject: Research

Main verb: has demonstrated

Complete idea: Yes!

It can stand alone. You just earned a new dishwasher. Now, try the second sentence:

Subject: critics

Main verb: continue

Complete idea: No—not with that "As" in the beginning. That turns the independent clause into a dependent clause, so it can't stand alone. That second "sentence" is really a fragment.

HEADS UP

One of the most common ways the ACT will create a sentence fragment is by adding a word to the beginning of a clause that can stand alone—for instance: *after, when, because, as, if,* etc.

Sentence:

She couldn't sleep.

Fragments:

After she couldn't sleep.
When she couldn't sleep.
Because she couldn't sleep.
If she couldn't sleep.

Those are all fragments!

That means Choice A is out. So, which one of the three remaining answer choices fixes the fragment and keeps the sentence meaning intact? Both C and D change the meaning of the two sentences. Positive things are being said about Horace in the first sentence and positive things are being said about him in the second. Adding a "however" or a "but" would indicate that someone should be bashing Horace in the second sentence, which no one is doing.

Now, if we were just considering sentence structure, both B and C would make the cut. They both fix the fragment correctly. Choice B, however, keeps the meaning intact, too. Choice B, you've won again, and reader, if you guessed correctly, you did, too.

Let's try another one:

> Tatiana's sister taught her to paint, and she mastered oil, acrylic and watercolor with such ease that Aunt Esther declared her talent a "gift from the heavens above."

Which one of the following alternatives to the underlined portion would NOT be acceptable?

F. paint; she

G. paint, and she then

H. paint she

J. paint. She

Okay, here your pencil will come in handy. When you see a "NOT" question like the one above, you'll need to treat the question like a true and false. Anything that **would be an acceptable alternative** gets a **"T"** for **TRUE** next to it. Anything that **wouldn't be an acceptable alternative** gets an **"F"** for **FALSE** next to it.

The best way to tackle this type of question is by plugging in the answer choices to see what would work.

Choice F would read: Tatiana's sister taught her to paint; she mastered oil, acrylic and . . .

Choice G would read: Tatiana's sister taught her to paint, and she then mastered oil, acrylic and . . .

Choice H would read: Tatiana's sister taught her to <u>paint she</u> mastered oil, acrylic and . . .

Choice J would read: Tatiana's sister taught her to <u>paint. She</u> mastered oil, acrylic and . . .

Go through each choice right now and write a "T" next to the ones that work and an "F" next to the one that doesn't. Write in the book with your pencil.

Choice F = T. Can it stand alone? Yes. The semicolon functions correctly.

Choice G = T. Can it stand alone? Yes. Adding a comma with the coordinating conjunction "and" puts the two clauses together nicely.

Choice H = F. Can it stand alone? No. That's a run-on.

Choice J = T. Can it stand alone? It works. Two sentences would be just fine, here.

So, the correct answer (because it is incorrect) is Choice H.

Did you notice anything about this question? It's not like the previous ones we completed.

Let's make a note that this is one of those instances where you'd be answering this question on your second pass through the English section. Why? It's a difficult one! Because there is a question in front of the answer choices, you would have circled this, along with the other tough questions, as one to come back to. *Also, it could use a different strategy, which I'll soon introduce.*

Parallelism

Parallelism is a similarity of structure in a pair or series of related words, phrases, or clauses.

Not Parallel*	Parallel
Last year, Jimmy ran the 5K, 10K, half-marathon, and full. *It's missing the "the" before each word in the series.	*Last year, Jimmy ran the 5K, the 10K, the half-marathon, and the full.*
Alison's concerns were mainly about Lisa's performance in school and how she gave her attitude at home. *The sentence uses a prepositional phrase for the first concern and a subordinate clause for the second.	*Alison's concerns were mainly about Lisa's performance in school and her attitude at home.*
In the summer, Jack usually likes swimming with dolphins and to jet-ski across the Gulf of Mexico. *The sentence uses a gerund and an infinitive.	*In the summer, Jack usually likes swimming with dolphins and jet-skiing across the Gulf of Mexico.*
As we got closer to the party, you could hear the bass thumping from Jay-Z's new one, and I felt certain the neighbors would call the police. *The sentence switches person in the pronouns.	*As we got closer to the party, we could hear the bass thumping from Jay-Z's new single, and I felt certain the neighbors would call the police.*
I don't know about you, but I think the value at McDonald's is much better than Wendy's. *The sentence uses a noun with a prepositional phrase at first, then switches to just the noun.	*I don't know about you, but I think the value at McDonald's is much better than the value at Wendy's.*

STRATEGY ALERT

How to Figure Out if a Sentence Is Parallel or Not

Play The "Name That Part of Speech" Game Show: Again, it's time to have a little fun and win some outstanding prizes, too. Let's play the "Name That Part of Speech" Game show, shall we!

Roger, tell 'em how to play!

Roger: "If you can label the parts of speech in the non-underlined part of the sentence, you'll be able to figure out if the underlined section is parallel to it or not. Sounds easy, doesn't it? It is! Try it here!"

You could either study diligently over a long period or <u>try cramming for a few hours before the test.</u>

A. NO CHANGE

B. attempt to cram for a few hours before the test.

C. cram quickly for a few hours before the test.

D. you could try cramming for a few hours before the test.

HEADS UP

Make sure to look for consistency with verbs, too. If a past tense verb is used in the first item of a list, it should be used in the second.

Poppy wanted a milkshake, but Ebony has the last one. = BAD

Poppy wanted a milkshake, but Ebony HAD the last one. = GOOD

To figure this out, identify the parts of speech in the non-underlined part of the sentence. It'll show you if there is a parallelism error in the underlined portion.

Present Verb	Adverb	Prepositional Phrase
study	**diligently**	**over a long period**

Present Verb	Gerund	Prepositional Phrase
<u>try</u>	**<u>cramming</u>**	**<u>for a few hours before the test.</u>**

It isn't parallel, so that means Choice A is out. Which one of the other choices follows the same pattern: present tense verb, adverb, prepositional phrase? Choice C. You're right!

Practice Sentence Structure and Formation

Use the **RGFM No? P or P** strategy. **R**ead the text until the first underlined section, **G**lance at the question for that underline to see what's being tested, **F**ix the problem (if there is one) yourself, and **M**atch your answer to the choices.

If you can't find your match, then **P**lug in the answer choices. Still not sure? Use the **P**rocess of **E**limination and get rid of at least two answers that are definitely incorrect.

During the closing months of World War I, England and the United States worked hand in <u>hand. As they formed</u> [1] the Allied Submarine Devices Investigation Committee, whose goal was to obtain effective underwater detection equipment from those experts in <u>technology fields and scientists.</u> [2] The committee developed <u>a trainable hydrophone and an innovative snorkel</u> [3] (a device for bringing air to the crew and engines when operating submerged on diesels).

At the end of World War II, the United States enhanced the snorkel and developed the Guppy (short for Greater Underwater Propulsion Power), a conversion of the fleet-type submarine of World War II fame. Performance increased greatly with the new electrical equipment, the additional battery capacity, and <u>the fact of the addition of the innovative Guppy</u>, [4] making the submarine a truly formidable craft. Reducing the surface area, streamlining every protruding object, and enclosing the periscope shears in a streamlined metal fairing <u>of the superstructure</u>. [5]

1.

A. NO CHANGE
B. hand: as they formed
C. hand. They formed
D. hand, because they formed

2.

F. NO CHANGE
G. the fields of technology and those experts in the field of science.
H. technology fields and experts in science.
J. the fields of technology and science.

3.

A. NO CHANGE
B. a trainable hydrophone and the innovative snorkel
C. both the trainable hydrophone and an innovative snorkel
D. both a hydrophone and an innovative snorkel

4.

F. NO CHANGE
G. adding the innovative Guppy,
H. the innovative Guppy,
J. streamlining and adding the innovative Guppy,

5.

A. NO CHANGE
B. of the superstructure, itself.
C. of the superstructure, and changing it.
D. improved the superstructure.

Answers on page 58.

Grammar and Usage

Ugh. Grammar. I know what you're thinking. Grammar!

Sure, grammar is not the most glorious of all English skills, but it *is* one of the most useful. Your writing can be stylish and succinct, accurate and agile, but if your grammar is poor, no one will care what you have to say.

The good news is that you don't have to be a grammarian to score well on these easy questions on the ACT. Just remember the RGFM No? P OR P strategy for solving easy questions, and I'll remind you of a few grammar things along the way.

Agreement

Agreement is when the subject and verb match in

- Person (first, second, third)
- Number (singular, plural)

Agreement is when a pronoun and its antecedent (the word it's replacing) match in

- Person (first, second, third)
- Number (singular, plural)
- Case (subject or object)
- Gender (he, she, or it)

This sounds harder than it is.

> **HEADS UP**
>
> Verbs also have to agree in **tense**. To see if a verb is in the right tense (past, present, future, etc.), match it up with other verbs or ideas:
>
> *The clock keeps accurate time for over three decades.*
>
> *The clock has kept accurate time for over three decades.*
>
> Present tense wouldn't work with the "over 3 decades" idea because it refers to both the past and the present.

Subject–Verb Agreement

That sweet old ***lady*** *with all seven of her dogs* ***walks*** *down to the bakery every morning.*

Subject: lady

Verb: walks

Agreement: Yes! The subject is singular (just one lady), so the verb must be singular. It is. If the sentence had included her dogs as part of the subject (lady *and* all of her dogs) the verb would have to be plural: "walk."

*Gosh, there **are** about a million **questions** from the audience.*

Subject: questions

Verb: are

Agreement: Yes. Why isn't the subject "there"? Just because the word "there" happens to come first in the sentence, does not make it the subject. When sentences start with "There are/is" you need to reverse the words to figure out where the subject and verb are, and hence, if they agree:

*Gosh, about a million **questions** from the audience **are** there.*

So, do the subject and verb agree? Yes! "Questions" is plural and "are" is a plural verb. Presto bango.

Pronoun–Antecedent Agreement

When any little girl dreams of becoming a superstar—although it's great to think big—she should probably try to get good grades in school just in case the whole fame thing doesn't work out.

Antecedent: girl

Pronoun: she

Agreement: Yes! They agree. Spoken English is much less formal than written English, so if you were to hear this sentence spoken, you might think that "they" would be an accurate replacement for "she." It isn't. Your friends will forgive you; the ACT will not.

That kid over there with the roller skates, at whom everyone seems to be staring, is my new boyfriend.

Antecedent: kid

Pronoun: whom

Agreement: Yes! They agree. Why? Pronoun case—remember that? "Who" is always used if it is replacing a subject, and "whom" will always be used if it is replacing some sort of object.

Tricky Subject/Verb and Pronoun/Antecedent Combos

The words *each, each one, either, neither, everyone, everybody, anybody, anyone, nobody, somebody, someone,* and *no one* are *singular* and require a *singular* verb and *singular pronoun* when used as the subject of a sentence.

> ***Nobody*** *on this entire planet, with the exception of Liz and her rowdy band of friends,* ***listens*** *to death metal anymore.*
>
> **Subject:** Nobody
>
> **Verb:** listens
>
> **Agreement:** "Nobody" is singular, so the verb "listens" is singular, too.
>
> *When* ***everyone*** *gives* ***his or her*** *undivided attention to the guest speaker, I will pass out the cookies.*
>
> **Antecedent:** everyone
>
> **Pronoun:** his or her
>
> **Agreement:** "Everyone" is singular, and the pronoun combo "his or her" is singular, too. "Their" is plural and cannot be used!

STRATEGY ALERT

How to Figure Out if Everything Agrees

Trash Anything in Between: If, after reading the underlined portion and glancing at the answer choices, you figure out that agreement is being tested (subject/verb or pronoun/antecedent), just draw a line on top of everything in between the two words in question.

Let's try it with a question similar to what you'll see on the ACT:

> Each one of the special children in her classroom fill Heather's heart with wonder, and, although she's contemplated resignation, she decides that she can't give up; she must continue to teach.
>
> **A.** NO CHANGE
>
> **B.** fills Heather's
>
> **C.** filled Heather's
>
> **D.** had filled Heather's

Trash anything in between the subject and verb:

> *Each ~~one of the special children in her classroom~~ fill Heather's heart with wonder, and she decides right then that she can't give up; she must continue to teach.*

"Each . . . fill" is not correct as it stands, remember? "Each" is one of those words that needs a singular verb. So cross out answer Choice A.

That leaves us with B, C, and D. B sounds good—it's singular too—but what about C and D? Should the verb tense be changed? Here's where you have to match the main verb with the other verbs in the sentence.

For Choice C, does "filled" (past tense) match with "decides" (present tense)? No. Choice C is out.

For Choice D, does "had filled" (past perfect tense) match with "decides" (present tense)? No. Choice D is out.

B is correct.

Verb tense can be tricky. Sometimes, verb tenses do not have to match, like in the following case, where the sentence changes from present tense to future:

> *As soon as **I am** off the phone, Mrs. Mott, **I will** get back to work.*

This is where your strategy for easy questions comes into play. If you can't fix the problem and match it to an answer, then plug in the choices one by one to see which works best. Eliminate at least two choices if you can, then make your best guess.

Modifiers

Modifiers are words that change the meaning of another word. That's what the word "modify" means: to change. Adjectives and adverbs are modifiers. Adjectives change nouns, and adverbs change everything else.

> *Michael's **eleventh** cupcake went **smoothly** down his throat just like the **previous** ten.*

Adjectives:	eleventh (cupcake), previous (ten)
Adverb:	smoothly (went)

We would never have known the enormity of Michael's cupcake obsession without those modifiers. The adjectives and adverb changed the nouns and verb to show us a new meaning.

The ACT will test your knowledge of modifiers in a couple of ways:

1. Correcting comparative and superlative mistakes
2. Correcting misplaced modifiers

Comparatives and Superlatives

Comparative adjectives and adverbs are used when two ideas are in play.

Superlative adjectives and adverbs are used when three or more ideas are in play.

HEADS UP

Most of the time, 3-syllable adjectives are made comparative and superlative with "more" and "most":

more lovable

most lovable

Comparative adjectives:

1. It's hard to tell whose voice is *louder* when Betty and Katie are yelling.
2. The steakhouse down the street is *more generous* with the salad toppings than that restaurant you suggested.

Superlative adjectives:

1. It's hard to tell whose voice is the *loudest* when Betty, Katie, and Annabelle are all yelling.
2. The steakhouse down the street is the *most generous* with the salad toppings out of all three of the restaurants you've suggested.

Comparative adverb:

1. Laura woke up *earlier* than you did.
2. I definitely agree that three-year-olds behave worse than two-year-olds.

Superlative adverb:

1. Out of all six of us, Cindy woke up the *earliest.*
2. Between two-year-olds, three-year-olds, and teenagers, three-year-olds behave the worst.

This only gets tricky when the comparatives and superlatives are really different. Like these:

Weird Adverbs		
Adverb	Comparative	Superlative
well	better	best

Weird Adjectives		
Adjective	Comparative	Superlative
bad	worse	worst
good	better	best
little	less	least
many	more	most

Misplaced Modifiers

Because modifiers change the meaning of the words in the sentence, their placement in the sentence is *very, very* important. Check this out:

> *The baby **almost** drank an entire can of diet soda while his older brother was watching football on YouTube.*

Here, the baby is just fine (and so is his older brother). He *almost* drank the soda, which means he didn't drink anything. Change the placement of the modifier and the older brother loses his Internet privileges for a month:

> *The baby drank **almost** an entire can of diet soda while his older brother was watching football on YouTube.*

Big difference, huh?

HEADS UP

In case you hadn't noticed, modifiers don't have to be one word. If a phrase changes the meaning of a word in some way, and can be removed without altering the sentence structure, then it's probably a modifying phrase—a group of words acting like an adverb or adjective.

Now, sometimes, modifiers will be nowhere near the word they're supposed to be modifying. And this is where the ACT test writers will get you.

Jack was gazing at the girl standing next to the fire hydrant ***wearing the leather pencil skirt.***

With the modifying phrase "wearing the leather miniskirt" in the wrong spot, we don't know whether the girl or the fire hydrant is wearing the leather pencil skirt.

Better: *Jack was gazing at the girl wearing the leather pencil skirt standing next to the fire hydrant.*

STRATEGY ALERT

How to Figure Out if a Modifier Is Right or Wrong

Make **Sure the Modifier Is Close to Its Word:** Modifiers like to be right next to the words they want to change. They also always have a type: Adjectives always look for nouns and pronouns; adverbs want to be close to adjectives, verbs, and other adverbs.

So, if you encounter an underlined section with an adjective or adverb inside it, you better make sure its word is nearby.

Let's try this strategy with a sentence similar to something you'd see on the ACT:

Cheek to cheek, the dance is performed to a sultry rhythm, and the band that lures the dancers to the floor often plays long past midnight.

F. NO CHANGE

G. Couples dance cheek to cheek to a sultry rhythm,

H. A sultry rhythm, the couples dance cheek to cheek,

J. Cheek to cheek, the sultry rhythm entices couples,

Let's first try to fix the problem (if there is a problem) ourselves. What's the issue here? Well, we don't know who is "cheek to cheek." We can assume that couples are dancing, but here they must be at the punch table or something because they are missing from the sentence. Here, the modifying phrase "cheek to cheek" is clearly slacking on its modifying duties.

So, let's put the word that's being modified back in the sentence—the "couples." That gets rid of Choice F.

Now, we have to be sure that the modifier is very close to the word it's modifying. That gets rid of Choice J for us. "Couples" is nowhere near "cheek to cheek."

Now, we're left with G and H, and the choice is easy. Choice H makes no sense, so the obvious answer is G.

Not as difficult as you thought, right?

Idioms

Idioms are phrases made up of verbs and prepositions that have come to be expected to go together for no particular reason.

> *After her mother gave her a "look," Francie agreed to* ***abide by*** *the rules.*
>
> *The reclusive old woman* ***accused*** *the teenager* ***of*** *trespassing, but the judge let him walk because the old woman also* ***accused*** *the judge of jury tampering.*

Most of the time, these will be really easy to figure out if you're a native English speaker. If you're not, you'll need to spend some time with an English idiomatic dictionary to get these correct because there are no real rules to follow.

STRATEGY ALERT

How to Figure Out if an Idiom Is Right or Wrong

Plug In Answers: These are so easy that all you'll really need to do is identify whether or not an idiom is in question (look for an underlined preposition), and then decide if it sounds correct as written. If not, just plug the answer choices into the sentence to see if one makes better sense.

Practice Grammar and Usage

Use the **RGFM No? P or P** strategy. **R**ead the text until the first underlined section, **G**lance at the question for that underline to see what's being tested, **F**ix the problem (if there is one) yourself, and **M**atch your answer to the choices.

If you can't find your match, then **P**lug in the answer choices. Still not sure? Use the **P**rocess of **E**limination and get rid of at least two answers that are definitely incorrect.

Mr. E. W. Hawkes has lately published, living at the mouth of the Yukon River, a valuable account of the ceremonies of two Eskimo tribes: [1] the Unaligmiut and Unalaklit on the Isle of St. Michael. Local rites, termed the Aiyaguk or "Asking" festival, and the Teauiyuk or "Bladder feast"—which is to placate the spirit of an animal already slain—is held [2] during the months of November and December. But more important [3] is the Aithukaguk or "Inviting-In" feast, for it is an appeal to the spirits represented by the masks, the totemic guardians, for future success in hunting. In the Eskimo ritual, this festival bests every other feast, even the Great Feast of the Dead.

In St. Michael the "Inviting-In" feast has lost much of its religious character and is now maintained chiefly for its social utility [4] of creating an opportunity for trade between two friendly tribes. An old chief remarked that they did not dance for pleasure alone, but to attract the game so that their families might be fed. If they did not dance, the spirits whom attended [5] the feast would be angry and the animals would stay away. The shades of their ancestors would go hungry since there would be no one to feed them, and their own names would be forgotten if no namesake could sing their praises in the dance.

1.
- **A.** NO CHANGE
- **B.** a valuable account of the ceremonies of two Eskimo tribes living at the mouth of the Yukon River:
- **C.** a valuable account of the ceremonies, living at the mouth of the Yukon River, of two Eskimo tribes:
- **D.** a valuable account of the ceremonies of two Eskimo tribes living at the mouth of the Yukon River:

2.
- **F.** NO CHANGE
- **G.** are being held
- **H.** are held
- **J.** has been held

3.
- **A.** NO CHANGE
- **B.** more importantly
- **C.** most importantly
- **D.** most important

4.
- **F.** NO CHANGE
- **G.** their social utility
- **H.** whose social utility
- **J.** his or her social utility

5.
- **A.** NO CHANGE
- **B.** who attended
- **C.** who are attending
- **D.** with whom they attended

Answers on page 59.

Knowledge of Language: 10–14 questions

We've covered the first type of questions asked by ACT English, Conventions of Standard English.

And now we're moving on to the second bullet point, Knowledge of Language. These types of questions involve

- Concision in word choice
- Precision in word choice
- Consistency in style
- Consistency in tone

These tend to be tougher than the punctuation, grammar, and sentence structure questions, but are *completely* solvable.

Remember, the tough questions are easy to spot—they'll actually ask you a question—and these pesky ones are meant to be answered *after* all those easy questions because they aren't worth any more points.

EASY

1. **A.** NO CHANGE

   B. day, using old thread for weaving,

   C. day, using old thread for weaving;

   D. day using old thread, for weaving,

TOUGH

2. Which of the following sentences would best continue the personal theme expressed here?

   A. As I grew older, I found I had a talent for numbers, and studied accountancy.

   B. Twenty years later, I had gone into engineering, and soon went to work for NASA.

   C. Throughout high school, I studied acting and drama, and began working with dinner theatre after graduation.

   D. It took me several years, but by the time I was 20, I had graduated from Clown College and begun working with a small family-run operation.

> **HEADS UP**
>
> Calling the questions in the section "tough" doesn't necessarily imply some sort of super difficulty. They aren't **that** tough. They will simply take you more time than those "easy" questions. Keep that in mind and don't psych yourself out!

So, before we plunge into the specifics of Rhetorical Skills, here is your strategy for solving tough ACT English questions:

Steps for Solving a Tough ACT English Question

RqRt P or A

READ QUESTION

Read the question above the answer choices.

↓

READ TEXT

Read the portion of the text in question. Remember, you will have just read the entire passage when you answered the easy questions, so you won't need to start at the beginning. Instead, begin with the sentence that includes the underline or the question material.

PLUG IN

Plug In answer choices to see which one works the best. One of them will be obviously wrong, so cross it off and choose among the remaining three letters.

OR

ANSWER

Answer the question. Some of these questions will not require you to plug anything into the sentence; you'll simply have to use your noggin to choose the best answer.

Let me show you how this works.

1. Read Question

2. Read Text
Keep the question in mind as you read. You're looking for a transitional sentence—one that would join sentence 2 to sentence 3.

[2] According to surveys and interviews, many young people today say that they want no children when they get older, or wish to postpone having children until their late thirties or even forties. [3] Often, couples cannot afford to have the woman stay home, even if she'd like to; she must contribute equally to the finances because one income is not enough to support the family's needs.

Which of the following makes the best transition between Sentence 2 and Sentence 3?

F. For some, even forty is too young to begin a family, and because life spans are relatively long, middle age is really the mid-forties.

H. Many men are satisfied to remain childless until their fifties, and, if they have married significantly younger women, they can become fathers then.

G. Because the financial situation in most families requires both the woman and man to work, a woman often has to make the choice to find a job.

J. Waiting until early middle age to have children allows women to leave the traditional role as homemaker and join the commercial workplace.

3. Answer: This is not a plug-in kind of question, so you'll just need to answer it. Which sentence best transitions the ideas from one to another? J because it involves having children, which is discussed in sentence 2, and working, discussed in sentence 3.

Concision and Precision in Word Choice

Keeping language concise and precise is when the words in the text are free from redundancy, ambiguity, and wordiness.

CONCISE AND PRECISE LANGUAGE IS FREE FROM:

REDUNDANCY

The sentence expresses an idea more than once.

The biography of Helen Keller's life was fascinating.

Better: *Helen Keller's biography was fascinating.*

Many uneducated people who have never been to school are coming to your house.

Uneducated people = people who have never been to school. Get rid of one of them.

AMBIGUITY

The antecedents for pronouns are unclear.

Jonah asked Noah if he'd bring his girlfriend with him to the pie-eating contest.

Whose girlfriend?

Jake told Josh he was a flippin' genius.

Who is the genius?

WORDINESS

The writer uses too many words instead of keeping the text precise.

Casey always thought that Stacey was attractive in appearance.

Better: *Casey always thought Stacey was attractive.*

Tanya was late for American Idol *auditions due to the fact that she tripped on her skirt and ripped a big tear up one side.*

Better: *Tanya was late for* American Idol *auditions because she tripped on her skirt and ripped it.*

One of your tasks on the ACT is to determine if sentences are clear. You'll see questions like these:

1. Which choice provides the most specific and precise information?
2. Which choice provides the most logical arrangement of the parts of this sentence?

Let's try a couple of these questions!

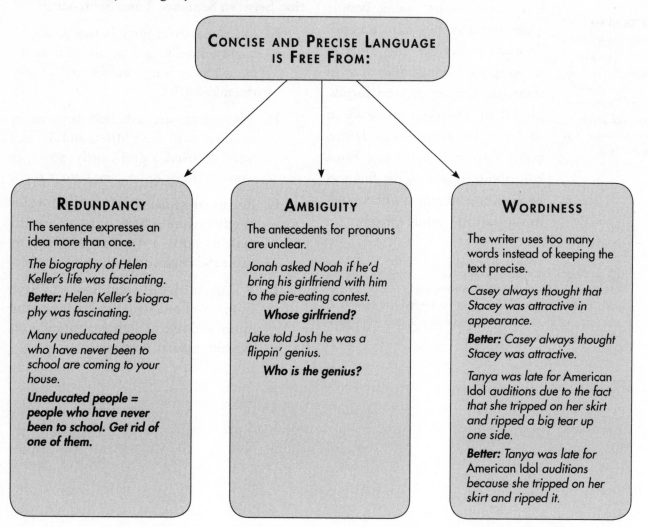

Today, plastic credit cards and plastic debit cards [1] are almost more common than paper money and coins. Although plastic is a relatively new invention, the concept of credit is over 3,000 years old. [2] Back in that time frame, Babylonians, Assyrians, and Egyptians could all settle one-third of a debt with cash, and also settle two-thirds of a debt with something called a "bill of exchange." Later, in 1730, Christopher Thornton first allowed his customers in London to make weekly payments for the furniture they bought from him. And in the eighteenth and nineteenth centuries, tallymen accepted weekly payments for clothing and other articles, using one side of a wooden stick to keep a tally of a customer's debt and the other side to keep a tally of a customer's payment.

1. Which choice provides the most specific and precise information?
   A. NO CHANGE
   B. plastic credit cards
   C. plastic debit and credit cards
   D. plastic, debit, and credit cards

2. Which choice provides the clearest information without altering the meaning of the text?
   F. NO CHANGE
   G. During that time frame, Babylonians, Assyrians, and Egyptians settled some of their debts with cash and most of their debts with something called a "bill of exchange."
   H. Babylonians, Assyrians, and Egyptians could settle their debts with cash and bills of exchange.
   J. In those days, Babylonians, Assyrians, and Egyptians could settle one-third of a debt with cash and two-thirds with a "bill of exchange."

For both questions, let's follow the strategy for solving toughies. First, we'll **R**ead the question, **R**ead the text, then either **P**lug-**I**n or **A**nswer.

When we read question 1, we see that we need to be on the look-out for clarity. So, after reading the text, "plastic credit cards and plastic debit cards," we can see an obvious redundancy issue: the words *plastic* and *cards* are used twice. That makes the sentence bulkier than it needs to be. Get rid of Choice A.

Let's Plug In. Which answer choice works the best without changing the meaning of the sentence?

Choice B: Today, plastic credit cards are almost more common . . .

Choice C: Today, plastic debit and credit cards are almost more common . . .

Choice D: Today, plastic, debit, and credit cards are almost more common . . .

Choice B is short, but it changes the meaning of the sentence because it doesn't include debit cards. It's out.

Choice C is clear and includes all the original info. Let's check Choice D to be sure . . .

Choice D equates the word *plastic* with "debit and credit" by putting it into a list, which makes the sentence ridiculous.

Choice C is our best choice!

STRATEGY ALERT

How to Choose the Most Concise and Precise Answer

Divide and Conquer: If you encounter a question that asks you to choose the clearest answer, and the text and answer choices are all *long*, then divide up the sentence into chunks by drawing brackets around portions of the sentence. Why? By dealing with each chunk individually to conquer this type of question, you won't get confused by all the words.

Let's read the text for question 2:

> Back in that time frame, Babylonians, Assyrians, and Egyptians could all settle one-third of a debt with cash, and also settle two-thirds of a debt with something called a "bill of exchange."

This is a long, complicated sentence to deal with in less than 30 seconds, and sounds wordy compared to some of the other options, so we'll get rid of Choice A. To deal with it, let's quickly divide it into chunks:

Chunk 1: {Back in that time frame,}

Chunk 2: {Babylonians, Assyrians, and Egyptians}

Chunk 3: {could all settle one-third of a debt with cash, and also settle two-thirds of a debt with something called a "bill of exchange."}

Now, which option offers the clearest, most precise language for Chunk 1? All three choices are still options. Choice G is shorter, Choice H gets rid of that part of the sentence altogether, and Choice J is shorter.

What about Chunk 2? Again, the three options are still there, because nothing was changed.

Chunk 3? Ah. Here's where we find some major differences. Because Choices G and H remove some necessary info (the one-third and two-thirds details), we have to choose Choice J. It's much clearer than the text, and doesn't change the meaning of the sentence.

G. During that time frame, Babylonians, Assyrians, and Egyptians settled some of their debts with cash and most of their debts with something called a "bill of exchange."

H. Babylonians, Assyrians, and Egyptians could settle their debts with cash and bills of exchange.

J. In those days, Babylonians, Assyrians, and Egyptians could settle one-third of a debt with cash and two-thirds with a "bill of exchange."

Consistency in Style and Tone

Consistency is when the writer's tone (the attitude conveyed) and the writing style (how that attitude is shared) stays the same throughout the text. The ACT *loves* consistent writing.

> *Above all else, Meredith relished the thought of lounging by the stream; the cacophony of the goslings intruded into her tranquility, however, and afforded her none of the solitude she'd hoped to acquire.*

The style of the sentence above is very formal. How can you tell? It's all about word choice. The writer made some stuffy word choices (*goslings* vs. *geese*; *cacophony* vs. *noise*), and in doing so, made the style sound rather overbearing, in my opinion. Here's the same information, with a different style:

> *More than anything, Meredith just wanted to lie down next to the river and daydream, but the annoying honking geese invaded her space, and destroyed her peace and quiet.*

This sentence is much more casual in style. And because of that, we can see that the writer's tone is less serious about the situation in the second example. The author's tone can be playful, witty, serious, outraged, etc. *Your* job on the ACT is to determine if the tone of the text you're reading is *consistent.*

You'll be asked questions like these:

1. Given that all the choices are true, which one provides the most specific detail and maintains the style and tone of the essay?
2. Which choice would be the most consistent with the figurative language provided elsewhere in the paragraph?
3. Which choice of words fits most specifically with the information at the end of this sentence?

HEADS UP

Writing style is how you *know* who has texted you without looking at the number on your phone. It's all about **word choice**. Your mom would probably never text curse words and slang. Your best friend would probably never use big words like a neurophysicist would.

Production of Writing: 22–24 questions

We've gone through both the first and second types of ACT English questions, Conventions of Standard English and Knowledge of Language.

And now, we're rounding third and heading home with the Production of Writing types of questions. Twenty-two to twenty-four questions will involve stuff like this:

- Topic Development:
  - — Evaluating the material's relevance
  - — Identifying whether a portion of text has met its goal
- Organization, Unity, and Cohesion:
  - — Using strategies to create logical organization
  - — Using strategies to ensure a smooth flow
  - — Ensuring effective introductions and conclusions

Topic Development

Most of the questions related to this reporting category will have to do with "relevance." Relevance is when supporting details are important and related directly to the topic of the essay, paragraph, or sentence.

After Tallulah got home from work, her growling stomach told her that she wanted pancakes for dinner. She got out the eggs, pancake mix, and griddle to start prepping. When Mortimer came home with chopsticks and chow mein five minutes later, she was pleased at his thoughtfulness, but irritated that she wouldn't get breakfast for dinner as planned. Mortimer forgot the soy sauce. Tallulah decided that she'd better let Mortimer know that she was planning a big pancake dinner for tomorrow night before he decided to come home with curry.

Which sentence above is not relevant to the point of the story? You got it: "Mortimer forgot the soy sauce." We could get rid of it without any change to the paragraph whatsoever. It's irrelevant. It's not an important detail necessary to the framework of the plot.

The ACT will test your ability to detect relevance in a number of ways. You'll be asked to judge if a sentence should be where it was placed. Should it be removed? Should a new sentence be added? Should a paragraph be changed? Does the paragraph fit with the author's intentions? Check out some of the examples of the kinds of strategy questions you'll see on the ACT:

1. Upon reviewing the paragraph and determining that some info has been left out, the writer composes the following sentence. Where should it be placed?
2. The writer would like to suggest . . . Given that all the choices are true, which one best accomplishes the writer's goal?
3. The writer is considering deleting the phrase . . . should it be kept or deleted?
4. If the writer were to delete sentence . . . , the essay would lose details that . . .
5. Which of the following true statements, if added here, would emphasize . . .
6. If the writer were to delete the final paragraph, the essay would lose information that:

HEADS UP

Remember that the ACT English section has tricky formatting: the paragraphs will have large spaces in between them! Be sure to note where one paragraph starts and stops before deciding that a sentence doesn't fit in with it. You may be looking at the text incorrectly!

7. If the writer were to delete the last part of the preceding sentence, the paragraph would lose:

Let's try solving one of these tough questions:

Today, plastic credit cards and plastic debit cards are almost more common than paper money and coins. Although plastic is a relatively new invention, the concept of credit is over 3,000 years old. Back in that time frame, Babylonians, Assyrians, and Egyptians could all settle one-third of a debt with cash, and also settle two-thirds of a debt with something called a "bill of exchange." [7] Later, in 1730, Christopher Thornton first allowed his customers in London to make weekly payments for the furniture they bought from him. And in the eighteenth and nineteenth centuries, tallymen accepted weekly payments for clothing and other articles, using one side of a wooden stick to keep a tally of a customer's debt and the other side to keep a tally of a customer's payment.

7. The writer is considering deleting the following sentence from the paragraph. If the writer were to make the deletion, the paragraph would primarily lose:

A. an important fact that shows the historical progression of the concept of credit.
B. excessive details that distract the reader from the topic of the paragraph.
C. information that indicates credit has changed drastically throughout the years.
D. statistics that explain the various usages of credit.

To solve, we'll use our Tough question strategy: **Rq Rt P** or **A**.

After reading the question, and the sentence that corresponds to the question, we see that we need to just answer it. If we took this sentence out of the paragraph, what would we lose?

> Later, in 1730, Christopher Thornton first allowed his customers in London to make weekly payments for the furniture they bought from him.

STRATEGY ALERT

How to Solve a Topic Development Question

Put Choices in Your Own Words: If you read through the questions and are stumped by all the choices, put the choices in your own words so you can make an informed decision.

Choice A: If I got rid of the Thornton sentence, I'd lose important info about credit's move through history.

Choice B: If I got rid of the Thornton sentence, I'd lose lots of details that are off-topic.

Choice C: If I got rid of the Thornton sentence, I'd lose info that shows how credit has REALLY changed.

Choice D: If I got rid of the Thornton sentence, I'd lose statistics that show different ways credit is used.

See? The correct choice is much easier to get to, now. The two obvious choices to get rid of first are Choice B and D. Since the Thornton sentence doesn't have lots of off-topic details, Choice B is out. Choice D mentions statistics, and there are none in the sentence. It's gone, too.

That leaves A and C. A sounds better than C, because although the Thornton sentence shows a slight change in credit, it isn't drastic. Choice A is the best answer.

Now, I wrote all these paraphrases out to explain the concept. In no way should you write your paraphrases out word for word; you'll lose time. Instead, just jot down one or two clarifying words near the choices so you don't get confused and have to reread.

Organization

Sure. You might not be the most organized of all your friends. Maybe your closet is an abyss and your backpack is a black hole. The ACT only cares about your language-related organizational skills. You know what I'm talking about—your ability to recognize appropriate transitional elements, sentence placement, introductions, and conclusions. The good news is that you'll be asked to deal with this in not one, but THREE different ways:

1. Organization of the passage as a whole
2. Organization of paragraphs
3. Organization of sentences

Passage Organization

For the most part, nonfiction essays on the ACT will be organized as you've come to expect essays to be arranged:

Introductory Paragraph	Contains the main idea of the essay
Supporting Paragraphs	Each contains • topic sentences that transition from the previous idea • supporting sentences that provide details about the topic sentences • concluding or transitional sentences that lead to the next idea
Concluding Paragraph	Contains sentences that provide extra insight; summarizes the essay

STRATEGY ALERT

How to Keep Essays Organized

Get Rid of the Fluff; Keep the Good Stuff: To help yourself answer questions related to the organization of the passage, summarize the main point of each paragraph when you're answering the easy questions. You can summarize in one of two ways:

1. **One Word:** If you only had one word to describe the paragraph, what would it be?
2. **Underline:** Draw a line under the word or phrase that seems to show the main point of the paragraph.

Why? When you come to a question like the following ones (which are *very* similar to the types of questions you'll see on the ACT), you won't need to reread the essay over and over again to figure out where things should be logically placed.

1. The writer wants to provide a sentence that will tie the conclusion to the introduction. Which choice does that LEAST effectively? (or) MOST effectively?
2. For the sake of logic and coherence, paragraph X should be placed after which paragraph?
3. Given that all the choices are true, which choice provides the most effective transition from the preceding paragraph to this one?
4. Which choice would best summarize the main point of the essay?
5. Given that all the choices are true, which one LEAST effectively introduces/concludes/summarizes the essay? Which one MOST effectively . . . ?

Paragraph Organization

Good writers use transitions from one paragraph to another and from one sentence to another to link ideas in the text. You simply need to be aware of what a transition is telling you.

Transitions	Why They Are Used
also, in the same way, just as, so too, likewise, similarly	to compare
accordingly, consequently, hence, so, therefore, thus	to show cause
but, however, in spite of, on the one hand, on the other hand, nevertheless, nonetheless, notwithstanding, in contrast, on the contrary, still, yet	to contrast
first, second, third, ... next, then, finally	to show a sequence of events
or, for example, for instance, namely, specifically, to illustrate, additionally, again, also, and, as well, besides, equally important, further, furthermore, in addition, moreover	to give examples or more info

Understanding the meaning behind the transition will help you keep a sense of the order and logic of the paragraph, and will help you answer these kinds of questions:

1. Which of the following sentence orders makes the paragraph the most logical?
2. The writer has decided to divide this paragraph into two smaller paragraphs. The best place to add the new paragraph break and new topic sentence would be at the beginning of which sentence?
3. Given that all the choices are true, which choice provides the most effective transition from the preceding sentence to this one?
4. For the sake of logic and coherence, sentence X should be placed after which sentence?

HEADS UP

Passages are like chains. Each sentence in the paragraph is a link in that chain. Watch out for missing links! A passage will never abruptly leave an idea and jump into the next one. Transitional sentences will lead from one paragraph to another, and transitional phrases will lead from one sentence to another. Remember—an effective transition will often address info from the two ideas it's linking.

Sentence Organization

Keeping sentences organized is pretty simple. Most of the sentence organization issues on the ACT will come from a modifier not staying close enough to the word it is modifying. Remember that? Modifiers (adjectives, adverbs, and modifying phrases) like to be close to the words they're modifying, and if they're sliding around in another part of the sentence, you'll need to be able to rearrange the words to correct it.

Let's try it:

The argument between the girls somewhat [1] originated in a strange way. When Josephine lowered her lashes and asked Kelsey's brother to help her reach "that large box—the one way up there," Kelsey suspected that Josephine was up to her tricks, yet again. This time, though, Kelsey determined that her brother would not bear the brunt of Josephine's feminine wiles and ultimate betrayal. She grabbed her brother's arm, which had just gotten a grip on the edge of the box, and pulled with all her might. The box teetered on the edge of the shelf, then toppled end over end, [2] spilling its contents, a massive collection of hair removal products, all over the floor. Red-faced, Josephine screamed at Kelsey, but Kelsey bore her no mind. She'd been justified, after all.

1. The best placement for the underlined word would be:

A. where it is *now*.
B. before the word *in*.
C. before the word *strange*.
D. before the word *a*.

2. The best placement for the underlined phrase would be:

F. where it is *now*.
G. after the word *spilling*.
H. between the word *contents* and the comma.
J. after the word *floor*.

Following the strategy for answering tough questions, **RqRt P or A**, you'd **R**ead the question first, then **R**ead the text encompassing the question, then either **P**lug in or **A**nswer it outright. Here, we need to plug in to figure it out. Here's what the sentence would look like if the choices were plugged in:

Choice A: The argument between the girls somewhat originated in a strange way.

Choice B: The argument between the girls originated somewhat in a strange way.

Choice C: The argument between the girls originated in a somewhat strange way.

Choice D: The argument between the girls originated in somewhat a strange way.

Here, you'll need to decide what word is being modified by the word "somewhat." Did the argument "somewhat originate"? No. That doesn't make sense. Choice A is out.

Choice B is merely a variation on that theme—placed there, it's still modifying the word *originate*, so that's out, too.

Choice C makes great sense. The argument started in a somewhat strange way, but let's check Choice D to be sure. What's the difference? That little "a" in between speaks to the sentence's style. Which choice makes the sentence the least bulky, the most fluid? Choice C.

Question 2 is solvable the same way. Read the question, read the text, then either plug in or answer it. Again, I'd just go ahead and plug in if I were you.

Here's what each choice looks like:

Choice F: The box teetered on the edge of the shelf, then toppled end over end, spilling its contents, a massive collection of hair removal products, all over the floor.

Choice G: The box teetered on the edge of the shelf, then toppled, spilling end over end its contents, a massive collection of hair removal products, all over the floor.

Choice H: The box teetered on the edge of the shelf, then toppled, spilling its contents end over end, a massive collection of hair removal products, all over the floor.

Choice J: The box teetered on the edge of the shelf, then toppled, spilling its contents, a massive collection of hair removal products, all over the floor end over end.

Don't let all the commas confuse you. Here, the question is just asking about the placement of the phrase "end over end." If we want to keep it as close to the word it's describing as is humanly possible, then it needs to be hanging out near "toppled." If you look at the choices, you'll see that Choice F, as the sentence is in the passage, does just that. Both Choices G and J make the sentence bulky-sounding and illogical, which are big no-no's. The only other option that could even be considered close is Choice H. There, you'd just have to ask yourself if a "box toppling end over end" makes more sense than "contents spilling end over end." If you picture it in your mind, you'll know Choice F is the right pick!

Practice Topic Development, Organization, Unity, and Cohesion

These questions are all toughies, so be sure to **Rq Rt P or A**: Read the question first, Read the text, and either Plug in or Answer the question outright.

[1]

The funeral was just stretching on and on that sweaty Sunday in the middle of the summer. I took a look at my fingers, clammy and swollen from the dizzy heat, and ached to be splashing around in the creek behind the church. Daddy promised that the rain from Friday would cool everything down, but the sun just sucked up all the water just the same as it did year after year. All the women, dressed in black with funny-looking hats, whispered at each other and blew their noses into hankies as they fanned themselves cooler. Preacher Tom yammered on and on in his booming voice like it was just another boring Sunday and no one had even died. Miss Patterson, my favorite Sunday school teacher, whispered 'cross the aisle to Daddy that "It's a cryin' shame, ya know." Daddy shrugged his big old coal-mining shoulders and said, "The good Lord knows what's best." I knew he wasn't really sad because he was a "hard-hearted man with no sense and no decency," like Momma used to say when he'd come home smelling like whiskey.

1. Which choice provides the most vivid description while maintaining the tone?
   - **A.** NO CHANGE
   - **B.** the hot sun
   - **C.** the agonizing rays of the sun
   - **D.** 90 degrees of scorching rays of sunshine

2. Which of the following choices provides the most specific and precise information?
   - **F.** NO CHANGE
   - **G.** like it always did year after year.
   - **H.** just as it always did.
   - **J.** like it did every year.

[2]

Before the end of the sermon, which lasted around five days to all us kids squirming around in the pews, I finally got to get up and stretch my scrawny legs. "Chicken legs," like Momma said.

3. Which phrase transitions into paragraph 2 the best?
   - **A.** NO CHANGE
   - **B.** At the end
   - **C.** Toward the end
   - **D.** Until the end

I spread my arms out to the side and yawned so wide my insides felt clean with new air, muggy as it was. Daddy pushed me up to the front with a "Git movin', Katie" and I gulped down the rest of the yawn in haste, [4] and made my way up to the casket. My frilly dress, made by Momma's own loving hands, pricked and bothered me something fierce as I stood restless by the coffin and pretended to like everyone hugging and pawing at me. [5] I thought that just because someone died, I shouldn't have to be scratched by some dress and squeezed to death like it was my own self that was laying up there cold as a cricket in the casket.

[3]

Although really, I wouldn't have minded.

[4]

At least then I'd get to see Momma again.

4. The best placement for the underlined phrase would be

F. where it is now.

G. after the word *down*.

H. in between the words *and* and *I*.

J. OMIT THE UNDERLINED PORTION

5. At this point, the writer is considering adding the following true sentence:

> I hated foo-foo dresses with all their lace, and hated sweaty people touching me just the same.

Should the writer add this sentence here?

A. Yes, because it adds new details that demonstrate how bothered Katie was by her dress and the hugging.

B. Yes, because it heightens the stress level of the story.

C. No, because these details were already explained thoroughly in the paragraph.

D. No, because the tone does not fit well with the rest of the paragraph.

6. If the writer were to delete paragraph 4, the essay would lose:

F. the author's purpose for writing the story.

G. a vital detail indicating how great Katie's loss really was.

H. extra information that Katie had already explained earlier in the story.

J. a fact that the reader wouldn't need to know until much later in the story.

Questions 7 and 8 relate to the story as a whole.

7. After reviewing earlier drafts of this story, the writer comes across this sentence:

    Momma had died last Tuesday, the day all the thunderstorms came rolling in through the hills.

    For logic and coherence, where should the writer put this sentence?

    A. As the first sentence in a new paragraph following paragraph 4.
    B. After the first sentence of paragraph 1.
    C. After the last sentence of paragraph 1.
    D. After the sentence in paragraph 3.

8. Suppose the writer's purpose had been to write a story that thoroughly explains the depth of feelings experienced by a child when his or her mother dies. Does this story accomplish this goal?

    F. Yes, because it provides specific examples of Katie's feelings of abandonment in paragraph 1, which demonstrate how much loss she experienced when her mother died.
    G. Yes, because the story hints at Katie's feelings of loss from a child's perspective, and allows the reader to experience her feelings secondhand.
    H. No, because although the story explains Katie's feelings of irritation about her dress and being touched, it does not thoroughly develop the underlying emotion behind her mother's death.
    J. No, because it does not mention or hint at Katie's feelings about her mother's death at all.

Answers on page 60.

Solutions to English Practice Questions

Punctuation, page 21

1. D.

Here you need a comma after both of the first items in a list. Remember to use the Comma Pause Test, because it will help you figure out where that comma should go!

2. G.

The word "it's" is the contraction for the words "it is." You're looking for the possessive form of the neuter pronoun "it," which is "its." Don't get confused!

3. D.

As it stands in the sentence, the comma forms a comma splice between those two sentences. Choice B makes it a run-on sentence. Choice C adds a colon, but doesn't use the Equality and Independence test to make sure it works. Choice D is correct because a semicolon can stand between two complete ideas.

4. F.

No change is necessary! The dashes are used correctly; they offset the interrupting material on both sides.

5. D.

There has to be punctuation between those two complete ideas, and a comma is not strong enough to separate them. So that gets rid of Choices A and C. The word "however" can follow a semicolon, but it's not strong enough to accompany just a comma, so Choice D is the only one that works.

Sentence Structure and Formation, page 28

1. C.

Leaving the sentence alone causes the second "sentence" to be a fragment. Choice C fixes the problem by getting rid of the "as." Choice B uses the colon incorrectly, and Choice D changes the meaning of the sentence.

2. J.

Here, we have a parallelism issue. As it stands, the two ideas joined by the word "and" are not parallel. Choice J fixes the problem while also reducing wordiness.

3. A.

No change is necessary. The sentence is parallel as it stands. Choice B changes the article to "the," and although Choice D sounds pretty good, it leaves out the adjective for the hydrophone, which changes the meaning and *loses* the best parallel structure.

4. H.

Here the only solution that keeps the sentence structure parallel is Choice H. You'd be able to determine it better if you played the "Name That Sentence Part" Game Show! The format in this series is an article, an adjective, and a noun. Choices F, G, and J do not follow that pattern.

5. D.

Every other choice is a fragment. Only Choice D adds that necessary verb, "improved."

Grammar and Usage, page 37

1. B.

As is, the sentence says that the writer, not the tribes, lives at the mouth of the Yukon River. So the sentence needs that modifying phrase to stay near the words it's modifying! Choice B provides the clearest sentence, with no additional punctuation or grammatical errors.

2. H.

X out anything in between the noun and the verb to figure out if they agree. Here the subject is "Local rites" and all that stuff in the middle is just distracting you from the verb, "is held." Since the word "rites" is plural, the verb has to be, too. "Are held" is the correct answer; it's plural and the tense is consistent with the rest of the sentence.

3. D.

Remember your superlatives! Here three feasts are being compared, so you have to use the superlative form, "most." You could switch the wording of the sentence around to read, "But the "Inviting-In" feast is the most important." The suffix "-ly" added to the word "important" changes that word to an adverb, which should only modify a verb, adverb or an adjective. Here a feast is described, which is a noun.

4. F.

No change is necessary. The feast is the subject of the sentence, so the pronoun describing it has to be the gender-neutral "it." It also has to be singular, so "his or her," "whose," and "their" do not work.

5. B.

The word "who" is taking the place of the word "spirits" in the subjective form; it's the subject of the sentence. Choice C changes the tense of the verb, Choice D changes the meaning of the sentence, and leaving it as it is puts that pronoun in the objective case.

Topic Development, Organization, Unity, and Cohesion, page 54

1. A.

No change is necessary. In this question, we needed to match the tone *and* keep the description vivid. Since the narrator is a little girl, she probably wouldn't use the words in Choices C and D, and Choice B is not vivid at all.

2. J.

Clarity is all about making the sentence free from wordiness, redundancy, and ambiguity. The sentence in the text has a redundant phrase. The choice that best fixes it is J, since it keeps the text the same and reduces wordiness.

3. B.

If you read the rest of the sentence carefully, you'll see that the word "At" is necessary to replace "Before." She wouldn't be allowed to get up *during* the sermon.

4. J.

There are two reasons this phrase should be omitted: 1. The tone is different from the rest of the passage, and 2. It's redundant. The writer already said that she gulped down the yawn. Adding "in haste" is unnecessary.

5. C.

This sentence is redundant. The writer already explained that people touching her bothered her, so it doesn't make sense to add another sentence that clearly says the same thing.

6. G.

If the writer were to get rid of the last line of the story, we wouldn't know how great Katie's loss was, which makes the story even more heartbreaking. Choice F is incorrect because this format doesn't really have a specific author's purpose in mind. Choice H is incorrect because the story doesn't explain that Katie's mother had already died and Choice J is incorrect because it's imperative that we find out whose funeral she was attending.

7. A.

The best answer here is Choice A. The most logical place to introduce new information, like this sentence does, is in a new paragraph. Adding it where Choices B and C suggest removes the element of surprise from the story and breaks up the first paragraph illogically. Adding it after paragraph 3 like Choice D suggests, also disrupts the flow of language. So, the most logical place to put it is in a new paragraph after she describes the funeral.

8. H.

If the purpose had been to "thoroughly explain the depth of feelings experienced by a child when his or her mother dies" then Choices F and G are obviously wrong. Katie's feelings about her mother's death are never fully explained. So that leaves Choices H and J. The last paragraph explains that Katie truly is saddened by her mother's death, which gets rid of Choice J. Therefore, Choice H is the best answer.

English Strategy Cheat Sheet

General Strategies:

- **Pace Yourself.** *36 seconds or less per question.*
- **Don't Change Every Answer.**
- Use "**OMIT.**"
- **Speak the Sentence Aloud.**
- **Don't Make a New Error.**
- **Pay Attention to Paragraph Breaks.**
- **Separate Tough Questions from Easy.** Easy ones will not have a question; they'll just have answer choices. Tough ones will start with a question.

Easy Questions: Use **RGFM No? P or P**: Read, Glance, Fix, Match. No? Plug In or POE

Tough Questions: Use **RqRt P or A:** Read question, Read text, Plug In or Answer.

Punctuation: Choose answers with proper comma, colon, dash, semicolon, apostrophe, and end mark usage.

- Do the **Comma Pause Test.**
- **Check for Independence and Equality** for colons and single dashes.
- **Trash the Interruption for double dashes.**
- **Replace Semicolons with End Marks.**
- **Turn Phrases with Apostrophes into Movie Titles** to check possession.

Grammar: Choose answers with proper agreement, modifiers, and idioms.

- **Trash Anything In Between** to check for agreement.
- **Make Sure the Modifier is Close to its Word.**
- **Plug It In** for idioms

Sentence Structure: Choose answers free from run-ons, comma splices, fragments, and parallelism errors.

- Play the "Can It Stand Alone?" Game Show to detect structure errors.
- Play the "Name That Part of Speech" Game Show to detect parallelism errors.

Organization: Choose answers with proper sentence, paragraph, and passage organization.

- **Get Rid of the Fluff; Keep the Good Stuff** to determine main idea.

Style: Choose answers that are consistent and clear (no ambiguity, redundancy, or wordiness).

- **Divide and Conquer** to find the clearest answer.

Strategy: Choose answers that are relevant to the passage.

- **Put Choices Into Your Own Words** to determine relevance.

Take the English Practice Test

Go to the REA Study Center

(www.rea.com/studycenter)

Now that you have completed this week's work, go to *rea.com/studycenter* and take the English Practice Test. This test is just like the English section of the actual ACT, with the added benefits of:

- **Timed testing conditions** – Gauge how much time you can spend on each question.
- **Automatic scoring** – Find out how you did on the test, instantly.
- **On-screen detailed explanations of answers** – Learn not just the correct answers, but also why the other answers are incorrect.
- **Diagnostic score reports** – Pinpoint where you're strongest and where you need to focus your study.

2

Week 2: Mathematics

ACT Mathematics Test Basics

The ACT Mathematics test has

- 60 multiple-choice questions.
- 5 answer choices per question.

You'll be tested

- for 60 minutes.
- in eight reporting categories: Integrating Essential Skills, Preparing for Higher Math (Including Number and Quantity, Algebra, Functions, Geometry, and Statistics and Probability), and Modeling (reported, but not factored into your final score).
- on mathematics that should be taught up to the beginning of Grade 12.

In order to score well,

- you must master ACT test-taking strategies.
- you must master the Mathematics content included in the ACT.

General Strategies for the Math Section

- **Pace Yourself with HAM.** Since you have 1 minute per question (on average), it will be important to categorize each question in your head as "Haven't Got Time," "Always," or "Maybe."
  - **H**—Haven't Got Time. These are questions you can't even start. You've read the question well, but aren't sure where to begin or which strategies to choose. It's best to guess with your standard guessing letter and move on.
  - **A**—Always. These are questions you have a good chance of getting correct. They are familiar and look like questions you've done before.
  - **M**—Maybe. These are questions you can start, but end up getting stuck or toggling between a couple choices.

  Once you get to a question, categorize it quickly in your head. Answer any "Haven't Got Time" (with your standard guessing letter) and "Always" questions immediately. Circle any "Maybe" questions and come back to them at the end.

- **X Out the Junk**. In order to test your brainpower, the ACT test writers sometimes put in unnecessary info—stuff you don't *need* to know to solve the problem—into the math questions. When you run into this extraneous information, cross it out with your pencil so you're not tempted to use it when you're solving the problem.
- **Break the Rules**. In your math classes, you probably learned certain ways to solve problems. Getting the right answer the "wrong" way wasn't good enough. The ACT is different. Since your score is based on the correct answer and not the process, feel free to use any method your heart desires to find the solution. Right is right no matter how you get there.
- **Rely on Your Calculator**. Getting to know your calculator can be the biggest timesaver for you on the test. There are components built into your Texas Instruments TI-83 that can save you lots of time (like pulling up the last entry by pressing "2nd" then "Enter"). Note: You cannot use a calculator with a CAS (Computer Algebra System) such as the TI-89 or higher. There are other restrictions for your calculator, too, so make sure you check the requirements before test day at ***https://www.act.org/calculator-policy.html***.

- **Use the Answers**. Although most of the time you will want to move "forward" with the problem (i.e., start with the given information and work from there), sometimes it will be helpful to consider the answer choices and work backwards. Often some answers are unrealistic, so you can narrow down the choices.

Integrating Essential Skills: 25 questions

"These questions address concepts typically learned before 8th grade, such as rates and percentages; proportional relationships; area, surface area, and volume; average and median; and expressing numbers in different ways. You will solve problems of increasing complexity, combine skills in longer chains of steps, apply skills in more varied contexts, understand more connections, and become more fluent."

—ACT.org, "Preparing for the ACT 2016–2017"

Two things:

1. Yes, if you are putting the title and the text together, 25 of the 60 questions on the ACT will be a review of 6th and 7th grade concepts.
2. Before you go turning cartwheels of glee, keep in mind that these problems ain't from your grandma's middle school. The problems are often layered; you might not just solve an equation that shows a proportion, for example. Instead, you may have to create a proportion and then use cross multiplication (or any other algebraic strategy) to solve.

Don't worry, though! We are going to explore many of the problem types so you can feel confident and ready.

Rates, Proportional Relationships, and Percentages

Important Vocabulary

Term	Definition	Examples
Ratio	A comparison of two amounts	150 for every 3, 12:4, $\frac{a}{b}$
Rate	A ratio of *different units*	150 sit-ups in 3 minutes, $\frac{12 \text{ eggs}}{4 \text{ omelets}}$
Unit Rate	A rate expressed as a quantity *of 1.*	50 sit-ups in 1 minute, $\frac{3 \text{ eggs}}{1 \text{ omelet}}$, 56 miles per hour
Proportion	A comparison of two equivalent ratios/rates.	$\frac{12 \text{ eggs}}{4 \text{ omelets}} = \frac{3 \text{ eggs}}{1 \text{ omelet}}$, $a : b = c : d$, $\frac{a}{b}$
Percentage	A rate with a denominator of 100—the percent symbol (%) can be thought of as "out of 100" and should be easy to remember because of its name—per cent (100 cents in $1)	25% of 100 people is 25 people. 10 bananas is 25% of 40 bananas. 100 pennies is 400% of 25 pennies.

Many of the questions that fall in the Integrating Essential Skills reporting category will be questions where you have to use ratios, rates, proportions, or percentages. So let's make sure to get these down first!

EXAMPLE

Shari measures the distance between her house and the college she wants to attend on a map and finds that they are $3\frac{1}{2}$ inches apart. If the map key says "$\frac{1}{4}$ inch = 12 miles," how many miles is Shari's house from the college?

A. 12

B. $15\frac{1}{2}$

C. 48

D. 95

E. 168

SOLUTION

The first thing to do is make sure we know what the problem is asking us to find. We are looking for the real distance between Shari's house and the college. Cool.

We are given a map legend and a measurement. Since the map shows that $\frac{1}{4}$ inch = 12 miles, then first, to help connect it to the $3\frac{1}{2}$ inches Shari found, we should figure out how many miles are in 1 inch. To do that, we find the **unit rate** by creating a **proportion** in which $\frac{1}{4}$ inch will become 1 inch by multiplying by 4:

$$\frac{12 \text{ miles}}{\frac{1}{4} \text{ inch}} = \frac{(12 \times 4) \text{ miles}}{\left(\frac{1}{4} \times 4\right) \text{ inch}} = \frac{48 \text{ miles}}{1 \text{ inch}}$$

Along the way, we kept in mind that the rate is connected to miles, so we multiplied our 12 miles by 4 as well. So now we know 1 inch = 48 miles. Woo hoo! With that, we can figure out how many miles are in three and a half inches.

$$3 \text{ inches} \times 48 \text{ miles/inch} = 144 \text{ miles}$$

$$\frac{1}{2} \text{ inch} \times 48 \text{ miles/inch} = 24 \text{ miles}$$

$$\left(4 + \frac{1}{2}\right) \text{ inches} = 144 \text{ miles} + 24 \text{ miles} = 168 \text{ miles.}$$

Our answer choice is E. There are 168 miles in $3\frac{1}{2}$ inches.

In that example, we had to use a rate that the problem gave us in order to find a specific value. However, you will find there are some questions that don't give a specific value just to make sure you're awake.

EXAMPLE

Blake has an assortment of cards (Pokémon, Yu-Gi-Oh!, and Magic the Gathering). The ratio of Pokémon cards to his entire card collection is 96:282, and the ratio of Yu-Gi-Oh! cards to his entire card collection is 17:47. If 1 card is chosen out of his entire collection at random, which type of card will most likely be drawn?

A. Pokémon

B. Yu-Gi-Oh!

C. Magic the Gathering

D. All three are equally likely

E. Cannot be determined from the given information

SOLUTION

Blake has too much time on his hands. However, we can help him solve his little quandary. You'll notice that ratios presented have rather big numbers. Not to fear. If values like those are used, there's a good chance that one of them is a multiple of another. On a question like this, you need to find a similar denominator. Since 282 is the bigger denominator when set up as a fraction, let's start with the ratio for Yu-Gi-Oh! cards and see if we can multiply our way to an equivalent denominator.

$$\frac{17}{47} = \frac{17 \times 6}{47 \times 6} = \frac{102}{282}$$

Since we found a common denominator, we can easily see that there are fewer Pokémon cards (96:282) compared to the Yu-Gi-Oh! cards (102:282). Now, to find out how many Magic the Gathering cards there are, we add up the two known values (Pokémon + Yu-Gi-Oh!), and subtract the sum from the total number of cards.

$$102 + 96 = 198$$

$$282 - 198 = 84$$

So the three ratios we now have are:

Pokémon	96:282
Yu-Gi-Oh!	102:282
Magic the Gathering	84:282

We can see that there are more Yu-Gi-Oh! cards and therefore if a card is drawn at random, it is most likely that it will be a Yu-Gi-Oh! card. Our choice is clear . . . B!

With those two problems under our belt, we can now dive into the murkier waters of the application of ratios and rates. What happens when our friend, the variable, comes to pay a visit?

EXAMPLE

A camel spits on five people every 4 days. At this rate, how many people will the camel spit on in $4 + d$ days?

A. $\frac{5}{4} + d$

B. $\frac{5}{4} + \frac{d}{4}$

C. $\frac{5}{4} + \frac{5}{4d}$

D. $5 + \frac{d}{4}$

E. $5 + \frac{5d}{4}$

SOLUTION

"I don't remember ever using variables in 6th and 7th grade" you might say to yourself. "I was more worried about getting <insert name here> to notice me." While the second statement may be true, let us jog your memory about the first. Here, we will need to set up a true proportion and solve it. Let's set up an equation with what we know and then we can solve for what we still need to know. We know our rate is 5 spits every 4 days. So we want to make a variable (let's say x) that will represent the number of spits in $4 + d$ days.

$$\frac{5(\text{spits})}{4(\text{days})} = \frac{x(\text{spits})}{4 + d(\text{days})}$$

Now, we can multiply both sides of the equation by $(4 + d)$ to get . . .

$$\frac{5(4 + d)}{4} = x$$

And now, looking at our choices . . . ah, drat! No such luck yet. We need to use our distributive property and fraction knowledge to make our expression $\frac{5(4+d)}{4}$ look like one of those choices.

$$\frac{5(4+d)}{4} = \frac{20+5d}{4} = \frac{20}{4} + \frac{5d}{4} = 5 + \frac{5d}{4}$$

And there we have it. Our answer is E.

Percentages are related to ratios and rates because they are a special kind of ratio that is always compared to $\frac{1}{100}$.

The Two Eggs of Percent Hatching

CHANGE A DECIMAL TO A PERCENT:

Move the decimal to the right 2 places.

$.359 = 35.9\%$

$1.97 = 197\%$

CHANGE A FRACTION TO A PERCENT:

Convert the fraction to a decimal with your calculator, and move the decimal to the right 2 places.

$\frac{5}{7} = .714 = 71.4\%$

$\frac{9}{4} = 2.25 = 225\%$

STRATEGY ALERT

How to Solve a Sales Percentage Problem

Learn the Native Language: When you're entering Math country, you need to learn the language. In percents, the word "of" will always mean "multiply" and the word "is" will always mean "equals." Don't start confusing the words, because the Math people aren't known for their outright friendliness, if you know what I mean.

Let's try our native language strategy with an ACT-like question:

A clothing store is currently having a 15% off sale on pants. If a certain pair of pants costs $28, how much would the pants be after the discount?

A. $3.20

B. $4.20

C. $6.80

D. $21.80

E. $23.80

So, we're looking for this: 15% **of** 28 **is** what? Or .15 **multiplied by** 28 **equals** = ?

$$28 \times .15 = 4.2.$$

The answer, however, is not Choice B. Why? We just figured out 15% of 28, and that *wasn't the question.* We need to know the *new price of the pants.* Now, we have to subtract the 4.2 from the original amount to get the discounted price.

$28 – $4.2 = $23.80, which is Choice E.

The pants that were originally $28 are now on sale for $23.80 because of a 15% discount. Learn the native language; get the answer correct.

Area, Surface Area, and Volume

Important Vocabulary

Term	Definition
Perimeter	The distance around a 2-dimensional shape.
Area	The size of a surface or the amount of space inside the boundary of a 2-dimensional shape.
Surface Area	The total area of the surface of a 3-dimensional object.
Volume	The amount of 3-dimensional space an object occupies.

Although some formulas will be given to you on the ACT, knowledge of the following formulas are assumed. Memorize them if you don't already have them down.

Perimeter, Circumference, and Area Formulas

Square

side length s

$P = 4s$

$A = s^2$

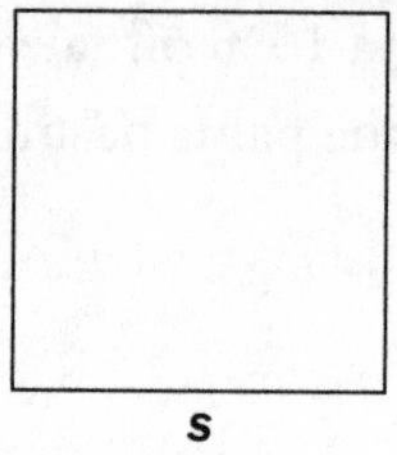

Rectangle

length l and width w

$P = 2l + 2w$

$A = lw$

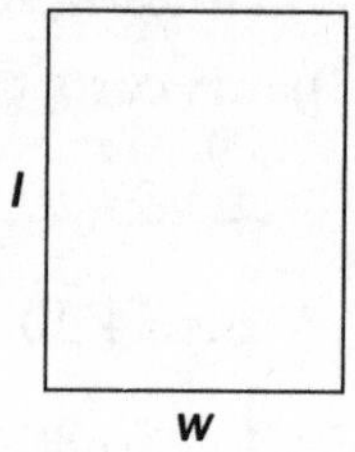

Triangle

side lengths a, b and c, base b, and height h

$P = a + b + c$

$A = \frac{1}{2}bh$

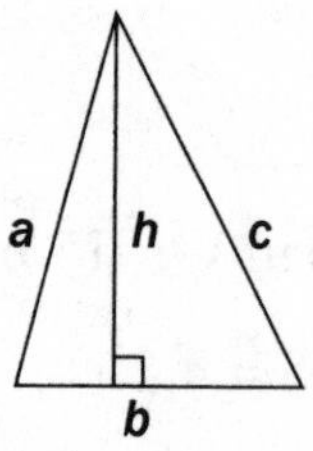

Circle

radius r

$C = 2\pi r$

$A = \pi r^2$

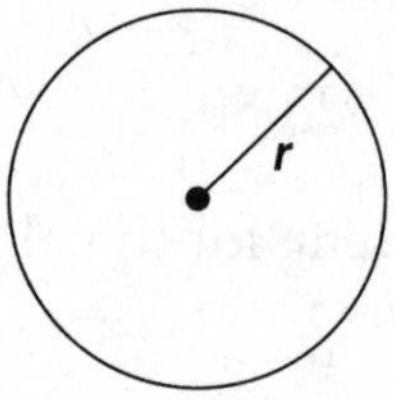

Rectangular Solid

l = length, w = width, h = height

Volume: $V = lwh$

Surface Area: $S = 2lw + 2lh + 2wh$

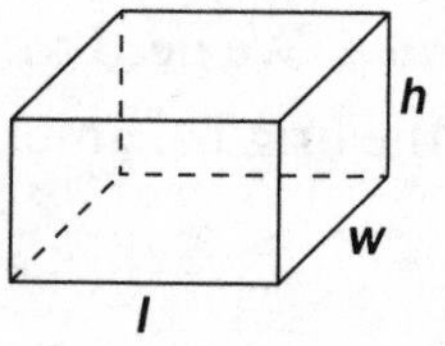

For this section, it's still not good enough to just know the formulas. You also need to know how to apply them in various contexts.

Let's try one:

EXAMPLE

A speaker box has a width of 8 inches and a length of 13 inches. How tall to the nearest inch can the speaker be if the volume should be no greater than 500 in^2?

A. 2

B. 3

C. 4

D. 5

E. 6

SOLUTION

For this problem, we need to remember the formula for volume and then work backwards.

Since $V = l \times w \times h$ for any rectangular prism, then we know $500 = 8 \times 13 \times h$, where h is the height of the speaker box. Since $500 = 104h$, then $h = \frac{500}{104} \approx 4.8$. Since the volume can be no more than 500 in^2, and we can only include a full inch, our height has to be 4 inches. C is the correct answer.

EXAMPLE

The formula for the perimeter of a rectangle is $P = 2(l + w)$ where l is the length and w is the width. If both the length and width were doubled, the perimeter would be multiplied by what factor?

A. $\frac{1}{2}$

B. 2

C. 4

D. 4.5

E. 10

SOLUTION

When a problem like this one asks you to do something to a variable in the formula and see the outcome, show what would happen to the formula and rewrite it to make sense of one of the answers.

If we were to double the length and the width, the formula would look like this:

$$P = 2(2l + 2w) = 2(2(l + w)) = 4(l + w)$$

At this point, it might be tempting to pick 4, but that is a *distractor*. Let's go back to our original equation and compare it.

Original formula: $P = 2(l + w)$

New formula: $P = 4(l + w)$

The only difference between the original formula and the new one is that the new one is the old one multiplied by 2. Our answer is B.

Average and Median

Mean: The mean is the average of a set of numbers. To find it, add up all the data and divide by the total.

Median: The median is the middle number when the numbers are arranged in numerical order. If there's an odd number of data, it's the middle one. If there's an even number of data, it's the average between the two middle numbers.

Here's an ACT-like problem:

The table below shows the number of songs on 45 different albums sold in the U.S. What is the average number of songs per album to the nearest 0.1 song?

Number of songs on an album	Number of albums with this total
9	8
10	12
11	11
12	6
13	5
14	3

HEADINGS ARE THE MOST IMPORTANT THING ABOUT A TABLE. I cannot shout this loud enough. Mess up the heading, mess up the problem.

For example, in the table above, it looks like you only have 6 or 12 pieces of data, and you know there are supposed to be 45. Well, if you pay attention to the headings, you'll see that there are actually 45 pieces of data here. Let's figure it out:

The first column has the number of songs on an album. The first entry in that column is 9. But, the other column tells me that there are 8 albums with 9 songs on them, so in actuality, there are 8 9s in that first row.

HEADS UP

When rounding, pay close attention to the number to the RIGHT of the place value you have to round to. If it's a 5 or higher, the number to the left will go up. If it's a 4 or lower, the number will stay the same.

Place values: thousands hundreds tens ones . tenths hundredths thousandths

54.7863 rounded to tenths is 54.8

54.7863 rounded to hundredths is 54.79

The question asks us to find the average number of songs per album. You could count them all up and divide, but that would be tedious and time-consuming. Here's a shortcut:

In this type of table, just take numbers *next to each other* and multiply them.

8 albums $\times$ 9 songs = 72 songs, $10 \times 12 = 120$, etc.

Then add up all of those totals.

$72 + 120 + 121 + 72 + 65 + 42 = 492$.

Then take that sum and divide it by your total number of albums. The question tells us there are 45.

$492/45 = 10.933333\ldots$

The question also tells us to round to the nearest tenth, so the answer is **10.9**. The mean (or average) of the 45 albums is 10.9.

Expressing Numbers in Different Ways

Put these values in order from smallest to largest: $\frac{16}{23}, \frac{3}{4}, 0.66, \frac{17}{24}, \frac{2}{3}$

You have your calculator, use it! Turn everything into a decimal by doing the division:

$$\frac{16}{23} = 0.695\ldots$$

$$\frac{3}{4} = 0.75$$

$$0.66 = 0.66$$

$$\frac{17}{24} = 0.708\ldots$$

$$\frac{2}{3} = 0.6666\ldots$$

Now arrange the decimals in order:

0.66 0.6666 . . . 0.695 . . . 0.708 . . . 0.75

Now arrange the fractions in order and you're finished!

$$0.66 \quad \frac{2}{3} \quad \frac{16}{23} \quad \frac{17}{24} \quad \frac{3}{4}$$

Absolute Value Equations

Absolute value equations are simply equations with absolute value signs $|x|$, which show how far away from zero a number is.

$|3| = x$. The answer is 3 because the number 3 is 3 spots away from zero on a number line.

$|-3| = x$. The answer is also 3 because the number –3 is 3 spots away from zero on a number line.

Now, let's ask the question this way:

$|x| = 4$. You know, the number 4 is 4 units away from zero, but you can also probably guess that –4 will be an answer. So there are two answers: $x = 4, -4$.

STRATEGY ALERT

How to Solve an Absolute Value Equation

Bump, Make 2, and Check: If you say this fast, it sounds an awful lot like a Russian ballet dancer. "Now introducing, Natalia Bumpmake2andcheck, who will perform a pas de deux with her partner, Ivan Pleasepickupthecheck." Silly? Da. Is the strategy silly? Nyet!

We'll try it with an ACT question:

Solve this equation for x: $|2x + 4| - 3 = 11$

A. 5

B. –9

C. 5, –9

D. –5, 9

E. No solution

Bump everything away from the absolute value sign by adding 3 to both sides

$|2x + 4| - 3 = 11$

$|2x + 4| = 14$

Make 2 equations, one with a negative answer and one with a positive, get rid of the absolute value signs, and solve both:

Equation 1: $2x + 4 = 14$
Subtract 4 from each side
$2x = 10$
Divide by 2
$x = 5$

Equation 2: $2x + 4 = -14$
Subtract 4 from each side
$2x = -18$
Divide by 2
$x = -9$

Check for *extraneous* solutions, a solution that just won't work. Sometimes, in these equations you will get two answers for x and one of them won't work, so check both solutions!

$$|2(5) + 4| - 3 = |10 + 4| - 3 = |14| - 3 = 14 - 3 = 11$$

$$|2(-9) + 4| - 3 = |-18 + 4| - 3 = |-14| - 3 = 14 - 3 = 11$$

These both check out, so your answer is Choice C: 5, –9.

Practice Integrating Essential Skills

1. In a recent poll, 18 people described their local police chief as being "very ethical." This number is exactly 30% of the people surveyed. How many people were surveyed?

A. 48

B. 56

C. 60

D. 70

E. 82

2. A triangle has one side that is twice the length of another side. If the remaining side is 6 inches and the perimeter is 18 inches, what is the length in inches of the longest side?

F. 6

G. 7

H. 8

J. 9

K. 10

3. If $a{:}b$ is 4:5 and $b{:}c$ is 9:5, what is $a{:}c$?

A. 9:1

B. 9:4

C. 4:9

D. 13:10

E. 36:25

4. If $|3x + 2| - 2x = 6$, then $x =$

F. 4

G. $-\frac{8}{5}$

H. 4 and $-\frac{8}{5}$

J. –4 and $-\frac{8}{5}$

K. No solution

5. What is the average of $\frac{1}{15}$ and $\frac{1}{25}$?

A. $\frac{1}{20}$

B. $\frac{3}{10}$

C. $\frac{2}{25}$

D. $\frac{4}{75}$

E. $\frac{26}{375}$

Answers on page 126.

Preparing for Higher Math: 35 questions

"This category captures the more recent mathematics that students are learning, starting when students begin using algebra as a general way of expressing and solving equations."

—ACT.org, "Preparing for the ACT 2016–2017"

Basically, this section pulls problems from 8th grade math, Algebra 1, Geometry, and Algebra 2. Before you start running for the hills, here's the good news: this math should be fresh in your memory and should feel familiar.

Number and Quantity: 4–6 questions

Real and Complex Numbers

Real numbers on their own are going to be addressed most likely with operations containing radicals (square roots and cube roots) and will be in fraction form. Let's jump right into a problem.

$\frac{2}{\sqrt{3}} + \frac{1}{\sqrt{5}} = ?$

A. $\frac{2\sqrt{5} + \sqrt{3}}{\sqrt{8}}$

B. $\frac{2\sqrt{5} + \sqrt{3}}{\sqrt{15}}$

C. $\frac{3}{\sqrt{3} + \sqrt{5}}$

D. $\frac{3}{\sqrt{8}}$

E. $\frac{3}{\sqrt{15}}$

Although you can definitely work this problem out, you don't need to, and that's the secret to not losing a bunch of time on a problem like this one. To get this problem correct, you really just need to remember the rules of fractions.

One rule is that when adding fractions, you cannot add them if they don't have common denominators. If I had $\frac{1}{2}$ of a candy bar and wanted to add to that $\frac{1}{4}$ of a candy bar, it would not make $\frac{2}{6}$ of a candy bar. Rather, I have to remember that $\frac{1}{2}$ is equivalent to $\frac{2}{4}$ and then I can add $\frac{2}{4}$ to $\frac{1}{4}$ to make $\frac{3}{4}$.

Looking at our answer choices, we can eliminate answers A, C, and D because all three denominators will only be created if you add across and that's not how fractions behave. Then between B and E, you have to remember that when you do multiply the denominators, you also must mimic the same multiplication across each numerator. Since E is unchanged in the numerator, the answer must be B.

For those of you who like to see the problem officially "done out," I've included it below, but know that this strategy is a big time commitment. I would do as much as I can to use what I know about numbers to avoid resorting to this strategy.

$$\frac{2}{\sqrt{3}} + \frac{1}{\sqrt{5}} = \frac{2 \times \sqrt{5}}{\sqrt{3} \times \sqrt{5}} + \frac{1 \times \sqrt{3}}{\sqrt{5} \times \sqrt{3}} = \frac{2\sqrt{5}}{\sqrt{15}} + \frac{\sqrt{3}}{\sqrt{15}} = \frac{2\sqrt{5} + \sqrt{3}}{\sqrt{15}}$$

Complex numbers are numbers made up of a real part and an imaginary part.

Unicorns are cool. Sure, they don't exist, but you would recognize a picture of one and could maybe even pick one out from a list of descriptions (a flying horse with a forehead horn; bikers get them tattooed on their shoulder blades; Voldemort drank the blood of one in HP1 so he could stay alive, etc.). In math, complex numbers are our unicorns. They are numbers that don't necessarily exist, but you still can recognize them and do cool stuff with them.

Every complex number will contain the number *i*. $i = \sqrt{-1}$. So $i^2 = \left(\sqrt{-1}\right)^2 = -1$. A complex number itself is usually reported in the form $a + bi$ where a is the *real* part and bi is the *imaginary* part. Numbers like $2 + 4i$ or $3 - 6i$ are complex. And all you'll really need to know about them is how to solve them on the ACT.

STRATEGY ALERT

How to Solve Complex Number Problems

FLIP and FOIL: This method will help you reduce your complex numbers so you don't feel like skewering *yourself* and lying down on the coals to sizzle when these types of math questions pop up on the ACT.

Let's try it:

Reduce to $a + bi$ form: $\dfrac{4+8i}{3-2i}$

A. $\dfrac{-4}{13} + \dfrac{32}{13i}$

B. $\dfrac{4}{3} - 4i$

C. $\dfrac{4}{3} + 4i$

D. $\dfrac{4}{13} - \dfrac{32}{13i}$

E. $\dfrac{28}{13} + \dfrac{32}{13i}$

First, let's **FLIP**!

We have to multiply the numerator and denominator after *flipping the denominator's sign.* In this case, when we flip the sign of 3 – 2*i*, we get 3 + 2*i*.

$$\frac{4+8i}{3-2i}\times\frac{3+2i}{3+2i}=\frac{(4+8i)(3+2i)}{(3-2i)(3+2i)}$$

That didn't help at all!!! Well, actually it looks like it didn't, but we're getting closer. Calm down. Now, we need the second half of our strategy: FOIL.

$$\frac{(4+8i)(3+2i)}{(3-2i)(3+2i)}=\frac{12+8i+24i+16i^2}{9+6i-6i-4i^2}=\frac{12+32i+16i^2}{9-4i^2}$$

"You've got to be kidding me!" says you. "That didn't make anything better!"

Well, that's because you left that i^2 in there, silly. Remember, that $i^2 = -1$, which is a little more manageable, right? Let's put a –1 everywhere we see an i^2.

$$\frac{12+32i+16i^2}{9-4i^2}=\frac{12+32i+16(-1)}{9-4(-1)}=\frac{12+32i-16}{9+4}=\frac{-4+32i}{13}=\frac{-4}{13}+\frac{32}{13i}$$

There. The final product in *a* + *bi* form is Choice A. Don't you feel smart?

Integer and Rational Exponents

Exponents and square roots are connected! An exponent is the number of times a base is multiplied by itself to get a particular number ($5 \times 5 \times 5 \times 5 = 5^4$). 4 is the exponent. A square root is what you get when you divide a number (say 16) by the two numbers that go into it equally (say 4). 4 is the square root of 16. And here's the connection: a square root is actually just an exponent in the form of a fraction. Check it out:

$$x^{\frac{1}{2}} = \sqrt{x},$$

$$4^{\frac{1}{2}} = \sqrt{4} = 2$$

Similarly, a cubed root is also a fraction:

$$x^{\frac{1}{3}} = \sqrt[3]{x},$$

$$8^{\frac{1}{3}} = \sqrt[3]{8} = 2$$

Notice the 3 in the denominator of the exponential fraction and the 3 in front of the square root (radical) sign. That is not a coincidence; that is the connection.

The Three Eggs of Exponent Hatching

To Multiply 2 Numbers with the Same Base/Different Exponents:

Add the exponents.

$$x^a \times x^b = x^{a+b}$$

To Divide 2 Numbers with the Same Base/Different Exponents:

Subtract the exponents.

$$\frac{x^a}{x^b} = x^{a-b}$$

To Solve Negative Exponents:

Flip it.

$$x^{-a} = \frac{1}{x^a}, \frac{x^{-a}}{y^{-b}} = \frac{y^b}{x^a}$$

On the ACT, you may see a question like this:

$$\text{Simplify } \frac{x^{-2}y^5z^{-3}}{x^{-4}yz^2}.$$

To solve, we'll need to use one of our handy-dandy strategies.

STRATEGY ALERT

How to Simplify an Exponential Expression

Flip-Flop and Chop: No, this isn't the subtitle to *Kung-Fu Panda 2* (although it should be). This is a quick way to remember how to cancel these funny little expressions. First, you Flip-Flop by moving the negative exponents to make them positive. If they are in the numerator, put them in the denominator and take away the negative. Vice versa if they're in the denominator:

$$\frac{x^{-2}y^5z^{-3}}{x^{-4}yz^2} = \frac{x^4y^5}{x^2yz^2 \times z^3}$$

Now, Chop: Hack away at canceling and combining like terms—get rid of as many x's and y's as you can with a couple of those eggs from exponent hatching:

$$\frac{x^4y^5}{x^2yz^2 \times z^3} = \frac{x^2y^4}{z^5}$$

There! We are done. All negatives have been taken away and all like terms have been combined.

Matrices

Matrices are groups of numbers (and sometimes variables) arranged by column and row in a box-like set of brackets.

There are lots of tricky maneuvers that you can do with matrices, but luckily the ACT limits the types of problems you will do. Let's take a look at one example you may see on the ACT.

STRATEGY ALERT

How to Solve Multiplication Matrices Problems

Let Your Fingers Do the Walkin': Those pointer fingers of yours, although great for all sorts of things — beckoning your love interest from across the room, pointing at UFOs, indicating the meal number you'd like at Happy Wok — are especially good at helping you solve matrices problems. Don't believe me? Check it out below.

Here's a question like you'll see on the ACT:

One ice skating arena hosts two hockey teams: X and Y. The owner is restocking the teams' equipment (helmets, sticks, and pucks). The matrices below show the numbers of each piece of equipment needed per team and the cost for each type of equipment. What is the total amount the owner will spend on restocking for both teams?

$$\begin{array}{c} \\ X \\ Y \end{array} \begin{array}{c} \begin{array}{ccc} H & S & P \end{array} \\ \left| \begin{array}{ccc} 7 & 13 & 35 \\ 5 & 9 & 45 \end{array} \right| \end{array} \quad S \quad \begin{array}{c} \$50 \\ \$35 \\ \$2 \end{array}$$

A. $560

B. $1,020

C. $1,305

D. $1,530

E. $2,035

Let your index fingers solve it for you! Here are the rules:

- Your left hand is in charge of the left matrix, and your right hand in charge of the right one.
- Your left hand ALWAYS moves left to right.
- Your right hand ALWAYS moves top to bottom.

Now, let's figure out the cost for team X first.

Point at the left-most entry with your left hand on the left matrix, and the topmost entry with your right hand on the right matrix.

You should be at 7 and \$50. Now multiply those two numbers together.

Then move one to the right with your left hand and one down with your right hand.

Now you are at 13 and \$35. Multiply those two numbers together.

Do the same thing with 35 and \$2.

Total up the numbers: \$350 + \$455 + \$70 = \$875.

Now complete the same process for the Y team to find a total:

\$250 + \$315 + \$90 = \$655.

Finally, add the two totals together and you will have your answer:

\$875 + \$655 = \$1,530. The total cost is \$1,530, Choice D.

See? Those index fingers are *handier* than you thought.

Algebra: 7–9 questions

Simplifying Expressions

On the ACT exam, you will encounter items where you will be required to perform operations with expressions. Let's look at a couple of examples below.

In scientific notation, 82,000,000 + 90,000,000 = ?

A. 1.72×10^{-9}

B. 1.72×10^{7}

C. 1.72×10^{8}

D. 1.72×10^{9}

E. 1.72×10^{15}

The first thing you will need to decide is whether you want to add the crazy big numbers presented here in standard form (as presented) or scientific notation (answers). I'm partial to adding as is and then interpreting to scientific notation, and since I'm driving this boat, you get to follow along.

$$82{,}000{,}000 + 90{,}000{,}000 = 172{,}000{,}000.$$

Word to the wise: the commas can help you keep your place values lined up—it's easy to make mistakes if you don't pay attention to those helpful place value markers.

Now we have to decide which of the expressions presented in scientific notation are equivalent to 172 million. We can rule out two right away—A and E. Since A includes a power of 10 with a negative exponent, that's going to be a teeny tiny decimal and definitely nowhere near the millions. E is a problem because if you remember the connection between a power of 10 and the number of zeroes, $10^{15} = 1{,}000{,}000{,}000{,}000{,}000$ (1 quadrillion). That's too big.

So we are left with B, C, and D. To get specific, we'll use the same strategy we did with E, keeping in mind our power of 10. We are looking for a number in the hundred millions, and the powers of 10 (ones, thousands, millions, billions, etc.) on each power of 3. So $10^3 = 1{,}000$ (1 thousand) and $10^6 = 1{,}000{,}000$ (1 million). Therefore $10^9 = 1{,}000{,}000{,}000$ (1 billion) which is one place value too big for our number, so if we back it up to $10^8 = 100{,}000{,}000$ and then multiply that by 1.72, we will get 172,000,000. Our choice is C.

Another topic you will see is an application of the distributive property in multiplying polynomials. We've been using the distributive property since the 3rd grade (although our teachers probably didn't start calling it that until middle school), so this should be familiar!

Which one of the following expressions is equivalent to $4x^3(5x - 2y + x + 3y)$?

A. $28x^3y$

B. $7xy$

C. $24x^3 - 4y$

D. $24x^4 - 4x^3y$

E. $24x^4 + 4x^3y$

For this problem, we need to apply the distributive property, but first, we can simplify the expression in the parenthesis, and then distribute. Just remember your exponent rules! When multiplying variables, they don't affect the value of the number in each term (known as the coefficient).

$$4x^3(5x - 2y + x + 3y) = 4x^3(6x + y) = 24x^4 + 4x^3y$$

From there you can see that our choice is E.

Using Equations

Although many types of equations are on the ACT, the most important to understand are linear and quadratic equations. The following examples deal with both in a very cool two-for-one kind of way.

A student was studying how fast a certain tank was being filled with water at a constant rate. The table below gives the height, h inches, of the water at 1 minute intervals from $t = 0$ minutes to $t = 5$ minutes.

t	0	1	2	3	4	5
h	12	20	28	36	44	52

Which of the following equations represents the relationship between h and t?

A. $h = t + 12$

B. $h = 8t + 4$

C. $h = 8t + 12$

D. $h = 12t + 8$

E. $h = 32t$

In a linear relationship, the rate of increase/decrease is always *constant*. When an item has the term "constant rate" you can always assume it's going to be linear which is represented in the form $y = mx + b$ with m representing the constant rate of change (slope) and b representing the initial value which always occurs when $x = 0$. In our problem, we will use h and t instead of x and y as the variables because that's what we were given.

So, first, we need to find h, so head on over to the table and find where $t = 0$. There, we can see that the h-value is 12 when t is 0. So our initial value is 12. This narrows our choices down to just A and C where both equations have "+ 12" at the end. Then we just have to look at how each value changes as our time changes. Head back to the table and notice that each t value increases by 1. When that happens, at the same time, the height increases by 8 inches, so our constant rate of change is 8 inches per minute meaning our slope is $\frac{8}{1}$. In the equation for A, our constant rate of change is 1, since every variable has an assumed 1 being multiplied by it. In the equation for C, however, we can see that $h = 8t + 12$ has both a slope of 8 and an initial value of 12. So our answer is, of course, C!

Quadratic Equations

Quadratic equations are $ax^2 + bx + c = 0$, where a, b, and c are numbers.

In the equation $x^2 - 3x - 18 = 0$, x^2 is the "a" term, -3 is the "b" term, and -18 is the "c" term.

On the test, you will be asked either to find the factors of a quadratic equation or to solve one. Below, you will find out how to do both.

Here's an easy quadratic equation that you will see on the ACT:

If $x^2 - 9x + 25 = 5$, what are the possible values for x?

A. –3, –5

B. –4, –5

C. –4, 5

D. 4, 5

E. –5, –5

With this type of equation, we could go through and solve it, but that would be dumb. It's easier and faster to plug in the numbers when you only have one step to the problem. First, plug in one of those –4s, because if it doesn't work, we're actually eliminating two answers.

$$(-4)^2 - 9 \times -4 + 25 = 77.$$

No. Choices B and C are wrong. If one of the numbers doesn't work, then the entire answer is incorrect.

Let's try Choice D:

$4^2 - 9 \times 4 + 25 = 5.$

It works! And since this is the only answer with a positive 4, and it happens to work, it must be the right one. We don't even have to check the positive 5.

Now not all of the quadratic equations on the ACT are going to be this simple. Check out this one:

What is the sum of the 2 solutions of the equation $x^2 - 9x + 25 = 5$?

A. –9

B. –8

C. 1

D. 0

E. 9

Here, we can't plug in numbers. We need to first find the two possibilities for x, and then add them up to get the answer choice. If we see one of these types of questions, we'll have to use a strategy to solve it.

STRATEGY ALERT

How to Solve a Quadratic Equation

ZIF it Up: ZIF stands for "Zero, Input, and Factor," which is a really handy way to solve quadratics. First you set everything equal to zero, input the + or – signs into your parentheses, and then factor it out to solve.

Let's try it with our problem from above:

What is the sum of the 2 solutions of the equation $x^2 - 9x + 25 = 5$?

Zero It Out:

Any time you are solving for x and you see x being raised to a power, combine like terms and set them equal to zero.

$$x^2 - 9x + 25 = 5$$

To zero this out, we need to subtract 5 from both sides:

$$x^2 - 9x + 20 = 0$$

Input the Signs:

First, set up the equation like this:

$$(x \quad)(x \quad) = 0$$

Then, you find and input the signs. Your "c" term in the quadratic equation always tells you whether the signs inside the parentheses will be the same or different. Here are the rules:

If "c" is negative, your first sign will be positive and the second will be negative.

$$(x + \quad)(x - \quad)$$

If "c" is positive and "b" is positive, then both signs will be positive.

$$(x + \quad)(x + \quad)$$

If "c" is positive and "b" is negative, then both signs will be negative.

$$(x - \quad)(x - \quad)$$

$$\underset{a}{x^2} - \underset{b}{9x} + \underset{c}{20} = 0$$

In our quadratic equation above, our c term (+20) is positive and our b term (–9) is negative, so our parentheses look like this:

$$(x - \quad)(x - \quad) = 0$$

Factor Your C, So It Adds Up to B:

Finally, you need to figure out what numbers go in the last spots, and this is easy to do!

First, find factors of your "c" term that will add up to your "b" term. So here, we need factors of the number 20 that will add up to –9.

(1, 20) (–1, –20) (2, 10) (–2, –10), (4, 5) (–4, –5).

Hmm, well, –4 and –5 add up to –9 but do they make the equation work? Let's see!

$$(x - 4) \times (x - 5) = 0$$

$$(-4 - 4) \times (-4 - 5) = 72$$

The negative answers don't work there, so we need to drop the negative signs to see if *that works*.

$$(x - 4) \times (x - 5) = 0$$

$$(4 - 4) \times (4 - 5) = 0$$

$$(5 - 4) \times (5 - 5) = 0$$

Yes! The positive 4 and 5 work. So, our answers are $x = 4, 5$, which when added together (the sum) gives us Choice E, which is 9. By the way, if you were to FOIL, you would find that the binomial ends up being what we started with. So we got it!

Solving Systems of Equations

System of Equations is any number of equations where more than one equation is in play.

Luckily, on the ACT, you will never see more than two equations at a time. Whew! One or two questions will give you two equations with an x and a y variable and ask you to solve them for both variables. In the past, you may have learned how to approach these problems a couple of different ways but on the ACT, you really just need this strategy:

STRATEGY ALERT

How to Solve a System of Equations

Use Kindergarten Math: To figure out the variables in a system of equations, all you need are your ten fingers and toes. Huh? Yep. Those sweet little digits, which first taught you to add and subtract in kindergarten, (i.e., If Johnny picks 2 apples and you pick 1 apple, how many apples have been picked?) are going to help you solve a system of equations because you really just need to add or subtract one from the other.

So, let's use our kindergarten math strategy on this ACT problem:

Solve this system of equations for x and y: $3x + 2y = 16$
$3x - y = 10$

A. (4, 2)

B. (–4, –2)

C. (–4, 2)

D. (4, –2)

E. (2, 2)

First, we add or subtract. Here, since there's a $3x$ in both equations, we'll just subtract the second from the first to get rid of the x variable.

$$\begin{array}{r} 3x + 2y = 16 \\ -(3x - y = 10) \\ \hline 3y = 6 \end{array}$$

Then, solve for y.

$$\frac{3y}{3} = \frac{6}{3}$$

$$y = 2$$

Plug y into either equation and solve for x.

$$\begin{array}{r} 3x - (2) = 10 \\ 3x + 2 = 10 + 2 \\ \hline 3x = 12 \end{array}$$

$$\frac{3x}{3} = \frac{12}{3}$$

$$x = 4$$

So your final answer is $x = 4$ and $y = 2$, which is Choice A.

Practice Number and Quantity and Algebra

1. A school is putting on a play with roles for Boys (B) and Girls (G). The director is ordering the costumes for the play including hats, coats, and shoes. The matrices below show the numbers of each costume item needed per gender and the cost to rent each costume piece. What is the total amount the director will spend on those costume pieces for the whole cast?

$$\begin{array}{c} \\ G \\ B \end{array} \begin{array}{c} \begin{array}{ccc} H & C & S \end{array} \\ \begin{vmatrix} 10 & 6 & 16 \\ 13 & 3 & 20 \end{vmatrix} \end{array} \qquad \begin{array}{c} \$5 \\ \$15 \\ \$10 \end{array}$$

   A. \$330

   B. \$450

   C. \$520

   D. \$585

   E. \$610

2. $6x^3y^4 \times 3xy \times 2xy^2$ is equivalent to:

   F. $11x^3y^6$

   G. $11x^5y^7$

   H. $36x^3y^6$

   J. $36x^5y^6$

   K. $36x^5y^7$

3. If $x \neq 0$, *and* $x^2 + 5x = 20x$, then $x = ?$

   A. 6

   B. 8

   C. 10

   D. 12

   E. 15

4. If –2 is a solution for the equation $x^2 - nx - 24 = 0$, what is the value of n?

F. –14

G. –10

H. 10

J. 14

K. Cannot be determined from the given information.

5. Reduce to $a + bi$ form: $\frac{5-6i}{3+4i}$

A. $\frac{5}{3}-\frac{3}{2}i$

B. $\frac{5}{3}+\frac{3}{2}i$

C. $\frac{-9}{25}-\frac{38}{25}i$

D. $\frac{-8}{19}+\frac{2}{19}i$

E. $\frac{3}{19}-\frac{2}{19}i$

Answers on page 127.

Functions: 7–9 questions

Function Definition, Notation, and Representation

Functions reveal a relationship between two variables. Functions are written a little differently than equations, but they're similar in an apples-to-oranges kind of way. Both are fruits, different trees produce them.

A function is usually named $f(x)$ or $g(x)$ and can be written this way:

$$f(x) = 2x - 4$$

which reads "*f* of *x* equals two *x* minus four."

The $f(x)$ does not mean that f is being multiplied by x. The function itself is "f" and the "(x)" is the variable that is most important in terms of the function. Everything after the equals sign defines that function.

One of the most basic things the ACT will ask you to do with functions is to evaluate them for a specific value. As long as you remember how to substitute (or "plug in") values into equations, you will be able to do this well.

If $f(x) = (2x - 3)^3$, then $f(3) = ?$

A. –1

B. 0

C. 1

D. 9

E. 27

Notice in the question, the value next to "f" is x at first and then 3. So it's asking you to substitute 3 in for x and evaluate the expression. Here's all you have to do:

$$f(3) = (2(3) - 3)^3 = (6 - 3)^3 = 3^3 = 3 \times 3 \times 3 = 27$$

Our answer is E.

STRATEGY ALERT

How to Solve a Two-Function Problem

Put a Sticker On It: Stickers are fun. We collected them as kids. We scratched and sniffed them. Our teachers put them on our exceptionally fantastic reports about honeybees in fifth grade. When you have to use one function to figure out another function, the easiest way to do it is to imagine that the second function is a sticker. You peel it off the page, being careful not to lose any stray parts, and place it directly where it needs to go.

Let's try our sticker technique with one of those ACT questions:

If $f(x) = \frac{1}{4} \times 12$ and $g(x) = 2x^2 + 12x + 16$, what is the value of $f(g(x))$?

A. 28

B. $\frac{1}{2}x^2 + 3x + 16$

C. $\frac{1}{4}x^2 + 12$

D. $2x^2 + \frac{49x}{4} + 28$

E. $2x^2 + 3x + 28$

Here, our "*x*" in the first term is being defined by the second term. We really need to find $f(g(x))$. All it's really asking us to do is put the entire $g(x)$ sticker everywhere you see an x in the function $f(x)$. It's actually not too bad once you know what you are doing.

So peel that $g(x)$ sticker off the page and stick it over the top of the x:

$$f(g(x)) = f(2x^2 + 12x + 16) = \frac{1}{4}(2x^2 + 12x + 16) + 12$$

Then solve:

$$\frac{1}{2}x^2 + 3x + 4 + 12 =$$

$$\frac{1}{2}x^2 + 3x + 16$$

Choice B is correct.

Important Features from Graphs

The reason why we graph any equation or function is to reveal key features that you might not be able to see in the equation as written. For instance, if you graph a quadratic function in the form $f(x) = ax^2 + bx + c$, then it will make a parabola either pointing upward or downward. One of the key features of a parabola is that it has a vertex—a point that is either the lowest point or the highest point on the graph. That means that there's exactly one x-value that will produce the highest or lowest y-value.

Another key feature of graphs will be revealed in the next problem.

> The equation $y = ax^3 + bx^2 + cx + d$ is graphed in the standard (x, y) coordinate plane below for real values of a, b, c, and d. When $y = 0$, which of the following best describes the solutions for x?

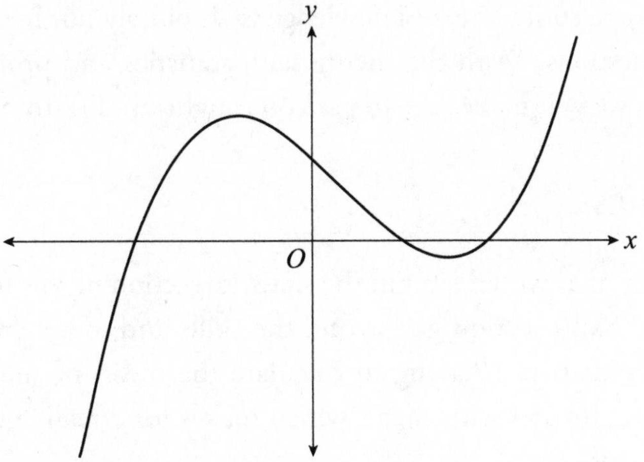

> **A.** 3 distinct positive real solutions
>
> **B.** 3 distinct negative real solutions
>
> **C.** 1 negative and 2 positive real solutions
>
> **D.** 3 real solutions that are not distinct
>
> **E.** 3 distinct solutions that are not real

Another important feature of a graph is it reveals the solutions for when the function is set equal to zero. These solutions occur when $y = 0$, or graphically, when the function touches the x-axis. Each time the curve does this, you will have a real solution. Therefore, we can easily see that this function has 3 real solutions. But now we have to figure out if they are positive or negative. The negative x-values are to the left side of the y-axis, and the positive values are to the right side of the y-axis. So we can see that the function crosses the x-axis once on the left side of the y-axis and twice on the right side, there is 1 negative solution and there are 2 positive solutions. Our answer is C.

Statistics and Probability: 5–7 questions

The statistics and probability concepts on the ACT are all addressed in middle school math, Algebra 1, and Algebra 2. So although you've probably had statistics or probability courses beyond those and have more familiarity with the concepts since then, a supersonic level of knowledge is absolutely not necessary to be successful on the ACT questions. With that being said, statistics and probability are often overlooked areas, so we will make sure to get you caught up. Presto bango.

Statistics

Questions that would land in the statistics section of this test and not in the Integrating Essential Skills section go beyond the skills and ideas already addressed in this book. So rather than just having to calculate the mean or median, you might have to do something further with them, which makes for a really great evening of mathematical shenanigans.

Here's an example:

What is the difference between the mean and the median of the set {3, 7, 9, 13}?

A. 0

B. 1

C. 4

D. 8

E. 12

You can see that we need to find both the mean and the median and then subtract because of that little word "difference."

Let's first find the mean (average).

$$\frac{3+7+9+13}{4} = \frac{32}{4} = 8$$

Now we need to find the median (middle number). When doing that, we know it's not 3 or 13 because those are on the ends. But how to choose between 7 and 9? You don't! Just average out those numbers to get an answer of 8.

Finally, to answer the question, we must subtract: 8 – 8 = 0. A is our choice! Bravo!

Probability

Questions in this section will test your ability to understand and apply concepts of probability.

Probability is all about chance. It's the likelihood of an event happening in the future.

If the words "what is the probability" ever pop up in a question, you can use this rule: **part divided by the whole.** This means, if you have a bag of six marbles and one is white, two are red, and three are blue, then you have a two out of six chance of drawing a red marble. So, the probability is $\frac{2}{6} = \frac{1}{3}$ or a 33.3% chance. The bottom number will always be the total number of marbles/basketballs/cousins/etc. in a question. The top number will be the part of the total you're looking for: the chance of pulling a red marble out of a bag, getting the deflated basketball out of the bin, identifying your second cousin from an old photo, etc.

STRATEGY ALERT

How to Solve Probability Problems

Chicken Scratch Your Possibilities: Probabilities are easy to solve if you take a quick second and scratch out a quick list of the possible outcomes. This can be in your secret, only-comprehensible-to-you handwriting. You'll be able to visualize the problem better and can solve toughies easier, like those probability questions that include the words "and" or "or."

Let's chicken scratch our possibilities with this ACT probability question:

> You are rolling one die twice. Knowing that there are 36 possible outcomes, what are the chances of rolling doubles <u>and</u> rolling a 5 as the first number of any roll?
>
> **F.** $\frac{1}{8}$
>
> **G.** $\frac{2}{3}$
>
> **H.** $\frac{1}{36}$
>
> **J.** $\frac{6}{36}$
>
> **K.** $\frac{11}{36}$

The good news is that we already know the number that will be on the bottom of the equation: 36. It's given to us in the question. Now, we just have to figure the odds of rolling the same number twice *and* a five landing up first in any given roll. Sounds tough, but it isn't if you start sketching out what you've got:

Chances of rolling doubles	Chances of rolling a 5 on the first roll
(Roll 1, Roll 2)	(Roll 1, Roll 2)
(1,1), (2,2), (3,3), (4,4), (5,5), or (6,6)	(5,1), (5,2), (5,3), (5,4), (5,5), or (5,6).
So there is a 6 out of 36 chance of rolling doubles	There is also a 6 out of 36 chance of rolling a five on the first roll.

Since we are given the word "and" in the question, we now need to look for the one roll that meets both criteria. (5,5) is the only element in both sets, and it is just 1 out of 36 possibilities. Don't count it twice! So the answer is $\frac{1}{36} \approx$ a 3% chance or Choice H.

Change up this problem and use the word "or" instead of "and":

> You are rolling one die twice. Knowing that there are 36 possible outcomes, what are the chances of rolling doubles <u>or</u> rolling a 5 as the first number of any roll?

If you reviewed your possibilities again, you'd see the same data as above: a 6 out of 36 chance of rolling doubles, and a 6 out of 36 chance of rolling a five on the first roll.

The difference between this problem and the last is that little conjunction "or." With "or" you need to count *every possibility,* making sure not to count anything repeated in each column twice. So, there are 6 chances of rolling doubles, 6 chances of rolling 5, but since (5,5) is a roll that appears in both columns, we only count it once. So, there are actually only 11 possible outcomes and the probability is 11 out of 36 or $\frac{11}{36} \approx$ a 31% chance.

Practice Functions, Statistics, and Probability

1. What is the value of $f(-2)$ where $f(x) = (24 + 9x) \times (x^2 + 3x + 12)$?

   A. –60

   B. –24

   C. 24

   D. 60

   E. 920

2. A pet store currently has 5 cats and 5 dogs. If a customer purchases at random one animal for herself and one animal for her partner, what is the probability that both will be dogs?

F. $\frac{1}{10}$

G. $\frac{1}{5}$

H. $\frac{2}{5}$

J. $\frac{2}{9}$

K. $\frac{1}{2}$

3. Which of the following describes a true relationship between the functions $f(x) = (x - 4)^2 + 4$ and $g(x) = \frac{1}{3}x + 2$ graphed below in the coordinate plane?

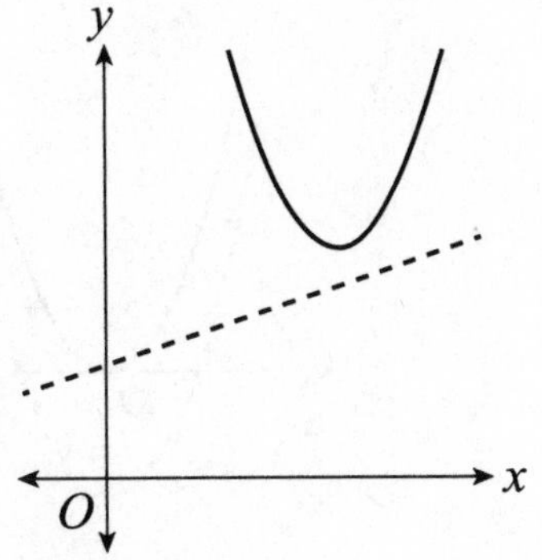

A. $f(x) = g(x)$ for exactly 2 values of x

B. $f(x) = g(x)$ for exactly 1 value of x

C. $f(x) < g(x)$ for all x

D. $f(x) > g(x)$ for all x

E. $f(x)$ is the inverse of $g(x)$

4. John has collected stamps over many years and the number of new stamps he's collected in the last 5 years is represented by the set {17, 16, 16, 22, 17}. This year, along with his other stamps, he ran across an old collection in his grandfather's attic and found 172 new stamps to add. If he added that data point to the original 5, which statement would be true?

   F. The median would increase.

   G. The median would decrease.

   H. The mean would increase

   J. The mean would decrease.

   K. Neither the median nor the mean would change.

5. The functions $y = x^2$ and $y = (x + a)^2 + b$, for constants a and b are graphed in the standard (x, y) coordinate plane below. The functions have the same maximum value. One of the following statements about the values of a and b is true. Which statement is it?

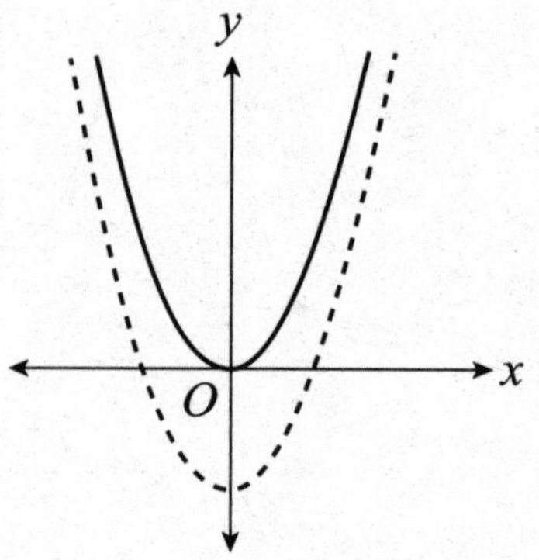

   A. $a < 0$ and $b = 0$

   B. $a = 0$ and $b < 0$

   C. $a = 0$ and $b > 0$

   D. $a > 0$ and $b = 0$

   E. $a > 0$ and $b < 0$

Answers on page 128.

Geometry: 7–9 questions

The geometry questions will test your knowledge of what you learned in Geometry class. (Makes sense, amiright?) However, there are also a few topics that you might remember from before Geometry, such as distance, midpoint, slope, and the equations of circles. Let's take a look-see.

Distance, Midpoint, and Slope

Distance, Midpoint, and Slope measure lines on the coordinate plane. Distance explains how far two points are apart, midpoint will show where the middle is between two points, and slope tells you the incline or grade of a line.

The Three Marshmallows of Coordinate Geometry

Distance Formula:	Midpoint Formula:	Slope Formula:
$d=\sqrt{(x_2-x_1)^2+(y_2-y_1)^2}$	$M=\frac{x_2+x_1}{2},\frac{y_2+y_1}{2}$	$m=\frac{y_2-y_1}{x_2-x_1}$

STRATEGY ALERT

How to Solve a Coordinate Plane Problem Involving Distance, Midpoint, or Slope

Pack the Marshmallows: Marshmallows are the glue that holds a good s'more together. You don't have marshmallows; you don't have a proper snack to nibble on around the campfire. These gooey, delicious little morsels above are the most important part of most of your Coordinate Geometry s'more sandwiches. So pack 'em up for your ACT camping trip!

Distance

A distance question on the ACT will look like this:

How many units apart are the points P (–3, –5) and Q (2, 7) in the standard (*x*, *y*) coordinate plane?

A. 10

B. 11

C. 12

D. 13

E. 14

It's easy for us to tell that this is a distance question because of the "How many units apart . . . " phrase. This will always tell you to pull out the old distance formula marshmallow. So, let's start putting in the numbers.

Let's let P be (x_1, y_1) and Q be (x_2, y_2):

$$d = \sqrt{((2)-(-3))^2 + ((7)-(-5))^2} = \sqrt{(2+3)^2 + (7+5)^2} = \sqrt{5^2 + 12^2} = \sqrt{169} = 13$$

Easy! We found that those two points are 13 units apart, which is Choice D.

Midpoint

A midpoint question might look like this:

In the standard (x, y) coordinate plane, points P and Q have coordinates (–3, 12) and (7, 4). What are the coordinates of the midpoint of $\overline{PQ}$?

A. (5, 8)

B. (3, 8)

C. (2, 8)

D. (3, 4)

E. (2, 4)

Let's grab our midpoint and plug in the points. We'll let P be (x_1, y_1) and Q can be (x_2, y_2).

$$M = \frac{x_2 + x_1}{2}, \frac{y_2 + y_1}{2}$$

$$= \frac{-3+7}{2}, \frac{12+4}{2} = \frac{4}{2}, \frac{16}{2} = (2,8)$$

HEADS UP

Make sure you're careful with your order of operations, here. The ACT's distractor questions will always involve ALMOST accurate answers. An easy slip-up is a PEMDAS mistake.

Our answer ends up as a point (Yes!) and that's just what we needed. Choice C is correct!

Slope

On the ACT, you'll be asked to read equations and name the slope as well as find the slope of two given points.

To name the slope based solely on the equation, you just have to get it in $y = mx + b$ form. That teeny m is your slope!

HEADS UP

The general line equation for slope is $y = mx + b$.

y is your *dependent variable*

m is the *slope* of the line

x is your *independent variable*

b is the *y-intercept*

Slope can be defined like this:

Increasing: going up

Decreasing: going down

Here's an ACT-type question:

What is the slope of the line passing through points P (9, –4) and Q (12, 5)?

A. 3

B. 4

C. –3

D. $\frac{1}{3}$

E. $-\frac{1}{3}$

Since you are given two points, and looking for slope, you can just use ol' slope marsh-mallow! We'll let P be (x1, y1) again:

$$m = \frac{5-(-4)}{12-(9)} = \frac{9}{3} = 3$$

The slope of the line passing through those points is 3, which also just happens to be Choice A. Brilliant!

Equations of Circles

Circles are round, have a radius, a center, and a coordinating formula that helps you figure them out:

$(x - h)^2 + (y - k)^2 = r^2$ where

- x and y correspond to the axes on the coordinate plane (as usual)
- (h, k) is the center of the circle
- r is the radius

Let's figure the parts of a circle out quickly, using just the formula and no computations:

In the circle $x^2 + (y - 3)^2 = 9$, what is the center?

Here, the center is (0, 3), which is easy to spot because the equation is already in the circle format. The "*h*" is missing, so we assume that's a zero. The "*k*" in the generic equation is preceded by a minus sign. Since the "3" in our equation is negative, the value of k is positive.

In the circle $x^2 + (y - 3)^2 = 9$, what is the radius?

No! It's not 9. The radius here is 3. Remember that the number to the right of the equal sign is an "r^2", not just a plain old r. So you have to take the square root of the 9 to get your radius, which is 3.

STRATEGY ALERT

How to Solve a Problem with Circles

Use Your Street Smarts: Everyone has street smarts — you know, that "practical" knowledge we carry around which allows us to get a nail into a wall if a hammer isn't handy and get into our house if we forgot our key. Practical knowledge shows you that a pair of shorts won't fit before you try them on, and that leaping from the apex of your apartment building onto a trampoline will not have a happy ending, unless your trajectory is just right. So, let's use our street smarts on this next question, okay?

Which of the following is an equation for the circle in the standard (x, y) coordinate plane that has its center at $(-3, 2)$ and passes through the point $(5, 8)$?

A. $(x - 3)^2 + (y + 2)^2 = 10$

B. $(x + 3)^2 + (y - 2)^2 = 10$

C. $(x - 3)^2 + (y + 2)^2 = 12$

D. $(x - 3)^2 + (y + 2)^2 = 100$

E. $(x + 3)^2 + (y - 2)^2 = 100$

First, we know that we're talking about a circle, so we have to use our circle equation:

$$(x - h)^2 + (y - k)^2 = r^2$$

Now, let's figure out what the vertex would look like in the equation. The points are (–3, 2), but we know that we have to obey those signs in the equation, so that negative gets canceled out in the "*h*" and becomes a regular ol' "3." The positive 2 becomes a –2 because it takes on the sign of the "*k*." (If it were a –2, it would cancel out.) So, just get rid of any answer choice that doesn't have a 3 in the "*h*" spot and a –2 in the "*k*" spot.

That leaves us Choices B and E.

And here's where those street smarts come in. You *could* plug in 5 for x and 8 for y and then find out if B or E is right, but it takes less time to just use your reasoning power. By looking at the numbers, wouldn't you figure that the radius is about 3.1 for B and 10 for E? Then, you'd realize that you'd need more than a distance of 3.1 to get from (–3, 2) to (5, 8)?

That's what I'd do, but I'm hardcore. But, if you don't trust your personal reasoning abilities, you could just plug in the numbers. Either way, you'd see that E works.

Angles, 2-D and 3-D Figures

Angles

Angles live wherever two lines meet. Some are acute, so tiny and light; some are obtuse, with great power and might!

Properties of Angles:

- **Straight Line:** 180°
- **Right Angle:** 90°

- **Angle Addition Rule:** two smaller angles within a larger angle will add together to the measure of the larger angle.
- **Opposite Angle Rule:** If two lines cross each other, 4 angles will be formed, and the opposites will be equal. If you look at the letter X, the angles at the top and bottom are equal, and the angles on the left and right side are equal. No matter where the line crosses, the top will match the bottom and the left will match the right.

Let's try solving an ACT angle problem, using the properties above as our guide:

In the figure below, $\overline{IL}$, $\overline{JM}$, and $\overline{KN}$ all intersect at point O. If the measure of $\angle IOJ$ is 45° and the measure of $\angle KOM$ is 115°, what is the measure of $\angle ION$.

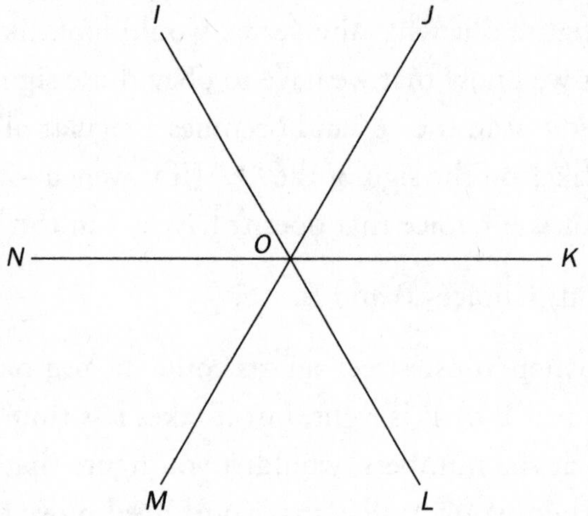

A. 60°

B. 70°

C. 80°

D. 90°

E. 100°

This problem tests your ability to recognize opposite angles and use the angle addition rule.

We are given angles *IOJ* and *KOM* which don't help us if we combine them.

But if we use the opposite angle rule for $\angle KOM$, we can figure out $\angle JON$.

Then we can use the angle addition rule since $\angle IOJ + \angle ION = \angle JON$. Here's the math:

$45° + \angle ION = 115°$

$115° - 45° = 70°$. Our answer is B.

Triangles

Triangles are shapes with three sides and three angles, and can be right, obtuse, equilateral, isosceles, or scalene.

Properties of Triangles:

- All *interior* angles add up to 180°.
- All *exterior* angles add up to 360°.
- The *perimeter* can be found by adding up the sides.
- The *area* of a triangle is $\frac{1}{2} \times \text{base} \times \text{height}$.

HEADS UP

In a right triangle, base and height are the two sides connected to the right angle. In other triangles, base is any side you want; height is that imaginary line drawn up the middle, which connects a side to its opposite angle. This creates a couple of right angles, which is something you can work with.

The Pythagorean Theorem:

$a^2 + b^2 = c^2$ where a and b are the sides hooked to the right angle, and c is the hypotenuse, the side opposite the right angle.

STRATEGY ALERT

How to Solve a Triangle Problem

Build a Table: One of the hardest things about solving one of these triangle problems is keeping everything straight. You're going to have to keep track of all sorts of angles and triangles, and if you get out your hammer and nails and craft a table in two nanoseconds, you may actually have a shot of answering correctly. Carpentry tools out? Let's go for it.

In the figure below, $\overline{BD}$ bisects $\angle ABC$. The measure of $\angle ABC$ is 110° and the measure of $\angle BAD$ is 50°. What is the measure of BDC?

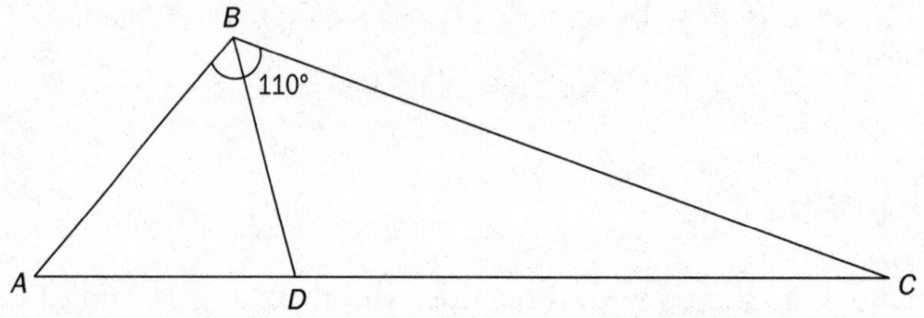

A. 75°

B. 85°

C. 95°

D. 105°

E. 115°

The first thing we'll do is rule out answer Choices A and B because $\angle BDC$ is obviously bigger than 90° and even though we're warned that the figures aren't drawn *exactly* to scale, we can usually trust them.

Then, we'll start our table with what we already know. We are given two angles of the large triangle *ABC*, and we're also given the measurement for the small angle *DBC*, because the question says that line *BD* *bisects* that 110° angle, which means it cuts it equally in two.

Triangle *ABC*:	Triangle *BCD*:
$\angle ABC = 110°$	$\angle DBC = 55°$
$\angle BAD = 50°$	$\angle BCD = ?$
$\angle BCD = ?$	$\angle BDC = ?$

Next, we figure out the rest and start adding to the chart. Since we know that $\angle ABC$ and $\angle BAD$ are 2 of the 3 angles of the big triangle *ABC*, we can find $\angle BCD$ since all interior angles add up to 180°.

$110° + 50° +$ angle $BCD = 180°$, so angle $BCD = 20°$

Let's add it to the chart.

Triangle *ABC*:	Triangle *BCD*:
$\angle ABC = 110°$	$\angle DBC = 55°$
$\angle BAD = 50°$	$\angle BCD = \mathbf{20°}$
$\angle BCD = \mathbf{20°}$	$\angle BDC = ?$

Now, let's look at the little triangle *BCD*. All we need is $\angle BDC$. We'll use the same 180° to solve:

$55° + 20° + \text{angle } BDC = 180°$. Then angle $BDC = 105°$

And the answer is Choice D, which would have been much more difficult to determine without a chart to keep us organized. You could also just label the angles right on the figure if that helps you keep it straight, too.

Quadrilaterals

Quadrilaterals are 4-sided figures, such as squares, rhombuses, parallelograms, trapezoids, and rectangles.

Properties of Quadrilaterals:

- All interior angles add up to 360°.
- Perimeter can be found by adding up all of the sides.
- Area is base × height.

STRATEGY ALERT

How to Find the Area of a Quadrilateral

Hack it Up: If you cut it into pieces, you will compute the area of this figure with accuracy and earn yourself more points on the ACT math portion.

Let's cut something into pieces:

What is the area of the trapezoid below?

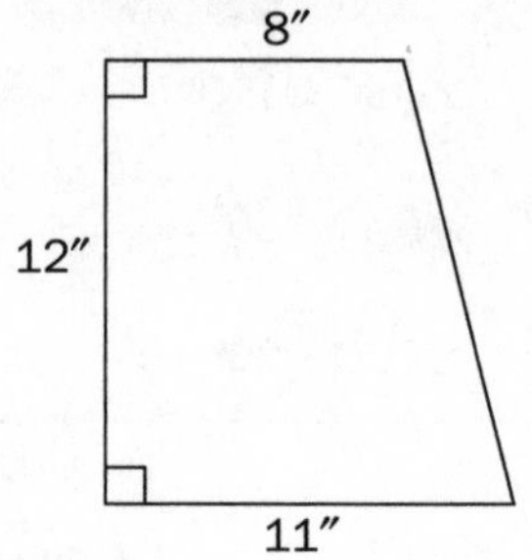

A. 96 in.^{2}

B. 107 in.^{2}

C. 114 in.^{2}

D. 132 in.^{2}

E. 1056 in.^{2}

First, you should always jump and cheer when you see right angles, which is what those little boxes indicate at the corners of the trapezoid.

Next, let's cut this one up. We'll need to cut off that extra piece on the right side of the trapezoid to turn this figure into a rectangle. We can do that by drawing a line straight down from the top right corner to the base. Do it, and see what you get.

Oooh! A rectangle on the left and a right triangle on the right. We can totally work with that.

To figure out the area of the rectangle, you just have to multiply 8″ by 12″ and you get 96 in.^{2} and then add that to the area of the triangle.

So, area for the triangle is $\frac{1}{2}$ base × height. We know the height: 12″, and since we hacked off 8″ from that 11″ line on the bottom, we know that the base of the triangle is 3″.

Now multiply $\frac{1}{2} \times 3'' \times 12''$ and you get 18 in.^{2}

Finally, add together 96 in.^{2} + 18 in.^{2} and you get 114 in^2. There's no part of the quadrilateral unaccounted for, so you are done, done, done. The answer is C!

Circles

Circles are round, and have a radius, diameter, circumference, area, sector, arc, chord, and tangent line.

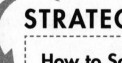

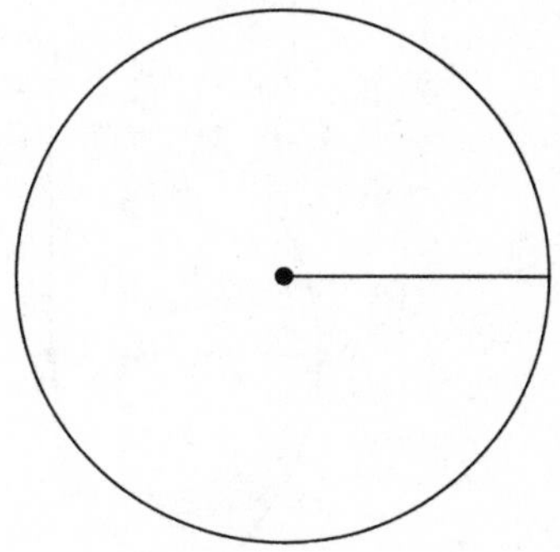

Properties of Circles:

- **Radius:** any line from the center of the circle to a point on the circle.
- **Diameter:** any line from a point on the circle to the opposite side which passes through the center
- **Circumference:** the perimeter of the circle. The formula is $C = 2\pi r$
- **Area:** all the space inside the circle. The formula is $A = \pi r^2$
- **Sector:** any triangular piece cut out by two radii. It's like a slice of pizza.
- **Arc:** the edge cut out by two radii. It's like the crust of a piece of pizza.
- **Chord:** any line connecting one point of a circle to another, but not necessarily opposite points (which would be a diameter). Every diameter is a chord, but not every chord is a diameter.
- **Tangent:** a line perpendicular to the radius that touches the circle in one spot. If you stood a coin up on its edge on a table, the coin would be the circle and the surface of the table would be tangent to the coin.

STRATEGY ALERT

How to Solve Circle Problems

Memorize: Open up skull; insert circle. Memorize those circle properties, or else you'll miss points on the ACT. These writers are sneaky. They know that terminology can trip you up. So if you commit sector, chord, tangent, and the rest of the terms to memory, you won't be stuck on test day when they're mentioned.

Here's one of those sneaky ACT questions for you:

> In the circle below, chord *AC* passes through the center of the circle *D*. If the radius *DB* is perpendicular to chord *AC* and has a length of 5 inches, what is the length of chord *BC* to the nearest tenth of an inch?

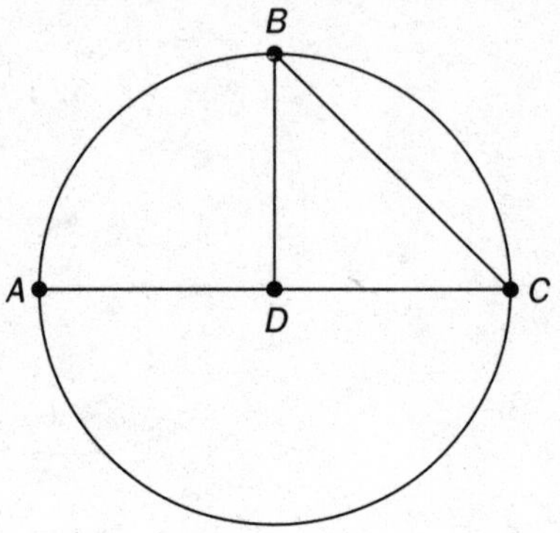

A. 6.4″

B. 7.1″

C. 9.3″

D. 10.0″

E. 12.3″

The first thing to recognize is that *DB* is a radius and *AC* passes through point *D*. That means that *AC* isn't just any old chord. It's a diameter of the circle and we can definitely do stuff with a diameter! It also means that *DA* and *DC* are also radii, so $DB = DA = DC$.

Most importantly, since $DB = DC = 5''$ and $\angle BDC$ is a right angle, triangle *BDC* is a right triangle. So, let's figure out the old hypotenuse with Pythagorean's Theorem:

$$5^2 + 5^2 = c^2$$

$$25 + 25 = c^2$$

$$50 = c^2$$

Use your calculator, and figure that the square root of 50 is 7.1″. There's our "*c*," the hypotenuse, which also happens to be Choice B.

Parallel Lines

Parallel lines are always the same length apart.

The Opposite Angle Rule comes into play when a line crosses two parallel lines. The opposite angles formed will be the same. In the figure below, $\angle a = \angle d$, $\angle e$, and $\angle h$. Likewise, $\angle b = \angle c$, $\angle f$, and $\angle g$.

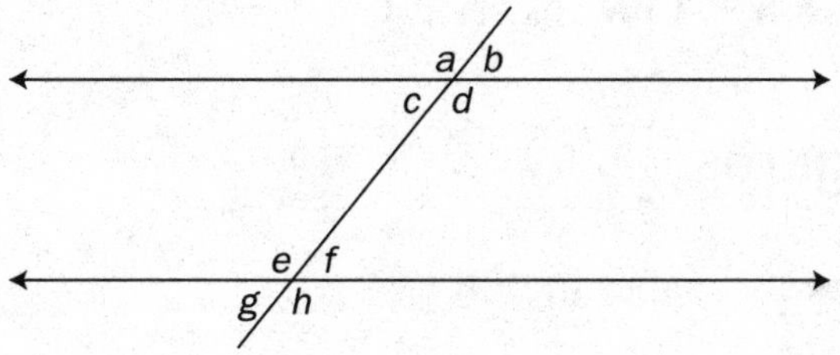

Let's keep the Opposite Angle rule in mind when we solve this ACT lines question:

> In the parallelogram *ABCD* below, points *E*, *A*, *D*, and *F* form a straight line. Given the angle measures as shown in the figure, what is the measure of angle *BDC*.

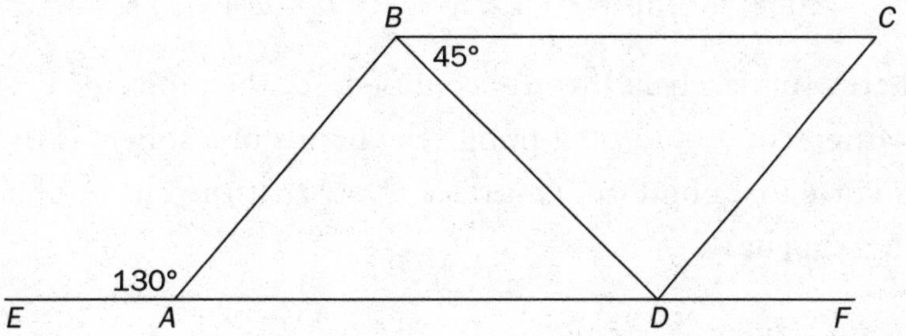

A. 45°

B. 55°

C. 85°

D. 115°

E. 130°

This is a parallelogram, which means that the opposite sides are parallel. Hence, the name.

We are looking for $\angle BDC$, so if we can figure out $\angle ADC$ and $\angle ADB$, then we can use the angle addition rule. Well, since BC and AD are parallel, then $\angle DBC$ and $\angle ADB$ are equal. Also, since AB and DC are parallel, $\angle EAB$ and $\angle ADC$ are equal.

So now we can use the angle addition rule.

$\angle BDC + \angle ADB = \angle ADC$

$\angle BDC + 45° = 130°$

$\angle BDC = 85°$. Our answer is C.

Solid Figures

Solid figures are shapes in 3D!

Solid figures of ACT interest:

Cube: a 6-sided figure that can look like a die (regular cube) or a shoebox (rectangular cube)

- *Volume:* Multiply length(l) × width(w) × height(h).
- *Surface Area:* If it's a regular cube, multiply $l \times w \times 6 = S$; if it's a rectangular cube, multiply $2 \times l \times w + 2 \times h \times w + 2 \times h \times l = S$

Sphere: This is a ball. If you're confused, see the projectile in soccer, basketball, baseball, bowling, tennis, and ping-pong. The radius of a sphere is the distance from the center of a circle to a point on its surface. Note that the radius of a sphere is usually denoted with a capital R.

- *Volume:* $V = \frac{4}{3}\pi R^3$
- *Surface Area:* $S = 4\pi R^2$

Cylinder: This shape is like a battery without the nubs. You can also think of it mathematically like a bunch of circles stacked on top of each other. There is a radius, but it is a little r not a big R because it corresponds to the circle that is consistent throughout the cylinder. The height of the cylinder is the distance between the top and bottom circle.

- *Volume:* $v = \pi r^2 h$
- *Surface Area:* $S = 2\pi rh$

Cone: Think of the little paper cups near water coolers.

- Volume: $V = \frac{1}{3}\pi r^2 h$
- Surface Area: $S = \pi r\sqrt{r^2 + h^2}$

Here's a question very similar to something you could see on the ACT:

What is the volume in cubic centimeters of the cylinder shown in the figure below?

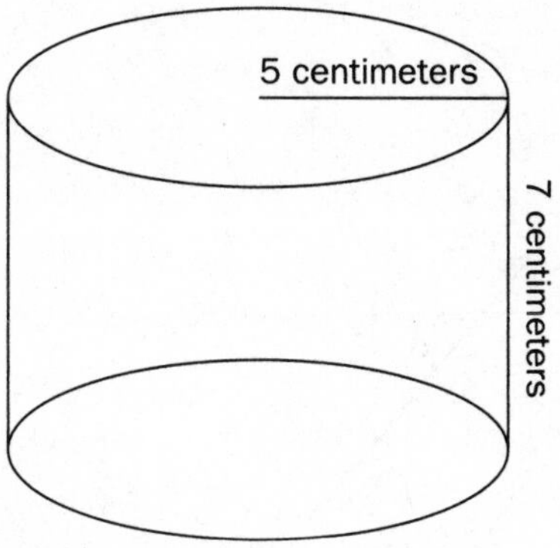

A. 35π

B. 70π

C. 115π

D. 150π

E. 175π

This is a pretty straightforward question, but you need your formula to answer it, and since you won't be receiving formulas on the test, you'd better have this memorized.

$V = \pi r^2 h$, so that's $5^2 \times 7 \times \pi = 175\pi$. That's it! E is the answer.

Trigonometric Ratios

Let's just review a couple of basic trig things and we'll jump directly into the practice questions so you can get on with your life today. We're keeping it short, since you've worked so hard this week!

Sine, Cosine, and Tangent

Sine, cosine, and tangent are the three main functions in trigonometry, and all have to deal with right triangles.

$$\text{Sine} = \frac{\text{Opposite}}{\text{Hypotenuse}},\ \text{Cosine} = \frac{\text{Adjacent}}{\text{Hypotenuse}},\ \text{Tangent} = \frac{\text{Opposite}}{\text{Adjacent}}.$$

Let's look at a basic right triangle to see what the heck I'm talking about.

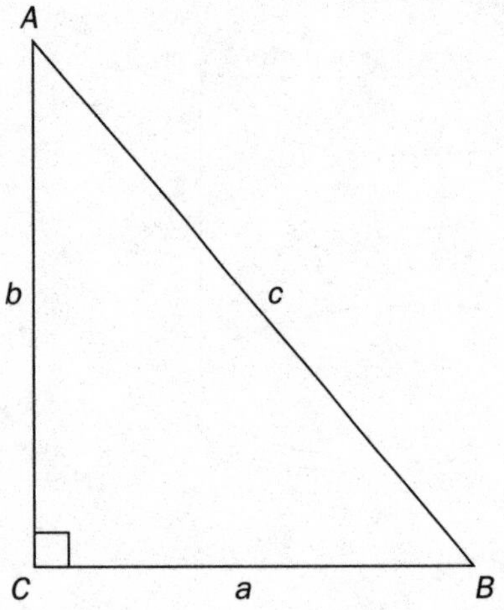

HEADS UP

Note that capital letters stand for angles and the lowercase letters stand for sides. Also note that it is the side opposite the angle that corresponds with the angle. See the placement of "A" and "a" in the example.

For kicks, let's identify the sine, cosine, and tangent of $\angle B$. The words "opposite," "adjacent," and "hypotenuse" all have to do with the sides of the triangle. So to figure out the identities, we just need to plug in whatever happens to be on the corresponding side:

$$\sin(B) = \frac{b}{c},\ \cos(B) = \frac{a}{c},\ \tan(B) = \frac{b}{a}$$

Get it?

STRATEGY ALERT

How to Compute a Basic Trigonometry Problem

Some Old Hitchhiker Caught a Horse Taking Oats Away: SOHCAHTOA is a quick way to remember the identities you'll need to solve every trig problem on the ACT. Learn them now; they'll never change.

$$\text{Sine} = \frac{\text{Opposite}}{\text{Hypotenuse}}, \text{Cosine} = \frac{\text{Adjacent}}{\text{Hypotenuse}}, \text{Tangent} = \frac{\text{Opposite}}{\text{Adjacent}}.$$

Let's use the old hitchhiker to solve a trig problem:

In right triangle *XYZ* below, the measure of segment *XY* is 24 centimeters, and the sine of angle *Z* is $\frac{3}{8}$. What is the length of segment *XZ* to the nearest tenth of a centimeter?

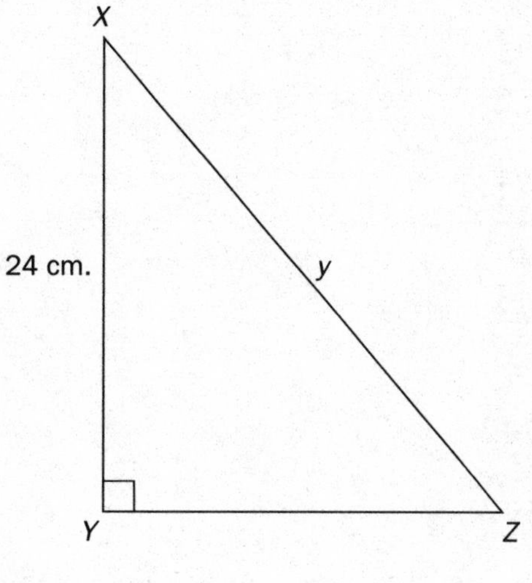

A. 24.0

B. 54.2

C. 59.3

D. 64.0

E. 110.2

We are given the sine of *Z*, which would involve line segments XY and XZ. We know line segment *XY*, so we can go ahead and solve $\frac{3}{8}=\frac{24}{y}\rightarrow(y)(3)=(24)(8)\rightarrow y=\frac{24\times 8}{3}=64$.

Our answer is D.

Another type of ACT problem will use both Pythagorean Theorem and the trig identities:

In the triangle below, what is the value of cos(angle *DEF*)?

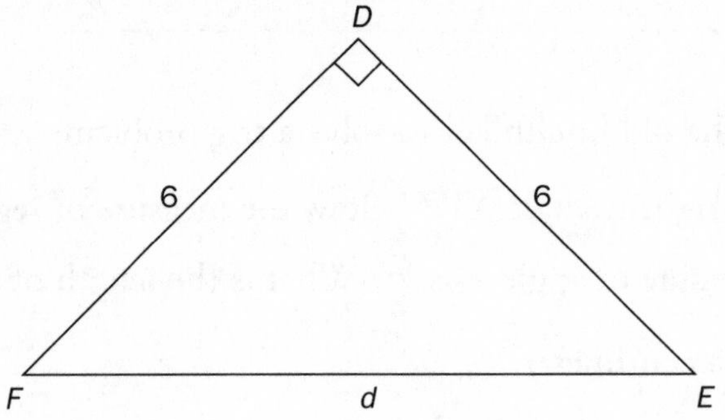

A. $\frac{\sqrt{2}}{8}$

B. $\frac{\sqrt{2}}{6}$

C. $\frac{\sqrt{2}}{2}$

D. $6\sqrt{2}$

E. $8\sqrt{2}$

Using Pythagorean's Theorem, you can find the hypotenuse, *d*. $6^2+6^2=d^2\rightarrow 72=d^2\rightarrow 6\sqrt{2}=d$.

Now, we are looking for the cosine of angle *DEF* which is adjacent/hypotenuse. That is $\frac{6}{6\sqrt{2}}=\frac{1}{\sqrt{2}}=\frac{\sqrt{2}}{2}$.

C is our final answer!

Practice Geometry

1. The circle in the figure below is inscribed in a square with a perimeter of 24 inches. What is the area of the shaded region in square inches?

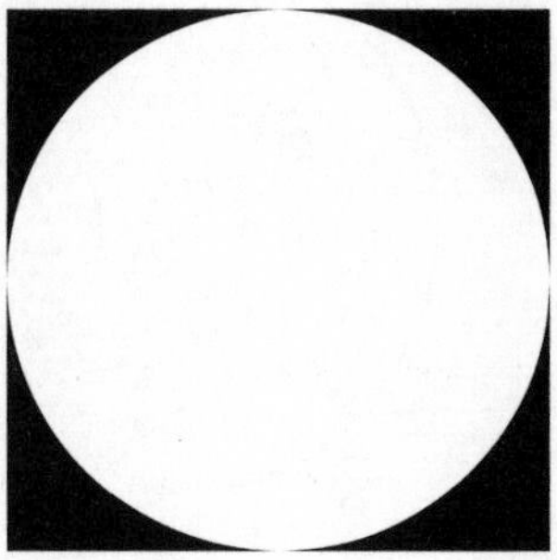

A. 6π

B. $36 - 9\pi$

C. $36 - 3\pi$

D. $18 - 9\pi$

E. $18 - 3\pi$

2. In triangle *ABC* below, line segment *AD* and line segment *DC* are 4 and 10 units, respectively. If the area of triangle *ABC* is 42 square units, how many units long is altitude *BD*?

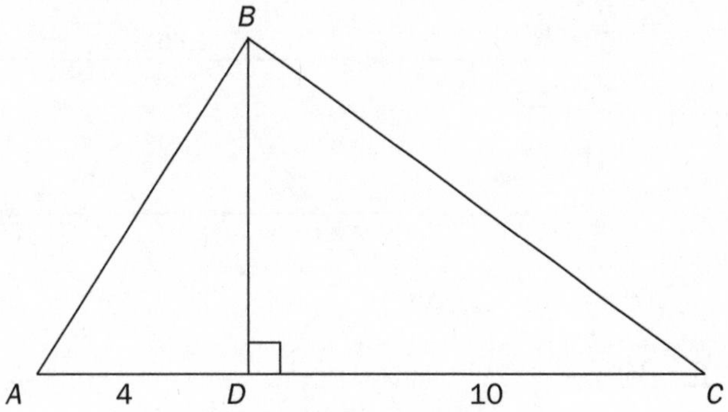

F. 2

G. 4

H. 6

J. 8

K. 10

3. The circumference of circle O is 10π and the circumference of circle P is 6π. What is the greatest possible distance between two points, one of which lies on the circumference of circle O and one of which lies on the circumference of circle P?

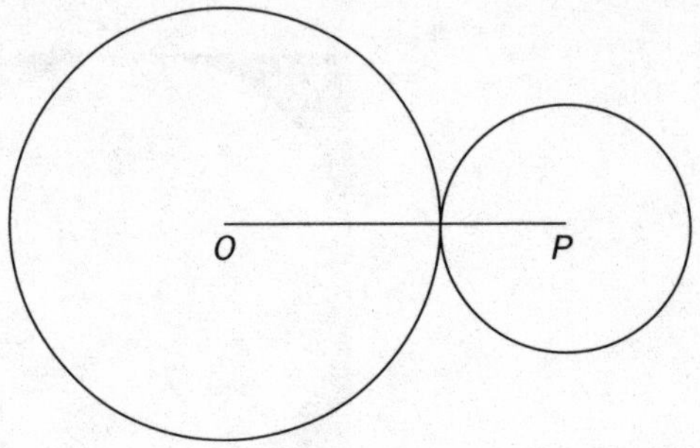

A. 8

B. 16

C. 20

D. 8π

E. 16π

4. In the figure below, lines m and l are parallel and angle $b = 42°$. What is the measure of angle e?

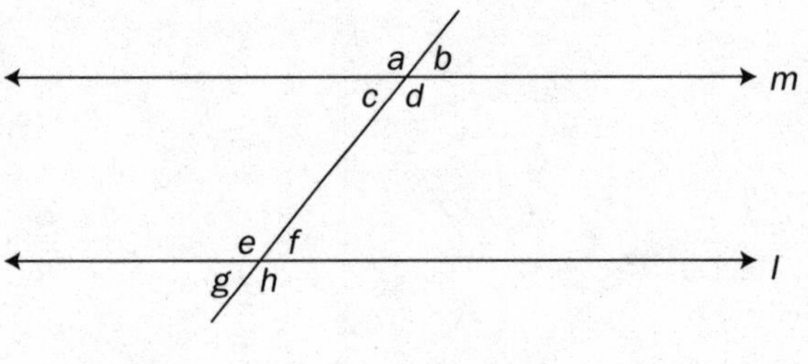

F. 30°

G. 42°

H. 48°

J. 100°

K. 138°

5. In the right triangle below, $AC = 13$ and $BC = 5$. What is the value of $\sin \angle ACB$?

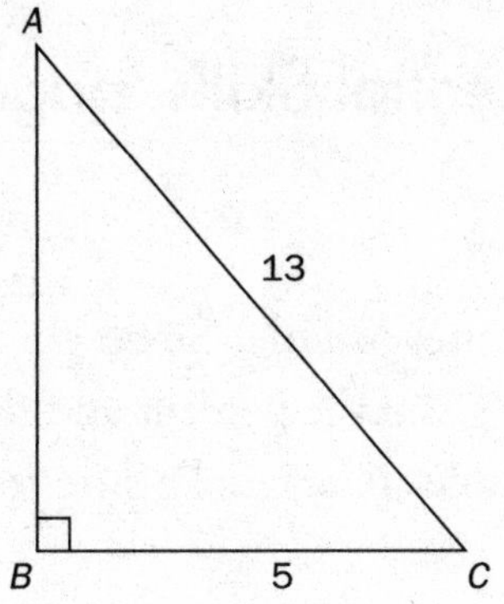

A. $\frac{5}{13}$

B. $\frac{5}{18}$

C. $\frac{12}{13}$

D. $\frac{2}{3}$

E. $\frac{13}{5}$

6. In the right triangle *DEF* below, *DF* is 14 inches, and angle *FDE* is 30°. What is the length of *DE*?

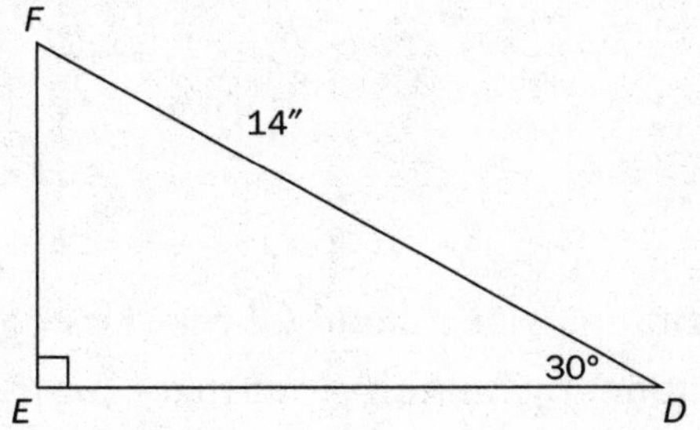

F. 7

G. $7\sqrt{3}$

H. 8

J. 9

K. 10

Answers on page 129.

Solutions to Math Practice Questions

Integrating Essential Skills, page 79

1. C.

Part = Percent times Whole. Since we are looking for the total number surveyed (Whole), and we are given the percent and the part, we can just plug it in to the formula and solve for the whole. First, make sure to change 30% into 0.3. Then $18 = 0.3 \times x$ and $x = \frac{18}{0.3} = 60$.

2. H.

Since all 3 sides of the triangle add up to 18 and one of the sides is 6, then we know the other two sides have to add up to 12. We also know a relationship about the two sides—that one side is twice the length of the other, so if we let x be the shorter side, then $2x$ would be the longer. So $x + 2x = 12 \rightarrow 3x = 12$, and $x = 4$. The three sides are 4, 6, and 8, and the longest of the three is 8.

3. E.

If we let $\frac{a}{b} = \frac{4}{5}$, then we can solve for b to find a. So $\frac{a}{b} = \frac{4}{5} \rightarrow 5a = 4b \rightarrow b = \frac{5a}{4}$. Now we can use that information to find the ratio for a:c.

$$\frac{b}{c} = \frac{9}{5} \rightarrow \frac{\left(\frac{5a}{4}\right)}{c} = \frac{9}{5} \rightarrow \frac{5a}{4c} = \frac{9}{5} \rightarrow \frac{a}{c} = \frac{36}{25}$$

4. H.

Remember—Bump, Make 2 and Check. First, get the absolute value by itself on one side of the equation, by bumping out that $-2x$. $|3x + 2| - 2x = 6 \rightarrow |3x + 2| = 6 + 2x$. Now, you have to Make 2 problems and solve them. For the first case, you just have to forget about the absolute value sign, not changing anything. $3x + 2 = 6 + 2x \rightarrow x = 4$. For the second case, you need to make the entire right side of the equation negative. So, $3x + 2 = -(6 + 2x) \rightarrow 3x + 2 = -6 - 2x \rightarrow 5x = -8 \rightarrow x = -\frac{8}{5}$. Now, Check! If you plug in 4 and $-\frac{8}{5}$ into the equation, you'll find that both answers work. So our answer is 4.

5. D.

Average = add 'em up and divide by how many there are. We need to add $\frac{1}{15}$ and $\frac{1}{25}$ and divide by 2 (the number of things we are adding up). $\frac{1}{15}+\frac{1}{25}=\frac{5}{75}+\frac{3}{75}=\frac{8}{75}$. Now divide that number by two and you get $\frac{8}{75}\div 2=\frac{8}{25}\times\frac{1}{2}=\frac{4}{75}$. The average of those two numbers is D: $\frac{4}{75}$.

Number and Quantity and Algebra, page 95

1. E.

Remember—Let Your Fingers Do the Walkin'! All you have to do is multiply the entries of the ROWS of the first matrix by the entries in the COLUMN of the second matrix. Then add them up. You can do all of that in just one step. $10 \times 5 + 6 \times 15 + 16 \times 10 + 13 \times 5 + 3 \times 15 + 20 \times 10 = 610$. As long as you plug everything into your calculator correctly, you should get an answer of 610.

2. K.

Just a mega-refresher on your exponent rules. Multiply the numbers in front and then add the exponents of like-term variables. $6 \times 3 \times 2 = 36$, $x^3 \times x \times x = x^5$ (remember there's a hidden "1" in the exponent of "x"), and $y^4 \times y \times y^2 = y^7$. We are, then, looking for $36x^5y^7$.

3. E.

Remember to ZIF it up with quadratics. First, zero it out: $x^2 + 5x = 20x \rightarrow x^2 - 15x = 0 \rightarrow x(x - 15) = 0$. So now we can split it up. Either $x = 0$ or $x - 15 = 0$. Since we are given that x doesn't equal zero, we have to use the second equation. $x - 15 = 0 \rightarrow x = 15$.

4. H.

First, plug in –2 for x (which would make it a solution). $(-2)^2 - n(-2) - 24 = 0 \rightarrow 4 + 2n - 24 = 0 \rightarrow 2n = 20$. Now just solve for n. $2n = 20 \rightarrow n = 10$. So n has to be 10 as long as $x = -2$.

5. C.

Flip and FOIL, kids. To reduce, you need to use the *flip* of the denominator's sign and FOIL the top and bottom (and don't forget that $i^2 = -1$):

$$\frac{5-6i}{3+4i} \times \frac{3-4i}{3-4i} = \frac{15-20i-18i+24i^2}{9-12i+12i-16i^2} = \frac{15-38i-24}{9+16} = \frac{-9-38i}{25} = \frac{-9}{25} - \frac{38}{25}i$$

Functions, Statistics, and Probability, page 102

1. D.

This problem tests your ability to read function language, but you basically just need to Put in your –2 Sticker! Just plug in "–2" everywhere you see an "x" in the function. $f(-2) = (24 + 9(-2)) \times ((-2)^2 + 3(-2) + 12) = (24 - 18) \times (4 - 6 + 12) = (6) \times (10) = 60$. So $f(-2) = 60$.

2. J.

Chicken Scratch Your Possibilities! The customer selects a pet two times, so you need to figure out each case first. The first time the customer selects a pet there is a $\frac{5}{10}$ or $\frac{1}{2}$ chance that she will get a dog. Then *once she has chosen the dog* there are 4 dogs left out of a total 9 animals. So for her second pick, she has a $\frac{4}{9}$ chance. The correct answer is then $\frac{1}{2} \times \frac{4}{9} = \frac{4}{18}$ or $\frac{2}{9}$. She has a $\frac{2}{9}$ chance of picking a dog twice.

3. D.

Since $f(x)$ is quadratic (because of the exponent of two enacting on the variable), it is the parabola. Since $g(x)$ is linear, it is the line. They never intersect, so A and B are out. They are also not reflections of each other over the line $y = x$, so they are not inverses of each other. However, one function will always have greater y-values than the other, and that is the parabola—represented by $f(x)$. So $f(x) > g(x)$ for all values of x.

4. H.

The original median of the data set is 17 and the mean is 17.6. Adding in the data point of 172 would not change the median, since the next highest value is also 17 and the average of 17 and 17 is 17. However, adding that point to the mean makes it 43.33 which is significantly higher than 17.6.

5. B.

The first thing to notice is the parabola going through the point (0, 0) and knowing that must be $y = x^2$. Once you know that, then it's a matter of how does the other parabola compare to it. Has it shifted left, right, up, and/or down? We can see that it's just shifted down, so any horizontal movement (indicated by a) is 0. So $a = 0$. Then to make a shift down, we know we must subtract outside the function. So $b < 0$. Therefore, the only statement that is true is $a = 0$, and $b < 0$.

Geometry, page 123

1. B.

There are two areas at work here: the area of the square and the area of the circle. Any time two shapes overlap and you are looking for the area, you can subtract the smaller area from the larger area. In this case, the square takes up more room, so you need to find the area of the square and subtract from that the area of the circle. The perimeter of the square is 24, so dividing that by 4 will give you 6, the length of one side. Square that, and you have the area of the square: 36. Now to find the area of the circle. To find r, note that it is $\frac{1}{2}$ the length of a side. So divide 6 by two and that gives you 3. The formula is $A = \pi r^2$, so the area of the circle is 9π. Now we just subtract: Area of the square – area of the circle = $36 - 9\pi$. The answer is B.

2. H.

In this problem, we have been given an area, and two segments that when added together will give us the base of the triangle. To find the altitude (or the height), we can use the formula for the area of a triangle: $A = \frac{1}{2} b \times h$. $42 = \frac{1}{2} \times 14 \times h \rightarrow 42 = 7h \rightarrow 6 = h$. The answer is H.

3. B.

The furthest point on two circles is if you drew a straight line through both of them and put a point at each furthest end where the line intersects the circles. In the figure, if we were to extend the line OP directly out so that it touched the outer wall of the circles, you can see that it is the furthest point. The line from O to the intersection of the circles is the tangent, and the same thing is true for P. Since we are given the circumference, we can figure out the radii of both circles and then multiply them by 2 and add them up to give us the answer. First, for circle O, $C = 2\pi r$, so $10\pi = 2\pi r \rightarrow 5 = r$. With P, $6\pi = 2\pi r \rightarrow 3 = r$. Now that we know the length of the radii, we just have to multiply them by two and add them up. $10 + 6 = 16$. Our answer is B.

4. K.

Remember when you have two parallel lines with a *transversal* (fancy name for the line going through two parallel lines), then there are only actually 2 different measures of angles. The measure of the given angle, and 180°—the measure of the given angle. If you look at b and then look at e, you can see that they are different. So e has to be $180° - b = 180° - 42° = 138°$. The answer is K.

5. C.

Here you will again need to use the Pythagorean Theorem first because the sine of ACB is going to be opposite AB (which we don't know yet) over hypotenuse AC (which we do). Just solve: $5^2 + c^2 = 13^2 \rightarrow 25 + c^2 = 169 \rightarrow c^2 = 144 \rightarrow c = 12$. Now we know side AB is 12 and the sine of ACB is $\frac{12}{13}$. C is our answer.

6. G.

Here, we are given a hypotenuse and an angle and are asked to find a side length. So we need to figure out which trig identity will help us. We know tangent is out because tangent never involves a hypotenuse. Is it sine or cosine? Well, we are looking for DE which is adjacent to the angle, so we need to use cosine. $\cos(30°) = \frac{\sqrt{3}}{2}$ (according to my trusty calculator), so we now just need to set it up. $\frac{\sqrt{3}}{2} = \frac{f}{14} \rightarrow \frac{14\sqrt{3}}{2} = f \rightarrow 7\sqrt{3} = f$.

Math Strategy Cheat Sheet

General Strategies:

- Pace Yourself with HAM. **H**aven't Got Time, **A**lways Answer, or **M**aybe. *1 minute or less per question*
- X Out the Junk
- Break the Rules
- Rely on your calculator
- Use the Answers

Integrating Essential Skills:

- Learn the Native Language to remember "of" means "multiply" and "is" means "equals" in sales percentage problems
- Bump, Make 2 and Check for absolute value equations

Preparing for Higher Math:

- FLIP and FOIL to solve complex number problems
- Flip-Flop and Chop to simplify an exponential expression
- Let Your Fingers Do the Walkin' to multiply matrices
- ZIF it up to solve quadratic equations
- Use Kindergarten Math to solve a system of equations
- Put a Sticker On It for two-function problems
- Plug It In for algebraic substitutions
- Use Your FOIL for multiplying binomials

Statistics and Probability:

- Chicken Scratch Your Possibilities for probability problems

Geometry:

- Pack the Marshmallows for distance, midpoint, or slope problems
- Use Your Street Smarts for circle problems
- Build a Table for triangle problems
- Hack it Up for quadrilaterals
- Stick the Circle in Your Noggin for circles in planes

Trigonometry:

- Some Old Hitchhiker Caught a Horse Taking Oats Away for sine, cosine, and tangent problems

Take the Math Practice Test

Go to the REA Study Center

(www.rea.com/studycenter)

Now that you have completed this week's work, go to *rea.com/studycenter* and take the Math Practice Test. This test is just like the Math section of the actual ACT, with the added benefits of:

- **Timed testing conditions** – Gauge how much time you can spend on each question.
- **Automatic scoring** – Find out how you did on the test, instantly.
- **On-screen detailed explanations of answers** – Learn not just the correct answers, but also why the other answers are incorrect.
- **Diagnostic score reports** – Pinpoint where you're strongest and where you need to focus your study.

Week 3: Reading

3

ACT Reading Test Basics

The ACT Reading test has

- 4 sections, each containing one long (80–90 lines) or two short (40–45 lines) passages of text.
- numbered lines.
- 10 multiple-choice questions per passage.
- 4 passages × 10 questions = 40 questions total.
- 4 answer choices per question.

You'll be tested

- for 35 minutes.
- in three areas: Key Ideas and Details, Craft and Structure, and Integration of Knowledge and Ideas.
- with questions that refer both to what is explicitly stated and what is implied.

In order to score well,

- you must master ACT test-taking strategies.
- you must master ACT Reading content strategies.

The Four Passages

These passages will be edited parts of novels, magazines, textbooks, biographies, journals, memoirs, personal essays, and short stories, and will always be presented in this order:

- **Prose Fiction:** content comes from short stories (either intact or edited) and excerpts from novels.
- **Social Science:** content comes from anthropology, archaeology, biography, business, economics, education, geography, history, political science, psychology, and sociology.
- **Humanities:** content comes from memoirs, personal essays, architecture, art, dance, ethics, film, language, literary reviews, music, philosophy, radio, television, and theater.
- **Natural Sciences:** content comes from anatomy, astronomy, biology, botany, chemistry, ecology, geology, medicine, meteorology, microbiology, natural history, physiology, physics, technology, and zoology.

General Strategies for the Reading Section

- **Pace Yourself:** And I mean that in the most literal sense. Bring a silent watch that allows you to set a timer, and set your watch to count down your remaining minutes according to the times listed in the third bullet below. You must—MUST—follow a reading strategy like the one I list on the next page in order to score well on this exam, unless you are an expert reader, or you'll run out of time.
- **Read Your Fave First:** You don't have to read in order; you can choose any of the four passages to read first. So, start this portion of the test by reading the passage that doesn't make you want to fall asleep. You'll answer more questions correctly if you're reading a subject that semi-interests you. If you're an English buff, then hit up the Prose Fiction passage first, followed by the Humanities text. If you're more in tune with the Science side of things, then start with the last passage, Natural Sciences, and follow it with the Social Science excerpt. Remember—your goal isn't to read and learn something the way it is in school; your goal is to get points.

- **Read the Pair of Passages Last:** Since you don't have to read the passages in order, never ever ever read the paired passages first. It's the toughest section, because you will have to answer questions that relate to *both* passages, which can get tricky. Save that passage until the very end.
- **Read 3 or Read 4:** Not everyone is an expert reader. If reading isn't your strong suit, it makes better scoring sense to read just 3 passages and answer everything accurately, rather than struggle through 4 passages and miss a bunch of questions because you're hurrying. Here's the math:

  Read 3

  11 minutes 40 seconds per passage

  3 passages × 8 of the 10 questions correct per passage = 24

  + 3 accurate guesses on the 4th passage = a raw score of 27

  Scaled ACT Reading score = 26 (78th percentile)

  Read 4

  8 minutes 45 seconds per passage

  4 passages × 6 of the 10 questions correct per passage = a raw score of 24

  Scaled ACT Reading score = 23 (66th percentile)

  See? It makes great sense! If you need more time, then just read the 3 passages and guess on the 4th passage. If you're a very strong reader and have confidence in your reading ability, by all means, go for four. But beware! This strategy only works if you improve your accuracy. If you read just 3 passages and only get 5 questions correct per passage, you're not doing yourself any favors by guessing on the 4th.
- **Separate Tough from Easy:** Just like on the other sections, you need to circle the numbers of the tough questions, so you can remember to come back to them after you answer the easy ones. Easy questions will reference a line number or paragraph, and tough reading questions will refer to the passage as a whole or a few words from the passage, but won't provide a specific location in the text.

EASY

16. In relation to the first paragraph's description of the Holocaust, the narrator's comments in lines 32–35 primarily serve to:

17. In the first paragraph, the author expresses the belief that scientists who help engage the minds of the disbelieving are likely to:

TOUGH

18. The passage suggests that Raphael's most important contribution to art was his:

19. Which of the following hypotheses is NOT tested in the passage?

6 Steps for Reading a Passage and Answering Questions

Reading isn't difficult, right? You've been doing it your whole life. You're doing it right now.

The physical act of reading isn't the issue on the ACT. In fact, reading isn't really what's being tested at all; here, you're tested on answering questions in a particular time frame. That's it. Sure, the questions are based on a passage, but you won't even need the whole passage to answer many of the questions correctly anyway, and what kind of a reading test is that?

Let's start by getting a handle on the steps you'll need to take to read the passage quickly and answer the questions in just 9 minutes or less.

Step 1: SEPARATE TOUGH from EASY

- Remember—tough questions do not reference a location in the text. Easy questions do!

Step 2: READ EASY QUESTION

- Read the first easy question. If necessary, put the question into your own words, so you understand what it's really asking you.

Step 3: READ and MARK UP the paragraph

- Read the paragraph that contains the lines indicated by the question. Always read a few lines above and below the reference, so you understand that portion of the passage. As you read the paragraph, mark it up in two ways:

1. Underline nouns and verbs (who did what).
2. Summarize the main idea of the paragraph in the margin. Use shorthand or even pictures because you won't have time to write complete sentences.

Step 4: POE and ANSWER the easy question. REPEAT for all easies.

- Look at the answer choices, and eliminate every single one that doesn't ring true. Then, choose the best answer. Repeat steps 2–4 for all the easies.

Step 5: READ and MARK UP the rest of the passage

- Once you've answered all the easy questions, go straight to the passage and skim it quickly, marking up the text as you did with the easy questions. Ignore the paragraphs you've already read.

Step 6: COVER, READ, and ANSWER TOUGHIES

- Read your first tough question and try to answer it in your head. Then, look for a match in the answers below it. If you don't know the answer right away or can't find it QUICKLY in the text, put a star next to the question and move on. You can come back to it if you have time at the end of the reading test. Repeat for all toughies.

I know this format doesn't look familiar at all. You're used to reading the passage, then reading the questions and answering them in order, and that method is definitely fine if you aren't being timed. Here, you're going to need to maximize your time, or you'll only end up reading just two of the passages instead of four, which guarantees that your reading score will be way less than it could be.

We're going to practice these steps as we move into the types of questions you'll see on this section of the test, so they'll become more familiar to you, okay?

Key Ideas and Details: 22–24 questions

One of the three areas on which you'll be tested on the Reading part of the ACT is Key Ideas and Details. Basically, you'll have to deal with the following reading comprehension skills you've known how to do since middle school:

- Determining the Main Idea
- Finding Supporting Details
- Making Inferences

Determining the Main Idea

You've been dealing with the main idea since you were in kindergarten. Perhaps even earlier. I don't know what kind of enthusiastic book pusher you had for a mother.

When I teach, I like to tell those students who never quite figured out how to find the main idea to think of it as the "big picture." It's the whole instead of the parts. It's the topic sentence versus the supporting details. It's what the writer wants you to understand from the whole passage. Here's a few ideas:

Main Idea of a Random Paragraph/Passage	Details That Support That Main Idea (aka—NOT THE MAIN IDEA)
It's never a good idea to come home with a dent in the fender of your dad's car.	Your parents will ground you. Dents are expensive to fix. Dents are difficult to hide, and if you try, such secrecy can ruin the "perfect little angel" reputation you've been cultivating for years.
Despite his death, Michael Jackson reigns as the king of pop.	He was a musical prodigy who brought vocal riffs into the mainstream market. He introduced legendary moves into the dance world. There's something superior about a guy who can make zombies look good dancing in a music video.
Test anxiety is *real*, but you can fix it.	Running a few laps around the block before you take the test will help calm those nerves. Laying off the caffeine before you test will help make your heart stop pounding so much. Repeating an uplifting phrase to yourself while you're waiting to begin will help make your stomach stop churning.

So, how do you find this main idea when you're reading a passage? For the most part, the main points of the paragraphs and passages you'll be reading will be *implied.* That means the main point will not be stated outright. You'll have to figure it out for yourself. The great news is that you'll have four answer choices to choose from. You won't need to compose a main idea. The bad news is that the answer choices will be tricky.

Easy Main Idea Questions

Easy main idea questions will ask you for the point (minus all the details) of a particular paragraph.

Finding the main idea of a paragraph is much easier than figuring out the main idea of a whole passage, because you have fewer details to dissect. When a main idea is implied, we have to follow a strategy to find it if it isn't obvious. And let's be honest—the ACT doesn't really go for obvious.

STRATEGY ALERT

How to Find the Main Idea of a Paragraph

Too Broad and Too Narrow Is Too Bad: When you're trying to find the main idea of a paragraph, you need to make sure you find the general idea that pulls all the info together without leaving anything out, but doesn't step *outside* the content of the paragraph, either. A summary that is "too narrow" is too specific; it only uses one or two ideas from the text. A summary that is "too broad" is too general; it says *more* than what's actually provided in the text. It includes bigger ideas than are actually given.

I'll show you what I mean with a paragraph similar to something you'll see on the ACT Reading test. This excerpt is from Henry David Thoreau's *Civil Disobedience*.

> Unjust laws exist: shall we be content to obey them, or shall we endeavor to amend them, and obey them until we have succeeded, or shall we transgress them at once? Men, generally, under such a government as this, think that they ought to wait until they have persuaded the majority to alter them. They think that, if they should resist, the remedy would be worse than the evil. But it is the fault of the government itself that the remedy is worse than the evil. It makes it worse. Why is it not more apt to anticipate and provide for reform? Why does it not cherish its wise minority? Why does it cry and resist before it is hurt? Why does it not encourage its citizens to put out its faults, and do better than it would have them? Why does it always crucify Christ and excommunicate Copernicus and Luther, and pronounce Washington and Franklin rebels?

So, let's use our reading strategy to begin:

Step 1: SEPARATE. This has already been done for you.

Step 2: READ the easy question. I'm leaving off the answers, because you're not supposed to read those yet.

11. The main idea of the first paragraph is that resistance to unjust laws:

Step 3: READ and MARK UP the text by underlining important words and summarizing in the margin.

Govmt is the problem bc they don't listen to wise people. Resistance is better than bad laws.

Unjust laws exist: shall we be content to obey them, or shall we endeavor to amend them, and obey them until we have succeeded, or shall we transgress them at once? Men, generally, under such a government as this, think that they ought to wait until they have persuaded the majority to alter them. They think that, if they should resist, the remedy would be worse than the evil. But it is the fault of the government itself that the remedy is worse than the evil. It makes it worse. Why is it not more apt to anticipate and provide for reform? Why does it not cherish its wise minority? Why does it cry and resist before it is hurt? Why does it not encourage its citizens to put out its faults, and do better than it would have them? Why does it always crucify Christ and excommunicate Copernicus and Luther, and pronounce Washington and Franklin rebels?

Step 4: POE and ANSWER the question. Practice it here. Check out the answer choices, and get rid of every single one that doesn't match your summary. Then, select the best letter:

11. The main idea of the first paragraph is that resistance to unjust laws:

A. is needed until the laws can be amended.

B. is a remedy worse than the evil of the government.

C. is a necessary evil caused by the government's failure to acknowledge the wisdom of the remedy.

D. is always better than allowing people to take advantage of you.

See anything that works?

Choice A is wrong because it is too narrow; it only utilizes part of the info in the paragraph.

Choice B calls resisting worse than the government, and that is the opposite of Thoreau's point.

Choice C is correct because it is the only choice that somewhat matches our summary in the margin and avoids being too broad or too narrow.

Choice D is incorrect because it is *too broad*: it includes ideas that weren't talked about at all in the passage.

HEADS UP

Don't choose an answer for a main idea question just because it uses the words from the first sentence of the paragraph. The first sentence is not necessarily the topic sentence, and probably will NOT contain the main idea. The test developers use words from the first sentence to distract you from the right answer.

Tough Main Idea Questions

Tough main idea questions will ask you for the point of the whole passage.

Of course, we wouldn't dare think of answering a tough question before finishing all of the easy questions. In one or two of the passages, though, you'll get a question that asks you about the main idea of the passage as a whole.

STRATEGY ALERT

How to Find the Main Idea of a Passage

Paragraph + Paragraph = Passage: In math, we know that 1 + 1 = 2, right? A passage is basically like a giant math problem. The sum of the main points of each paragraph equals the main point of the passage. So, to find the main idea of the passage, you just need to read the main points that you've scribbled in the margins and add them altogether.

So, you already know how to find the main idea of a paragraph. Let's suppose, after reading a passage of text, we scratch out these main ideas from the five paragraphs that make up the passage:

Paragraph 1: Airlines discovered that windows were deteriorating on airplanes.

Paragraph 2: Airlines thought faulty suppliers or engineers were to blame, but that wasn't it.

Paragraph 3: A volcano erupted that put sulfuric acid into the stratosphere.

Paragraph 4: Airplanes went into the stratosphere and windows melted from the acid.

Paragraph 5: Engineers felt responsible, but it was an unusual circumstance no one could predict.

So, try to add up all those ideas into one statement. What could it be?

Which of the following statements best expresses the main idea of the passage?

F. After airlines discovered deteriorating windows on their airplanes, they launched an investigation to discover the cause.

G. Airline engineers should always utilize every safety precaution when creating materials for airplanes.

H. Sulfuric acid can be projected into the air by volcanoes, and wreak havoc on airplane parts, as was discovered by airline executives.

J. When airplane windows began to deteriorate, airplane officials investigated and discovered that sulfuric acid was to blame, not the engineers.

Choice F is too narrow.

Choice G is too broad.

Choice H is too narrow.

Choice J is correct.

Practice Reading for the Main Idea

Vaulting played a great part,—perhaps the greatest, though certainly not the only part in developing Gothic architecture; but it will not do to define it as simply the expression of scientific vaulting. The Romans were masters of the art of vaulting long before; they used,—probably invented,—the cross-vault, and understood the concentration of thrusts on isolated points. It was from them, and from Eastern Rome as well, that the Romanesque builders learned how to make their stone roofs, and they in their turn passed the art on to their Gothic successors, who improved and developed it in their own way, making in the end almost a new art of it. But it must be remembered that most of the problems of scientific vaulting had presented themselves before their time, and had been partially solved by their predecessors, though not so completely.

Nor is it correct to regard vaulting as an essential feature of the style, however great its influence may have been on the structure of great churches. In England, except on a grand scale, it is exceptional: and yet if Westminster Hall with its stupendous timber covering, and the Fen churches with their glorious wooden roofs, and the splendid ceiling of the nave at St. David's are not Gothic, what are they? And what else can we call the countless village churches, gems of modest art that stud our country far and wide, and constitute one of its greatest charms, though it is only here and there that they aspire to the dignity of a vaulted ceiling?

Again if the test of Gothic is to be the logical expression of a vaulted construction what becomes of domestic architecture both here and abroad, in which vaulting certainly does not play an important part? Are the town halls of Brussels, Ypres, and Louvain not Gothic, nor the Broletto of Como, the pontifical palace at Viterbo, or that of the popes at Avignon, or the ducal palace at Venice?

Still less is Gothic architecture, as it has appeared to Gothic not the ordinary layman, a matter of quatrefoils and trefoils, form but of cusps and traceries, of crockets and finials, pinnacles and flying buttresses. These are but the accidents of the style, though no doubt they resulted naturally from the application of certain principles behind them. But they might all fly away and yet leave a Gothic building behind them. Many an old tithe barn of rough timber framework is as truly a piece of Gothic architecture as York Minster or Salisbury Cathedral.

If then none of these attempted definitions are really coextensive with the Gothic style of architecture, for a building may be Gothic and yet have none of these characteristics, how are we to define it?

The true way of looking at Gothic art is to regard it not as a definite style bound by certain formulas—for the spirit is infinitely various—but rather as the expression of a certain temper, sentiment, and spirit which inspired the whole method of doing things during the Middle Ages in sculpture and painting as well as in architecture. It cannot be defined by any of its outward features, for they are variable, differing at different times and in different places. They are the outward expression of certain cardinal principles behind them, and though these principles are common to all good styles, Gothic among them, the result of applying them to the buildings of each age, country, and people will vary as the circumstances of that country, that age, and that people vary.

1. Which of the following best expresses the main point of the first paragraph?

A. Although vaulted ceilings were not invented by the Gothic architects, they improved them.

B. Vaulted ceilings are a consistent aspect of Gothic architecture.

C. The Romans invented the vaulted ceilings.

D. Although vaulting plays a significant role in Gothic architecture, it can't be defined by vaulting, since the Romans invented it.

2. Which of the following statements best expresses the main idea of the passage?

F. Despite vaulted ceilings' prevalence in all aspects of Gothic architecture, it is not an *original* feature of the method; rather, vaulting is more customary to palaces.

G. Vaulting, although a primary component of Gothic architecture, is not the only important feature of the method.

H. Gothic architecture cannot be defined by any of its outward features, including vaulting; rather, it's best defined by the spirit of the method.

J. The features of Gothic architecture are indefinable because they vary widely from people to people and place to place.

Answers on page 182.

Finding Supporting Details

Supporting details questions are generally on the easy side because they rely more on your eyeballs than your brain. Many of the questions basically ask you to *locate* the correct answer, rather than actually think about anything, and for that, we have to thank the ACT writers. These questions are a break, considering some of the inference questions coming up.

So let's practice finding stuff in the text.

Easy Supporting Details Questions

Easy Supporting Details Questions will literally ask you to find an idea in the text, while providing the spot to look for it.

HEADS UP

Trying to locate information in the passage is the No. 1 reason students score lower than they should on the ACT Reading portion. Underlining important nouns and verbs and summarizing in the margin as you read it the first time around will help you when you get to questions that require you to search the text.

These are literally as easy as a word search. You just have to *find* the answers to get points and I truly couldn't be happier for you. Here are two examples:

1. In line 13, the author uses the remark "the merriment of moving forward" to illustrate:

A. the young woman's hopes for the future.

B. the young man's prospects for his career.

C. the young woman's responsibilities toward her cousin's family.

D. the young man's desires for personal freedom.

This question is really simple. The ACT writers give you a line number *and* a direct quote. All you have to do is locate the line, find the phrase and answer the question.

2. The author calls which of the following events a "potent warning of the human condition"?

F. The Bubonic Plague in Europe

G. The Red River Flood in Vietnam

H. The 1988 Armenian earthquake

J. The Great Caribbean Hurricane of 1780

Now, for this one, you aren't given a line number or paragraph indicator, but it's not *that* difficult to locate an exact phrase in the text. Plus, the answer choices tell you where to find the info, too. Look for those exact words/dates plus the phrase in the quotation marks.

3. The last paragraph establishes all of the following about being thin EXCEPT:

A. that being thin can also come with major health deficits.

B. that being thin is an androgynous look—one that many women try to emulate.

C. that being thin is seen as ideal.

D. that teenage girls are the most susceptible to buying the belief system that thin is beautiful.

Where this can get slightly more trying is with an "EXCEPT" question like the one above. And here's where a strategy comes into play.

STRATEGY ALERT

How to Solve an EXCEPT Question

True and X it Out: This is a slight variation on the True and False questions you got tripped up on as a first-grader. Go through each answer choice and mark it true or false, as it relates to the question. If the statement is true, X it out. It's no longer a contender for the correct answer. If the statement is false, keep it. It could be correct. Yes, I know this is counterintuitive (true is wrong and false is right?). But trust me on this, the strategy will help you keep it straight.

Let's use our **True and X it Out** strategy on the "thin" question (number 3, above):

Many female idols—models, movie stars, and musicians—are much thinner than the average person. But because these women seem ideal—what many teenage girls and women strive to become—their body weight is also seen as perfection. Often the result is women and teenage girls having poor body images which lead to destructive dieting behaviors, sometimes to the extreme of anorexia nervosa or bulimia. Teenage girls as well as women unrealistically seek the androgynous look by which they define beauty. They have trouble grasping the fact that real beauty lies not in how many pounds they weigh, nor in the size of the clothes they wear; it comes from general health. Focusing on weight to the detriment of other healthful activities is clearly imprudent. Eating too little may very well result in a thin body; however, the consumption of too few necessary vitamins and minerals also results in thinning hair, jaundiced, wrinkled skin, and a loss of energy. These results are often not taken into account before extreme measures to reduce weight are taken.

3. The last paragraph establishes all of the following about being thin EXCEPT:

   A. that being thin can also come with major health deficits.

   B. that being thin is an androgynous look—one that many women try to emulate.

   C. that being thin is seen as ideal.

   D. that teenage girls are the most susceptible to buying the belief system that thin is beautiful.

First, read it with the reading strategy! Read the question, then read the text, underlining important nouns and verbs and summarizing in the paragraph. Then, you can spot the true statements more easily:

Choice A is true. Lines 35–37 clearly provides health issues associated with being thin. Use your pencil and X out Choice A. Wrong.

Choice B is also true. Lines 30–31 explain that women associate androgyny with beauty. X it out. Wrong.

Choice C is definitely established throughout the entire paragraph, so X that out, too. Wrong again.

Choice D is neither stated nor implied in the text—the passage clearly points out in lines 28–31 that both women and teens are susceptible to the belief—so it is false, which means Choice D is the correct answer.

Tough Supporting Details Questions

Tough supporting details questions will ask you to find info in the text without giving you a line number, paragraph number, or quotation marks to help you locate the info. They take the most time out of any other type of reading question and hence, are the most dangerous!

> Which of the following is NOT listed in the passage as a factor contributing to the Ice Age?

The example above seems easy, right? You just look back at the text, locate the info, and answer the question.

Wrong. This question requires you to skim the passage again. You will not be able to answer it, and all the other tough supporting detail questions, without going back to the text, which is why it takes so long. These questions are dangerous because they slowly take your precious time away from you, which is why we need a strategy.

HEADS UP

Use the words inside the question to help you locate info in the text. If the question mentions a "purchase from the Freedom Center," then keep your eyes peeled for the words "Freedom Center" as you hunt for the info. Once you've scoured a paragraph that *doesn't* contain the answer, put an "X" next to it so you're not tempted to look again. Since these are the last questions you'll answer per passage, you can scribble as much as you'd like.

STRATEGY ALERT

How to Solve a Tough Supporting Detail Question

Skip, Clock It, and Search: Although this sounds like some sort of method the LAPD might use for finding a thief holed up in an abandoned warehouse, this technique is your No. 1 ally in your detective work to uncover supporting details. First, you'll just go ahead and SKIP these types of questions when you're answering the toughies. Then, before going back to them, you'll CLOCK the time. If you have at least a full minute left on your watch for the passage you're on, then go ahead and SEARCH the text for the answer. If not, guess and move onto the next passage. There are easier questions waiting for you to answer them!

Examples of some more of those tough supporting detail questions:

- According to the passage, one of the woman's worries about her present situation is that she:

- According to the passage, which of the following places is the last one Jackie was said to have visited?
- Which of the following situations is NOT described in the passage?
- The author calls the interactions that produced the Crimean Wars:
- Which of the following is NOT listed as an item Josie most wanted to purchase from the Freedom Center?
- The author cites all of the following as causes of the Wars of the Roses EXCEPT:
- All of the following details are used in the passage to demonstrate Scott's musical genius EXCEPT that he:
- According to the passage, the black color of the valleys of the mountains in the Atlantic basin is:
- The passage mentions that the onset of illness would be caused by any of the following EXCEPT:

Practice Reading for Supporting Details

A cave or cavern is an opening in the side of a mountain or underneath the surface of the Earth, usually formed by some natural action such as water trickling through the cracks or flowing in underground streams. Caves are often formed in limestone or some other soft rock when the water drips and wears away the stone. If the water carries the mineral called calcite, or calcium carbonate, it produces a phenomenon of nature in the form of color rock formations inside the caves. These decorative dripstone features are called speleothems (from the Greek *spelaion* for *cave* and *thema* for *deposit*). When lanterns or electric lights highlight these structures, they transform a cave into a natural wonderland.

The most familiar speleothems are stalactites and stalagmites. Stalactites hang downward from the ceiling and are formed as drop after drop of water slowly trickles through cracks in the cave roof. As each drop of water hangs from the ceiling, it loses carbon dioxide and deposits a film of calcite. Successive drops add ring below ring, the water dripping through the hollow center of the rings, until a pendant cylinder forms. Tubular or "soda straw" stalactites grow in this way; most are fragile and have the diameter of a drop of water, but some reach a length of perhaps a yard or more. The large cone-shaped stalactites begin as these fragile tubes and then enlarge to cones when enough water accumulates to flow along the outside of the soda straws. Deposition of calcite on the outside of the tubes, most of which are near the ceiling and taper downward, results in the familiar cone shapes.

1. According to the passage, water can do all of the following EXCEPT:

   A. flow underground in mountain streams to form caves.

   B. stream alongside stalactites, depositing calcite to create conical shapes.

   C. wear away stalagmites by trickling through cracks in caverns.

   D. add to the height and depth of a speleothem by depositing films of calcite.

2. Information in the last paragraph indicates that "soda straw" stalactites:

   F. are formed on cavern floors and have the diameter of a drop of water.

   G. start as brittle tubes, but gain strength as water flows around them.

   H. can reach over a yard in length and breadth.

   J. slowly gain length as drops of water deposit speleothems into the tubes.

3. The passage provides information that answers which of the following questions?

   I. Do cone-shaped stalactites begin as tubular stalactites?

   II. Are stalactites and stalagmites considered colored rock formations?

   III. Does the length of time water drips into the cave effect the height of the stalagmite?

   A. I only

   B. I and II only

   C. I and III only

   D. II and III only

4. The author calls which of the following "a natural wonderland"?

   F. a cave

   G. a stalactite

   H. a stalagmite

   J. a speleothem

HEADS UP

When you get a question like #3, treat the roman-numeral questions listed like short-answer questions; find the answers in the text (or answer them with a yes or no), for as many as you can. Then, choose the right answer.

Answers on page 182.

Making Inferences

Sure, you can *find* details in the passage; so could a trained pachyderm. However, here's the kind of stuff that separates us from most of the other mammals on the planet: drawing conclusions. Can you use the information in the text another way? Can you infer the meaning behind the words? Can you interpret the text to make a reasonable judgment?

See, if you can do this, you have the goods to stand tall at the end of the ACT Reading section.

Tough Inference Questions

Tough making inferences questions are really all the ACT will give you. For the most part, when you're asked to interpret information, you will not be given a particular line number or paragraph. The questions that provide locations are often just looking for details, rather than inferences.

So what does it mean to make an inference?

You read the presented information and you think it over a bit to draw more meaning from it. An inference is an educated guess based on specific information.

This sounds tricky, but you literally make inferences all day long. If your mom stares at you, you infer that she's annoyed with you. If your uncle says "Nice outfit," then snickers into his collar, you infer that 1) he's got issues and 2) he doesn't like your new acid-washed jean shorts. Neither of them came out and told you, "Sally/Tommy, I'm annoyed with you" or "Your outfit is pretty bad," but since you're paying attention, you get their drift.

Let's take a look at some inferences we could make based on the details from this passage:

> "God gave me the child!" cried Hester. "He gave her in requital of all things else, which he had taken from me. She is my happiness! She is my torture, nonetheless! Pearl keeps me here in life! Pearl punishes me, too. See ye not, she is the scarlet letter, only capable of being loved, and so endowed with a millionfold the power of retribution for my sin? Ye shall not take her! I will die first!"

What are some things we can conclude, based on this passage, even if we didn't know anything beyond just these few sentences?

- A mother is talking/shouting.
- The mother has done something wrong and the child reminds her of it.
- The mother is passionate and desperate, which means she's in a situation where she sees no way out.

The text didn't tell us these things, but we can guess based on the info given.

Now what if we were to get this question on the ACT?

According to the passage, we can reasonably infer that when it comes to Pearl, Hester believes:

A. that although Pearl is Hester's saving grace, this child will ultimately destroy her.

B. that Pearl has saved Hester's own life, although the child causes her pain every day.

C. that Pearl will never have a better life without Hester.

D. that although Pearl will inevitably turn away from her, Hester is desperate to keep her.

> **HEADS UP**
>
> All of the answer choices are going to sound good! That's why they're good answer distractors. Do not select an answer choice because it's similar to another or complicated—there will always be a distinct reason why one is incorrect and one is correct. Often, the test designer will mask incorrect answers in complicated language, so you'll have to pay close attention to get it right.

This is where things get a little trickier, eh? As always, when things get tricky, we need a strategy for breaking stuff down.

STRATEGY ALERT

How to Solve an Inference Question

Translate and Add the Tag: When you come across a question that makes no sense, translate it so it does. Then, add the question tag to the answers so you can have a shot at getting this thing right.

Here's how:

> *According to the passage, we can reasonably infer that when it comes to Pearl, Hester believes:*

This is unnecessarily long. Why don't we translate it to:

> *Hester believes:*

We already know that the question is about Pearl. All the answer choices refer to her. So, instead of confusing yourself with a lengthy question, just translate it into something that you can understand. Let's do the same for the answers and add the tag, so they're less confusing, too:

A. that although Pearl is Hester's saving grace, this child will ultimately seek to destroy her.

Translation: *Hester believes that Pearl is wonderful, but she'll want to hurt Hester.*

B. that Pearl has saved Hester's own life, although the child causes her pain every day.

Translation: *Hester believes that Pearl saved her, but Pearl hurts her.*

C. that Pearl will never have a better life without Hester.

Translation: *Hester believes that Pearl's life will be terrible without her.*

D. that although Pearl will inevitably turn away from her, Hester is desperate to keep her.

Translation: *Hester believes Pearl will want nothing to do with her, but she wants Pearl as her daughter anyway.*

Okay. That's better. So which one of these can we reasonably infer from the text? It has to be Choice B. Choice A says that the kid *will want* to hurt her mom, and in no way does the text imply this. Choice C is out, too. The passage says nothing about Pearl's life—Hester only talks about herself.

Choice D is out, too, because we never hear anything about Pearl's feelings; we just hear about Hester's, so we'd have no way of knowing if Pearl wants her or not.

Hence, Choice B is the right one.

Practice Making Inferences

[I chose a reading passage that's as long as an actual passage on the Reading section of the ACT. Don't fail me now! Be sure to use your reading technique (page 138) as you go, to get the most correct answers.]

There is a certain church in the city of New York which I have always regarded with peculiar interest, on account of a marriage there solemnized, under very singular circumstances, in my grandmother's girlhood. That venerable lady chanced to be a spectator of the scene, and ever after made it her favorite narrative. Whether the edifice now standing on the same site be the identical one to which she referred, I am not antiquarian enough to know; nor would it be worthwhile to correct myself, perhaps, of an agreeable error, by reading the date of its erection on the tablet over the door. It is a stately church, surrounded by an enclosure of the loveliest green, within which appear urns, pillars, obelisks, and other forms of monumental marble, the tributes of private affection, or more splendid memorials of historic dust. With such a place, though the tumult of the city rolls beneath its tower, one would be willing to connect some legendary interest.

The marriage might be considered as the result of an early engagement, though there had been two intermediate weddings on the lady's part, and forty years of celibacy on that of the gentleman. At sixty-five, Mr. Ellenwood was a shy, but not quite a secluded man; selfish, like all men who brood over their own hearts, yet manifesting on rare occasions a vein of generous sentiment; a scholar throughout life, though always an indolent one, because his studies had no definite object, either of public advantage or personal ambition; a gentleman, high bred and fastidiously delicate, yet sometimes requiring a considerable relaxation, in his behalf, of the common rules of society. In truth, there were so many anomalies in his character, and though shrinking with diseased sensibility from public notice, it had been his fatality so often to become the topic of the day, by some wild eccentricity of conduct, that people searched his lineage for an hereditary taint of insanity. But there was no need of this. His caprices had their origin in a mind that lacked the support of an engrossing purpose, and in feelings that preyed upon themselves for want of other food. If he were mad, it was the consequence, and not the cause, of an aimless and abortive life.

The widow was as complete a con[illegible] to her third bridegroom, in everything but age, as can well be conceived. Compelled to relinquish her first engagement, she had been united to a man of twice her own years, to whom she became an exemplary wife, and by whose death she was left in possession of a splendid fortune. A southern gentleman, considerably younger than herself, succeeded to her hand, and carried her to Charleston, where, after many uncomfortable years, she found herself again a widow. It would have been singular, if any uncommon delicacy of feeling had survived through such a life as Mrs. Dabney's; it could not but be crushed and killed by her early disappointment, the cold duty of her first marriage, the dislocation of the heart's principles, consequent on a second union, and the unkindness of her southern husband, which had inevitably driven her to connect the idea of his death with that of her comfort. To be brief, she was that wisest variety of woman, a philosopher, bearing troubles of the heart with equanimity, dispensing with all that should have been her happiness, and making the best of what remained. Sage in most matters, the widow was perhaps the more amiable for the one frailty that made her ridiculous. Being childless, she could not remain beautiful by proxy, in the person of a daughter; she therefore refused to grow old and ugly, on any consideration; she struggled with Time, and held fast her roses in spite of him, till the venerable thief appeared to have relinquished the spoil, as not worth the trouble of acquiring it.

1. Which of the following statements about Mrs. Dabney is best supported by the passage?

A. She is a severe, unkind woman.

B. She is a generally happy woman.

C. She is a woman content with her fate.

D. She is a woman saddened by loss.

2. The passage suggests that Mr. Ellenwood's primary problem was his:

F. insanity, inherited from his family.

G. lack of purpose and drive.

H. selfishness, which prevented him from accomplishment.

J. shortage of womanly suitors.

3. It can be reasonably inferred from the passage that Mrs. Dabney desires to keep intact which of the following characteristics the more she ages?

A. Her beauty

B. Her duty

C. Her wisdom

D. Her happiness

4. Based on the information in the passage, it could be suggested that the narrator believes Mrs. Dabney's prior marriages to be:

F. uncomfortable, but convenient to Mrs. Dabney.

G. satisfactory and dull to Mrs. Dabney.

H. cold and displeasing to Mrs. Dabney.

J. awful, but worthwhile to Mrs. Dabney.

Answers on page 183.

Craft and Structure: 10–12 questions

The second area on which you'll be tested in this, Craft and Structure. Here, you'll focus on the following skills:

- Understanding Vocabulary in Context
- Determining the Author or Narrator's Voice and Purpose

Understanding Vocabulary in Context

Relax. The ACT is not like the standardized tests of the past with mountains of vocabulary words to memorize and synonyms to recognize out of context. In fact, the only vocabulary you'll even really need to know is *in context,* which means you get to use the clues around the word to help you figure it out.

And as always—you'll have answer choices to help you hone in on your target.

Easy Vocabulary Questions

Easy vocabulary questions are the only kind there are on the ACT. You'll never have to guess where the word is that you're trying to define; you'll always be given a line number for reference.

As it is used in line 57, the word *adjustment* most nearly means:

The most important part of this question is the phrase, "as it is used." The ACT will always provide you several correct definitions of the word, so, without looking at the context, you'll have no idea which to choose.

For example, the word *adjustment* can mean all sorts of things:

- You can go into a chiropractor's office for an *adjustment* after your accidental fender bender.
- You can fiddle with the *adjustments* on your TV to get the best sound while you're streaming Netflix.
- Your aunt can be going through an *adjustment* while dealing with an "empty nest."

Let's try substituting another word in each case:

- You can go into a chiropractor's office for an *alignment* after your accidental fender bender.
- You can fiddle with the *buttons* on your TV to get the best sound while you're streaming Netflix.
- Your aunt can be going through a *trial* while dealing with an "empty nest."

So if your question was:

> As it is used in line 57, the word *adjustment* most nearly means:

And your choices were:

A. correction

B. alignment

C. buttons

D. trial

You may be tempted to choose Choice A if you don't read the text, because the word "adjustment" always means, "correction," right? Obviously not. The *context* tells you how to choose.

STRATEGY ALERT

How to Solve a Vocabulary in Context Question

Put Me In, Coach! Just like when you begged your 8th grade baseball coach to let you pitch to that batter, there are words warming up in the bullpen of your brain just waiting for their chance to get into the game. The best way to solve one of these "most nearly means" questions is by putting one of those little players into the sentence.

Let's try it:

> Although tragedy must arouse our pity for the tragic hero as he endures his catastrophe and must fright us as we witness the consequences of a flawed behavior, there must also be a cleansing of these emotions which should leave the audience elated. The assumption is that while the tragic hero endures a crushing reversal, somehow he is not thoroughly defeated as he gains new stature through suffering and the knowledge that comes with suffering.

17. As it is used in line 5, the word *stature* most nearly means:

Before reading the answer choices, put in one of your second-stringers. The word *stature* is out of the game. (He's been throwing too many pitches inside.) Who should replace him? If I were the coach, I'd put in someone like "strength" or "greatness." They've been pretty accurate this season.

Let's take a look at the bench and see who we've got to work with.

A. height

B. achievement

C. power

D. status

Well, I'm not seeing "strength" or "greatness" exactly, but I know for sure that "height" is out. "Stature" can mean "height," but not in this context. "Status" also doesn't seem to work—that's more of a social standing kind of thing, and the context seems to point to inner strength.

That leaves us with "achievement" and "power." Which one is gonna strike out this last batter and end the game? I'm going to have to choose "power" because the word "achievement" doesn't fit into the sentence as well. "He gains new achievement through suffering" sounds strange, whereas "He gains new power through suffering" sounds good. Choice C—You're in!

Determining the Author or Narrator's Voice and Purpose

This sounds so intimidating, doesn't it? Author or narrator's voice and purpose? How stodgy can you get? Very, as it turns out.

These types of questions on ACT Reading deal with how the author or narrator sounds (voice) and why the author writes or why the narrator says or does something (purpose). You've already dealt with voice during the English section. These questions just take it one step further to see if you can identify the techniques used to create the passage.

When the question asks about the *narrator's* take on everything, you'll remember that the narrator is *not* necessarily the author. Yes, you will. You already know that the difference between the narrator and the author is that the author wrote the passage, and the narrator is the person the author uses to tell the story in a fictional piece. Yep. You knew that.

Easy Voice and Purpose Questions

Easy voice and purpose questions will ask you to figure out why or how the author wrote something in a given section of the text.

You'll see a question like this:

> The author most likely includes the info in lines 54–57 in order to:
>
> **A.** identify the root causes of evil as described by the village chief.
>
> **B.** contrast the beliefs of the chief with those of the visiting tribesman.
>
> **C.** describe a new way of thinking brought to the village by the visiting tribesman.
>
> **D.** critique the arrogance of the chief's beliefs by demonstrating a superior system.

Your job will be to figure out which one of those four choices explains why the author included the information.

The best way to do this is with a strategy!

STRATEGY ALERT

How to Solve an Easy Author's Voice and Purpose Question

Find the Signal Words: Signal words are little flags in the passage that tell you *how* the author chose to get information to you, the reader. The author could have *described* a recipe, *criticized* a play, *compared* two generals, etc. It's your job to figure out which technique the author used in the passage, and each one of those reasons comes with little signal words to help you figure it out!

Here's what I mean:

Word Used in Answer Choice	If the answer choice uses this word, it means that the author . . .
compare	. . . shows ***similarities*** between ideas. **Example:** If the author compared the North and South during the Civil War, then you could read about valiant soldiers, dedicated generals, and shortages of supplies on both sides. **Signal Words:** *both, similarly, in the same way, like, just as*
contrast	. . . shows ***differences*** between ideas. **Example:** If the author contrasted Michigan and Florida lakes, then you could read about Florida lakes being home to alligators and larger flying insects, and Michigan lakes having more edible fish and sporting events. **Signal Words:** *however, but, dissimilarly, on the other hand*
criticize	. . . shows a ***negative opinion*** of an idea. **Example:** If the author criticizes a sculptor's use of marble, then you could read about the waste of a popular building material, the lack of skill demonstrated, and the poorly constructed statue. **Signal Words:** look for words that show the author's negative opinion. Judgment words like *bad*, *wasteful*, and *poor* all demonstrate negative opinions.
describe/ illustrate	. . . ***paints a picture*** of an idea. **Example:** If the author describes a baby's cry, then you could read about the first soft whimpers, the increasing throaty wails when his mother doesn't respond, and the calming hiccupping sobs when she finally swaddles him in her arms. **Signal Words:** look for words that provide descriptive detail. Adjectives like *red, lusty, morose, striped, sparkling,* and *crestfallen* are all illustrative.

Word Used in Answer Choice	If the answer choice uses this word, it means that the author . . .
explain	. . . ***breaks down*** an idea into simple words. **Example:** If the author explains the process of creating brown butter, you could read about adding butter to a hot pan, stirring until sediment forms, waiting for the butter to turn golden, then straining. **Signal Words:** look for words that turn a complicated process into simple language. A "descriptive" text will use more adjectives. An "explanatory" text will usually be used with a complicated idea.
identify or list	. . . ***tells*** the reader about an idea or series of ideas. **Example:** If the author identifies the types of red wine available on the menu, you could read about merlot, cabernet sauvignon, and malbec. **Signal Words:** Text that identifies or lists, will name an idea or series of ideas, without providing much description or opinion.
Intensify/ heighten	. . . makes an idea ***greater***. **Example:** If the author intensifies a description of a fire consuming a house, you could read about the blazing inferno roaring out of control, the increased temperatures, or the sweat-soaked faces of the firefighters. **Signal Words:** Text that intensifies will add more specific details to the idea. Look for superlative adjectives and "bigger" concepts. A hot fire is descriptive, but a blazing inferno is more intense.
suggest	. . . ***proposes*** an idea. **Example:** If the author suggests that cows are the most useful farm animal, you could read about their strength, ability to produce milk, and source of meat. **Signal Words:** "Suggest" answers are usually positive opinions, and try to sway the reader to believe. The author will provide a point, then use details to prove it.

See? Find the signal words; figure out the reason/purpose for writing.

Let's look for some signal words in the following paragraph:

> The next day, the 22nd of March, at six in the morning, preparations for departure were begun. The last gleams of twilight were melting into night. The cold was great; the constellations shown with wonderful intensity. In the zenith glittered that wondrous Southern Cross—the polar bear of Antarctic regions. The thermometer showed 12 degrees below zero, and when the wind freshened it was most biting. Flakes of ice increased on the open water. The sea seemed

everywhere alike. Numerous blackish patches spread on the surface, showing the formation of fresh ice. Evidently the southern basin, frozen during the six winter months, was absolutely inaccessible. What became of the whales in that time? Doubtless they went beneath the icebergs, seeking more practicable seas. As to the seals and morses, accustomed to life in a hard climate, they remained on these icy shores.

The author's description of the temperature in lines 41–45 primarily serves to:

F. explain the hardships the boatmen were about to go through.

G. intensify the setting, so the reader can experience the boatmen's difficult journey.

H. compare the differences between boatmen who have experienced hardships and those who haven't.

J. identify the causes of the temperature decrease.

Let's follow our reading steps to answer this question:

Step 1: SEPARATE tough from easy (already done).

Step 2: READ the easy question.

Step 3: READ and MARK UP the text by underlining important words and summarizing in the margin. For this type of question, make sure you look for those SIGNAL WORDS. Why did the author include that information?

HEADS UP

Be careful not to choose an answer that is only half right. Often, the test writers will include an answer choice that not only uses words from the paragraph, but also includes **some** accurate information. Make sure to read the entire answer choice before selecting. Half right is also completely wrong and will lower your score!

Step 4: POE and ANSWER the easy question.

Here, if you've followed the method, you'll see some obvious choices to get rid of.

Choice H is definitely out because two things aren't being compared.

Cross it off.

Choice J is out, because although the author talks about the temperature being cold, he doesn't say *why* it's gotten colder.

Choices F and G are close!

So, we need to check the signal words! When you underlined, did you notice that you were underlining adjectives that *increasingly* described the dropping temperature? At first, the author indicated that it was just cold. Then, in the lines related to the question, he added more intense details to heighten the feeling. So, our choice has to be Choice G.

Tough Voice and Purpose Questions

Tough voice-and-purpose questions will ask you to figure out why or how the author wrote something in the entire passage.

Okay. These questions can be tough. Why? They don't give you a spot to refer back to. You'll have to get a feel for the entire passage after reading it. It can be intimidating, but if you follow those easy reading steps before you attempt any of these tough questions, you'll have a much better shot at answering correctly.

- Which of the following best describes the structure of the passage? (a dialogue? a character sketch? a narration?)
- Based on the passage, which of the following statements best describes the overall attitude of the narrator?
- The author most nearly characterizes the role of earthquakes in continent formation as one that:
- Based on details in the passage, the author's general attitude about extreme sports could best be described as:

So for these toughies, read the text and mark it up, underlining important nouns and verbs. Then, summarize each paragraph with a word or phrase in the margin, so you'll remember what you've read.

Try to answer the question in your head as best as you can, then look for a match in the answers below. If you can't knock out two answer choices right away and choose wisely from the last two choices, then put a star next to the question number to come back to it, and move on.

Try not to refer back to the text when you're answering the tough questions. Your goal is to understand it as you read it the first time, so you don't *have* to go back and search in order to answer the tough questions. You'll waste valuable answering time by searching, and you get 0 points for reading and looking. The only way to score ACT Reading points is by answering correctly, so don't waste your time!

Practice Reading for Vocabulary, Author's Voice, and Purpose

Until the early 1900's, Americans were not extremely concerned about their futures as they became older. The major source of economic security was farming, and the extended family cared for the elderly. However, the Industrial Revolution brought an end to this tradition. Farming gave way to more progressive means of earning a living and family ties became looser; as a result, the family was not always available to take care of the older generation. The great Depression of the 1930's exacerbated these economic security woes. So in 1935, Congress, under the direction of President Franklin D. Roosevelt, signed into law the Social Security Act. This act created a program intended to provide continuing income for retired workers at least 65 years old, partially through the collection of funds from Americans in the work force. Much organization was required to get the program under way, but the first monthly Social Security checks were issued in 1940. Over the years the Social Security Program has metamorphosed into benefits not only for workers but also for the disabled and for survivors of beneficiaries, as well as medical insurance benefits in the form of Medicare.

Today there is some concern that Social Security is not so "secure." Rumors and prediction contend that by 2020, if not sooner, the system will be running in the red, distributing more money in benefits than it is taking in. Life expectancy is lengthening while birth rates are declining, so the number of people receiving benefits is steadily increasing while the number of workers contributing to the Social Security coffers is dwindling. Fifty years ago, the ratio of workers to Social Security beneficiaries was approximately 16 to 1. In 2008, it was 3 to 1. Theories about how to solve this problem are plentiful, but what approach would be most effective—and what the government decides to do—remains to be seen.

1. The author most likely mentions the Depression to:

A. identify the primary purpose for Social Security.

B. criticize FDR's adoption of a program that would run out of money.

C. contrast the effectiveness of the Social Security Program with that of family care.

D. list another factor that contributed to the need for the Social Security Program.

2. The author most likely includes information in lines 35–39 in order to intensify:

F. the argument that the Social Security Program is no longer effective.

G. the premise that without aid, the Social Security Program will continue as it always has.

H. the belief that the Social Security Program's lack of security poses a threat to the U.S.

J. the approach of solving the Social Security crisis before it's too late.

3. The main function of the first paragraph (lines 1–28) is to:

A. suggest the vital nature of FDR's role in the Social Security Program's inception.

B. explain the basic need for, and a brief history of, the Social Security Program.

C. illustrate the decline of the Social Security Program and the steps required to fix it.

D. compare the beginning of the Social Security Program with its decline.

4. Based on the passage, the author's attitude toward the government's solutions to the Social Security Program's problems could best be described as:

F. hopeful.

G. grim.

H. neutral.

J. skeptical.

5. As it is used in line 7, the word *tradition* most nearly means:

A. practice.

B. belief.

C. ritual.

D. habit.

Answers on page 184.

Integration of Knowledge and Ideas: 5–7 questions

The third area on which you'll be tested is how you can analyze the Integration of Knowledge and Ideas. Sounds vague and strange, doesn't it? No worries! It isn't so bad! Plus, there are only a handful of these toughies. In short, you will need to make connections between two texts, evaluating reasoning and evidence to do so.

Most of these questions will apply to the two-passage portion of the test. A couple though will get into the analysis of an author's arguments or claims. And here's how you go about solving these types of questions.

Analyzing an Author's Arguments or Claims

Arguments. Aren't they grand? You get in them with your siblings over the very best seat in the living room and you get in them with your parents over your increasing need to be in charge of your own life. Fortunately for you, you have a *ton* of experience with arguments, am I right? Unfortunately for you, there are a few things the ACT arguments questions expect you to understand that you may not already know.

Tough Arguments Questions

There's no way around it. The arguments questions are going to be challenging. But we can make it a little bit easier by explaining the basics of arguments so you can look for those basics in the text if you have to figure out the author's claim and how he or she constructed the reasoning and evidence to support it.

Argument Basics

Any argument worth its salt will have these things: one or more premises and one conclusion.

Premises are statements that present evidence. They're the "proof" an author presents to make his or her case.

"**Cats with long hair shed all over the house** so you should not get a long-haired cat. I have heard that **they also have lots of fleas.**"

The premises or evidence here, is that long-haired cats shed and have lots of fleas.

Conclusions are the claims the perspectives make. It's what the statement says will, did, or should happen because of the premise. It's the argument the author is making.

"Cats with long hair shed all over the house so **you should not get a long-haired cat**. I have heard that they also have lots of fleas."

Let's try another statement. Underline the premise or premises and circle the conclusion.

"Scientific discoveries are continually disproving religious myths. Further, science provides the only hope for solving the many problems faced by humanity like overpopulation and global warming. Hence, science provides a more accurate view of human life than does religion."

Go ahead. I'm waiting.

Tick. Tock. Tick. Tock.

Okay! Ready. Did you get this?

"Scientific discoveries are continually disproving religious myths. Further, science provides the only hope for solving the many problems faced by humanity like overpopulation and global warming. Hence, science provides a more accurate view of human life than does religion."

The author argues that science is a more accurate view of human life than religion and uses the premises of science disproving religious myths and solving humanity's problems as proof.

Let's try one of those pesky ACT argument questions to see how this looks in action.

In William Shakespeare's *Hamlet*, Gertrude is a woman who means no harm but whose poor judgment contributes greatly to the terrible events that occur. There are only two female characters in the play, and neither one—Gertrude or Ophelia—is an evil, assertive character. But the decisions Gertrude *does* bring herself to make, eventually lead to her death and the downfall of others as well.

We first realize in Act I, Scene 2 that poor judgment is her major character flaw. As the mother of a grieving son, Gertrude should have been more sensitive to Hamlet's feelings. Instead, less than two months after King Hamlet's death, Gertrude remarries Claudius, her dead husband's own brother. Gertrude should have realized how humiliated Hamlet would feel as a result, because at that time it was considered incestuous for a widow to marry her husband's brother. There is also jealousy on the part of a son, who feels that his mother should be giving him more attention during the mourning period. Gertrude is not in touch with her own son's feelings to see why he is angry. Hamlet expresses this outrage during his first soliloquy:

O, most wicked speed, to post
With such dexterity to incestuous
sheets! (I.ii 156–157)

Gertrude is shown to be a loving mother but a parent who cannot read into her son's behavior. When answering Hamlet, she says that it is common for all men to die. But this is not just any man who died; it was Hamlet's own father!

Which of the following reasons does the author suggest is the primary cause of the deterioration of Gertrude and others in the play?

F. King Hamlet's death

G. Gertrude's poor decisions

H. The marriage between Claudius and Gertrude

J. Hamlet's jealousy

So, if we're following the argument parameters, let's look for the evidence in the text. In this scenario, the best thing to do is to look for the phrase (or a paraphrase of it) "the deterioration of Gertrude and others" in the text to see if we can figure out what the evidence says.

Since the text says, "But the decisions Gertrude *does* bring herself to make, eventually lead to her death and the downfall of others as well." we can safely assume that

Choice G is correct. The premise, "the decisions Gertrude *does* bring herself to make" is the cause of her and others' *downfall*, which is a synonym of the word *deterioration.*

And although Choice H is one of those poor decisions, it is not broad enough in scope. The author claims that all of her decisions—not just one—caused the problem.

Drawing Conclusions Based on Evidence

Some of these Integration of Knowledge and Ideas questions take it a step further. They won't want you to simply study the author's arguments and find their conclusions, they will ask you to draw your *own* conclusions based on the information in the text.

It may sound familiar to you, because drawing conclusions is a common type of inferencing skill. When you draw a conclusion, you form a judgment or opinion that is not implicitly stated or implied in the text. How do you do that? You base your conclusion on details in the passage. You study the facts to get absolute proof of your conclusion.

For example, if your friend shows you that the sole of her left shoe is coming loose, insists you drive her to the shoe store, and stands in the aisle contemplating shoes that are similar to the ones with the loose sole, a reasonable conclusion is that she is shopping for new shoes. She didn't tell you that, or even imply it, but, using the evidence at hand, you can draw that conclusion based on the facts.

What conclusion can you draw from the following passage?

> "Jessie has studied all week for her algebra test. She spent two hours every night working on the review exercises in her textbook. Last night, she could not sleep very well because she was afraid she would sleep through her alarm."

Based on the information presented in the passage, which conclusion can we draw about Jessie?

A. Jessie will pass her test.

B. Jessie wants a good score on her algebra test.

C. Jessie gets nervous when she has to take tests.

D. Jessie enjoys taking tests.

Choice A is not a conclusion. It's a prediction. Someone who studies that much and is completely prepared will probably pass her test. However, we can't reasonably conclude that because she could have worked on all of the review exercises incorrectly.

Choice B is a logical conclusion. Whether or not she gets a good score, we know she wants one. Someone who studies all week, spends two hours a night and cannot sleep because she doesn't want to miss her alarm, is concerned about that score.

Choice C is not a conclusion but a generalization. It's too broad in scope. We only know how she reacts to algebra tests, not all tests, and we can't be sure she's nervous before all of her big tests. We can't even say for certain she's nervous before this test. She seemed nervous about missing her alarm, but not necessarily about taking the test.

Choice D is not a conclusion because the passage does not imply that Jessie is enjoying anything.

Tricky? It can be. Let's try a strategy to help us out.

STRATEGY ALERT

Face the Facts

When confronted with a question that asks you to form your own conclusion, you have to face the facts, whether you like it or not. You are not assuming anything. You are not reading between the lines. You are reading the lines and what they tell you—exactly.

Let's try facing the facts with another passage.

> Fran was a born worrier. She worried about everything. When she went on a business trip, she worried that she might forget her ticket or that the plane might be late and she wouldn't get to her meeting on time. When she drove, she worried that traffic would be terrible and that she'd get in a car wreck before arriving at her destination. When she went on vacation, she worried that she would arrive at a hotel and somehow her reservation would be mixed up and she wouldn't have a room.

Suppose Fran got a new job. Which of the following thoughts would Fran MOST LIKELY have the day before she started?

F. I wonder when I'll get a pay raise.

G. I hope I don't get lost in such a big building.

H. I wonder if my new boss will promote me.

J. I hope I get an office with a great view.

Choices F and H are not logical conclusions, since, if we face the facts, Fran's primary worries tend to be negative in slant.

"forget her ticket"

"plane might be late"

"wouldn't get to her meeting"

"traffic would be terrible"

"get in a car wreck"

Choice J is a positive hope. She wants something, which is great. If the answer choice had been reworded to say, "I hope I don't get an office with a parking lot view" then that would be a logical conclusion.

Hence, Choice G, which shows a negative worry similar to Fran's line of thinking (poor Fran), it's the most logical conclusion and the correct answer.

Making Connections Between Texts

You've done Venn diagrams since you were a little kid. You draw two circles, intersecting them slightly, and then write what's similar between the two things you're studying in the intersection. As it turns out, that's a pretty valuable skill, according to the ACT. One of the skills on which you'll be tested is your ability to make connections between two similar texts.

Tough Connections Questions

Yep. You guessed it. The Making Connections questions on ACT Reading can get a little complicated. Luckily for you, we're going to go through them, every step of the way.

Connection questions can only happen in the Reading passage that uses two correlated passages. Although the ACT test writers will use their discretion when deciding which passages to use, they could potentially put passages together like this:

Passage A	Passage B
An excerpt about an author's life, written by a close friend	An excerpt from the same author's most popular book
One essayist's firsthand account of watching a historic event	Another essayist's firsthand account of watching the same historic event
An excerpt from a scientific journal about a natural phenomenon	A reporter's account while watching the natural phenomenon firsthand
An excerpt of an author's short story about growing up.	An excerpt of a different author's short story about growing up.

Your job will be to find the similarities and differences as you go so you can answer questions like these:

1. Both Passage A and Passage B highlight the author's use of ____?
2. Based on the author's description of his childhood home in Passage A, which of the following conclusions can you draw about the author of Passage B's remembrance of *her* childhood home?
3. A great orator once said, "I am everything my life has intended me to become." How does this statement apply to both the information about the author's approach to storytelling in Passage A, and the main character's quest for greatness in Passage B?
4. Compared to the narrator in Passage B, the narrator of Passage A provides much more information about:

So, as you can see, you'll need to put your thinking caps on to solve these bad boys. Let's practice with some sample Passages that could be found under the "Humanities" passage.

Passage A, detailing Charles Dickens' first visit to the White House, is an excerpt from a nonfiction book, *American Notes for General Circulation* by Charles Dickens (©1842 by Chapman and Hall). Passage B, which describes a live-cattle market in London, is an excerpt from a nonfiction book, *A Child's History of England* by Charles Dickens (©1851 Bradbury and Evans).

Passage A

The President's mansion is more like an English club-house, both within and without, than any other kind of establishment with which I can compare it. The ornamental ground about it has been laid out in garden walks; they are pretty, and agreeable to the eye; though they have that uncomfortable air of having been made yesterday, which is far from favourable to the display of such beauties. My first visit to this house was on the morning after my arrival, when I was carried thither by an official gentleman, who was so kind as to charge himself with my presentation to the President. We entered a large hall, and having twice or thrice rung a bell which nobody answered, walked without further ceremony through the rooms on the ground floor, as diverse other gentlemen (mostly with their hats on, and their hands in their pockets) were doing very leisurely. Some of these had ladies with them, to whom they were showing the premises; others were lounging on the chairs and sofas; others, in a perfect state of exhaustion from listlessness, were yawning drearily. The greater portion of this assemblage were rather asserting their supremacy than doing anything else, as they had no particular business there that anybody knew of. A few were closely eyeing the movables, as if to make quite sure that the President (who was far from popular) had not made away with any of the furniture, or sold the fixtures for his private benefit. After glancing at these loungers; who were scattered over a pretty drawing-room, opening upon a terrace which commanded a beautiful prospect of the river and the adjacent country; and who were sauntering, too, about a larger state-room called the Eastern Drawing-room; we went up-stairs into another chamber, where there were certain visitors, waiting for audiences.

Passage B

If you look at a Map of the World, you will see, in the left-hand upper corner of the Eastern Hemisphere, two Islands lying in the sea. They are England and Scotland, and Ireland. England and Scotland form the greater part of these Islands. Ireland is the next in size. The little neighbouring islands, which are so small upon the Map as to be mere dots, are chiefly little bits of Scotland, broken off, I dare say, in the course of a great length of time, by the power of the restless water.

In the old days, a long, long while ago, before Our Saviour was born on earth and lay asleep in a manger, these Islands were in the same place, and the stormy sea roared round them, just as it roars now. But the sea was not alive, then, with great ships and brave sailors, sailing to and from all parts of the world. It was very lonely. The Islands lay solitary, in the great expanse of water. The foaming waves dashed against their cliffs, and the bleak winds blew over their forests; but the winds and waves brought no adventurers to land upon the Islands, and the savage Islanders knew nothing of the rest of the world, and the rest of the world knew nothing of them.

It is supposed that the Phoenicians, who were an ancient people, famous for carrying on trade, came in ships to these Islands, and found that they produced tin and lead; both very useful things, as you know, and both produced to this very hour upon the sea-coast. The most celebrated tin mines in Cornwall are, still, close to the sea. One of them, which I have seen, is so close to it that it is hollowed out underneath the ocean; and the miners say, that in stormy weather, when they are at work down in that deep place, they can hear the noise of the waves thundering above their heads. So, the Phoenicians, coasting about the Islands, would come, without much difficulty, to where the tin and lead were.

Let's start with an easier question.

Both Passage A and Passage B highlight Dickens' usage of:

F. terse, controlled word choice.

G. a light, often sarcastic, tone.

H. long, complex sentence structure.

J. a swift-moving plot.

If we were to make a Venn diagram of the passages (which I do not recommend that you do when taking the actual test because it will take too much time, but we'll do so here for illustration's sake) we'd see a few things about these two passages. Remember that a Venn diagram highlights the similarities and differences between two things. Similarities go in the cross-section, while things only associated with one go in the outside portion of the circle.

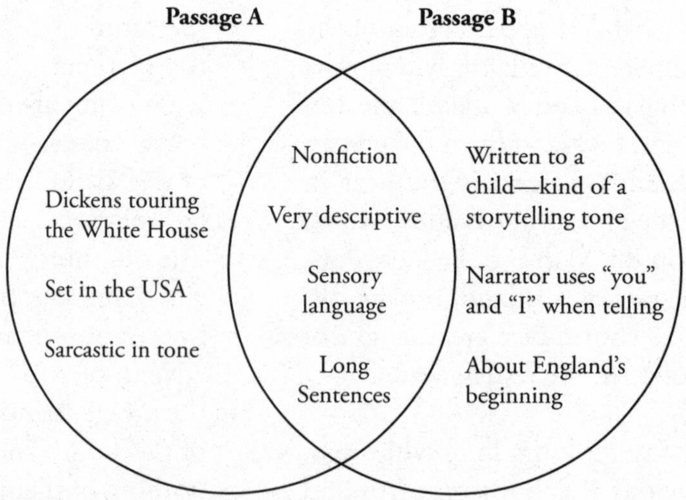

Both passages are nonfiction. The heading to the passages before we even start reading tell us that. Both passages are chock full of Dickens' descriptive language. Passage A relates Dickens' somewhat sarcastic tour of the White House in the United States, while Passage B is more of a lyrical telling of the very beginning of England to a child.

So, if we're looking at the question, we can get rid of a couple of those answer choices.

Choice F is incorrect, because Dickens' word choices are anything but terse (which means short and succinct). Choice J is also incorrect because nonfiction does not have a plot. That leaves Choices G and H. Choice G only refers to Passage A, and since the question asked for the similarity between both passages, it is out. That leaves Choice H, which is quite easy to see from the long, unbroken sentences and prevalent usage of the semicolon.

Now, let's dive into a slightly more difficult question because of the complexity.

Anton Chekhov, Russian playwright and short story writer, once said:

"Don't tell me the moon is shining; show me the glint of light on broken glass."

How does this statement apply to Dickens' writing style in both Passage A and Passage B?

A. Passage A uses more descriptive, sensory language than Passage B and, as such, does more showing than telling.

B. Passage B uses more descriptive, sensory language than Passage A and, as such, does more showing than telling.

C. Both Passages A and B use incredibly vivid, descriptive sensory language equally and, as such, both show their subjects equally.

D. Neither Passage A nor B use much vivid, descriptive sensory language, and, as such, both tell about their subjects.

The simplest way to go about solving this comparative question is by going back through the passage to underline the descriptive, sensory language. If you do that, you'll see that Choice B is the correct answer because Passage B utilizes more descriptive sensory language, language that makes you hear, see, smell, touch, and even taste the scene.

Now, let's practice a few of these Integration of Knowledge and Ideas questions so you can *really* get a handle on this section!

Practice Analyzing Author's Arguments and Making Connections

Passage A is adapted from "Clamor in the East: East Berliners Explore Land Long Forbidden" by Ferdinand Protzman (©1989 The New York Times). Passage B is adapted from "Fall of the Berlin Wall opened a world of opportunity" by Liam Halligan (©2014 by The Telegraph).

Passage A

The 28-year-old Berlin wall opened up Thursday and by midnight thousands of East Berliners—of all ages, from every way of life—were walking, biking and driving to crossing points in the wall and entering the western half of the city, a place of freedom—a place they could only gaze at just hours before. A place of returned dignity and hope.

At Checkpoint Charlie, where Allied and Soviet tanks were locked in a tense face-off while the Berlin wall was being erected in August 1961, lines of cars and people began to file across the border by late evening. Cheers, sparkling wine, flowers and applause greeted the new arrivals. On the West Berlin side of the wall, at the Brandenburg Gate, the most prominent landmark of the city's division, hundreds of people chanted, '"Gate open! Gate open!"

"I can't believe I'm here," an elderly East Berliner told reporters as he crossed into the West. "This is what we have dreamed of all these years. Freedom. Freedom, finally."

"It's over, it's all over, I can't believe it," said an East German as he ducked to get under the red-and-white barriers at the Bornholmer Strasse crossing, an act that might have cost him his life several months ago.

Most of the people interviewed said they would return shortly to their homes; that they just wanted to see what crossing the border was like.

Reacting to the late-night flood of people into the city, Walter Momper, West Berlin's Mayor, made a televised appeal to East Berliners not to rush into his city.

"Please, come tomorrow or the next day," Mr. Momper said late Thursday evening. But he also greeted the East German decision. "We've fought against this division for 40 years," he said. "We cannot shrink now from the task that has been given us. Since we are really a great metropolis, we will find a way to cope with this rush."

"This is what we have dreamed of since we were little children," said a 23-year-old East Berliner, moments after he crossed at Checkpoint Charlie. He asked to be identified as Knobi. "We heard the news at 11:30 P.M., then when we heard they were letting people through, well, here we are. Of course, we're coming back home," he said. "After this, there can be no turning back. This is the turning point everyone has been talking about."

Passage B

On this historic weekend, I have two economic observations related to the fall of the Berlin Wall. The first is that while many post-Communist states are seen here in the West as failures, and a sense of doom and missed opportunity pervades our view of the former "Eastern bloc," I think that's misguided.

As the Wall came down, of course, the entire Soviet power structure—with its closed borders, economic oppression and mind-controls—started to fall with it. A wealth of previously closed, declining economies across Eastern Europe, the Former Soviet Union and Central Asia spluttered into life, enduring much hardship and uncertainty, yes, but clearly lurching forward.

These 30 or so countries, their citizens often bewildered at how quickly lives and livelihoods had been upended, began rapidly to adopt free markets and open up.

Across the region, economies had been centrally-planned. Most or all private property had been illegal and little happened without the authoritarian hand of a gargantuan state. Oppression and thought-control prevailed, with prison camps housing those who dared show dissent.

Yet, during the hectic years after 1989, prices were liberalized and voucher privatizations doled out vast amounts of property—from land, to machinery and real estate. Constitutions were rewritten and companies began to incorporate. As a result, people once living under communism, in their hundreds of millions, are today able to work for themselves, get a normal job, do business, travel, consume vibrant local and foreign media and be part of the rest of the world. Their kids, the coming generation across Eastern Europe, Russia and Central Asia, having never known Communism, are in my experience exceptionally dynamic and ambitious. Now they have a chance to make a good go of their lives.

Yes—the "transition" years were confused, chaotic and, for some, deeply unfair. And, most certainly, in many countries, there's still a very long way to go. But, on balance, it has to be good that economic and political freedoms have been extended and totalitarian nostrums smashed.

Some former Communist countries—such as Poland and the Baltic States—we now view as allies, welcoming them into the European Union and NATO. Others, not least Russia, are typically still seen as Cold War foes.

The reality is, though, that in practically all these countries, lives are now richer, happier and longer than they were during the years when the Berlin Wall, and everything it represented, was in place. That shouldn't be forgotten.

Questions 1 and 2 ask about Passage A.

1. Which of the following claims is best supported by Passage A?
   - A. The fall of the Berlin wall led to severe unrest that did not justify its destruction.
   - B. The fall of the Berlin wall offered freedom to many people who had been denied it for years.
   - C. The effects of the fall of the Berlin wall can still be felt, many decades after its demise.
   - D. The effects of the fall of the Berlin wall caused short-term freedom, but long-term unrest in Berlin.

2. Which of the following claims would the author most likely support the LEAST?
   - F. The gift of personal liberty is worth the sacrifice of chaos.
   - G. Freedom must be meted out slowly, so as not to give rise to tension.
   - H. The ability to choose one's fate can mitigate the suffering of repression.
   - J. One single event can positively impact the lives of thousands of people.

Questions 3 and 4 ask about Passage B.

3. Which of the following facts does the author NOT use to support his argument that it's misguided to say that many post-Communist states are failures:
   - A. After the fall of the Berlin wall, countries began rapidly to adopt free markets and open up.
   - B. We now view some former Communist countries as Allies
   - C. People once living under communism are currently able to work for themselves.
   - D. The entire Soviet power structure—with its closed borders, economic oppression and mind-controls—started to fall with the Berlin wall.

4. Which details best support the author's conclusion that "lives are now richer, happier and longer than they were during the years when the Berlin Wall, and everything it represented, was in place"?
   - F. After the Berlin wall fell, people today are able to do business, travel, consume vibrant media and be part of the rest of the world.
   - G. Citizens were quickly surprised how easily their lives were upended after the fall of the Berlin wall.
   - H. After the Berlin wall fell, prices were liberalized and voucher privatizations doled out vast amounts of property—from land to machinery and real estate
   - J. The "transition" years after the fall of the Berlin wall, were confused, chaotic and, for some, deeply unfair.

Questions 5 and 6 ask about both passages.

5. Horst Köhler, President of Germany from 2004 to 2010, once said:

> **"The Wall was an edifice of fear. On November 9th… it became a place of joy."**

How does this statement apply to both the quotations provided by the newspaper reporter in Passage A and the author's opinion about the fall of the Berlin wall in Passage B?

A. The quote proves that the elation felt by Berliners on November 9th was in direct opposition to the pain East Berliners felt for years while the wall was still standing.

B. The quote reveals the euphoria Berliners felt at the crumbling of the wall, but highlights the ensuing tension the fall caused in post-Communist countries.

C. The quote reinforces the immediate happiness felt by the East Berliners who experienced freedom for the first time in years and hints at the eventual joy of post-Communist countries who experienced freedom years later.

D. The quote indicates that the Communist influences that allowed the wall to continue were finally dismantled, but negates the mixed feelings Berliners had when the rush of people crossed the barrier for the first time.

6. Compared to the author of Passage A, the author of Passage B provides LESS information about:

F. the feelings of the Berliners during the fall.

G. the economic climate after the fall.

H. the historic significance of the fall.

J. the ripple socioeconomic effects of the fall.

Answers on page 186.

Solutions to Reading Practice Questions

Main Idea, page 144

1. D.

Here you have to remember the "Too Broad and Too Narrow" rule. The point of the paragraph is Choice D because it includes all the aspects of the paragraph, and not just a few. Plus, it doesn't step outside the bounds of the paragraph, either.

2. H.

Although the passage talks quite a bit about vaulting, it specifically gets at the point that the *spirit* of the method is the primary way it is distinguished from other methods. Choice F strays outside the bounds of the passage. Choice G is too narrow. Choice J is incorrect because vaulting is obviously a facet of the style.

Supporting Details, page 151

1. C.

Okay, so this is one of those questions where you must use the True and X it Out strategy. If it's true, it's not the right answer. Line 5 tells us that Choice A is correct, so it's out. Lines 24–25 tells us that Choice B is true, so it's not your answer. Lines 18 through the end of the passage tell us that Choice D is correct, so that leaves Choice C. If you didn't want to go the POE direction, you could simply have read Choice C and discover that it's wrong—water doesn't wear away stalagmites; it creates them.

2. G.

Choice G is the only one supported by the passage. Choice F is wrong because stalactites are formed on cavern ceilings. Choice H is wrong because although the passage says that stalactites can reach a yard in length, it says nothing about breadth. (That would be huge, by the way.) And Choice J is incorrect, because if you were paying attention to the passage, you'd realize that *speleothem* is the generic term for a stalactite, so one couldn't be deposited inside. Impossible.

3. B.

You can find the right answer here by simply answering the questions. If you can answer them, then the information has been provided. The only question that you *can't* answer based on the information in the passage is III, which means that Choice B is correct because Choices C and D contain III. The passage never talks about the height of stalagmites.

4. F.

The phrase "a natural wonderland" is used in lines 16–17, and describes the cave. Although speleothems are inside the cave, the writer specifically uses the descriptive phrase to explain how the cave would look if lights highlighted the formations.

Making Inferences, page 156

1. C.

With these questions, you have to use a bit of reasoning skill, and if necessary, you'll need to Translate and Add the Tag to get the question correct. With this one, you have to gauge your overall *impression* of Mrs. Dabney, but not move outside the scope of the passage. Lines 74–80 go into detail about her state of being; Choice C seems to offer the most succinct views of her. Nothing indicates that she's an unkind woman, so Choice A is out. Choice B is the best distractor, because it seems like she may be generally happy, but if we read lines 55–59, we see that she has let go of true happiness for mere contentment.

2. G.

The key to this question is the word *primary*. Mr. Ellenwood seems to have a bunch of problems, but his main problem—the most important one—is his lack of purpose. He's done a lot of things, but is described over and over again as kind of lazy without a real point to his life. We know that Mr. Ellenwood is not insane—the text tells us this in lines 49–51, and nothing indicates that he's selfish, either. It's true that he's had a lack of womanly suitors (hence the celibacy comment), but that was a detail thrown in there and doesn't affect his life overall.

3. A.

This one's tricky! Although Mrs. Dabney *does* maintain her duty the most by staying married to men she didn't really feel passionate about, that's not the characteristic she *desires* to keep intact as she ages. Choice B is out. Lines 84–85 indicate that Mrs. Dabney has "held fast her roses" in spite of Time, which means that she's clung to her youth and beauty as much as possible. We already know that she's given up her happiness for contentment, which gets rid of Choice D, and although she's a wise woman, she doesn't seem to care about it.

4. H.

The most important words in the answer choices are "to Mrs. Dabney." How does the narrator believe Mrs. Dabney feels about her prior marriages? This is definitely a case where you need to Translate and Add the Tag. Does Mrs. Dabney think her marriages were uncomfortable, but convenient? Nope. Choice F is out. I doubt anyone would think being in a marriage where your husband's death would aid your comfort (lines 72–73) is convenient. Does Mrs. Dabney find her marriages satisfactory? Again, no for the same reason. Does she find them worthwhile in any way? No. Choice J is also out, which leaves us Choice H.

Vocabulary, Author's Voice, and Purpose, page 166

1. D.

You should ask yourself, "Why was this paragraph written?" If you've read it, you'll realize that it couldn't be Choice A. The Depression contributed to the need for Social Security, but wasn't the primary reason it was started. The paragraph didn't use any negative words to describe the program, so Choice B is out, and since nothing was being contrasted (no contrasting signal words), Choice C is out, too.

2. F.

Intensify means to "up the ante," so to speak. If we see that the ratio of workers versus beneficiaries is rapidly going down, then that intensifies *something* that's for sure. Choice G is wrong—the first half of the sentence makes you believe that it could be right, but the last part is definitely incorrect. Choice H doesn't make sense, and Choice J is incorrect because the author never offers an opinion about solving the crisis.

3. B.

Those verbs at the beginning are your friends! The question incorporates a "main idea" with a purpose—what was the main reason the author wrote that first paragraph? Was it to suggest how important FDR was in creating the Social Security Program? Nope. Choice A is out. Was it to paint a picture of the Social Security Program's decline? No. Choice C is gone. Was it to compare anything to anything? No! It has to be B. The paragraph, along with the rest of the passage, is mostly explanatory—straightforward information without any real opinions.

4. H.

This is an explanatory piece, which sounds like it comes from a textbook or newspaper. It's straightforward with little or no opinion at all. The events are merely described, vs. critiqued or supported, which is why the author's attitude is definitely neutral. He or she is neither for nor against the government's solutions to the Social Security Program. If you chose incorrectly, you probably guessed Choice G or Choice J. Choice G describes the state of the program, but not the author's attitude, which is what the question asks for. Choice J describes how most people feel about the government, but apparently, not the author. Choice H it is.

5. A.

The context is so important for answering this question. If you just use the word "tradition," any one of those answers could be correct. However, it can't be all of them! To figure it out, it helps to ask, "What *tradition* is the Industrial Revolution ending?" The *tradition* referred to is "extended family caring for the elderly." So the answer choice has to be able to serve as a description of that phrase. Would Choice B do it? Is "extended family caring for the elderly" a *belief*? No. Choice B is out. Is "extended family caring for the elderly" a *ritual*? That seems weird. It's out. Is "extended family caring for the elderly" a *habit*? That one lacks purpose. A habit is something you do without thinking about it. The word doesn't imply any deliberate choice. But practice implies choice. Hence, it's the best answer!

Analyzing Author's Arguments and Making Connections, page 178

1. B.

Although none of the claims mentioned in the answer choices are explicitly stated or even implied, you must draw the conclusion of Choice B. People celebrated in the quotes, praising the fact that they'd become free: "Freedom. Freedom, finally." There is no evidence for Choices A, C, or D in the text.

2. G.

Again, here we need to use the evidence to determine which of the following claims the author would LEAST likely support. By reporting about the jubilation of the East Berliners as they crossed the wall and by stating that they had returned to "a place they could only gaze at just hours before. A place of returned dignity and hope," we can assume that the author was in favor of the wall falling and the circumstances surrounding it. Every statement besides G supports the freedom that came with the fall.

3. D.

The author's premise—that believing that the fall of Communism led to the failure of many Communist states is FALSE—is supported by evidence in Choices A, B, and C. He says, actually, these new post-Communist states are successful because of those three reasons. Choice D is simply a fact about what happened when the wall fell and simply adds info to the essay. He doesn't use it to support his argument.

4. F.

Here, the question asks you to determine which supports the idea that lives post-fall of the wall are richer, happier, and longer. Choice F shows how people have freedom, can make choices, and are filling their days with things previously unavailable to them. Choice G could be taken positively OR negatively, so that's out. Choice H, although a positive impact, doesn't speak about people's lives directly. And Choice J is a negative consequence, and does not support the conclusion.

5. C.

This is tricky, because you have to make sure that the answer relates to the quote, Passage A and Passage B. Choice A doesn't relate to Passage B, so it's out. Choice B incorrectly relates to both the quote and Passage B because the quote does not highlight any tension and neither does Passage B. Choice D incorrectly relates to Passage A, since no one in that passage expressed "mixed feelings" about the fall. Choice C is correct because the quote does reinforce the immediate happiness by stating the actual date, which correctly relates to Passage A, and also mentioning continuance, which we can only assume is positive, as well.

6. F.

Passage B focuses on the socioeconomic and political climate after the fall along with its historic impact. But, whereas Passage A focused on the feeling of being free, Passage B leaves much of that out. Hence, Choice F is the best answer.

Reading Strategy Cheat Sheet

General Strategies:

- **Pace Yourself.**
- **Read Your Fave First.**
- **Read 3 or Read 4 Passages.**
- **Separate Tough from Easy**—Tough questions will not give you a location to find the information. Easy questions will give you quotation marks, a line number, or a paragraph number in which to search.

6 Steps for the Reading Section:

1. **Separate Tough from Easy.**
2. **Read Easy Question.**
3. **Read and Mark Up** the paragraph.
4. **POE and Answer.** Repeat for All Easies.
5. **Read and Mark Up** the rest of the passage.
6. **Cover, Read, and Answer** toughies.

Main Idea Questions:

- **Too Broad and Too Narrow is Too Bad.**
- **Paragraph + Paragraph = Passage.**

Supporting Details Questions:

- **True and X It Out for EXCEPT** questions.
- **Skip, Clock It, and Search** for Tough Supporting Details Questions.

Making Inferences:

- **Translate and Add the Tag.**

Vocabulary Questions:

- **Put Me In, Coach!**

Author or Narrator's Voice and Purpose Questions:

- **Find the Signal Words.**

Analyzing an Author's Arguments or Claims:

- **Face the Facts**

Take the Reading Practice Test

Go to the REA Study Center

(www.rea.com/studycenter)

Now that you have completed this week's work, go to *rea.com/studycenter* and take the Reading Practice Test. This test is just like the Reading section of the actual ACT, with the added benefits of:

- **Timed testing conditions** – Gauge how much time you can spend on each question.
- **Automatic scoring** – Find out how you did on the test, instantly.
- **On-screen detailed explanations of answers** – Learn not just the correct answers, but also why the other answers are incorrect.
- **Diagnostic score reports** – Pinpoint where you're strongest and where you need to focus your study.

4

Week 4: Science Reasoning

ACT Science Reasoning Test Basics

The ACT Science Reasoning test has

- 6–7 sets of passages
- 5–7 multiple-choice questions per passage
- 40 questions total
- 4 answer choices per question

You'll be tested

- for 35 minutes
- with three different types of passages:
  - Data Representation (Charts, Graphs, Tables, and other Graphics)
  - Research Summaries (Experiments)
  - Conflicting Viewpoints (Two Different Hypotheses)
- in reading and analyzing data from the fields of biology, chemistry, physics, geology, astronomy, or meteorology

You'll receive

- a single subject Science Reasoning score on a scale of 1–36.
- three competency scores in these subareas: Interpretation of Data, Scientific Investigation, and Evaluation of Models, Inferences and Experimental Results. More on these in a second.

In order to score well,

- you must master ACT test-taking strategies.
- you must master ACT Science content strategies.

General Strategies for the Science Reasoning Section

- **Pace Yourself**: Since you'll be reading 6–7 passages and answering 40 questions in 35 minutes, you'll have 5–6 minutes per passage. Do not spend 2 minutes on just one tough question—it isn't worth any more points than the easy ones!
- **Use Reading Skills**: The ACT Science test is less about science and more about reading and reasoning. Sure, you'll have to take a gander at science stuff, but you will NOT be tested on your vast knowledge of the biological processes. Instead, you'll merely have to read about some scientific information, and in some cases, analyze it. You'll use lots of the skills you used in the previous Reading section.
- **Pep Yourself Up**: Now would be a great time to stick a piece of candy in your mouth. Why? Ordinarily, I'd never recommend sugar as a way to energize yourself, but because this is the fourth multiple-choice section on a long test, eating a piece of candy right before you test will help give you a burst of energy that you'll need to stay focused. (Watch out for the crash after the test!)
- **Read "Charts" Passages First**: After the sugar explosion of your Jolly Rancher, you'll be firing on all four cylinders. But before you plunge into the test without regard to content, head straight to the first Data Representation passage and dig in. These passages are easier than the others because they have less material to read, and hence, take less time.
- **Put It In Your Own Words**: You'll be reading lots and lots of scientific facts, here. Sometimes, that stuff sounds crazy and seems more difficult than it actually is. If you put some of the technical terms into simpler words, you'll have an easier time answering the question (i.e., call a "graduated cylinder" a test tube; call NaCl, salt, makes sense!).

Science Reasoning Reporting Categories

Unlike the other sections of this book, this section will not be organized according to the reporting categories listed below. Why? Well, because there are specific strategies you must master for each of the three types of passages no matter the questions asked. But be informed that these are the types of skills you will have to display throughout the entire test section, and we will touch on each as we go.

- **Interpretation of Data**: recognizing trends in data, translating data from tables into graphs, reasoning mathematically based on data, interpolating and extrapolating info and more.
- **Scientific Investigation**: identifying variables and controls in experiments, comparing, contrasting, changing and extending experiments, predicting results and more.
- **Evaluation of Models, Inferences, and Experimental Results**: judging the validity of scientific experimentation, formulating conclusions, determining which conclusion is supported by new findings and more.

Data Representation: 12–16 questions

You read charts, graphs, and tables every day of your life. If you want to know how many calories were in that little package of chocolate-frosted doughnuts you just deposited into your gullet, you look at the *table* of nutritional information and discover that yes, it wasn't wonderful for your heart!

When you grab the ESPN magazine from the table in the waiting room at the doctor's office, you might find a *bar graph* of the batting averages of the top 10 hitters in the American League and discover that, yes, Jose Bautista is best at bat like everyone thought.

If your family is interested in moving to Tornado Alley, you might first consult a *chart* that indicates the number of tornado hits in the southern plains in the last few years.

Charts, graphs, and tables help us to interpret complex information in a way that words simply can't. Luckily for you, this section is an easy one because all you'll need to do is brush up on your chart-reading skills rather than comprehending any new complex, scientific material.

Data Representation Reading Strategy

Before hitting the questions, we need to figure out the best way to conquer these passages on the Science test. Our goals are to maximize our time (the precious few minutes we'll have!) and get as many answers correct as is humanly possible. So, inject this Data Representation Strategy directly into your brain before you test, okay? Trust me, it'll help!

1. **Separate Tough from Easy:** This is the only type of passage on this test in which you'll need to separate tough questions from easy ones. Here, the long questions are tougher; short ones are easier. Why? You'll have less information to analyze with the easier ones, and with scientific data, it's easy to get confused with more details.
2. **Read the Question:** Read the question AND the answer choices here. There is no way you'll solve these in your head and then be able to find a match.

   1. The question

   A. Choice A

   B. Choice B

   C. Choice C

   D. Choice D
3. **Hit The Charts:** Read the chart, table, or graph related to the question. DO NOT read the paragraph above the chart, table, or graph unless you're missing key information to help you answer. Often, it contains extra information you don't need.

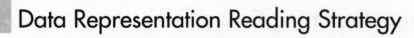

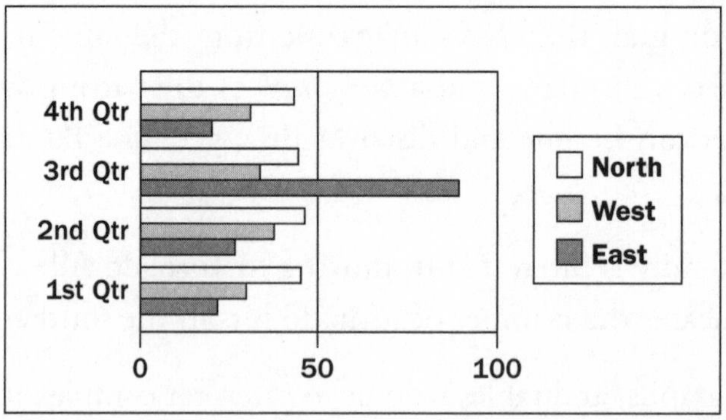

4. **Take Notes:** Scratch out a few words to help you remember what the charts were showing you.

   3rd quarter ↑ East to about 90
   N and W stayed same

5. **Answer:** Use Process of Elimination and answer the question. Remember to physically cross off incorrect answer choices.

   1. Question, question, question, question, question, question, question, question, question, question, question, question

      ~~**A.** Choice A~~

      ~~**B.** Choice B~~

      (C) Choice C

      ~~**D.** Choice D~~

Easy Data Representation Questions

Easy Data Representation Questions are short, and can be answered using just the charts, graphs, or tables as a reference. These are the easiest types of Interpretation of Data questions you will encounter during the Science Reasoning test, so sit back and enjoy!

On all the Data Representation passages, you'll be given 2–3 related charts, tables and graphs with a paragraph or two at the beginning to help explain them. The paragraph is often unnecessary for answering most of the questions. Take this question, for example. It's solvable without any extra info besides Figure 1.

1. According to Figure 1, approximately how many tornadoes, NOT classified as F2–F5, occurred during the year 1966?

   A. 200

   B. 350

   C. 550

   D. 750

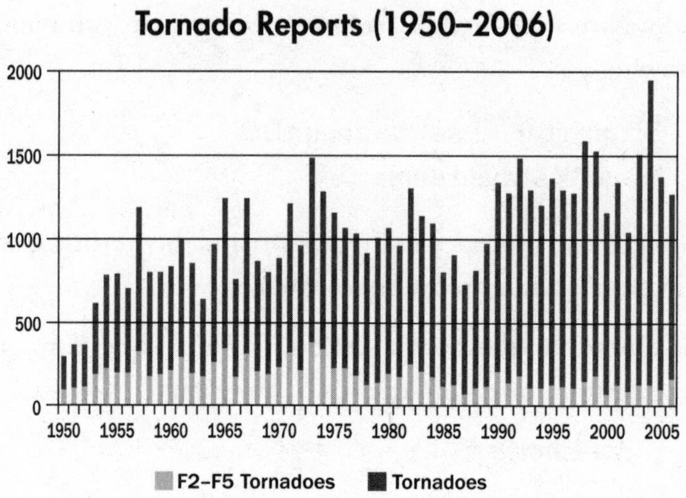

Figure 1

(Source: *http://dotearth.blogs.nytimes.com/tag/tornadoes/*)

Here, all you have to do is read the chart, which involves just a couple of steps, and to help us make the best usage of our time, we'll use a strategy.

STRATEGY ALERT

How to Solve an Easy Data Representation Question

Lock Down the Details MIA: Okay, detectives. I'd like to put out an APB for a few numbers and details missing from this chart. It appears as though these suspects headed off the page into unknown territory. Your task is to apprehend the missing persons and bring them down to headquarters for questioning. Do you copy? Roger that.

In order to solve this problem, we need to lock down those missing in action details on the chart. Because of space, a graphics designer cannot put every single detail on the chart—you have to do some detective work to locate those missing details. Your first job is to figure out exactly which one of those little lines on the bottom of the chart is the year 1966, because it's unclear which line goes with a particular column. The best way to do this is to count from left to right.

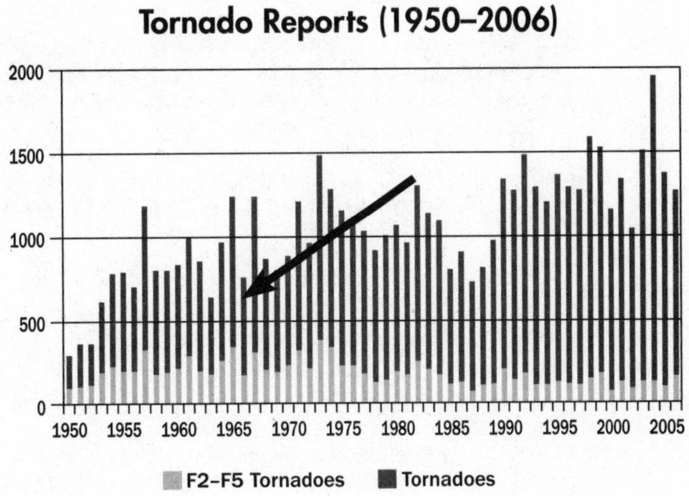

Ah. There it is.

We've counted and discovered the column associated with 1966. Now we just need to find the total number of tornadoes that WERE NOT categorized as F2–F5, which according to the key, are the top portion of those columns. That's where those numbers that went MIA on the left would really help. Let's fill them in ourselves.

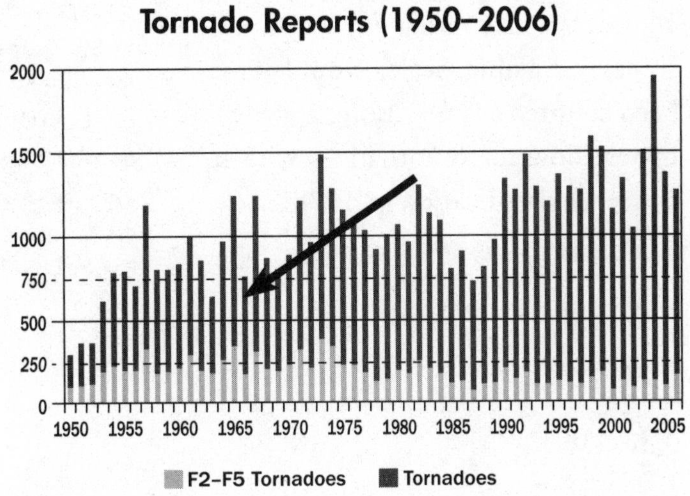

So the total number of reported tornadoes in 1966 was about 750, according to our MIA numbers. But, we need just the total number of tornadoes NOT categorized as F2–F5. So, let's just subtract all the F2–F5s from the total. It looks like there are about 200 or so of them, so if we subtract, we get about 550, Choice C.

Now, you're never going to see just one chart, table, or graph in each passage. So, here's a table related to the first one and another question.

ORIGINAL FUJITA SCALE		ENHANCED FUJITA SCALE	
F5	261–318 mph	EF5	+200 mph
F4	207–260 mph	EF4	168–200 mph
F3	158–206 mph	EF3	136–167 mph
F2	113–157 mph	EF2	111–135 mph
F1	73–112 mph	EF1	86–110 mph
F0	<73 mph	EF0	65–85 mph

Figure 2

(Source: *http://www.helpcharts.com/Tornado-Fujita-Scale.html*)

2. Based on the information provided in Figure 1 and Figure 2, a particular tornado *K*, with wind speeds of 111 mph with a rating of EF2 on the Enhanced Fujita Scale, would have been counted as one among approximately how many tornadoes within the same classification in 1978?

F. 175

G. 550

H. 725

J. 900

HEADS UP

Most of the time, you won't have to understand all of the technical words in the graphics. You could just as easily call chlorofluorocarbons "goopsies" or "bungaloos" and arrive at the same correct answer on the test. Remember, your goal is to answer questions correctly, not truly understand the science behind the figures.

We need information from both Figures 1 and 2 to answer the question, but the language can get tricky. Let's just jot down the stuff we know so we don't get confused, okay?

- A tornado with wind speeds of 111 mph is rated as an EF2 on the Enhanced Fujita Scale.
- But a tornado with wind speeds of 111 mph is rated as an F1 on the Original Scale, and the Original Fujita Scale was used in the first figure.
- An F1 tornado is in the "tornadoes" classification in Figure 1 (as opposed to the F2–F5 classification).

- In order to find the total number of tornadoes, we just repeat the process we used in the first question:
  - Find the correct column.
  - Find the total number of tornadoes in that column (about 900).
  - Subtract the total number of F2–F5 tornadoes (about 175) from the 900.
  - The approximate number of tornadoes is about 725, or Choice H.

Tough Data Representation Questions

Tough Data Representation Questions are longer and may present new information, ask you to consider two or three of the figures, ask you to predict results, ask you to analyze the data more thoroughly, and will always take more time.

Take a look at Question 3, which relates to Figure 3, below:

U.S. Reported Tornadoes and Average Number of Deaths Per Year 1961–1990

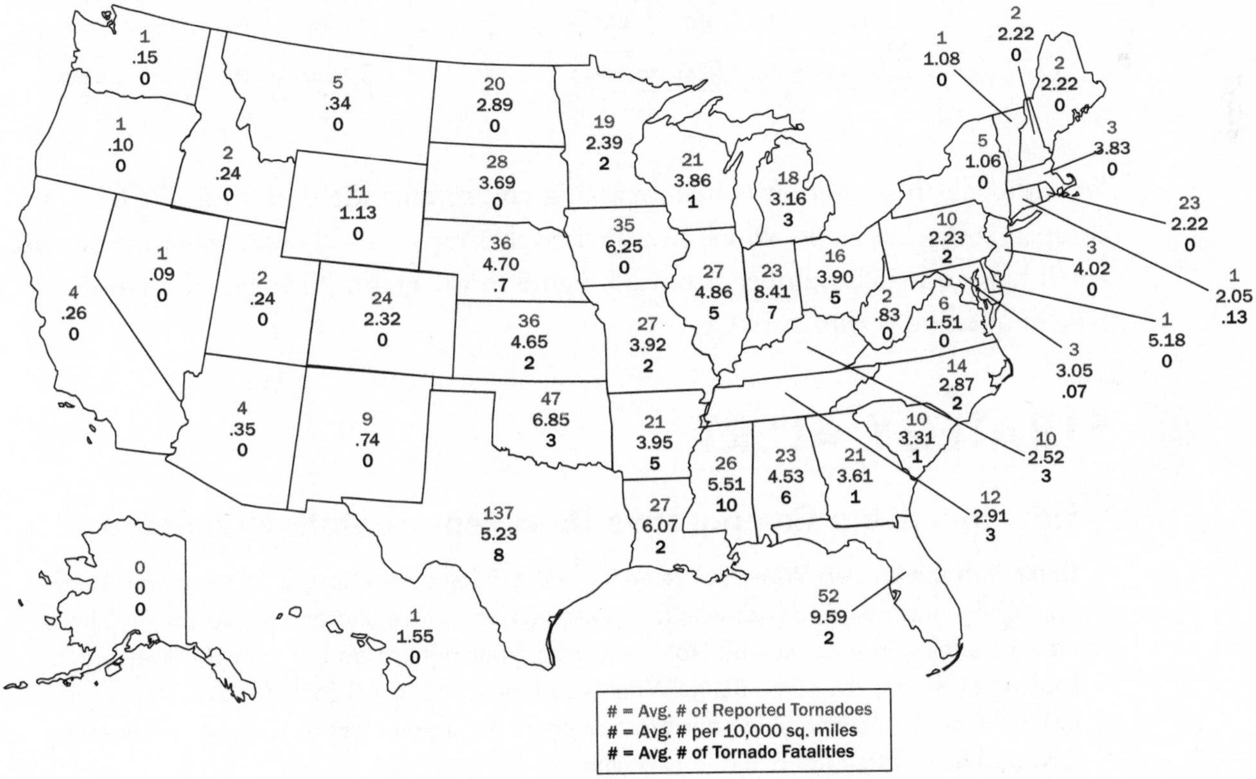

Figure 3

(Source: *http://www.examiner.com/weather-in-richmond/death-and-tornadoes-per-state-photo*)

3. According to Figure 3, which of the following graphs best represents the average number of reported tornadoes and tornadoes reported per 10,000 sq. miles for Michigan, Florida, Oklahoma, and Louisiana?

A.

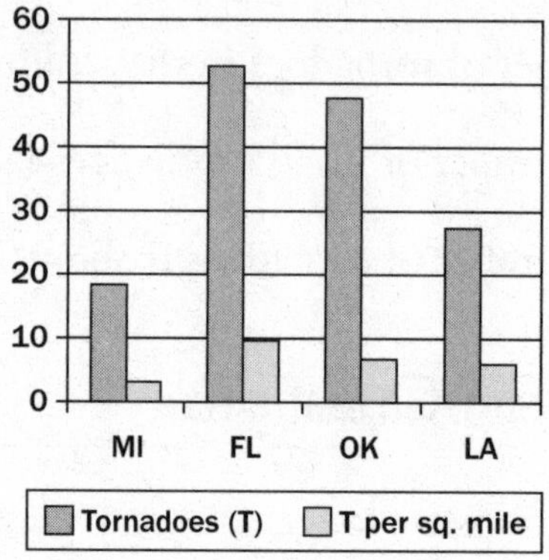

B.

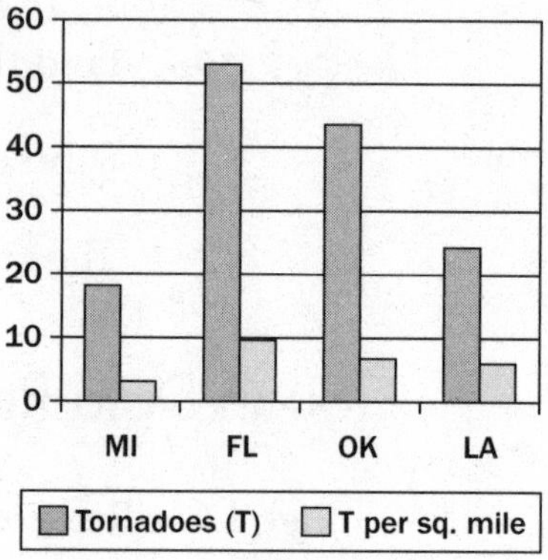

C.

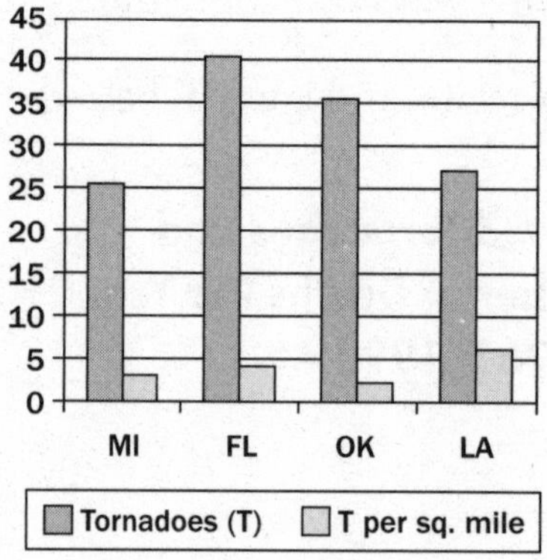

D.

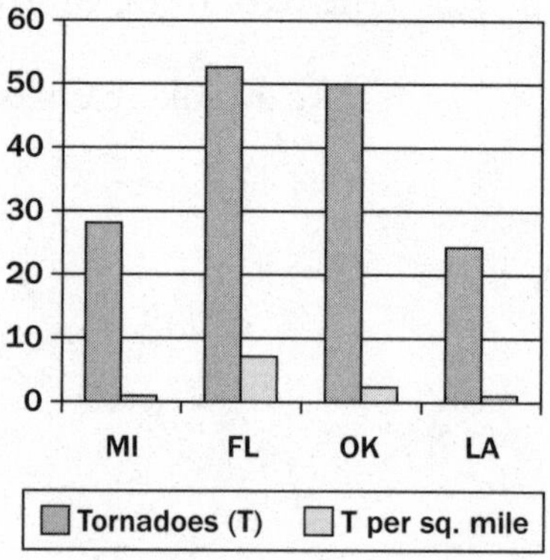

So, although this question is merely asking you to take the data from Figure 3 and compare it to a bar graph, which seems relatively simple, it will take some time because you'll have to match numbers from the figure to the graphs. The best way to do this type of question is with a strategy!

STRATEGY ALERT

How to Solve a Comparative Data Representation Question

Don't Stuff the Burger: When you're eating a big, juicy cheeseburger dripping with ketchup, oozing mustard, piled high with tomatoes, pickles, lettuce and onions, do you just shove the whole thing in your mouth? Not if you want your date to go out with you ever again. Looking at data is the same thing. When you have a bunch of facts to take in, your first instinct is to just shove it all in your brain at once! But if you want any chance of digesting it, you'd better take it just one bite at a time.

Let's take a bite out of question 3 from the previous page.

Because Michigan is listed first in the graphs, let's start with that state. If we look at the map, we see that Michigan has this info:

- 18 = average number of reported tornadoes
- 3.16 = average number of reported tornadoes per square mile
- 3 = average deaths per year

> **HEADS UP**
>
> Many of the questions and graphics will contain information that you don't need to understand to answer correctly. Don't be confused by extra info! Cross it off or ignore it and stick with the details you DO need.

Let's go to the charts to see which one might correspond with Michigan.

Right away, we can see that we don't need the death toll info, so we can ignore it. We also see that graphs A and B fit the bill—both 18 and 3.16 seem to be represented pretty accurately on each, but C and D do not. So, we can get rid of C and D, because if one part of the graph isn't correct, the whole thing isn't correct.

So, we'll have to move on to the next state, which is Florida, but wait! If we use our brains, we can see that they both look the same in the charts—we aren't going to be able to differentiate between the right and wrong answer with the Florida info, so we'll move onto Oklahoma, because those bars are showing different numbers.

Oklahoma info:

- 47 = average number of reported tornadoes
- 6.85 = average number of reported tornadoes per square mile

Which one of those graphs represents the information for Oklahoma? Choice B shows a total number of reported tornadoes around 43, which is incorrect. And since we've found one error, we can eliminate it.

That means Choice A is correct.

Let's try one more toughie:

> Which of the following conclusions is best supported by Figures 1 and 2?
>
> **F.** That although the number of tornadoes with wind speeds of 112 mph or below has increased, the total reported tornadic activity has decreased.
>
> **G.** That although the number of tornadoes with wind speeds of 112 mph or below has decreased, the total reported tornadic activity has increased.
>
> **H.** That although the number of tornadoes with wind speeds of 113 mph or above has increased, the total reported tornadic activity has decreased.
>
> **J.** That although the number of tornadoes with wind speeds of 113 mph or above has decreased, the total reported tornadic activity has increased.

Since the language is all so similar, we'll simply use our strategy again, and just bite off what we can chew.

First, let's define our terms according to something useful, since mph of tornadoes isn't used in Figure 1.

- Any tornado with wind speeds of 112 mph or below is considered an F1 or F0. Such a tornado is classified under "tornadoes" in Figure 1.
- Any tornado with wind speeds of 113 mph or above is an F2–F5 and labeled just that in Figure 1.

Choice F says "tornadoes" have ↑ and total # has ↓.

Choice G says "tornadoes" have ↓ and total # has ↑.

Choice H says "F2–F5" have ↑ and total # has ↓.

Choice J says "F2–F5" have ↓ and total # has ↑.

When you look at the chart, you'll see that Choice J is correct. The number of reported F2–F5 tornadoes has gone down, even though the total number of reported tornadoes has gone up.

If we just take in the information bit by bit, we can actually solve one of these tough questions!

Practice Data Representation

Adapted from *Response to ammonium and nitrate by a mycorrhizal annual invasive grass and native shrub in southern California* Author(s): Yoshida LC ; Allen EB Source: AMERICAN JOURNAL OF BOTANY Volume: 88 Issue: 8 Pages: 1430–1436 DOI: 10.2307/3558450 Published: AUG 2001

The goal of the research study presented was to determine the interaction of mycorrhizae, a fungus that colonizes its host, and two N sources, ammonium (NH_4) and nitrate (NO_3) on the growth of a coastal sage scrub species, *Artemisia californica* and an exotic grass, *Bromus madritensis*. Nitrogen deposits may be causing *A. californica* to die off, and *B. madritensis* to replace it.

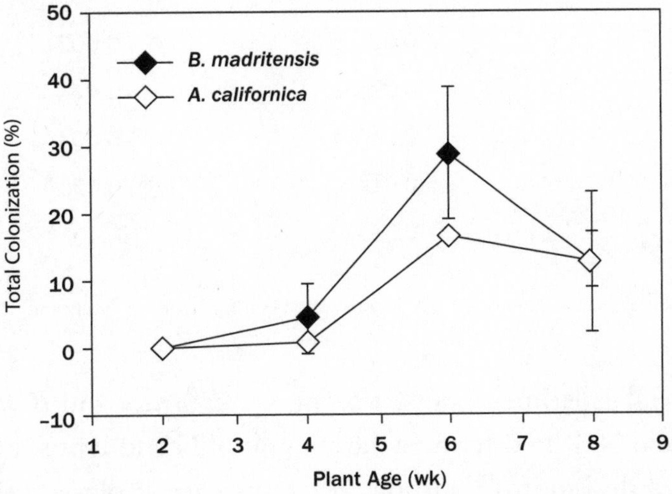

Figure 1: Progress of mycorrhizal colonization in *Bromus madritensis* and *Artemisia californica* over 8 weeks in soil with typical N (nitrogen) amount.

Table 1: Growth Value Results Between N and Mycorrhizal Treatments in Shoot, Root, and Total Mass of *Artemisia californica* and *Bromus madritensis*

Statistical Comparisons	Shoot	Root	Total
Artemisia californica			
C, NH_4	0.048	0.538	0.094
C, NO_3	0.042	0.122	0.033
NH_4, NO_3	0.954	0.351	0.634
M, NM	0.304	0.772	0.394
N × M	0.054	0.219	0.048
Bromus madritensis			
C, NH_4	0.001	0.003	0.001
C, NO_3	0.085	0.914	0.418
NO_3, NH_4	0.063	0.004	0.011
M, NM	0.014	0.035	0.021
N × M	0.063	0.131	0.091

C = controls, M = mycorrhizal, NM = nonmycorrhizal. *P* values set in boldface type are significantly different ($P < 0.05$) between treatments.

In several experiments, a portion of *A. californica* and *B. madritensis* was *not* given the NO_3 and NH_4 to determine the amount of N and P present without the additions. This is called the "control" portion. The results are displayed below.

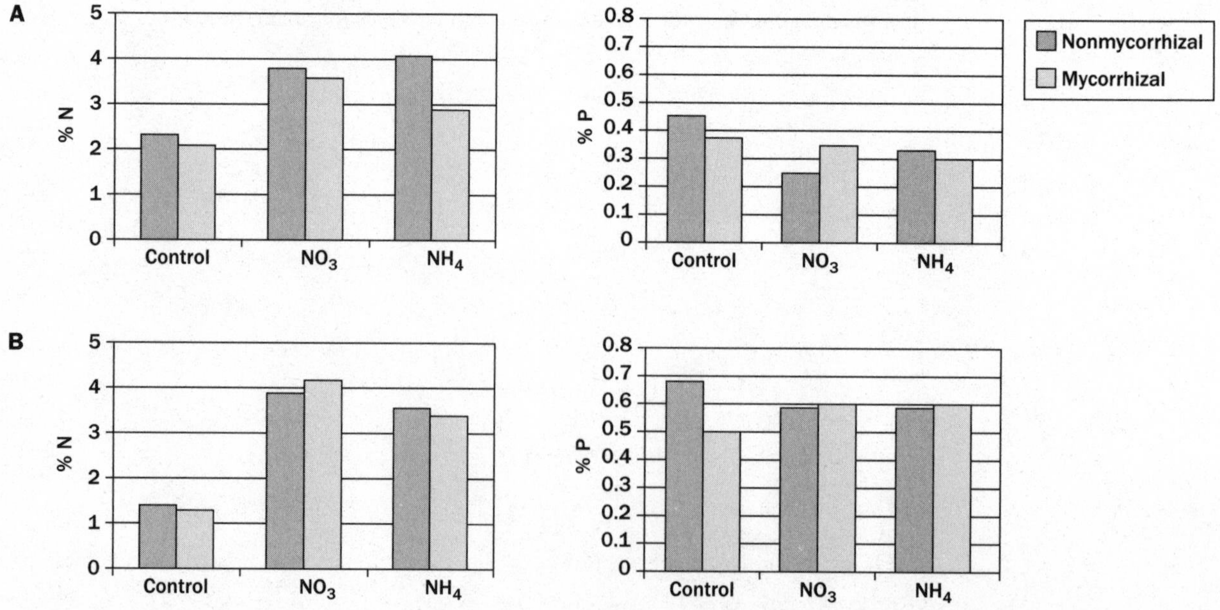

Figure 2: Concentrations of N (nitrogen) and P (bicarbonate) in shoots of (A) *A. californica* and (B) *B. madritensis*.

1. The information in Figure 1 supports the conclusion that

A. *B. madritensis* was colonized much more quickly by the mycorrhizae than *A. californica.*

B. The mycorrhizae colonized *B. madritensis* at a higher percentage than it colonized *A. californica.*

C. The mycorrhizae colonized *A. californica* at half the rate of *B. madritensis.*

D. *B. madritensis* was colonized by the mycorrhizae at a lower percentage than *A. californica.*

2. Based on the information in Table 1, which of the following configurations produced the highest number of combined shoot and root growth for *A. californica*?

F. $N \times M$

G. M, NM

H. NH_4, NO_3

J. C, NH_4

3. According to the information in Figure 2, the situation that produced the highest percentage of nitrogen in the shoots is

A. Mycorrhizal *B. madritensis* with the addition of NO_3.

B. Mycorrhizal *A. californica* with the addition of NO_3.

C. Nonmycorrhizal *B. madritensis* with the addition of NH_4.

D. Nonmycorrhizal *B. madritensis* in the control sample.

4. According to the information in Table 1 and Figure 2, what conclusion can one draw about the N source, nitrate (NO_3)?

F. NO_3 negatively impacts the percentage of N in *B. madritensis*, but creates the smallest mass of *B. madritensis* when measured with NH_4.

G. NO_3 positively impacts the percentage of P in *A. californica*, but creates the largest mass of *A. californica* when measured with the control portion.

H. NO_3 positively impacts the percentage of N in *B. madritensis*, but creates the smallest mass of *B. madritensis* when measured with the control portion.

J. NO_3 negatively impacts the percentage of P in *A. californica,* but creates the largest mass of *A. californica* when measured with NH_4.

5. Does the addition of the N sources NH_4 and NO_3 seem to be contributing to the decline of *A. californica* and the replacement by *B. madritensis*, according to Table 1?

   A. Yes, because the addition of both of those elements creates a much larger mass in *B. madritensis*, which would mean that if those N sources were equally present in both grasses, *A. californica's* smaller size would contribute to its decline and eventual takeover by *B. madritensis*.

   B. Yes, because the addition of both of those elements creates a much larger combination of root and shoot in *B. madritensis*, which would mean that if those N sources were present equally in both grasses, *B. madritensis* would be the hardier of the two, and more likely to thrive.

   C. No, because the addition of both of those elements creates a much larger shoot in *A. californica* than it does in *B. madritensis*, which would mean that if those N sources were present equally in both grasses, *A. californica* would get more sun and eventually grow larger than *B. madritensis*.

   D. No, because the addition of both of those elements creates equal masses between the grasses, so the growth patterns of both *B. madritensis* and *A. californica* would remain the same because of their equal exposure to the sun.

Answers on page 249.

Research Summaries: 18–22 questions

"Research summaries" is just a sassy way of saying "experiments." These passages will give you this stuff:

1. A paragraph or sentence describing the goal of the experiments.
2. 2–3 experiments and the methods the scientists/researchers used.
3. Graphics to help explain the results or methods of the experiments (not always, but typically).

Research Summaries Reading Strategy

Again, the best way to go at these passages is NOT with a "dive-in-head-first" kind of strategy. That's not a great way to get the most out of your time. But, since these passages are significantly different from the charts passages, you're gonna need a different reading strategy and it involves your pencil in a major way.

1. **Start Reading:** This section is unlike the others—you *DO NOT* need to separate tough from easy questions because they are virtually indistinguishable at a glance, so start reading immediately with your pencil in hand—you're going to be using a lot of it in this section.
2. **Underline the Reason for the Experiment:** The first paragraph of each research summaries passage will give you a *REASON* for the experiment—what the researchers were hoping to accomplish. (Does a barrel roll farther when filled with water, air, or sand? How much higher do plants grow when supplied with varying types and amounts of fertilizer, etc.) **When you find it, underline it, and put a star (☆) next to it.** If you don't know the reason for the experiments, you'll have a hard time getting answers correct.
3. **Summarize Each Experiment Paragraph:** Since you'll be moving quickly through loads of data, it's important to read so you *understand* what is going on. Summarize as you go! Your pencil is your friend. It will help you get more points the more you use it.
4. **Answer Questions in Order—Circle Anything Tough:** Remember, you only have 5 minutes per passage, and that includes answering every question. You'll want to take at least 2 minutes to read, and about 3 to answer the questions. If you don't immediately understand how to answer a question or where to look for the answer, then circle the number and come back to it.

Summarizing the Experiments

Summarizing the experiments is key to understanding the whole passage and getting the most points out of those questions.

Once you've started reading your first research summaries passage, your primary concern is to locate the reasons for the experiment pronto, and summarize them until you know exactly what's going on. Check out a typical research summaries passage on the next page:

Passage I

A student performed 2 studies to investigate the differences in weather fronts as determined by temperature, barometric pressure (millibar, mb), precipitation, wind direction, and humidity. She made observations in six different U.S. cities in the Northeast, Midwest, and South.

Study 1

A warm front is a specific air pressure system where warm air replaces cool air. It is associated with a low pressure system and usually moves from a southerly direction to the north. A warm front can be depicted by an increase in temperature and humidity (higher dew point temperatures), a decrease in the air pressure, a wind change to a southerly direction, and the likelihood of precipitation. A series of weather observations were taken for Boston, Atlanta, and Trenton. (Table 1)

Table 1

Location	Temperature	Wind Direction	Dew Point Temperature	Precipitation	Time
Boston	45	Easterly	40	Cloudy	1:05 PM
Boston	45	Easterly	40	Cloudy	2:15 PM
Boston	62	South	62	Cloudy	3:25 PM
Atlanta	72	Northeasterly	72	Mostly Cloudy	8:25 AM
Atlanta	78	Southeasterly	77	Rain	10:30 AM
Atlanta	77	Southeasterly	76	Mostly Cloudy	11:35 AM
Trenton	65	Easterly	50	Cloudy	1:15 PM
Trenton	67	Southerly	64	Cloudy	1:25 PM
Trenton	67	Southerly	64	Rain	1:30 PM

Study 2

A cold front is another specific front that is also associated with a low pressure system. During a cold front, cold air replaces warm air. A cold front usually moves from a northerly direction southward. A cold front can be depicted by rapidly falling temperatures and barometric pressure, a wind shift to the north or west, and a moderate chance of precipitation. The barometric pressure, after falling, usually rises very sharply after the passage of a cold front. A series of weather observations were taken from Columbus, Houston, and Mobile. (Table 2)

Table 2

Location	Temperature	Wind Direction	Barometric Pressure	Precipitation	Time
Columbus	80	Southerly	1010	Cloudy	3:05 PM
Columbus	80	Southerly	1000	Cloudy	3:30 PM
Columbus	63	Northwesterly	950	Clear	3:35 PM
Houston	94	Southeasterly	1020	Clear	5:00 PM
Houston	93	Southerly	1022	Thunderstorms	5:15 PM
Houston	78	Westerly	955	Clear	5:30 PM
Mobile	85	Westerly	988	Partly Cloudy	8:10 PM
Mobile	84	Westerly	1005	Partly Cloudy	8:25 PM
Mobile	83	Westerly	1010	Clear	8:40 PM

If you were like the average student taking the ACT, you would've just read all that information and thought to yourself, "I'll come back to this information if I need it. It's always there for reference. I get the gist of the experiment—I'll just come back and reread anything I need to in order to answer the questions correctly. What a fantastic plan!"

Sound shockingly familiar?

Here's the problem with that. Unlike school, you are being TIMED BY A GIANT STOPWATCH. You don't have time to reread and reanalyze. You don't have time to go back to the text to understand everything. You need to stick the info in your brain the first time around!

So, let's follow our reading plan and go get some points:

Step 1: Start Reading

Okay. You will.

Step 2: Underline the Reason for the Experiment

What in the world was the study trying to show? Pick up your pencil and read the first paragraph to see:

☆ A student performed 2 studies to investigate the differences in weather fronts as determined by temperature, barometric pressure (millibar, mb), precipitation, wind direction, and humidity. She made observations in six different U.S. cities in the Northeast, Midwest, and South.

Most of the time on the ACT, the test writers will come right out and tell you what the purpose of the study is. This is not like finding the main idea, where you'll have to put all the pieces together and make a guess. Scientists like things plain and simple. Here, I went ahead and underlined the point of the study and put a star by it. Keep this objective in mind as you read the rest of the study!

HEADS UP

The Research Summaries passages are very different from the Data Representation passages, because you will typically use ALL of the info inside the paragraphs to help answer questions. This is why it's imperative to understand every part of the experiment. You could miss getting an answer correct if you miss one little detail!

Step 3: Summarize Each Experiment Paragraph

For now, you'll skip trying to analyze the tables, graphs, and charts that go along with the paragraphs, because the *paragraphs* hold the key to answering the questions. Yes, the tables of data are important, but not at first. First, you need to understand the process, and wrap your head around the little details inside the paragraphs because they can make or break you. Any tiny fact can be used in a question, which is why you must use the best, most efficient way to read and process the info inside the experiments. Sounds like someone needs a strategy!

Let's take a look at Study 1:

Study 1

> A warm front is a specific air pressure system where *(1)* warm air replaces cool air. It is associated with a *(2)* low pressure system and usually moves from a southerly direction to the north. A warm front can be depicted by an *(3)* increase in temperature and humidity (higher dew point temperatures), a *(4)* decrease in the air pressure, a *(5)* wind change to a southerly direction, and the *(6)* likelihood of precipitation. A series of weather observations were taken for Boston, Atlanta, and Trenton.[1]

Let's doodle a summary. Your brain remembers pictures and symbols much more easily than words, so we'll use symbols when we can to process all the info in the paragraph. Use arrows to show effects and direction. Use pictures to signify tangible objects. Use abbreviations, acronyms, and weird associations you have that will help you remember the data. Here's the smart doodle I came up with for this study. Naturally, yours could look different.

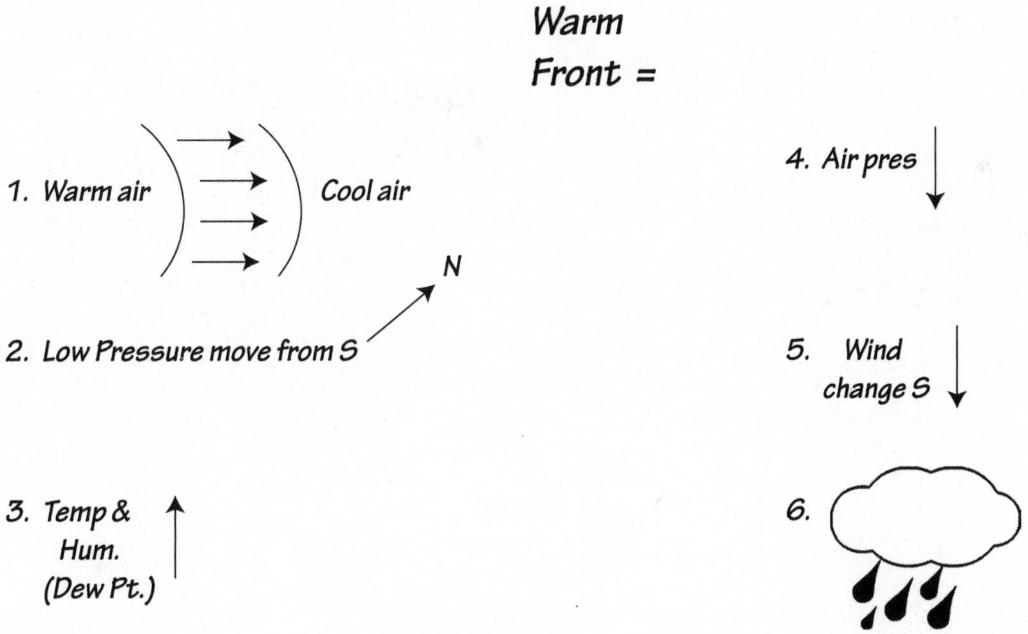

Basically, we took all those little facts—the ones you're never going to remember by just reading them—and made them into a key of sorts. If a question wanted you to

[1] *I added numbers to the paragraph to show the info to which the doodles refer.*

figure out if Boston was experiencing a warm front, let's say, then it'd be much easier to determine using our key then it would be to reread the paragraph. You could just X out the stuff that didn't match to make your observation that much easier.

Now, I want YOU to try it. Take a look at Study 2, and doodle your brains out. Make your own kind of shorthand to go along with the passage to help you understand and more importantly, REMEMBER the info. You don't need to number the info inside the paragraphs (that was a reference for you) and you don't need to make yours exactly like mine. You may, however.

Study 2

A cold front is another specific front which is also associated with a low pressure system. During a cold front, cold air replaces warm air. A cold front usually moves from a northerly direction southward. A cold front can be depicted by rapidly falling temperatures and barometric pressure, a wind shift to the north or west, and a moderate chance of precipitation. The barometric pressure, after falling, usually rises very sharply after the passage of a cold front. A series of weather observations were taken from Columbus, Houston, and Mobile.

Cold Front

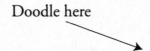

Doodle here

And now, you know more about warm and cold fronts than you may need.

Right now, let's focus on the paragraphs themselves by trying our hand at summarizing another one!

Passage II

A scientist wanted to study the effects of the substrate hydrogen peroxide (H_2O_2) and pH on the enzyme catalase, and determine the optimum pH and reaction time for catalase and other enzymes as well. Enzymes, such as catalase, are protein molecules found in living cells. Catalase, in particular, speeds up the decomposition of hydrogen peroxide into water and oxygen.

$$H_2O_2 \xrightarrow{\text{Catalase}} \rightarrow \rightarrow \rightarrow \rightarrow H_2O + O_2$$

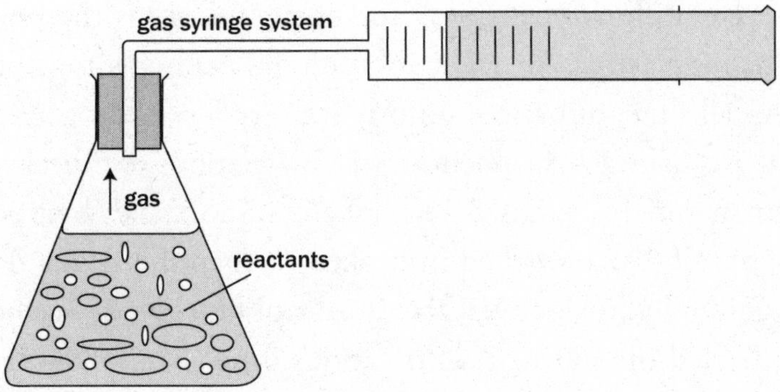

Figure 1

Experiment 1

For the first experiment—the effects of the substrate H_2O_2 (a weak acid) on catalase—the scientist wanted to measure the reaction time, or how long it took a gas syringe system to move 30cm^3 when H_2O_2 was introduced to catalase. He added 2cm^3 of yeast, an easily measured catalase, to a beaker. He then added 4cm^3 of hydrogen peroxide at various concentrations to a test tube. He poured the H_2O_2 solution into the beaker and started a stopwatch the moment the gas began to move. He recorded the reaction time in seconds for each concentration.

Enzyme	H_2O_2 concentration	Reaction time (seconds)
Trial 1	4 %	47.3
Trial 2	8 %	18.4
Trial 3	10%	17.3
Trial 4	12%	14.5
Trial 5	16%	10.6
Trial 6	20%	9.7

Experiment 2

The scientist also wanted to find the optimum pH value and reaction time of several different enzymes. The optimum pH is the point where the enzyme is the most active. An acidic solution has many hydrogen ions ($H+$) and a pH < 7. An alkaline, or basic solution, has very few hydrogen ions and a pH >7. A pH of 7 is neutral. The scientist set up 7 stations of 3 beakers, with pH strips in all. At station 1, he added $4cm^3$ of a common acid, hydrochloric acid (HCl) until a pH of 3 was reached in beaker 1. Then, he added $4cm^3$ of a common base, sodium hydroxide ($NaOH$) until a pH of 10 was reached in beaker 2. Next, he adjusted the pH to 7 with various drops of the $NaOH$ and HCl in beaker 3. He repeated this process until all seven stations contained identical solutions in each beaker. Finally, he added $2cm^3$ of seven different enzymes (one per station) to chart reaction time and discover optimum pH.

Enzyme	pH Optimum	Reaction time (seconds)
Pepsin	1.5–1.6	68.9
Trypsin	7.8–8.7	15.6
Urease	7.3	22.8
Invertase	4.5	47.3
Maltase	6.1–6.8	28.2
Malt Amylase	4.6–5.2	41.5
Catalase	7.0	20.9

Let's doodle our way through Passage II, okay?

Step 1: Start Reading

Okay. You will.

Step 2: Underline the Reason for the Experiment

Passage II

A scientist wanted to study the effects of the substrate hydrogen peroxide (H_2O_2) and pH on the enzyme catalase, and determine the optimum pH and reaction time for catalase and other enzymes as well. Enzymes, such as catalase, are protein molecules found in living cells. Catalase, in particular, speeds up the decomposition of hydrogen peroxide into water and oxygen.

$$\overset{\text{Catalase}}{H_2O_2 \rightarrow \rightarrow \rightarrow \rightarrow \rightarrow H_2O + O_2}$$

Step 3: Summarize Each Experiment Paragraph

Experiment 1

For the first experiment—the effects of the substrate H_2O_2 (a weak acid) on catalase—the scientist wanted to measure the reaction time, or how long it took a gas syringe system to move 30cm^3 when H_2O_2 was introduced to catalase. He added 2cm^3 of yeast, an easily measured catalase, to a beaker. He then added 4cm^3 of hydrogen peroxide at various concentrations to a test tube. He poured the H_2O_2 solution into the beaker and started a stopwatch to record the reaction time in seconds for each concentration.

Lucky for us, the ACT actually gave us a beaker to show us how the experiment works. All we have to do is add some numbers to help us remember the amounts, define some terms and we're all set for this paragraph.

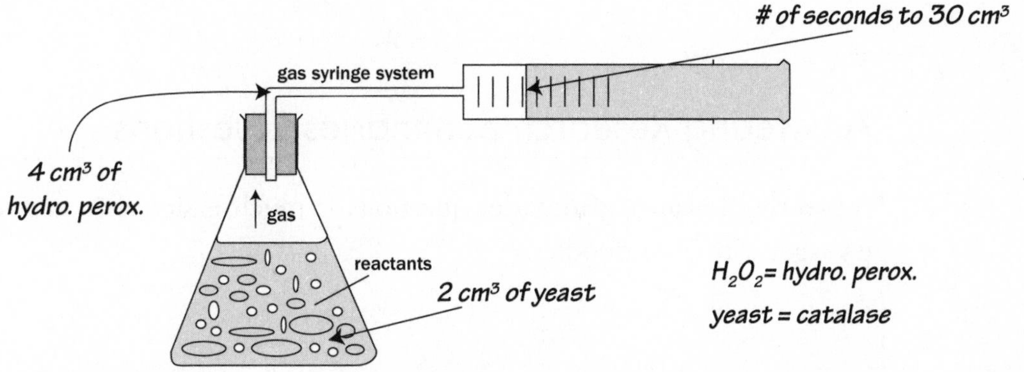

Now, it's your turn! Do some doodling on Experiment 2. This one is a bit tougher, but it's in your best interest to try to understand how the experiment was laid out—give it a whirl below!

Experiment 2

The scientist also wanted to find the optimum pH value and reaction time of several different enzymes. The optimum pH is the point where the enzyme is the most active. An acidic solution has many hydrogen ions (H+) and a pH < 7. An alkaline, or basic solution has very few hydrogen ions and a pH >7. A pH of 7 is neutral. The scientist set up 7 stations of 3 beakers, with pH strips in all. At station 1, he added 4cm^3 of a common acid, hydrochloric acid (HCl) until a pH of 3 was reached in beaker 1. Then, he added 4cm^3 of a common base, sodium hydroxide (NaOH) until a pH of 10 was reached in beaker 2. Next, he adjusted the pH to 7 with various drops of the NaOH and HCl in beaker 3. He repeated this process until all seven stations contained identical solutions in each beaker. Finally, he added 2cm^3 of seven different enzymes (one per station) to chart reaction time and discover optimum pH.

Doodle here →

Answering Research Summaries Questions

Answering research summaries questions is much easier after you've summarized the passages with your doodles.

Step 4 of our Reading Summaries Reading Strategy involves answering those six questions that will follow each passage. Remember, with these passages, you won't be separating the toughies from the easies because on this section, it's not the fastest way to the right answer. However, it's a great idea to see the *kinds* of questions you'll be asked on this section, so let's work our way through them so our science score isn't hovering in the low teens.

Recall Questions

Recall Questions will ask you to simply pull information directly from the paragraphs or graphics without any significant interpretation of the material at all.

These kinds of questions are your friends. They basically will ask you to *find* information or *identify* details using the paragraphs or graphics as a reference. Here are some examples:

1. In Experiment 1, which of the strains of viruses infected Host 1?

A. Virus X only

B. Virus Y only

C. Virus X and Virus Y only

D. Virus Y and Virus Z only

2. In Experiment 2, the density of the $NaNO_3$ solution was found to be:

F. less than 1.624 g/mL

G. 1.624 g/mL

H. 2.649 g/ML

J. greater than 2.649 g/ML

3. Based on the results of Experiments 1 and 2, in which of the following trials, after the additional tilling, was the soil found to be the most permeable?

A. Trials 1 and 2

B. Trials 2 and 3

C. Trials 2 and 4

D. Trials 3 and 5

Answering these questions is really a matter of looking at the details and making a selection. Let's try one using the details from Study 1 from the weather passage.

> A student performed 2 studies to investigate the differences in weather fronts as determined by temperature, barometric pressure (air pressure), precipitation, wind direction, and humidity. She made observations in six different U.S. cities in the Northeast, Midwest, and South.

Study 1

> A warm front is a specific air pressure system where warm air replaces cool air. It is associated with a low pressure system and usually moves from a southerly direction to the north. A warm front can be depicted by an increase in temperature and humidity (higher dew point temperatures), a decrease in the air pressure, a wind change to a southerly direction, and the likelihood of precipitation. A series of weather observations were taken for Boston, Atlanta, and Trenton. (Table 1)

1. What types of weather characteristics would most accurately determine that a warm front has come?

- **A.** increase in barometric pressure, precipitation, wind change to a southerly direction
- **B.** barometric pressure falls, then rises sharply, low pressure system, precipitation
- **C.** increase in temperature, low pressure system, system moves from a northerly direction southward
- **D.** low pressure system, increase in temperature, wind change to a southerly direction

Even though these questions rely solely on the information from the paragraph and not any analyzing on your part, they can be tricky if you're not careful. The best way to answer these questions is with a strategy!

STRATEGY ALERT

How to Answer a Recall Question

Target Practice: Get out that pencil and cross out every possibility that is NOT correct. When you get a recall question like this, often the answers are confusing because they are all so darn similar. So if you imagine that every word in each answer choice is a target, you can just knock them out if they're incorrect and narrow down to the correct answer.

We could reread the paragraph about Experiment 1, where a warm front is described, but that would be dumb. So, let's use our warm front smart doodle on page 211 to move even faster.

Here's what our answer choices look like when we cross out everything that doesn't describe a warm front:

~~**A.** increase in barometric pressure~~[1], precipitation, wind change to a southerly direction

B. barometric pressure falls, ~~then rises sharply~~[2], low pressure system, precipitation

C. increase in temperature, low pressure system, ~~system moves from a northerly direction southward~~[3]

D. low pressure system, increase in temperature, wind change to a southerly direction

That must mean Choice D is our answer! When we check it against our smart doodle, all three characteristics fit the description of a warm front. Yes!

Analytical Questions

Analytical Questions will ask you to interpret information, apply knowledge, reason through circumstances, draw conclusions based on evidence and use info in a new way. This is where your reasoning skills really come in handy. These types of questions would most typically fall under the Scientific Investigation Reporting Category.

If you checked your brain at the door when you answered the recall questions, you're gonna want to go get it. Take a look at some of these questions:

1. Suppose a scientist determines that a formerly unidentifiable virus can be identified given the information from Experiment 1. If this virus reacts the same way as Virus X in solution Q, and reacts the same way as Virus Y in solution M, which host would the virus most likely infect?

A. Host 1

B. Host 2

C. Host 3

D. Host 4

---

[1] *Warm fronts have a decrease in air pressure, which we know is the same thing as a decrease in barometric pressure from the introductory paragraph.*

[2] *Cold fronts have a falling barometric pressure that rises sharply; warm fronts do not.*

[3] *The system moves from a southerly direction northward in a warm front.*

2. Is the scientist's hypothesis, that all of the solutions were basic, supported by the results of Experiment 2?

   F. Yes, because all of the solutions had many positive H ions and a pH > 7.

   G. Yes, because all of the solutions had very few positive H ions and a pH >7.

   H. No, because all of the solutions had many positive H ions and a pH < 7.

   J. No, because all of the solutions had very few positive H ions and a pH < 7.

3. Suppose that a sixth solution had been measured in Experiment 1 with a mass of 45.9g. The density of this solution, according to the results in Table 1, would most likely have been closest to the density of which solution?

   A. H_2O_2 at 20%

   B. H_2O_2 at 16%

   C. HCl at 20%

   D. HCl at 16%

See? These require a little more of that *reasoning* which is what the Science Reasoning test is all about, anyway. Let's try a couple of these with the weather passage again. You can use the doodle I created for the warm front (p. 211) and your doodle (p. 212) for the cold front you created to help you answer the question.

Study 1

A warm front is a specific air pressure system where warm air replaces cool air. It is associated with a low pressure system and usually moves from a southerly direction to the north. A warm front passage can be depicted by an increase in temperature and humidity (higher dew point temperatures), a decrease in the air pressure, a wind change to a southerly direction, and the likelihood of precipitation. A series of weather observations were taken for Boston, Atlanta, and Trenton. (Table 1)

Table 1

Location	Temperature	Wind Direction	Dew Point Temperature	Precipitation	Time
Boston	45	Easterly	40	Cloudy	1:05 PM
Boston	45	Easterly	40	Cloudy	2:15 PM
Boston	62	South	62	Cloudy	3:25 PM
Atlanta	72	Northeasterly	72	Mostly Cloudy	8:25 AM
Atlanta	78	Southeasterly	77	Rain	10:30 AM
Atlanta	77	Southeasterly	76	Mostly Cloudy	11:35 AM
Trenton	65	Easterly	50	Cloudy	1:15 PM
Trenton	67	Southerly	64	Cloudy	1:25 PM
Trenton	67	Southerly	64	Rain	1:30 PM

Study 2

A cold front is another specific front which is also associated with a low pressure system. During a cold front, cold air replaces warm air. A cold front usually moves from a northerly direction southward. A cold front can be depicted by rapidly falling temperatures and barometric pressure, a wind shift to the north or west, and a moderate chance of precipitation. The barometric pressure, after falling, usually rises very sharply after the passage of a cold front. A series of weather observations were taken from Columbus, Houston, and Mobile. (Table 2)

Table 2

Location	Temperature	Wind Direction	Barometric Pressure	Precipitation	Time
Columbus	80	Southerly	1010	Cloudy	3:05 PM
Columbus	80	Southerly	1000	Cloudy	3:30 PM
Columbus	63	Northwesterly	950	Clear	3:35 PM
Houston	94	Southeasterly	1020	Clear	5:00 PM
Houston	93	Southerly	1022	Thunderstorms	5:15 PM
Houston	78	Westerly	955	Clear	5:30 PM
Mobile	85	Westerly	988	Partly Cloudy	8:10 PM
Mobile	84	Westerly	1005	Partly Cloudy	8:25 PM
Mobile	83	Westerly	1010	Clear	8:40 PM

2. Suppose a meteorologist received the computer data in the following table to help forecast the weather for Sunday evening. What would be the best temperature forecast?

Time	Wind Direction	Barometric Pressure	Precipitation
Saturday Night	Southwest	1005	Cloudy
Sunday Morning	Northwest	974	Showers
Sunday Afternoon	Northwest	1020	Clearing

F. It's going to be warmer.

G. It's going to be colder, then warmer later.

H. It's going to be colder.

J. The temperature will not change.

Here, you not only have to use the information in the passage to figure out what causes temperatures to increase, you have to apply it to a new scenario. Whew. Let's try a strategy so we don't overload our brains with info. We're going to recycle one from the Chart section, since it seems to apply: **Don't Stuff the Burger.** Let's take this question piece by piece so we don't get overwhelmed.

HEADS UP

You'll learn a lot about the experiments as you answer questions in these passages. Don't be afraid to jot down things you discover as you answer a question—things that may not have been as clear to you at first. Sometimes, the facts you learn from the questions will help you get the next answer correct since you're delving deeper into the material.

First, we need to determine what the answer choices mean. It seems obvious that "warmer" means the temperatures will increase, which means that a warm front is coming. "Colder" means the temperatures will decrease, which means a cold front is coming. Okay. We know how to determine warm and cold fronts—by comparing the info to our Doodles.

So, let's go ahead and look at *Wind Direction* first. A warm front indicates that the wind will head south, and a cold front indicates that the wind will head north or west. Sunday afternoon has experienced a northwest wind, so that's one point for the "cold front" side—Choice G or H. Let's keep digging though, because there are many factors to a forecast.

Let's check out the *Barometric Pressure* column. It looks like the pressure went down on Sunday morning, then went back up sharply by Sunday afternoon. If we check out the studies, that fits with a cold front, too! Another point in the "cold front" category. But how do we choose between Choices G and H? Let's check the last column—Precipitation.

It looks as though on Sunday afternoon, the precipitation is clearing up. If a warm front were following a cold front, we could expect it to keep raining because a warm front has a "likelihood" of precipitation. Therefore, we can safely choose Choice H—it's going to be colder.

Let's try another one.

3. What would be the most accurate meteorological description about what occurred in Mobile?

A. There was a cold frontal passage, but it was followed by a warm frontal passage.

B. There was a cold frontal passage, but it occurred before the earliest observation was made.

C. There was no cold frontal passage.

D. A warm frontal passage occurred.

With this one, we'll take it bit by bit again. First, we'll get a grasp on what happened in Mobile.

> **HEADS UP**
>
> When a question repeats info in the answer choices (like the phrase "There was a cold frontal passage" in question 3), read that information in the passage first. You can knock out a couple of answer choices at a time if the info is NOT correct. Often, though, if info is repeated, then one of those answer choices IS correct.

If we look at the charts, we see these facts:

- Mobile experienced a westerly wind all three days.
- Barometric pressure rose sharply from 8:10 to 8:25 and rose slightly from 8:25 to 8:40.
- Partly cloudy skies cleared up by 8:40.

Next, we'll follow the heads-up advice and read about the cold fronts first to see if any of that info fits into a cold front.

- Mobile experienced a Westerly wind all three days.

  Cold fronts have winds that shift to the north or west.

- Barometric pressure rose from 8:10 to 8:25 and rose slightly from 8:25 to 8:40.

  Cold fronts have a dropping barometric pressure that rises sharply.

- Partly cloudy skies cleared up by 8:40.

  Cold fronts have a moderate chance of precipitation.

Well, it appears as though Choice B fits really well. If a cold front passage occurred before the first observation, then that sharp rise of barometric pressure fits, as does the clearing skies and the wind shift to the west. Choices A and D are incorrect because we see no signs of a warm front happening. Choice C is incorrect because the barometric pressure would have stayed the same.

Practice Research Summaries

Don't forget to use your reading strategy!

Passage II

A scientist wanted to study the effects of the substrate hydrogen peroxide (H_2O_2) and pH on the enzyme catalase. Enzymes, such as catalase, are protein molecules found in living cells. Catalase, in particular, speeds up the decomposition of hydrogen peroxide into water and oxygen.

Catalase

$$H_2O_2 \rightarrow \rightarrow \rightarrow \rightarrow \rightarrow H_2O + O_2$$

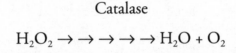

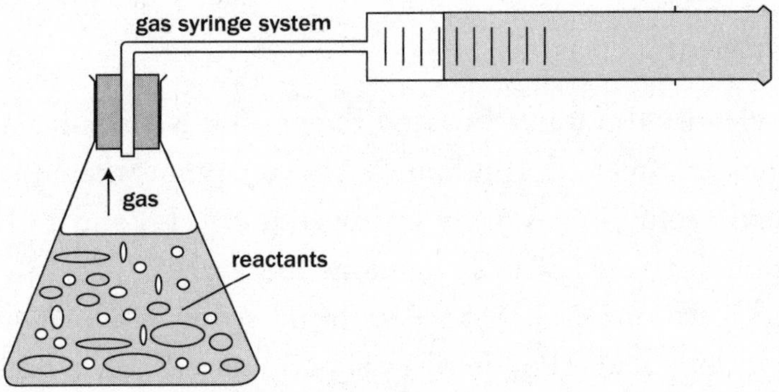

Figure 1

Experiment 1

For the first experiment—the effects of the substrate H_2O_2 (a weak acid) on catalase—the scientist wanted to measure the reaction time, or how long it took a gas syringe system (gss) to move 30 cm^3 when H_2O_2 was introduced to catalase. He added 2 cm^3 of yeast, an easily measured catalase, to a beaker. He then added 4 cm^3 of hydrogen peroxide at various concentrations to a test tube. He poured the H_2O_2 solution into the beaker and started a stopwatch the moment the gas began to move. He recorded the reaction time in seconds for each concentration (see Table 1).

Table 1

Trial	H_2O_2 concentration	Reaction time
Trial 1	4 %	47.3
Trial 2	8 %	18.4
Trial 3	10%	17.3
Trial 4	12%	14.5
Trial 5	16%	10.6
Trial 6	20%	9.7

Experiment 2

The scientist also wanted to find the optimum pH value and reaction time of several different enzymes. The optimum pH is the point where the enzyme is the most active. An acidic solution has many hydrogen ions (H+) and a pH < 7. An alkaline, or basic solution, has very few hydrogen ions and a pH >7. A pH of 7 is neutral. The scientist set up 7 stations of 3 beakers, with pH strips in all. At station 1, he added $4cm^3$ of hydrochloric acid (HCl) until a pH of 3 was reached in beaker 1. Then, he added $4cm^3$ of a common base, sodium hydroxide (NaOH) until a pH of 10 was reached in beaker 2. Next, he adjusted the pH to 7 with various drops of the NaOH and HCl in beaker 3. He repeated this process until all seven stations contained identical solutions in each beaker. Finally, he added $2cm^3$ of seven different enzymes (one per station) to chart reaction time in seconds and discover optimum pH (see Table 2).

Table 2

Enzyme	pH Optimum	NaOH Reaction time	Reaction time (seconds)
Pepsin	1.5–1.6	136.1	68.9
Trypsin	7.8–8.7	82.8	15.6
Urease	7.3	90	22.8
Invertase	4.5	114.5	47.3
Maltase	6.1–6.8	95.4	28.2
Malt Amylase	4.6–5.2	108.7	41.5
Catalase	7.0	88.1	20.9

1. Based on the information in Experiments 1 and 2, in which of the following situations were the reaction times the same?

A. The enzyme trypsin's reaction with NaOH and the reaction time in Trial 2.

B. The enzyme catalase's reaction with HCl and catalase's reaction with 20% of H_2O_2.

C. The enzyme urease's reaction with NaOH and the reaction time in Trial 4.

D. The enzyme invertase's reaction with HCl and catalase's reaction with 4% of hydrogen peroxide.

2. Suppose the scientist had added $4cm^3$ of hydrogen peroxide in a 24% concentration to $2cm^3$ of catalase. Based on the information provided in Experiment 1, how long, approximately, would it take the gas syringe system to move $30cm^3$?

F. 1.5 seconds

G. 7.3 seconds

H. 9.6 seconds

J. 16.5 seconds

3. One of the scientist's initial hypotheses was that an enzyme's reaction times to both the HCl and NaOH would be faster the higher the pH Optimum. Based on the information in Table 2, was his hypothesis correct?

A. No, because the faster the enzyme's pH Optimum, the faster the reaction time to NaOH, but the slower the reaction time to the HCl.

B. No, because the reaction times did not correlate to the pH Optimum in any way.

C. Yes, because the lower the enzyme's pH Optimum, the slower both the NaOH and HCl's reaction times were.

D. Yes, because the higher the pH Optimum, both the NaOH and the HCl's reaction times dropped proportionately.

4. Does the enzyme malt amylase reach its pH Optimum in a basic or acidic solution?

F. both

G. neither

H. basic

J. acidic

5. Based on the information in Experiment 1, which of the following is NOT a reason the scientist used a gas syringe system and a stopwatch together?

A. The gss system accurately measures the different concentrations of hydrogen peroxide.

B. It's impossible to accurately record the amount of gas escaping during a reaction with just a stopwatch.

C. By measuring reaction times with a gss system, the scientist can more accurately compare reaction times of various concentrations of solutions.

D. By allowing the gas released during the reaction to move the plunger, the gss gives an exact place for the scientist to stop the stopwatch and record the time.

6. Based on the information from Experiments 1 and 2, the enzyme catalase reacts the fastest in which situation?

   F. when it is mixed with an acid

   G. when it is mixed with a neutral solution

   H. when it is mixed with a base

   J. when it reaches a pH of 7

Answers on page 250.

Conflicting Viewpoints: 6–8 questions

It's no secret that people across the world have **gasp!** differing points of view. Some fashion designers believe that burnt orange corduroy is a great fabric for crafting a pair of ladies' trousers. I happen to believe that this is a crime on several different levels.

Others have the opinion that some young reality stars have subzero talent. I happen to concur.

When it comes to science, though, you'd think that people would kinda get along. That all the physicists and geologists and paleontologists would get together and kinda *agree* on scientific theories that are supposed to be, well, scientific.

You'd be wrong. Science is only science because it's proven, and before it can be proven, it is debated. Hence, you have this illustrative passage—just one of them—on the ACT Science section: Conflicting Viewpoints. Here, you'll see two or more scientists battling it out verbally over a scientific theory or giving two or more hypotheses with different assertions. Your job will be to answer the questions accompanying this one passage correctly. Think you can wade through the theories to get the right answers? You certainly can and MUST. Let's learn how to do it.

Conflicting Viewpoints Reading Strategy

Unlike the two previous types of science passages, this passage will have more reading. It definitely has *less* reading than the Reading test, but just enough that you'll need to pay close attention to everything in the passage. Because these passages aren't long, the writers cram a lot of info into just a few sentences. Your *Primary Goal* in life when reading this passage is to understand it the first time around, so you can whip through the questions without having to refer back to the passage more than a couple times.

Here's the strategy that will help you do just that:

Step 1: Grasp the Intro: The conflicting viewpoints passage will always be set up with an intro paragraph that gives a little background to the argument, defines some terms, and tells you why the two scientists or theorists are fighting.

> **HEADS UP**
>
> Treat each part of the passage as a separate entity. Read and understand the intro. Then read and understand Theory 1. Then read and understand Theory 2. If you think of them as separate ideas, and focus ONLY on the portion you're reading, you won't be as confused when more and more data is thrown at you.

Step 2: Grasp Theory or hypothesis 1: Theory 1 will be the first scientist's persuasive paragraph about his or her side of the story. You'll read the main point—usually the first sentence—that explains what the scientist believes on the matter. Then, you'll read supporting details and facts that prove this scientist's point.

Step 3: Grasp Theory or hypothesis 2: Theory 2 will be the second scientist's persuasive paragraph about his or her viewpoint on the subject and the facts to prove it.

Step 4: Grasp Theory or hypothesis 3: If necessary, repeat the step if there is another theory or hypothesis.

Step 5: Answer the Questions: Once you're completely sure you understand the info inside the passage, have at the questions. Go in order. Circle anything you can't answer quickly and come back to it if you still have time.

Things you don't have to worry about when you're reading:

1. **Which scientist is right or wrong.** You'll never be asked to figure out who's telling the truth, so you should not care.
2. **Which questions are tough and which are easy.** Just like the experiments passages, you don't need to separate these questions before you read. Just read the text so you understand it, then hit the first question in the queue. If you can't answer it within a few seconds of reading it, or don't remember where to get the info quickly, circle it, and come back to it.

Grasping the Conflicting Viewpoints Passages

Grasp the Intro

Grasp the Intro and comprehend the whole point of the passage.

Unlike the charts passages, the intro in the Conflicting Viewpoints passage is very, very important. That first paragraph will not only set the scene for you so you know what the conflict is all about, it contains info that will definitely be used in the questions. Our primary goal is to understand what this paragraph is trying to get across, so the best way to catch what they're tossing to us is with a strategy:

STRATEGY ALERT

How to Understand the Conflicting Viewpoints Paragraphs

Star, Underline, Define, and Refine: We can understand the intro the best by starring the reason for the conflict, underlining anything important, defining all terms, and refining any language that's too clunky to understand.

Let's try it with a typical introduction you'd see in a Conflicting Viewpoints passage on the ACT Science Reasoning test:

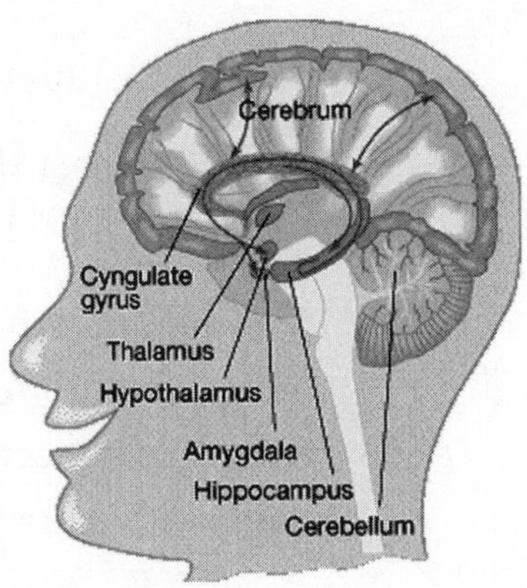

The limbic system is a set of brain structures located at the top of the brain stem, buried beneath the *cerebral cortex* (the sheet of neural tissue that covers the cerebrum of the brain). This system is responsible for controlling various functions in the body like storing memories, regulating hormones, perceiving senses, controlling motor function, and regulating bodily temperature. The limbic system is also responsible for emotional responses, but the ways in which emotional responses tie into physiological functioning has long been debated. In the 19th century, two theorists debated whether emotional responses occurred after or during a person's physical response to an outside event.

So, did you see anything to star? What's the big debate about? Obviously, it has something to do with the brain, since there's a giant cross-section of an oddly smiling head next to the paragraph. Luckily for us, the reason for the conflict is pretty easy to find. It's typically going to be one of the last few sentences of the introductory paragraph. And in this case, it certainly is:

> The limbic system is a set of brain structures located at the top of the brain stem, buried beneath the *cerebral cortex* (the sheet of neural tissue that covers the cerebrum of the brain). This system is responsible for controlling various functions in the body like storing memories, regulating hormones, perceiving senses, controlling motor function, and regulating bodily temperature. The limbic system is also responsible for emotional responses, but the ways in which emotional responses tie into physiological functioning has long been debated. In the 19th century, two theorists debated whether emotional responses occurred after or during a person's physical response to an outside event.

If you don't quite understand the debate, it's a great idea to refine the language, because understanding the debate is key to getting the questions correct. Let's try it here:

> In the 19th century, two theorists debated whether emotional responses occurred after or during a person's physical response to an outside event.

We can definitely refine that clunky sentence into:

Conflict's 2 sides:

Emotions occur AFTER physical reactions

Emotions and physical reactions occur AT THE SAME TIME.

You can expect that one theory will cover the "AFTER" side and the other theory will cover the "AT THE SAME TIME" side.

So, we starred the reason for the conflict and refined the language so we could actually understand it! Yes! The next job is to underline, define, and refine some more. We'll underline important nouns and verbs—especially anything italicized—and will define them with refined language (a paraphrase) on the side of the page.

Cortex covers cerebrum

Limbic controls phys. AND emo.

The limbic system is a set of brain structures located at the top of the brain stem, buried beneath the *cerebral cortex* (the sheet of neural tissue that covers the cerebrum of the brain). This system is responsible for controlling various functions in the body like storing memories, regulating hormones, perceiving senses, controlling motor function, and regulating bodily temperature. The limbic system is also responsible for emotional responses, but the ways in which emotional responses tie into physiological functioning has long been debated. In the 19th century, two theorists debated whether emotional responses occurred after or during a person's physical response to an outside event.

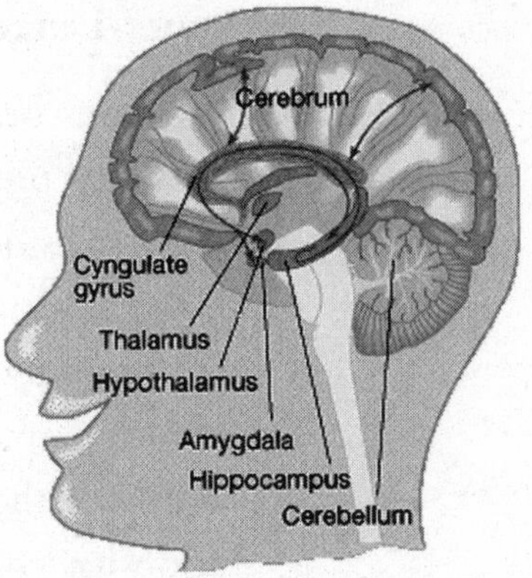

That ought to do it.

If you just take the time to Star, Underline, Define, and Refine while you read the intro, you will remember it more easily and in many cases, won't even have to refer back to the text when you're answering questions!

Grasp the Theories

Grasp the Theories one at a time. Treat them as separate ideas and get a hold of the idea inside the paragraph firmly before moving onto the second idea.

Just like the intro, we need to comprehend this theory and the quicker we do it, the quicker we get to the questions. Let's use the **Star, Underline, Define, and Refine** strategy from above:

Instead of underlining and starring the *reason for the conflict* like we did in the intro, we will be looking for the theorist's main point—his or her view on the subject. Here, we'll find out if Theorist 1 believes that emotions happen AFTER or AT THE SAME TIME AS physical responses. Typically, in these passages, the main point is in the first few sentences. Thank goodness something is ridiculously easy.

James-Lange Theory of Emotion

Emotions occur after a body has responded to an event; hence, emotions are caused by physiological reactions. When a human being responds to experiences in the outside world, the *thalamus* (part of the limbic system) sends a message to the autonomic nervous system to create physiological reactions in the body like a rapidly beating heart, sweating hands, dryness of mouth, perspiration, or dilating pupils. Then, the autonomic nervous system sends the response to the cortex for the interpretation of the impulses it has received, and that interpretation has come to be known as an emotion. (My heart is beating rapidly, so I must be scared.)

This theory is proven time and again by those who suffer psychological impairments like panic disorders. Those who suffer from panic disorders often experience emotional trauma after certain physiological responses, like hyperventilation and bodily tics, have already occurred. Once the affected person feels the bodily changes start to happen, the emotion follows. With therapy, panic disorder sufferers can learn to disassociate the physical response with the emotional state. If physical responses did not control emotional responses, then therapy would not be necessary to help them recover; they wouldn't feel the disturbing feelings in the first place.

So, what's this theory's main point? Which side is James-Lange taking?

1. Emotions occur AFTER physical reactions
2. Emotions and physical reactions occur AT THE SAME TIME.

I'm sure you chose point 1. Why? Because the theory all but comes right out and smacks you with it in the first sentence:

☆ Emotions occur ***after*** a body has responded to an event; hence, emotions are caused by physiological reactions.

Starred it.

Now, we need to underline, define, and refine yet again. In these paragraphs, we're looking for the theorist's *proof.* Why do they believe what they do and how do they prove it? These paragraphs are like little persuasive essays. These scientists are trying their best to get you to believe their point! So, what evidence do they put in the paragraph to make you believe it?

Let's take another look at the theory. What facts does the theorist rely on? Let's go through it, and underline anything that proves the point. Then, we'll define any terms and refine the language in the margin.

James-Lange Theory of Emotion

Thalamus = part of limbic system

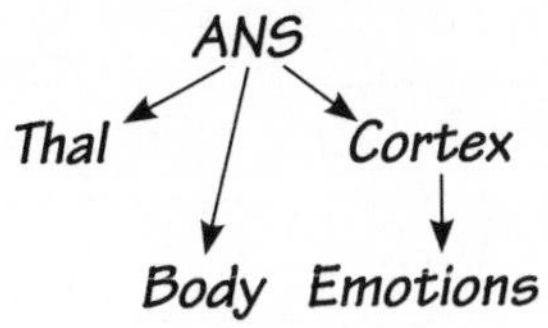

Emotions occur after a body has responded to an event; hence, emotions are caused by physiological reactions. When a human being responds to experiences in the outside world, the *thalamus* (part of the limbic system) sends a message to the autonomic nervous system to create physiological reactions in the body like a rapidly beating heart, sweating hands, dryness of mouth, perspiration, or dilating pupils. Then, the autonomic nervous system sends the response to the cortex for the interpretation of the impulses it has received, and that interpretation has come to be known as an emotion. (My heart is beating rapidly, so I must be scared.)

Panic disorder = *body changes THEN emo. *therapy blocks emotion caused by body

This theory is proven time and again by those who suffer psychological impairments like panic disorders. Those who suffer from panic disorders often experience emotional trauma after certain physiological responses, like hyperventilation and bodily tics, have already occurred. Once the affected person feels the bodily changes start to happen, the emotion follows. With therapy, panic disorder sufferers can learn to disassociate the physical response with the emotional state. If physical responses did not control emotional responses, then therapy would not be necessary to help them recover; they wouldn't feel the disturbing feelings in the first place.

Okay, so what do we know for sure after our strategy? What points does the James-Lange theory use to convince us that emotions occur AFTER physical responses?

- The thalamus, which is part of the limbic system, is important to emotional response, and the limbic system (as mentioned in the introduction) controls both physical and emotional responses.

HEADS UP

Although you'll never be completing a bulleted list of what you've learned from the theory like I did, your brain will do this automatically (sort of). When you write while you read, your brain processes the information much more thoroughly—making connections, forming opinions, and scuttling anything unnecessary—than it does when you just read.

- The order of emotional response is this: the thalamus sends an impulse to the ANS (controls the body's responses). The ANS then sends an impulse to the cortex (controls emotions).
- People with panic disorders experience the bodily response first, followed by the emotion, but therapy can block the emotional response.

Are you convinced? It doesn't matter. All we've done is process the paragraph so we comprehend the James-Lange theory and can answer questions correctly.

Now it's YOUR turn. I want you to **Star, Underline, Define and Refine** the heck out of Theory 2. Go ahead. Don't be shy. Do it right now. Hopefully, you'll understand the main point and the proof the theorist offers you.

Get crackin!

Cannon-Bard Theory of Emotion

Emotions occur simultaneously with physiological responses; hence, emotions are not caused by bodily responses. This theory has been proven scientifically through case studies of traumatic brain injury patients. People who have experienced brain trauma and have severed neural connections to the cortex of the cerebrum still exhibit emotional responses appropriately (cry at funerals, laugh at jokes).

The reception time also plays a factor when considering the emotions. In case studies of human interaction, for example, where brain function is monitored via *electroencephalography* (the recording of electrical activity along the scalp), a person's brain emits signals to the various portions of the brain in milliseconds. A *visceral* or physiological reception time is largely indistinguishable from the reception time of other basic brain functions. The thalamus sends messages to the cortex for an emotional response; it also sends messages to the autonomic nervous system for the physiological response. In both cases, the *reception time* (the time it takes the message to be received) is nearly the same, proving that one cannot occur before, nor cause the other.

Answering Conflicting Viewpoints Questions

Answering Conflicting Viewpoints Questions isn't as simple as you'd think, but with the right strategies, will help bolster that ACT Science Reasoning score.

Step 4 of our Reading strategy for the Conflicting Viewpoints section tells us to answer the 6–8 questions accompanying the theorists' paragraphs. Soooo . . . .we better get on it. Since this is the only way to get points, we're going to want to do this quickly and efficiently, ONLY referring back to the passages when absolutely necessary. Hopefully, though, your skills at the **Star, Underline, Define, and Refine** strategy will help make this process go a little more quickly.

Agreement Questions

Agreement Questions are the ACT test writers' way of asking you whether or not a statement would logically go along with, fit into, or be consistent with one or both of the theories. You may also see questions that ask you to compare new findings or results to one of the viewpoints, and those types of questions would fall under the Evaluation of Models, Inferences, and Experimental Results reporting category.

You will typically find at least two or three of these agreement types of questions on the Conflicting Viewpoints passage, because it's an easy way to check whether or not you've truly understood the paragraphs. These agreement questions can be asked in all sorts of ways:

Which claim is supported by . . .

Which statement is consistent with . . .

Which fact would be accepted by . . .

Which theory is strengthened by this evidence . . .

Which hypothesis is best supported by the new findings presented by this chart . . .

These questions can refer to one of the theories, two of the theories, or all of the theories, which is why it's important to understand everything in the theories before you plunge into the questions! Here are some samples:

Which of the following claims would be supported by both scientists in Hypotheses 1 and 2?

A. When the depolarization reaches –55Mv a neuron will fire an action potential.

B. When a neuron reaches its threshold, it will fire.

C. When the depolarization reaches –55Mv, a neuron will cease to fire an action potential.

D. When a neuron reaches its threshold, it will cease to fire.

Which of the following statements is most consistent with Scientist 1's theory?

F. The Sudan was once covered by oceanic water because of the marine fossils found in its sedimentary layers.

G. The Sudan, although purported to have been covered by oceanic water, remains free from fossilized sea life.

H. The Sudan is an example of how a land mass can incur sedimentary fossilized marine life without ever having been covered by oceanic water.

J. The Sudan was neither covered with oceanic water; hence, it is free from sedimentary fossilized marine life.

According to the information provided, which of the following descriptions of allopathic medicine would be accepted by both physician 1 and physician 2, but NOT physician 3?

A. Allopathic medicine is a viable scientific method of treating patients.

B. Allopathic medicine is closely related to homeopathic medicine.

C. Allopathic medicine has long been disregarded by the medical community.

D. Allopathic medicine had its place in time, but current practices warrant more useful techniques.

To solve these questions and figure out if everything agrees, you'll need to use a strategy!

STRATEGY ALERT

How to Answer an Agreement Conflicting Viewpoints Question

Open Up a Chakra* or Two: Often, your subconscious knows things before you do. You know for a fact that you shouldn't accept a friend request from that guy who everyone else thinks is cool. Your gut tells you something is wrong at midnight and you wake up the next morning to find you've left the lights on in your car. (HATE that.) You can miraculously state the name of that kid who sat next to you in summer camp eight years ago when you bump into him at Target. We have some sort of sixth sense that allows us to process info even when we don't realize it. So, for agreement questions, you're gonna want to tap into that.

If you've done your assignment, you will have already underlined all the important words in the Cannon-Bard theory as well as defined any terms and refined the language. If so, you will have subconsciously picked up a lot of info from the text! Let's take a look at the passage again, and then use our Chakra method to answer some questions:

HEADS UP

The ACT Conflicting Viewpoints section will also throw a few "recall" questions at you: the ones that ask you to "find the information." Since you've conquered these in both the Reading section and the Experiments part of Science already, I won't get into them again here.

Passage

The limbic system is a set of brain structures located at the top of the brain stem, buried beneath the *cerebral cortex* (the sheet of neural tissue that covers the cerebrum of the brain). This system is responsible for controlling various functions in the body like storing memories, regulating hormones, perceiving senses, controlling motor function, and regulating bodily temperature. The limbic system is also responsible for emotional responses, but the ways in which emotional responses tie into physiological functioning has long been debated. In the 19th century, two theorists debated whether emotional responses occurred after or during a person's physical response to an outside event.

**A chakra is a main energy center in your body.*

James-Lange Theory of Emotion

Thalamus = part of limbic system

ANS → Thal → Body; ANS → Cortex → Emotions

Emotions occur after a body has responded to an event; hence, emotions are caused by physiological reactions. When a human being responds to experiences in the outside world, the *thalamus* (part of the limbic system) sends a message to the autonomic nervous system to create physiological reactions in the body like a rapidly beating heart, sweating hands, dryness of mouth, perspiration, or dilating pupils. Then, the autonomic nervous system sends the response to the cortex for the interpretation of the impulses it has received, and that interpretation has come to be known as an emotion. (My heart is beating rapidly, so I must be scared.)

Panic disorder = *body changes THEN emo. *therapy blocks emotion caused by body

This theory is proven time and again by those who suffer psychological impairments like panic disorders. Those who suffer from panic disorders often experience emotional trauma after certain physiological responses, like hyperventilation and bodily tics, have already occurred. Once the affected person feels the bodily changes start to happen, the emotion follows. With therapy, panic disorder sufferers can learn to disassociate the physical response with the emotional state. If physical responses did not control emotional responses, then therapy would not be necessary to help them recover; they wouldn't feel the disturbing feelings in the first place.

To let our subconscious *really* work, we'll just read the question and scan the four answers briefly. Then, remembering what you've read—and trusting your instincts—make a choice.

> Which statement would be consistent with both the James-Lange and Cannon-Bard theories of emotion?
>
> **A.** The autonomic nervous system is necessary for an emotional response.
>
> **B.** The thalamus is necessary for an emotional response.
>
> **C.** The cortex has nothing to do with an emotional response
>
> **D.** The limbic system creates bodily responses after emotional responses.

Well? How'd you do? Are your chakras in alignment or open or whatever it is they say? Did you choose Choice B?

If your subconscious is a little more sub than you'd like and you chose something else, here are the facts:

Choice A is consistent with only the James-Lange theory, because the ANS, which creates the bodily response, sends a message to the cortex for the emotional response. So, it's definitely not agreeing with my chakras.

Choice B seems correct because both theories assert that the thalamus, part of the limbic system, sends the impulses after an outside event happens.

Choice C agrees with neither theory because the cortex creates the emotional response.

Choice D is also not in agreement with either theory because the Cannon-Bard theory puts the responses as spontaneous and the James-Lange theory says the bodily response comes first.

Let's try it again. Read the question and the four choices briefly. Go ahead and cross off anything that seems "off." Then, select the best choice.

> A man, after experiencing damage to the neural pathways leading from the thalamus to the autonomic nervous system, suddenly stops expressing horror at graphic photos of destruction, crying at funerals, and laughing at jokes that used to be funny to him. This example is evidence that strengthens which theory?
>
> **F.** The Cannon-Bard theory, because the neural pathways connecting the limbic system to the thalamus carry the signal to emit an emotional response.
>
> **G.** The James-Lange theory, because the neural pathways connecting the limbic system to the thalamus carry the signal to emit an emotional response.
>
> **H.** The Cannon-Bard theory, because it shows that the man's emotions were severed after damage to the autonomic nervous system, which controls initial bodily responses to an outside event.
>
> **J.** The James-Lange theory, because it shows that the man's emotions were severed after damage to the autonomic nervous system, which controls initial bodily responses to an outside event.

Do you have a gut reaction to this one?

Choice F and Choice G are way off because the thalamus is PART of the limbic system, so one can't be connected to the other with neural *anythings*. That's like saying you poured sugar into your coffee, and drank the coffee but not the sugar. Doesn't make sense.

Choice H is incorrect because it wouldn't matter if the man's pathways to the autonomic nervous system were damaged because the theory states that the ANS does not send a message to the cortex to emit an emotion; the responses occur at the same time (from two different pathways).

That leaves Choice J, which definitely explains this theory to a T, and yes, my chakras are totally fine with this answer. Are yours?

Disagreement Questions

Disagreement Questions are the ACT writers' way of asking you whether or not a statement would logically contradict one or both of the theories.

Again, you could possibly see a couple of these "disagreement" types of questions, and they'll be asked in a couple of different ways:

> This evidence contradicts evidence stated in which hypothesis . . .
>
> Which statement is the strongest evidence against theory 1 . . .
>
> Which fact would NOT be accepted by . . .
>
> Which theory is *weakened* by the evidence the most . . .

And yet again, these questions can refer to one or all of the theories or hypotheses. Here are some more samples:

> The theorist who favors further research into biological transmutation implies that his opponent's hypothesis is *weakened* by which of the following observations?
>
> **A.** During the synthesis of egg shells, there is an anomalous increase in calcium and decrease in magnesium levels.
>
> **B.** During the synthesis of egg shells, there is an anomalous decrease in calcium and decrease in magnesium levels.
>
> **C.** Magnesium never increases during the excreting process.
>
> **D.** Magnesium is only found during the synthesis of the egg shells.

With which of the following statements would Scientist 1, Scientist 2, and Scientist 3 most likely disagree?

F. Strong interactions that take place in known nuclear processes do not rule out that other nuclear processes may rely on "weak" interactions.

G. Weak interactions will never produce the start of a nuclear process.

H. Nuclear processes typically begin with a strong interaction in oppositional forces.

J. Nuclear processes typically begin with a weak interaction in oppositional forces.

Which of the following statements about mitochondria's role in cell functioning would be inconsistent with Scientist 1's theory?

A. These organelles play a vitally necessary role in energy transformation.

B. These organelles are located in the cytoplasm.

C. Mitochondria are present in the nucleus of a cell and contain their own genetic material

D. Mitochondria is abundant in both the nucleus and cytoplasm.

Since you'll be getting a couple of these questions, we need to know how to tackle them. And how do we spell "tackle" in this book? That's right, "S-T-R-A-T-E-G-Y."

STRATEGY ALERT

How to Solve a Disagreement Conflicting Viewpoints Question

The Glass is Half Full: Are you a Debbie Downer? Do you rain on everyone's parade? Do you continuously point out the flaws in your Facebook friends' arguments about whether "Smackdown" should be allowed on the air? If so, you have something in common with the writers of these questions. In these "disagreement" questions, the answer choices are just brimming — *brimming!* — with facts that are consistent with the original statement. But, like the Negative Nancys they are, they have to make you find the one tiny little answer that doesn't fit. Well, I say, look on the bright side of things. Find all the blessings in the answer choices. See the glass as half full.

Let's have a go:

Passage

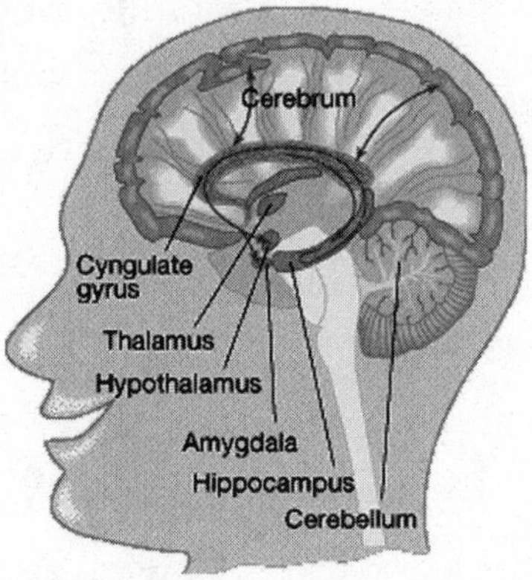

The limbic system is a set of brain structures located at the top of the brain stem, buried beneath the *cerebral cortex* (the sheet of neural tissue that covers the cerebrum of the brain). This system is responsible for controlling various functions in the body like storing memories, regulating hormones, perceiving senses, controlling motor function, and regulating bodily temperature. The limbic system is also responsible for emotional responses, but the ways in which emotional responses tie into physiological functioning has long been debated. In the 19th century, two theorists debated whether emotional responses occurred after or during a person's physical response to an outside event.

James-Lange Theory of Emotion

Thalamus = part of limbic system

ANS → Thal → Body; ANS → Cortex → Emotions

Emotions occur after a body has responded to an event; hence, emotions are caused by physiological reactions. When a human being responds to experiences in the outside world, the *thalamus* (part of the limbic system) sends a message to the autonomic nervous system to create physiological reactions in the body like a rapidly beating heart, sweating hands, dryness of mouth, perspiration, or dilating pupils. Then, the autonomic nervous system sends the response to the cortex for the interpretation of the impulses it has received, and that interpretation has come to be known as an emotion. (My heart is beating rapidly, so I must be scared.)

*Panic disorder = *body changes THEN emo. *therapy blocks emotion caused by body*

This theory is proven time and again by those who suffer psychological impairments like panic disorders. Those who suffer from panic disorders often experience emotional trauma after certain physiological responses, like hyperventilation and bodily tics, have already occurred. Once the affected person feels the bodily changes start to happen, the emotion follows. With therapy, panic disorder sufferers can learn to disassociate the physical response with the emotional state. If physical responses did not control emotional responses, then therapy would not be necessary to help them recover; they wouldn't feel the disturbing feelings in the first place.

Cannon-Bard Theory of Emotion

Emotions occur simultaneously with physiological responses; hence, emotions are not caused by bodily responses. This theory has been proven scientifically through case studies of traumatic brain injury patients. People who have experienced brain trauma and have severed neural connections to the cortex of the cerebrum still exhibit emotional responses appropriately (cry at funerals, laugh at jokes).

The reception time also plays a factor when considering the emotions. In case studies of human interaction, for example, where brain function is monitored via *electroencephalography* (the recording of electrical activity along the scalp), a person's brain emits signals to the various portions of the brain in milliseconds. A *visceral* or physiological reception time is largely indistinguishable from the reception time of other basic brain functions. The thalamus sends messages to the cortex for an emotional response; it also sends messages to the autonomic nervous system for the physiological response. In both cases, the *reception time* (the time it takes the message to be received) is nearly the same, proving that one cannot occur before, nor cause the other.

Which of the following statements would be inconsistent with the Cannon-Bard theory of emotion?

A. The thalamus sends a signal to the autonomic nervous system, which then signals the body to react.

B. A body's reception time to a stimulus is largely the same as the emotional reception time.

C. The time it takes an external factor to affect the emotions should be taken into consideration when assessing the factors that cause emotional responses.

D. The body's physiological response to a stimulus affects the emotions because of the connection to the neural pathways.

When we look at the glass as being half full, we see that ¾ of the answer choices are actually correct statements. Isn't that fantastic??!!! We have three little statements that fit nicely into the theory. How sweet.

So, let's figure out which three are *consistent* or *agree* with the Cannon-Bard theory, because we don't always want to focus on the negative, do we?

Choice A is definitely one of those choices that fit in. The thalamus *does* send signals to the ANS, and the Cannon-Bard theory supports that.

Choice B is also one of those responses that fit in. We found yet another fact to be thankful for.

Choice C is almost a direct quote from the second paragraph, so again, it fits with the theory. Aren't we grateful for so many nice facts that fit into the theory? I know I am.

Choice D. Sigh. We have to look at the half-empty piece, now don't we? Choice D doesn't fit in at all. Cannon-Bard never believed that the body's reactions affected the emotions, so this little Negative Nelly is the right answer.

When you look at the glass as half full and pick out the facts that *do* support the theory, it's easier to narrow down to the correct answer, which is always, in disagreement questions, the one that doesn't fit in.

So, are you ready to practice? Read the practice Science questions, and don't forget your strategies!

Practice Conflicting Viewpoints

Don't forget to use your reading strategy!

The most common type of mountains on the Earth's surface is the *folded* mountain. Typical characteristics of this type are thick layers of sedimentary rock and fossils of marine organisms embedded within the layers. Large mountainous regions such as the Alps, the Himalayas, and the Appalachians are all folded mountains.

The formation of mountains has long been a curiosity to scientists. Many theories have been formulated over time concerning mountain formation. Most theories of the last one hundred years use the idea that the *asthenosphere* (the liquid rock layer of the Earth's mantle, below the lithosphere and a thin layer of crust, in which there is relatively low resistance to flow and convection) plays a major role in mountain formation. Just how the asthenosphere helps form these mountain regions, however, had always been heavily debated before the 20th century.

Theory 1

James D. Dana, an American geologist, proposed a theory of mountain formation called global cooling or the contracting Earth theory. Global cooling suggested that the Earth's asthenosphere had been in a molten state at one time, and mountains formed as it cooled due to various ice ages and other catastrophic events. When it cooled, it shrank, causing the rigid crust to crumple and form mountain ranges.

The global cooling theory is proven by the abundance of volcanoes and earthquakes present in mountainous areas in the world. As the outer layers of the Earth cools, the Earth's internal temperature increases with increasing depth. This increased internal temperature heats the groundwater and forms steam. Usually the downward pressure of the contracting Earth contains the steam, but in mountainous areas, around the sites of fissures in the Earth's crust, the steam escapes, causing a bubbling in the asthenosphere. This bubbling causes waves, which subsequently causes volcanoes and earthquakes.

Theory 2

A more recent theory, the plate tectonics theory, states that shifting continental plates in the Earth's lithosphere forms mountains. On Earth, there are currently seven or eight major and many minor plates. The lithospheric plates shift as the asthenosphere moves in waves. The plates move in relation to one another at one of three types of plate boundaries or fissures in the Earth: collisional boundaries, divergent boundaries, and conservative transform boundaries. All of the major Earth changes—earthquakes, volcanoes, mountain formation, and oceanic trench formations—can be attributed to the plates shifting between 0 and 100 mm laterally at any one of these boundaries.

Theory 3

The concept of catastrophism was first popularized by the early 19th-century French scientist Georges Cuvier, who proposed that new life forms had moved in from other areas after local floods. He used fossilized tropical botany found in Europe to prove his theory.

His theory holds that major mountain chains and subsequent earthquakes were formed by violent and sudden natural catastrophes such as great floods. Plants and animals living in the parts of the world where such events occurred were killed off, being replaced abruptly by the new forms whose fossils defined the geological strata. Some catastrophists attempted to relate at least one such change to the Biblical account of Noah's flood.

1. Which of the following best describes how the three theories explain how earthquakes formed on the Earth?

	Theory 1	Theory 2	Theory 3
A.	shifting tectonic plates	liquid rock shrinking and cooling	The Great Flood
B.	liquid rock shrinking and cooling	shifting tectonic plates	natural catastrophes
C.	steam causes bubbles in asthenosphere	shifting tectonic plates	natural catastrophes
D.	steam causes bubbles in asthenosphere	Earth's internal temperature increasing	shifting tectonic plates

2. Assume Theory 2's assertions are correct. Based on this assumption and the information provided, which of the following is *least* likely to occur along a collisional fissure?

F. the formation of mountains

G. steam escaping to the asthenosphere

H. the formation of an oceanic trench

J. lithospheric crumpling

3. Which of the following statements about the asthenosphere would be consistent with Theories 1 and 2, but NOT Theory 3?

A. The asthenosphere affects the formation of mountains.

B. The asthenosphere forms earthquakes and volcanoes when it is heated from the Earth's internal steam.

C. The asthenosphere caused the Earth's crust to crumple in the past, and continues to do so in the present.

D. The asthenosphere forms mountains when it bubbles from internal heat.

4. Which of the following illustrations is consistent with the description of Theory 1's description of mountain formation in the passages?

F. Earth is molten → Earth cools → crust shrinks → asthenosphere forms waves → waves bubble → crust crumples → mountains formed

G. Earth is molten → Earth cools → asthenosphere forms waves → asthenosphere bubbles → asthenosphere forms waves → mountains formed

H. Earth is molten → catastrophic event → Earth cools → Earth shrinks → crust shrinks → crust crumples → mountains formed

J. Earth is molten → catastrophic event → Earth cools → Earth shrinks → Earth compresses steam → steam erupts through fissure → mountains formed

---

Answers on page 252.

Solutions to Science Reasoning Practice Questions

Data Representation, page 203

1. B.

Here, you have to pay close attention to the words and what they mean. It also helps if you can read a figure. The bottom of the figure was the plant age in weeks, and both the *B. madritensis* and the *A. californica* were colonized at the same rate, so that rules out Choice A and Choice C, which both talk about rate of colonization. The left side of the figure refers to the colonization percentage, and both Choices B and D deal with percentages. Obviously, the graph reads that *B. madritensis* was colonized at a *higher* percentage than *A. californica*, so the answer is B.

2. H.

This is a really easy question, because all you need to do is look at the table to figure it out. Which one of the choices underneath *A. californica* (the top group) had the most shoot AND root growth? If you look at the numbers next to NH_4 and NO_3, you'll see your answer clearly without too much tough math.

3. A.

Again, this is a place where you have to simply check out the details of the tables. Make sure, though, that you're looking at Figure 2 and not Table 1! The graphs on the left of Figure 2 are dealing with the percentage of nitrogen found. The graphs on the right are dealing with the percentage of bicarbonate found in the plants. Here, we're looking for the highest percentage of N in the shoots, so we'll be looking at just the graphs on the left. The highest percentage of N looks like the middle light-colored bar on the bottom graph, which is Choice A, mycorrhizal *B. madritensis* with the addition of NO_3.

4. J.

Question 4 is testing your reasoning ability a little bit. Here, you're asked to draw a conclusion, or use the information to make a guess about something. When you have a number of factors to look at, just draw a summary of each question so you don't get confused. If you draw it all out, you'll end up with the correct answer, which is J.

5. C.

Again, the question is asking you to "suppose." Based on the information, which plant is hardier? Choice C is correct because of the information given in the answer. When you compare the answer's evidence to the charts, you can't help but conclude the correct answer.

Research Summaries, page 225

1. D.

Technically, you could go down the list and match up every example to see which had the same reaction time. Or, you could hit up the tables *first* and find the two matching reaction times, then match it to the answers. That would take infinitely less time. If you did, you'd see that Choice D is correct.

2. G.

Remember, you're not going to be asked to do any complex math on the Science Reasoning section. Looking at all the numbers, you may be fooled into thinking you need to do some sort of math equation to solve. However, all you *really* need to do is put that 24% concentration of H_2O_2 at the bottom of Table 1 underneath the 20%, and guesstimate the reaction time. It's not going to be 1.5 seconds (Choice F) because the reaction times aren't going down much. It also isn't going to be 9.6 seconds (Choice H) because the reaction times are going down more than that. It can't be Choice J either, because the reaction time going back up wouldn't make sense. That leaves G!

3. C.

This question requires you to do some doodling to keep everything straight. The scientist thought that the faster the reaction times to both HCl and NaOH, the higher the pH Optimum, and you need to see if he was right. So check out the table. The faster the reaction time, the lower the number. Do the lowest numbers of reaction times correlate positively with the higher pH optimums? The highest pH Optimum is for Trypsin with an 8.7, and the reaction times are the lowest of both the NaOH and HCl. If you work your way down from the next highest pH Optimum to check reaction times, you'll see that they slowly move up, which means he was right.

4. J.

This question requires you to understand the information inside the paragraphs. If you did some doodling, you would have already noted that an acidic solution has a pH less than 7, so Malt Amylase is acidic, Choice J.

5. A.

Here's a question that requires you to play the true/false game like you did in elementary school. Every answer that's true gets crossed off—it's not correct for the question. Any answer that's false is your bingo. By asking you which one of those is NOT a reason, the question is automatically asking you which ones ARE reasons. Choices B, C, and D are all very good reasons for him to use both pieces of equipment together, so Choice A is our winner.

6. F.

The fastest reaction time is also going to be the lowest number in the tables. The lowest number is on Table 1, in Trial 6, when catalase reacts with H_2O_2 in a 20% concentration. Since the paragraph tells us that H_2O_2 is a weak acid, Choice F has to be correct.

Conflicting Viewpoints, page 246

1. C.

This question is tricky because you assume that the question is asking you how *mountains* are formed, since that's the main idea behind the theories. However, this question is asking about *earthquake* formation, not mountains, and earthquakes are discussed in each theory! Choice C explains the formation of earthquakes according to all three theories.

2. J.

Again, this one is tricky! Because Choice G uses language present in Theory 1, you may be tempted to choose it. However, you'd be wrong. Because escaping steam is part of what takes place in volcanic eruptions, that is more likely to happen rather than crumpling of any kind. Remember to choose the answer that is *least* likely.

3. A.

Both theories 1 and 2 discussed the asthenosphere's place in mountain formation, but Theory 3 never discussed the asthenosphere at all. Thus, Choice A is correct. Choice B refers to Theory 1 only. Choice C is incorrect because, according to Theory 2, the earth's crust is no longer crumpling. Choice D is wrong because that's not what Theory 2 purports about mountain formation.

4. H.

This process is definitely one that you should've doodled when you defined terms in the margin! Only Choice H goes through the process of mountain formation without missing or replacing any steps.

Science Reasoning Strategy Cheat Sheet

General Strategies:

- **Pace Yourself.**
- **Use Your Reading Skills.**
- **Pep Yourself Up.**
- **Read "Charts" Passages** (Data Representation) First.
- **Put It in Your Words.**

Data Representation Reading Strategy

1. **Separate Tough From Easy.**
2. **Read the Question.**
3. **Hit the Charts.**
4. **Take Notes.**
5. **Answer.**

Data Representation General Strategies

- **Lock Down the Details MIA** for Easy Data Representation Questions
- **Don't Stuff the Burger** for Tough Data Representation Questions

Research Summaries Reading Strategy

1. **Read the Passage.**
2. **Underline the Reason for the Experiment.**
3. **Summarize the Experiments.**
4. **Answer the Questions in Order.**

Research Summaries General Strategies

- **Smarten Up Your Doodles** to summarize the paragraphs.
- **Target Practice** to Answer a Recall Question.

Conflicting Viewpoints Reading Strategy

1. **Grasp the Intro.**
2. **Grasp Theory 1.**
3. **Grasp Theory 2.**
4. **Answer the Questions.**

Conflicting Viewpoints General Strategies

- **Star, Underline, Define, and Refine** to understand the passage.
- **Open Up a Chakra or Two** to answer an agreement question.
- **The Glass is Half Full** for a disagreement question

Take the Science Practice Test

Go to the REA Study Center

(www.rea.com/studycenter)

Now that you have completed this week's work, go to *rea.com/studycenter* and take the Science Practice Test. This test is just like the Science section of the actual ACT, with the added benefits of:

- **Timed testing conditions** – Gauge how much time you can spend on each question.
- **Automatic scoring** – Find out how you did on the test, instantly.
- **On-screen detailed explanations of answers** – Learn not just the correct answers, but also why the other answers are incorrect.
- **Diagnostic score reports** – Pinpoint where you're strongest and where you need to focus your study.

5

Week 5: Writing

Enhanced ACT Writing Test Basics

The Enhanced ACT Writing Test has

- 1 prompt discussing a controversial issue.
    - ▶ 3 perspectives about the issue.
    - ▶ 1 writing task
- 4 sheets of lined paper where you'll be writing your essay.
- 2–3 sheets of blank paper where you can plan your essay.

You'll be tested

- for 40 minutes.

You'll receive

- a single subject Writing score on a scale of 1–36.
- an English Language Arts (ELA) score on a scale of 1–36.
- 4 Writing competency scores on a scale of 2–12 in these areas: Ideas and Analysis, Development and Support, Organization, and Language Use and Conventions.

In order to score well,

- you must master ACT test-taking strategies.
- you must master ACT Writing strategies.

General Strategies for the ACT Writing Test

- **Pace Yourself:** Like every other portion of the test, you'll need to watch the time. If you spend 20 minutes making a detailed outline, you're in big trouble when it comes time to expand your wonderful ideas.
- **Avoid Chicken Scratch:** If the graders can't read it, they can't score it. Avoid using your fancy curlicues and "unique" way of writing the letter *G*. Keep your text legible so you have a chance at getting your essay scored.
- **If It Ain't Broke . . . Don't Fix It.** Don't try to come up with a shiny new way of writing your essay like skipping the introduction or writing a bulleted list instead of composing a well-thought-out piece. The writing techniques your teachers have taught you throughout high school will (mostly) work. Use them.
- **Use Your Life Experiences:** That time you saw the two drivers shouting at each other after an accident would illustrate a compelling reason why firearms should be regulated. Use your personal anecdotes to help make your point stronger.

The Enhanced ACT Writing Prompt

When you open up your testing booklet to the Writing portion, you'll see a prompt that looks like this example:

Social Media and Free Speech

Among other cherished values, the First Amendment protects the freedom of speech. People can exercise their freedom by choosing not to speak at all, by using offensive words and phrases to convey political messages, and even by burning the American flag. People value their protected right to say what they want without the threat of punishment from the government. Free speech is generally seen as a very good thing, but when it comes to social media, concerned citizens argue that the U.S. Supreme Court should regulate it. Although free speech does not include the right to incite actions that would harm others, like shouting "fire" in a crowded room or spreading libelous falsehoods, there are no regulations concerning cyber-bullying on social media. Given the accelerating usage and prevalence of conversations on social media, it is worth examining the implications of free speech when it comes to this medium of expression.

Perspective One	Perspective Two	Perspective Three
The government regulating what citizens say on social media annihilates free speech and leads to the loss of even more freedoms. The government should not have the power to silence anyone for any reason, even if the speech causes harm.	Giving up a portion of your free speech creates safety for humanity. Is a citizen's right to belittle, disparage, and make fun of another person worth more than a person's right to life? Cyberbullying often leads to suicide and keeping people alive and happy is more important than someone's right to say terrible things.	Regulating speech on social media would only be a temporary fix for the problem of bullying. It's up to society to discourage bullying in every form.

Below the prompt, you'll get this essay task: Write a unified, coherent essay in which you evaluate multiple perspectives on free speech and its relevance to social media. In your essay, be sure to:

- analyze and evaluate the perspectives given
- state and develop your own perspective on the issue
- explain the relationship between your perspective and those given

Your perspective may be in full agreement with any of the others, in partial agreement, or wholly different. Whatever the case, support your ideas with logical reasoning and detailed, persuasive examples.

The ACT Writing Process

So, then you need to write. And writing is so easy, right? You put your pencil on the paper, think of a few transitions, an anecdote or two, the basic 5-paragraph outline your fifth-grade English teacher taught you and go. Write your brains out. Easy A. Or, in this case, easy 36.

If this is what you think, then you're in the vast *minority* of the population. Most teenagers find it difficult to write a coherent, clear, concise, focused essay in 40 minutes on a subject they've neither chosen nor researched. And I'm guessing that even those bragging about how "easy" writing a good essay is, could learn a trick or two from the next few pages.

Let's proceed with the previous prompt by utilizing the **4 C's of the ACT Essay**:

1. **Critique**
2. **Condense**
3. **Compose**
4. **Correct**

Critique (5 minutes)

Your first task will be to quickly read the prompt and analyze the arguments given. Since part of your score on the essay comes from your ability to analyze those perspectives, using them to boost your thesis, you're going to need to find the strengths and weaknesses before you write a single word.

Condense (7–8 minutes)

Your next task is to condense all of your ideas about the prompt into one single idea: a thesis. Then, put together an outline that proves your thesis correct and keeps you organized.

Compose (22–23 minutes)

Now's the time to strut your stuff. Use your very best clear, fresh, effective language to write a compelling, developed argument for your perspective on the controversial issue. Make the readers weep with gratitude that they were blessed enough to get to read your essay.

Correct (4–5 minutes)

Save a few minutes for reviewing to ensure your essay is as much of a rock star as you are.

How to Critique the Prompt

Critiquing the prompt and perspectives is important to formulating your own opinion and argument on the issue. Why? You need fuel to propel your essay forward! These perspectives will give you ideas to shoot down and ideas to develop in your own essay, which you MUST do on the Enhanced ACT essay. You will not get a top score if you fail to use those perspectives in your essay. Here's what to do:

1. Underline the "cause" or premise of each perspective. The premise is the collection of "facts" given in the statement. From Perspective One, for example, the premise is underlined below:

   "Regulating what citizens say on social media annihilates free speech and leads to the loss of even more freedoms."

2. Circle the conclusions of each perspective. Conclusions are the claims the perspectives are making. It's what they say will happen because of the premise.

   "Regulating what citizens say on social media annihilates free speech and leads to the loss of even more freedoms."

3. On a separate sheet of paper, brainstorm ideas, questions, logical errors, and other thoughts while you read. Some of those conclusions given in the perspectives will be logically inaccurate or overreaching and you can use those mistakes to fuel your own ideas. In the instance above, you could brainstorm things like this when you're reading the perspectives:
   1. Free speech is already regulated; libel and slander are not allowed.
   2. One freedom being taken away does not mean more taken away. We can't carry assault rifles, but can carry firearms with a permit.
   3. Negative consequences of regulation? What does this mean for the future? Who decides what is acceptable?
   4. Who would pay for regulation? Country is already in debt.
   5. Consequences of not regulating: suicides, bullying, angry/depressed teens.
   6. Cyberbullying does not always lead to suicide.
   7. Other ways to regulate outside of government?

How to Condense Your Ideas

Your next step in creating a masterpiece is to take all of those critiques and ideas presented by the prompt and figure out where in the world you stand on the issue. That's called developing a thesis.

For this essay, your thesis will be the one perspective you can support the most and it must specifically make an argument for or against the controversial topic. If, when going through the perspectives, one resounded with you—yes! This makes total sense—then you can choose to agree with that perspective or some form of that perspective. If none of the perspectives really seem to fit what you believe, you can definitely develop an idea of your own, but you'd better be able to support it.

An easy way to write a quick thesis is to simply write down the statement about the issue that is the truest according to you. It's easier to defend a thesis that you actually believe. Now, you do not have to agree with your own thesis in order to write a great essay. If you know more information about the opposing viewpoint, then by all means, play the devil's advocate and write as if you believe the opposing side.

Here are a few possible theses for the above prompt:

1. Regulating speech on social media is an absolute must, but the government needs to stay out of it.
2. The government should never regulate speech on social media because of the terrible, long-lasting consequences for society.
3. Regulating speech on social media is a great idea, but impossible to implement with any kind of control.
4. The government's regulation of speech on social media would create a police state, one in which even more people than are currently affected by cyberbullying would be harmed.
5. There is no need to regulate speech on social media as the system works well as it stands.

Once you've condensed your thoughts into a provable thesis, you'll need to condense all the information you have into a quick outline, making sure to address the three perspectives given in a thoughtful, analytical way.

Our ideas are not naturally organized. We often think unrelated things like, "I wish my Math teacher was kidnapped by aliens. Why can't aliens ever kidnap anyone that annoys me? My left foot itches. Whatever happened to Dora the Explorer?," all at the same time.

We can't just start writing using a few notes about logical errors and a quick thesis and get a top-scoring essay. Nope! We need an organizational system to help us manage our info and write a stellar essay that doesn't veer off topic (off topic = reduced points). That's where the outline comes in.

I'll show you a couple of ways to outline, based on the type of essay you want or are able to write.

5-Paragraph Point-Point-Counterpoint (PPC) Outline

Organizing your thoughts into a PPC essay outline is all about placement. If you decide to go with this 5-paragraph structure to organize your essay, you'll need to take a look at your notes from your critique session and form your ideas into the following outline:

Introduction with Thesis

Body Paragraph 1: Point 1

- support 1 which proves point 1
- support 2 which proves point 1

Body Paragraph 2: Point 2

- support 1 which proves point 2
- support 2 which proves point 2

Body Paragraph 3: Counterpoint

- support 1 which attacks the counterpoint
- support 2 which attacks the counterpoint
- Better solution

Conclusion with restated thesis

Introduction with Thesis

You've already written your thesis, so this part is easy. Just write it at the top of your scratch paper. Don't worry about the entire introduction just yet. Trust me, we'll get there.

Points

Body paragraphs 1 and 2 are where you're going to argue that your thesis is correct, so these points should, without any doubt, prove it.

Supports

The supports listed under the body paragraphs are the evidence with which you prove your points. They're the facts, statistics (if you happen to know them), anecdotal evidence, logical arguments, and thorough reasoning that proves you are correct. Here is where you'll analyze the given perspectives, making sure to use them to further your arguments.

Counterpoint

The counterpoint is the statement that directly contradicts your thesis. This could be one of the ways you analyze one of the given perspectives if one of them directly contradicts your point. If so, you'll spend this paragraph shooting down the counterpoint and providing a better solution than what is offered.

Conclusion with Restated Thesis

The restated thesis is where you bring everything back together in the conclusion. You'll state your thesis in a new way, go back over your points and hammer down your incredible solution to the problem.

Here's the prompt again as a reminder:

Social Media and Free Speech

Among other cherished values, the First Amendment protects freedom of speech. People can exercise their freedom by choosing not to speak at all, by using offensive words and phrases to convey political messages, and even by burning the American flag. People value their protected right to say what they want without the threat of punishment from the government. Free speech is generally seen as a very good thing, but when it comes to social media, concerned citizens argue that the U.S. Supreme Court should regulate it. Although free speech does not include the right to incite actions that would harm others, like shouting "fire" in a crowded room or spreading libelous falsehoods, there are no regulations concerning cyberbullying on social media. Given the accelerating usage and prevalence of conversations on social media, it is worth examining the implications of free speech when it comes to this medium of expression.

Perspective One	Perspective Two	Perspective Three
The government regulating what citizens say on social media annihilates free speech and leads to the loss of even more freedoms. The government should not have the power to silence anyone for any reason, even if the speech causes harm.	Giving up a portion of your free speech creates safety for humanity. Is a citizen's right to belittle, disparage, and make fun of another person worth more than a person's right to life? Cyberbullying often leads to suicide and keeping people alive and happy is more important than someone's right to say terrible things.	Regulating speech on social media would only be a temporary fix for the problem of bullying. It's up to society to discourage bullying in every form.

If we decided to go with sample thesis 2, then a PPC outline based on this prompt could end up looking something like this:

Thesis: The government should never regulate speech on social media because of the terrible, long-lasting consequences for society.

Paragraph 1: It gives too much control to the government.

- The government would have to gain access to personal information
- Our First Amendment rights would slowly disintegrate (partial agreement with perspective 1)

Paragraph 2: Organization-led regulation has a way of imposing morality, which is a notion our country opposes.

- Differences in religion, creed, culture—who decides what's right/wrong?
- Separation of church and state.

Paragraph 3: Counterpoint: The consequences are too dire *not* to intervene.

- Statistically not enough of a trend to get government involved. (disagreement with perspective 2)
- Impossible to control by government with strict monitoring of everyone in a police state.
    - ▶ Another Option: Regulation needs to happen by family and friends. Concerned citizens. (agreement with perspective 3)

Restated thesis: Although legislators seem to have citizens in mind, regulating speech on social media can lead to disaster.

4-Paragraph Point-Counterpoint, Point-Counterpoint (PCPC) Outline

You may not be quite as familiar with this outline form. Here, you'll come up with arguments against your own ideas and dismiss them, which will make your point even stronger. You'll focus on elaborating two main points, while digging deep into your ideas. You'll also offer a better solution in the conclusion to leave your reader something to think about.

Here's how the PCPC outline looks:

Introduction with Thesis:

Paragraph 1:

- support 1 + elaboration
- support 2 + elaboration
- counterpoint and dismissal

Paragraph 2:

- support 1 + elaboration
- support 2 + elaboration
- counterpoint and dismissal

Conclusion with restated thesis and a better option

Let's have at it with the same thesis we used in the prior outline.

Thesis: The government should never regulate speech on social media because of the terrible, long-lasting consequences for society.

Paragraph 1: Social media regulation gives too much control to the government

- The government would have to gain access to personal information.
- Our First Amendment rights would slowly disintegrate. (partial agreement with perspective 1)
- **Counterpoint:** Current regulations on our speech have not led to further loss of First Amendment rights.
- **Dismissal:** We haven't yet broached the type of regulation this implies which would only be effective with infiltrative monitoring.

Paragraph 2: Organization-led regulation has a way of imposing morality, which is a notion our country opposes.

- Who gets to decide what is right?
- Vast cultural/moral/ethical differences, separation of church and state
- **Counterpoint:** Statistically destructive nature of social media bullying

- **Dismissal:** Not enough of a problem (disagreement with perspective 2) and it's overshadowed by the "good" that social media brings like connection, entertainment, and friendship—qualities everyone agrees are great.

Restated thesis: Although legislators seem to have citizens in mind, regulating speech on social media can lead to disaster.

A Better Option: Regulating social media is like putting a bandage on a gushing wound—only a surface fix. Concerned citizens should help monitor each other by calling out cyberbullying when they see it. (agreement with perspective 3)

Now, it's your turn. Choose a thesis related to the topic. You can choose one of the sample theses I've provided or approach the topic in your own way and come up with TWO outlines—one for the 5-paragraph PPC essay and one for the 4-paragraph PCPC essay. Be sure to incorporate the three perspectives into your outline or you will lose points on your essay!

Practice Outlining

5-Paragraph PPC Outline

Thesis

Paragraph 1: Point 1

- support 1
- support 2

Paragraph 2: Point 2

- support 1
- support 2

Paragraph 3: Counterpoint

- attack counterpoint
- attack counterpoint
- Better option

Restated thesis

4-Paragraph PCPC Outline

Thesis

Paragraph 1: Point 1

- support 1
- support 2
- **Counterpoint:**
- **Dismissal:**

Paragraph 2: Point 2

- support 1
- support 2
- **Counterpoint:**
- **Dismissal:**

Restated Thesis and A Better Option

How to Compose Your Essay

We've talked about prewriting and all the jazz that comes with it; now, it's time to cram all that information into a coherent, logical essay in about 23 minutes. If that doesn't set your knees to quivering, I'm not sure what will.

Look, the ACT test-makers *wanted* to create a test that would challenge you. What kind of college admissions exam would be easy enough so that everyone and his or her third cousin who's been living under a rock for the last 18 years could breeze through it? Not a very selective one, I can tell you that.

This test is designed to push your limits, so you'll be able to give those admissions officers something to consider when they're thinking about admitting you to their college or university.

And the ACT essay is the last step. Once you're finished writing and reviewing your masterpiece, you're all done. You can breeze out of the testing center confident that you've done the best you can do. So, let's get to work!

The Introduction

The introduction opens the gate into the essay, and needs to draw your reader in, stage the scenario, and illuminate your topic.

A poorly-written introduction is a great way to turn off your readers, which is never a great way to get points on the essay. We're going to want to keep our readers engaged, and we'll do this by making sure we write an awesome introduction.

STRATEGY ALERT

How to Write an Introduction

Climb from Base Camp to Pinnacle:
Have you ever read about those climbers who, during their attempts at conquering Mount Everest, slip to the edge of a crevasse and dangle for hours before plummeting to their bone-crushing deaths? Yes. That would not be a great way to die. So, let's not do that to our readers, okay? Our introductions are like giant mountains turned upside down, balancing precariously on their snow-covered peaks. You need to build a sensible path for our upside-down hikers to follow.

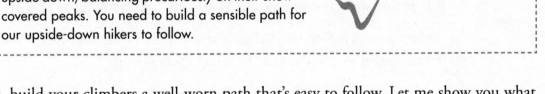

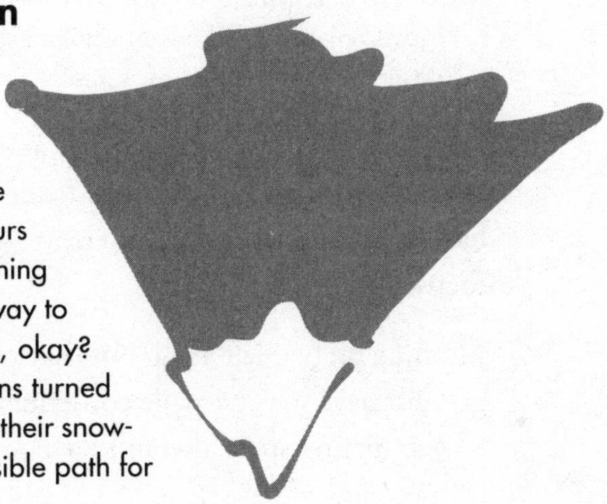

So, build your climbers a well-worn path that's easy to follow. Let me show you what this will look like:

Broad statement about topic with sensory details that sets
up topic for discussion. Slightly less broad statement
building on previous statement. A slightly
narrower statement that builds
toward thesis statement. An
even narrower state-
ment that leads
to thesis.
Thesis.

The reason we use an inverted triangle or upside-down mountain as a visual for the intro is because you'll start with a statement about a topic broader than what you're writing about. You'll move on to make little connections that lead you from the broad statement to your thesis. Here's what an intro for the prompt about the FCC regulating TV might look like:

Big idea = poor decisions lead to scars

When I was six, I was jumping on my bed and, as my mother had warned me again and again, toppled off and crashed face-first against my dresser. I screamed as blood dripped from a gash adjacent to my right eye. To this day, I still wear the scar. This white scar is a lasting effect from a poor decision, one I have to explain to inquisitive strangers. Typically, our foolish decisions aren't laid so bare for the entire world to see. We can hide a lie. We can ignore hurt feelings. But sometimes, those choices are very apparent, with societal-wide consequences. The regulation of speech on social media is just such an instance where a poor decision could potentially disfigure an entire generation. The government should never regulate speech on social media because of the terrible, long-lasting consequences for society.

I used the thesis we've been working with in our outline, and narrowed it down to hook my readers. Here's how I went from a big idea to a small one and took my readers from base camp (first sentence of essay—draws readers in) to pinnacle (thesis, very narrow, focused idea):

Jumping on bed left a scar → That was a poor decision → Other poor decisions are bigger and have societal-wide consequences → Regulating speech is one of those instances → Regulating speech would have terrible consequences and would scar/harm society.

These little arrows join the trail of ideas that will lead your happy climbers from the base of the mountain to the pinnacle. Don't let them down!

The Body

The body is the main part of your essay, where you'll spend the majority of your time filling in the blanks from your outline.

The body of the essay is where all the good stuff happens. You will elaborate on those ideas you developed in prewriting, use transitions to tie everything together, and make sure your language is fresh and clear.

Elaborating

To elaborate means to explain in a logical, precise, focused way. We created a pair of pretty awesome outlines, if I do say so myself, but to fill out the body of our essay, we need to take that outline and expand on it.

Here's a basic first paragraph someone might use in an ACT essay (who doesn't want a good score):

> To begin, the government should not regulate speech on social media because it gives the government too much control over people's lives. To monitor social media, the government would have to take access of very personal information like passwords and account numbers. The government has no business inside of people's personal lives. In addition, citizens' First Amendment rights, the rights to free speech, would slowly begin to disintegrate under such constant scrutiny. People would censor themselves out of fear, and that is just one of the terrible consequences our society cannot afford.

This is a paragraph many teenagers will write. It contains two supporting points to the topic sentence, with a sentence or two "elaborating" on each point. Although it's focused and logical, it says next to nothing and it doesn't bring up any of the perspectives. It only scratches the surface of the issue, and the ACT writers need you to dig much deeper than that for the higher scores.

Here's an elaborated paragraph in a PPC essay with the same topic sentence:

> Giving the government too much control over the lives of citizens is one of the insidious consequences of handing over the reins of social media regulation. Doesn't this elected entity already have enough control? The government regulates water. Light bulbs. It regulates the facts kids are taught and the food kids are fed in school. It even regulates citizens' bodies to a certain extent, but so far, it does not have too much control over the words that come out of people's mouths. That cannot change. In order to control speech on social media, people would be forced to forfeit privacy and passwords. They would give up the freedom of a first response. Not only would they regulate citizens, but citizens would also regulate themselves out of fear. The First Amendment right to free speech would disintegrate under such scrutiny because the notion that "big brother is watching" would scare people into self-censorship, eradicating free thought. They would end up thinking what the government wanted them to think and, even more dangerously, believing the lies they told themselves.

See the difference? With the first paragraph, one typically found in a standard essay, the ideas aren't investigated as closely. The points aren't connected or elaborated upon. The second paragraph says the same thing, but it touches on so much more: fear, censorship, governmental control over every aspect of people's lives. It makes logical points—ones you'd make to your friends if you were arguing the idea—and stays focused, never veering too far off topic.

Using Transitions

To get from one paragraph to the next, and to join ideas within the paragraphs, you'll have to pull out some transitions to cue the reader that you're switching your thought process.

The first paragraph above uses some very basic transitions. "To begin" and "in addition" are just fine if you want an average score. If you want a better score, I'd use some of the following transitions in your essay:

To show agreement, addition, or similarity	To show opposition, limitation, or contradiction	To show examples, support, or emphasis
As a matter of fact,	In contrast,	To clarify,
Coupled with	Although this may be true,	To repeat,
Correspondingly,	Nevertheless,	In other words,
Additionally,	Conversely,	For this reason,
Even more,	On the contrary,	Chiefly,
Not only...but also	In spite of,	Namely,
In the first place,	Despite,	To be sure,
Equally,	Be that as it may,	Important to realize,
Identically,	Regardless,	Another key point,
Not to mention,	Otherwise,	With this in mind,

But for heaven's sake, mix it up already. Don't start every new paragraph with a transition. That gets repetitive and boring. When you write your practice essays, try out new ways of putting transitions together to see which ones fit you the best.

Fresh Language

Gosh, nothing is worse than reading boring material, right? I know you know what I mean. Textbooks of the past (and some in the present) used the more stagnant language possible because the writers wanted to sound smart.

Here's a newsflash: you can use smart language while still keeping your readers awake.

Regular sentence: The bird flew out of the cage and headed for the hills.

Smart (but boring) sentence: The *Grus japonensis* took flight from its abode and set course toward the distant hills.

Smart (but interesting) sentence: The red-crowned crane burst from her cage and with wings pumping madly, zigzagged south toward those low-lying hills—toward freedom.

Your essay should be exciting, even if the topic you've received is not. Let your language grab your readers and shake them around in their seats. You want them to *feel* something so they feel led to give you a top score!

Let's use a strategy to figure out how to do this:

STRATEGY ALERT

How to Use Fresh Language:

Check the Three S's: **S**ensory words, **S**pecific words, and **S**entence patterns. In every paragraph you need to offer your reader a feast for the eyes. Things like ***sensory*** images (smell, taste, touch, sight, sound), ***specific*** versus boring words (azure vs. blue, skintight acid-washed leggings vs. pants) and varied ***sentence*** patterns keep your writing as fresh as a crisp apple on a red-checked table cloth.

Sensory Words

When you are trying to describe something in your essay, it makes sense (get it!) to use sensory words to convey meaning. You can tell your ACT grader that you think metal detectors should be banned from schools, but it would be more convincing to describe how your cheeks flamed red hot when you were roughly tugged out of the line to get into school while your bag was snatched away and searched. You can convey nuances of meaning with sensory words that are lost when you use a "normal" sentence.

Here are some sensory examples:

- **Smell:**
  - **Normal sentence:** The trash can smelled awful to Rose.
  - **Sensory sentence:** The nauseating blast of decaying food from the trash bin hit Rose full in the face as she opened the garage door.

- ▶ **Normal sentence:** The old woman felt afraid when she smelled the nursing home.
- ▶ **Sensory sentence:** Walking into the nursing home, the *powerful stench of carnations and cooked cabbage* made the old woman clutch her guts as if to prevent them from spilling out.

- **Sound:**
  - ▶ **Normal sentence:** The house was old.
  - ▶ **Sensory sentence:** The floor, crafted of old pine worn smooth from years of use, *creaked and groaned as the house settled with a sigh* for the evening.
  - ▶ **Normal sentence:** He kicked the bottle into the alley.
  - ▶ **Sensory sentence:** He kicked the glass bottle sending it *pinging* across the cobblestones until it skittered against a dumpster and *clanked* stridently to a stop.

Specific Words

Always try to use precise language, so your meaning isn't skewed when you write. Choose the exact word you want versus a more general term. The clearer your meaning is, the more your readers will understand what you're trying to say, and as always, if they *get* you, you'll be rewarded.

General Words = Just Okay	Specific Words = Better
a doctor	a pediatrician, an obstetrician, a podiatrist
college	U of M, Yale, Hillsborough Community College
girl	the 13-year-old brat wearing her big sister's elastic hair band
happy	ecstatic, enthralled, content, exuberant, pleased
talk	scream, miscommunicate, mumble, whisper, chit-chat

Varied Sentence Patterns

You know when you're reading sentences that sound shockingly alike. You read them in many children's stories: Dick and Jane went to the store. Dick and Jane bought toothpaste. Dick and Jane's car broke down on the way home and they unwittingly thumbed a ride from a drug lord. You don't want your essay to read like Humpty Dumpty. So, vary your sentence patterns so your essay is smoother and more interesting.

Typical sentence: "The most shocking news of the day was that Elvira bought a test prep book and threw it away."

Possible rewrites to vary sentence pattern:

- After purchasing a test prep book, Elvira shockingly threw it away.
- Shockingly, Elvira purchased a test prep book then threw it away.
- To everyone's shock, Elvira threw away a test prep book she had just bought.
- Elvira, to everyone's shock, purchased a test prep book then threw it away!
- In a shocking move after a recent test prep book purchase, Elvira threw it away.

HEADS UP

Don't just vary your sentence structure; vary the length of the sentences, too. If you traditionally write 7- to 10-word sentences, try adding some shorter intentional fragments to spice things up a bit. They're totally legal as long as they're intended! Trust me, though, the graders will know the difference.

See? You can change up your sentence structure to make your paragraphs more interesting.

Practice Your Vivid Language

Rewrite these boring sentences so they're as fresh and sparkly as a raindrop!

Make these sentences fresh with sensory words:

1. Jack helped himself to his grandmother's cake.

2. The judge concluded the trial and dismissed the accused.

3. Unbelievably, the hawk swallowed the lizard in one bite!

Make these sentences fresh with specific words:

1. That man over there just asked for my number.

2. Standing on top of the hill, Elliot started singing.

3. When Jenica came back from the store, she realized she'd purchased shampoo instead of socks.

Make these sentences fresh with varied sentence patterns:

1. Lyle Armweak won the Tour de France and then fired his mechanic in a fit of winner's machismo.

2. Astrid read her horoscope every day and when it told her she'd be meeting a tall, dark stranger she never assumed it would be a grizzly bear.

3. If you never try to do anything, you'll never fail at anything, but you'll never succeed at anything, either.

The Conclusion

The Conclusion is your last chance to make a good impression. In it, you'll restate your thesis in broad terms and leave the readers something to think about, present another option, offer a bigger picture or give further implications.

You know how some girls spend tons of time on the front of their hair (flat ironing or creating perfect waves), but forget to check out the rest so they look beauty-pageant when they face you and freak show when they walk away? Yes. That's a bit like writing a great essay and ignoring the conclusion. *You* may not be able to tell that it's a train wreck, but it'll be obvious to everyone else.

The conclusion is your chance to pull out all the persuasive stops. To help you remember what to toss in there, let's use a strategy.

STRATEGY ALERT

How to Write a Conclusion for the ACT Essay

Tie, Restate, Sum, and Offer: These four little words are your ticket to big points in the concluding paragraph. **Tie** the first sentence of the conclusion to the first few sentences of your intro. **Restate** your thesis in a brand new way. **Sum** up your strongest points. And **offer** a better option or something for the reader to think about.

Here's an example of a conclusion written using the 5-paragraph PPC Outline on page 267:

> I never realized when I was a kid how much my bad decisions could affect the rest of my life. Believe me, I wouldn't have been jumping on my bed[1] if I'd realized that years later I'd be describing the injury to store clerks in Target. Just as I didn't realize the long-term implications of short-term mistakes, many people don't recognize the extent of their poor decisions, either. Although legislators seem to have citizens in mind, regulating speech on social media because of cyberbullying can lead to disaster.[2] Essentially, we would be giving the government too much control over our lives[3]—a forfeit that could cost us our ability to think for ourselves. Furthermore, supporting forced values[4] in a country that fights against such separation of the ideological and theological would create irreparable controversy. Citizens of this country can band together and stop cyberbullying in its tracks.[5] Regulating social media is like taking medicine for a cold; it's much better to prevent it in the first place by washing your hands. Self-regulation is better and lasts longer than forced regulation, so the people who support this type of censorship should find a better cause around which to rally.

1. **Tie:** I tied the conclusion to the introduction by referring back to the jumping on the bed incident.
2. **Restate:** I restated the thesis just as I'd planned in my outline.
3. **Sum:** I summed up the first body paragraph by paraphrasing my topic sentence.
4. **Sum:** I summed up the second body paragraph by paraphrasing my topic sentence.
5. **Offer:** I offered the reader a better alternative.

This conclusion fits perfectly with our strategy.

Now, I'm going to show you how it all fits together. Here is an example of an essay based on the prompt we've been talking about.

Note—there are intentional errors in this essay because we will be editing it later. In the meantime, see if you can spot them!

Sample 5-Paragraph PPC Essay

When I was six, I was jumping on my bed and, as my mother had warned me again and again, toppled off and crashed face-first against my dresser. I screamed as blood dripped from a gash next to my right eye. To this day, I still have the scar. This white scar is a lasting effect from a poor decision, one I have to explain to inquisitive strangers. Typically, our foolish decisions aren't laid so bare for the entire world to see, because we can hide a lie or can ignore hurt feelings. But sometimes, those choices are very apparent, with societal-wide consequences. The regulation of speech on social media is just such an instance where a poor decision could potentially disfigure an entire generation. The government should never regulate speech on social media because of the terrible, long-lasting consequences for society.

Giving the government too much control over the lives of citizens is one of the terrible consequences of handing over the reins of social media regulation. Doesn't this elected entity already have enough control? The government regulates water. Light bulbs. It regulates the facts kids are taught and the food kids are fed in school. It even regulates citizens' bodies to a certain extent, but so far, it does not have too much control over the words that come out of our mouths. That cannot change. In order to control speech on social media, people would be forced to forfeit privacy and passwords. They would give up the freedom of a first response. Not only would they regulate citizens, but citizens would also regulate themselves out of fear. The First Amendment right to free speech would disintegrate under such scrutiny because the notion that "big brother is watching" would scare people into self-censorship, eradicating free thought. They would end up thinking what the government wanted them to think and, even more dangerously, believing the lies they told themselves.

Second, anyone supporting social media regulation didn't pause to consider the enormous consequences when choosing sides in a moral debate, one that would start if social media standards were up for grabs. Who gets to decide what sort of speech is right? What is moral? There are a number of basic things the country can generally agree upon as "good" and we already have laws to protect those things: personal freedom, the right to life, and the right to innocence to name a few. But as to what constitutes good speech? That is another story. Some people would want to prevent any speech promoting homosexuality. Others would want to censor speech about The Bible. There is a separation of church and state for a reason. Personal values related to speech for one person are different from those of another; people from all religious, moral and ethical creeds have been fighting for thousands of years about this very fact. Organizational-led regulation would force morality because someone would have to choose which words and phrases were acceptable and which were not; as such, the entire country should balk against a system that would inflict this kind of moral judgment.

Advocates for social media censorship state that the effects of cyberbullying like suicide and teen depression are just too dire not to get involved. However, statistically, when compared to the vast majority of the population, the instances and affects of cyberbullying are relatively low when you think about the amount of surveillance that would be required by thorough social media regulation. This kind of censorship would turn our country into a police state. Phones, computers, tablets and other devices would have to be monitored every second of the day. The amount of time and money this would take would be enormous. Instead, community leaders should join forces to create anti-bullying campaigns to spread the dangers. People can call out cyberbullies on social media and support those who have been hurt. The amount of negativity on social media can be regulated; it just shouldn't be the government doing it.

I never realized when I was a kid how much my bad decisions could affect the rest of my life. Believe me, I wouldn't have been jumping on my bed if I'd realized that years later I'd be describing the injury to store clerks in Target. Just as I didn't realize the long-term implications of short-term mistakes, many people don't recognize the extent of their poor decisions, either. Although legislators seem to have citizens in mind, regulating speech on social media because of cyberbullying can lead to disaster. Essentially, we would be giving the government too much control over our live—a forfeit that could cost us our ability to think for ourselves. Furthermore, supporting forced values in a country that fights against separation of the ideological and theological would create irreparable controversy. Citizens of this country can band together and stop cyberbullying in its tracks. Regulating social media is like taking medicine for a cold; it's much better to prevent it in the first place by washing your hands. Self-regulation is better and lasts longer than forced regulation, so the people who support this type of censorship should find a better cause around which to rally.

Practice Writing Your Essay

Okay guys and girls! Feeling inspired? Let's hope so. It's your turn to put it all together. Get out some paper and set a timer for 23 minutes. Then, using your outlines, write until your little hand breaks. Once the time is up, set your pencil down and go get a snack or something. You've earned it.

Good luck!

How to Correct Your Essay

You made it! You wrote the essay and you're just a few short days shy of finishing this book and taking the test. Jackpot!

Before you get light-headed from your extreme good fortune of completing this stuff, let's get this last part of essay-writing under our belts, shall we? This could be the step that makes or breaks you. Reviewing what you've written is a complete necessity. You wouldn't head out to the movie with the best looking person in school without giving yourself a once-over on the way out the door, would you? Gosh, I hope not. You ate spinach for dinner and a big chunk of green is stuck between your two front teeth.

So, let's go searching for stray bits of chewed-up food particles in our essay. We don't want to keep your date waiting.

Essay Rubric

So, I've given you pointers for getting your topics out of your head and onto paper. Now, let's see what you've learned! Here's the score you can expect based on the ACT essay rubric, a quick, easy way of showing you exactly what each score requires.

	Ideas and Analysis	Development and Support	Organization	Language Use
Score 6: Effective skill in writing an argumentative essay	Critically analyzes the issue and three perspectives in an insightful context Thesis is precise and shows shades of meaning in thought and purpose. Insightfully discusses the issue by naming causes and effects, discussing values, critiquing assumptions, and detailing complexities and tensions.	Development of ideas and support for claims deepen understanding and apply to concepts outside of the issue. Reasoning and usage of examples are skillful and demonstrate the importance of the argument. The limits and complications improve the argument and take it further.	Response is skillfully organized. Response has a strong thesis that is supported throughout. Ideas progress logically and increase the argument's success. Transitions between and within paragraphs strengthen the relationships among ideas.	The use of language enhances the argument. Word choice is skillful and precise. Sentence structures are consistently varied and clear. Stylistic and register choices, including voice and tone, are strategic and effective. While a few minor errors in grammar, usage, and mechanics may be present, they do not disrupt understanding.

	Ideas and Analysis	Development and Support	Organization	Language Use
Score 5: Well-developed skill in writing an argumentative essay	Productively analyzes the issue and three perspectives in a thoughtful context. Thesis is precise in thought and purpose. Thoughtfully discusses the issue by naming causes and effects, discussing values, critiquing assumptions, and detailing complexities and tensions.	Development of ideas and support for claims deepen understanding. Reasoning and usage of examples are mostly skillful and demonstrate the importance of the argument. The limits and complications improve the argument.	Response is productively organized. Response has a strong thesis that is mostly supported throughout. Ideas progress logically and contribute to the argument's success. Transitions between and within paragraphs consistently clarify the relationships among ideas.	The use of language services the argument. Word choice is precise. Sentence structures are clear and varied often. Stylistic and register choices, including voice and tone, are purposeful and productive. While minor errors in grammar, usage, and mechanics may be present, they do not disrupt understanding.
Score 4: Adequate skill in writing an argumentative essay	Discusses the issue and three perspectives in a relevant context. Thesis is clear in thought and purpose. Recognizes causes and effects, values, assumptions, and complexities and tensions.	Development of ideas and support for claims clarify meaning and purpose. Reasoning and usage of examples are clear and adequately demonstrate the importance of the argument. The limits and complications extend the argument.	Response is clearly organized. Response has an emerging thesis or controlling idea that is mostly supported throughout. Ideas are logically grouped and sequenced. Transitions between and within paragraphs clarify the relationships among ideas.	The use of language conveys the argument clearly. Word choice is adequate and somewhat precise. Sentence structures are clear and demonstrate some variety. Stylistic and register choices, including voice and tone, are appropriate for the purpose. While errors in grammar, usage, and mechanics are present, they rarely disrupt understanding.

(continued)

	Ideas and Analysis	Development and Support	Organization	Language Use
Score 3: Some developing skill in writing an argumentative essay	Generates an argument that responds to the three perspectives on the issue in a limited context. Thesis is somewhat clear in thought and purpose. Analysis is simplistic or somewhat unclear.	Development of ideas and support for claims are mostly relevant, but are overly general or simplistic. Reasoning and examples largely clarify the argument, but may be somewhat repetitive or imprecise.	Response is basically organized. Most ideas are logically grouped. Transitions between and within paragraphs sometimes clarify the relationships among ideas.	The use of language is basic and somewhat clear. Word choice is general and occasionally imprecise. Sentence structures are usually clear, but show little variety. Stylistic and register choices, including voice and tone, are not always appropriate for the purpose. Distracting errors in grammar, usage, and mechanics may be present, but they generally do not disrupt understanding.
Score 2: Weak or inconsistent skill in writing an argumentative essay	Generates an argument that weakly responds to the three perspectives. The thesis, if present, demonstrates little clarity in thought or purpose. Attempts at analysis are incomplete or are primarily restatements of the issue or perspectives.	Development of ideas and support for claims are weak, confused, or disjointed. Reasoning and illustration are inadequate, illogical, circular and fail to clarify the argument.	Response is organized in a very basic way. Grouping of ideas is inconsistent and often unclear. Transitions between and within paragraphs are misleading or poor.	The use of language is inconsistent and often unclear. Word choice is very basic and frequently imprecise. Sentence structures are sometimes unclear. Stylistic and register choices, including voice and tone, are inconsistent and not always appropriate for the purpose. Distracting errors in grammar, usage, and mechanics are present, and they sometimes disrupt understanding.
Score 1: Little or no skill in writing an argumentative essay	Fails to generate an argument that responds to the task. Intentions are difficult to interpret. Attempts at analysis are unclear or irrelevant.	Ideas lack development and claims lack support. Reasoning and illustration are unclear, incoherent, or mostly absent.	No organizational structure. Little grouping of ideas. When present, transitions fail to connect ideas.	Fails to demonstrate skill in responding to the task. Word choice is imprecise and often difficult to understand. Sentence structures are often unclear. Stylistic and register choices are difficult to identify. Errors in grammar, usage, and mechanics are often present and disrupt understanding.

Correcting Your Essay

Reviewing your essay takes just a few minutes and can get you a few extra positive marks.

The rubric lets you know how you'll be scored, but you won't be able to go back through your essay and change everything. So, let's get a strategy under our belts so we know what to fix when we're all done writing.

STRATEGY ALERT

How to Correct Your ACT Essay

Go WEST, Young Man: Strap on your cowboy boots, and hit the trail. We're headin' into the sunset of your essay, and you're gonna wanna finish in time for chow. You will not have time to change anything besides WEST (**W**ord choice, **E**rrors, **S**entences, and **T**ransitions) when you're reviewing. Logic, thesis, organization, and development have to stay exactly as they are, which is why we lassoed our ideas and slung them into an outline before we ever wrote anything. So, saddle up them horses, guys and gals. We'll giddyup into my essay from yesterday to see what kind of varmints we can pull outta there.

When I was six, I was jumping on my bed and, as my mother had warned me again and again, toppled off and crashed face-first against my dresser. I screamed as blood dripped from a gash next to my right eye. To this day, I still have the scar. This white scar is a lasting effect from a bad decision, one I have to explain to inquisitive strangers. Typically, our foolish decisions aren't laid so bare for the entire world to see, because we can hide a lie or can ignore hurt feelings. But sometimes, those choices are very apparent, with societal-wide consequences. The regulation of speech on social media is just such an instance where a poor decision could potentially disfigure an entire generation. The government should never regulate speech on social media because of the terrible, long-lasting consequences for society.

Giving the government too much control over the lives of citizens is one of the terrible consequences of handing over the reins of social media regulation. Doesn't this elected entity already have enough control? The government regulates water. Light bulbs. It regulates the facts kids are taught and the food kids are fed in school. It even regulates citizens' bodies to a certain extent, but so far, it does not have too much control over the words that come out of our mouths. That cannot change. In order to control speech on social media, people would be forced to forfeit privacy and passwords. They would give up the freedom of a first response. Not only would they regulate citizens, but citizens would also regulate themselves out of fear. The First Amendment right to free speech would disintegrate under such scrutiny because the notion that "big brother is watching" would scare people into self-censorship, eradicating free thought. They would end up thinking what the government wanted them to think and, even more dangerously, believing the lies they told themselves.

Second, anyone supporting social media regulation didn't pause to consider the enormous consequences when choosing sides in a moral debate, one that would start if social media standards were up for grabs. Who gets to decide what sort of speech is right? What is moral? There are a number of basic things the country can generally agree upon as "good" and we already have laws to protect those things: personal freedom, the right to life, and the right to innocence to name a few. But as to what constitutes good speech? That is another story. Some people would want to prevent any speech promoting homosexuality. Others would want to censor speech about The Bible. There is a separation of church and state for a reason. Personal values related to speech for one person are different from those of another; people from all religious, moral and ethical creeds have been fighting for thousands of years about this very fact. Organizational-led regulation would force morality because someone would have to choose which words and phrases were acceptable and which were not; as such, the entire country should balk against a system that would inflict this kind of moral judgment.

Advocates for social media censorship state that the effects of cyberbullying like suicide and teen depression are just too dire not to get involved. However, statistically, when compared to the vast majority of the population, the instances and affects of cyberbullying are relatively low when you think about the amount of surveillance that would be required by thorough social media regulation. This kind of censorship would turn our country into a police state. Phones, computers, tablets and other devices would have to be monitored every second of the day. The amount of time and money this would take would be enormous. Instead, community leaders should join forces to create anti-bullying campaigns to spread the dangers. People can call out cyberbullies on social media and support those who have been hurt. The amount of negativity on social media can be regulated; it just shouldn't be the government doing it.

I never realized when I was a kid how much my bad decisions could affect the rest of my life. Believe me, I wouldn't have been jumping on my bed if I'd realized that years later I'd be describing the injury to store clerks in Target. Just as I didn't realize the long-term implications of short-term mistakes, many people don't recognize the extent of their poor decisions, either. Although legislators seem to have citizens in mind, regulating speech on social media because of cyberbullying can lead to disaster. First, we would be giving the government too much control over our lives— a forfeit that could cost us our ability to think for ourselves. Also, supporting forced values in a country that fights against separation of the ideological and theological would create irreparable controversy. Citizens of this country can band together and stop cyberbullying in its

> tracks. Regulating social media is like treating a cold; it's much better to prevent it in the first place by washing your hands. Self-regulation is better and lasts longer than forced regulation, so the people who support this type of censorship should find a better cause to rally around.

Let's go ahead and dive into the essay above, checking for the WEST. I see a ton of changes we could easily and quickly make that would improve the essay immensely! To help you out, I've underlined a few words and phrases throughout the essay that we can change to make it better. While you're reading, go ahead and underline anything else you think you could improve.

- **Introduction:**
    - **Word Choice:** Change "next" to "adjacent"
    - **Word Choice:** Change "have" to "wear"
    - **Word Choice:** Change "bad" to "poor"
    - **Sentence Variety:** Change "Typically, our poor decisions aren't laid so bare for the entire world to see, because we can hide a lie and ignore hurt feelings." to "Typically, our poor decisions aren't laid so bare for the entire world to see. We can hide a lie. We can ignore hurt feelings."
- **First Body Paragraph**
    - **Word Choice:** Change "terrible" to "insidious"
    - **Errors:** Change "our mouths" to "people's mouths"
- **Second Body Paragraph**
    - **Transition:** Replace "Second" with "Of even graver importance,"
    - **Word Choice:** Change "start" to "ensue"
    - **Word Choice:** Change "good" to "appropriate"
    - **Word Choice:** Change "prevent" to "eradicate"
- **Third Body Paragraph**
    - **Errors:** Replace "affects" with "effects"
    - **Word Choice:** Change "you think about" to "pitted against"
    - **Errors:** Delete this sentence as it is irrelevant to the argument: "The amount of time and money this would take would be enormous."

- **Conclusion**
  - ▶ **Transitions:** Replace “First” with “Initially”
  - ▶ **Transitions:** Change “Also” to “Furthermore”
  - ▶ **Errors:** Change “cause to rally around” to “cause around which to rally.”

Now, it’s your turn! Following the Go WEST strategy, take a look at the essay that you wrote and review it. Look for obvious and less obvious ways you can improve it.

Writing Strategy Cheat Sheet

General Strategies

- **Pace Yourself.**
- **Avoid Chicken Scratch.**
- **If it Ain't Broke . . . Don't Fix It.**
- **Use Your Life Experiences.**

ACT Writing Strategy

- **Use the 4 C's**
  1. **C**ritique the issue and three perspectives.
  2. **C**ondense your ideas into a thesis and outline.
  3. **C**ompose your essay with clear, fresh, effective language.
  4. **C**orrect your essay.

Writing Strategies

- Climb from **Base Camp** to **Pinnacle for Writing the Introduction**.
- **Check the 3 S's** for using fresh, effective language.
- **Tie, Restate, Sum,** and **Offer** for writing the conclusion.

Reviewing Strategy

- **Go WEST, Young Man** to review your essay.

Take the Writing Practice Test

Go to the REA Study Center

(www.rea.com/studycenter)

Now that you have completed this week's work, go to *www.rea.com/studycenter* and take the Writing Practice Test. This test is just like the Writing section of the actual ACT, with the added benefits of:

- **Timed testing conditions** – Gauge your time when writing your essay.
- **On-screen detailed sample response** – Guides you to an accurate essay score.

ACT Practice Test

Also available at the REA Study Center *(www.rea.com/studycenter)*

This practice exam is available at the online REA Study Center. We recommend that you take the online version of the practice exam for the added benefits of:

- Instant scoring
- Enforced time conditions
- Detailed score report of your strengths and weaknesses

Practice Test
English

TIME: 45 minutes
75 questions

DIRECTIONS: In the five passages that follow, certain words and phrases are underlined and numbered. In the right-hand column, you will find alternatives for the underlined part. In most cases, you are to choose the one that best expresses the idea, makes the statement appropriate for standard written English, or is worded most consistently with the style and tone of the passage as a whole. If you think the original version is best, choose "NO CHANGE." In some cases, you will find in the right-hand column a question about the underlined part. You are to choose the best answer to the question. You will also find questions about a section of the passage, or about the passage as a whole. These questions do not refer to an underlined portion of the passage, but rather are identified by a number or numbers in a box.

For each question, choose the alternative you consider best and fill in the corresponding oval on your answer document. Read each passage through once before you begin to answer the questions that accompany it. For many of the questions, you must read several sentences beyond the question to determine the answer. Be sure that you have read far enough ahead each time you choose an alternative.

Passage I

The following paragraphs may or may not be in the most logical order. Each paragraph is numbered in brackets, and question 15 will ask you to choose where Paragraph 3 should most logically be placed.

Vincent van Gogh: Mad, Genius, or Both?

[1]

It has been exactly 100 years since artist Vincent van Gogh <u>almost</u> (1) propped his easel against a haystack near the Chateau d'Auvers in France and fired a bullet into his chest. Doctors were summoned and the artist's younger

1. The best placement for the underlined word would be:
   A. where it is now.
   B. after the word *been.*
   C. after the word *exactly.*
   D. after the word *years.*

brother, Theo, rushed[2] by train from Paris as soon as he heard the news: that Vincent had tried to kill himself.[3] [4]

2.
F. NO CHANGE
G. brother, Theo rushed
H. brother Theo, rushed
J. brother Theo rushed

3.
A. NO CHANGE
B. news; that Vincent had tried to kill himself.
C. news: Vincent had tried to kill himself.
D. news, Vincent had tried to kill himself.

4. Upon reviewing paragraph 1 and determining that some information has been left out, the writer composes the following sentence:

> "He managed to crawl back to the house of a family named Ravoux, with whom he was living."

Where should it be placed?
F. It should be left out of the paragraph
G. Before sentence 1
H. Before sentence 2
J. After sentence 2

[2]

Like van Gogh's artistic works, many questions remain to this day.[5] Was Vincent addicted to absinthe? Did he really chase Paul Gauguin with a razor, or was that a story embroidered

5. Which sentence states the information most clearly?
A. NO CHANGE
B. Many questions are remaining to this day like van Gogh's artistic works.
C. Many questions, like van Gogh's artistic works, have been remaining to this day.
D. Like van Gogh's artistic works remaining to this day, many questions do, too.

by Gauguin to justify leaving van Gogh, completely abandoning him, [6] in Arles? Did Theo die—six months after his brother, at the age of 22 in an asylum near Utrecht—from grief over Vincent's suicide? Was the artist epileptic or manic depressive or did he suffer [7] from an inner-ear disorder, as a recent article in the *Journal of the American Medical Association* suggests, that finally drove him in the winter of 1888 to lop off part of his left ear in a desperate attempt to alleviate the pain?

[3]

[8] "I wish I could pass away like this," Vincent said as he lay beside his brother, shortly before dying in the early morning of July 29, 1890, who left behind hundreds of paintings and drawings no one wanted. Theo had tried for years to sell them in the hope of recouping a fraction of the money he had shelled out to support his hapless brother

6. Which choice offers the most precise information?
- **F.** NO CHANGE
- **G.** with abandonment,
- **H.** abandoning him,
- **J.** OMIT the underlined portion and remove the comma after van Gogh

7.
- **A.** NO CHANGE
- **B.** Was the artist epileptic, manic depressive, and did he suffer
- **C.** Was the artist epileptic or manic depressive or suffering
- **D.** Was the artist epileptic or was he manic depressive or did he suffer

8. Which choice offers the clearest, most precise information?
- **F.** NO CHANGE
- **G.** Shortly before dying in the early morning of July 29, 1890, Vincent said, "I wish I could pass away like this," as he lay beside his brother, leaving behind hundreds of paintings and drawings no one wanted.
- **H.** Leaving behind hundreds of paintings and drawings no one wanted, Vincent said, "I wish I could pass away like this," as he lay beside his brother, who died in the early morning of July 29, 1890.
- **J.** "I wish I could pass away like this," Vincent said shortly before dying in the early morning of July 29, 1890, as he lay beside his brother, who left behind hundreds of paintings and drawings no one wanted.

over the course of more than a decade. He had no luck, neither did the Paris dealer, Julien François (Pere) Tanguy, who had agreed to keep some of Vincent's paintings in the attic of his shop.

[4]

As an earlier generation of van Gogh biographers wove such fanciful tales of the pathetic starving painter driven to drink and lunacy that the latest crop of historians and writers have found it necessary to undo at least in part the myth that has obscured the man.

9. The writer is considering deleting the underlined phrase. Should it be kept or deleted?

A. It should be kept because it adds relevant details that demonstrate how long Theo had been supporting Vincent.

B. It should be kept because it adds relevant details that support how Vincent was mistreated throughout his short life.

C. It should be deleted because the phrase adds misleading data to the paragraph.

D. It should be deleted because it provides nearly identical information to details in the beginning of the sentence.

10.

F. NO CHANGE

G. no luck, and neither did the Paris dealer,

H. no luck: neither did the Paris dealer,

J. no luck; and neither did the Paris dealer,

11.

A. NO CHANGE

B. Despite an earlier generation of van Gogh biographers

C. While an earlier generation of van Gogh biographers

D. An earlier generation of van Gogh biographers

12.

F. NO CHANGE

G. crops of historians and writers have had

H. crop of historians and writers has

J. crop, of historians and writers, has

As David Sweetman, author of the engaging new "Van Gogh: His Life and His Art," says of the old biographies: [13] "The one significant conclusion that can be reached from them is that whatever he was suffering from cannot be determined by his art the image of Vincent as an isolated Holy Fool, artist-sage, deranged or

13.

A. NO CHANGE

B. "The one significant conclusion that can be reached from them is that whatever he was suffering from cannot be directly 'read' into his art; the image of Vincent as an isolated Holy Fool, artist-sage or whatever, has finally been exposed as the nonsense it always was . . ."

C. "The one significant conclusion that can be reached from them is that whatever he was suffering from cannot be directly 'read' into his art; as the image of Vincent as an isolated Holy Fool, artist-sage or whatever, has finally been exposed as the nonsense it always was . . ."

D. "The one significant conclusion that can be reached from them is that whatever he was suffering from cannot be directly 'read' into his art, the image of Vincent as an isolated Holy Fool, artist-sage or whatever, has finally been exposed as the nonsense it always was . . ."

whatever, has finally been exposed as the nonsense it always was . . . " [14]

Michael Kimmerlman, "Vincent Obsessed," from The New York Times Book Review, August 12, 1990, New York: copyright 1990, pp. 1, 22, 23.

14. The writer wants to add a sentence to the end of the essay that will tie the conclusion to the introduction. Which choice does that LEAST effectively?

F. Regardless of Vincent van Gogh's suicide and the controversy that followed it in France, his work as an artist, regarded as much less than it actually was in his day, will always be remembered for the true excellence it demonstrated.

G. Despite Vincent van Gogh's suicide and his obvious personal afflictions in which biographers may never fully be educated, his legacy as a masterful artist unappreciated in his time will remain untouched for untold millennia.

H. Vincent van Gogh's physiological and emotional impairments, no matter what they are called, did nothing to take away from the genius of his artistry despite his early death; his masterful works should and will be celebrated for generations to come.

J. Biographers and historians may never fully have a grasp on the impairments leading to Vincent Van Gogh's death, but they cannot and will not take away from the artist that he was and the enjoyment future generations will have by studying this master painter.

> Question 15 asks about the preceding passage as a whole. (Starts on page 293.)

15. For the sake of logic and coherence, paragraph 3 should be placed:

A. where it is.

B. before paragraph 1.

C. after paragraph 1.

D. after paragraph 4.

Passage II

Getting Educated

"Have a seat, Marguerite. Over there by the table."

She carried a platter and a tea towel embroidered with a design based after a rose garden in spring[16]. I was sure that like everything else about her, the cookies would be for certain be perfect, although she warned that she hadn't tried her hand at baking sweets for some time. [17]

16.
- **F.** NO CHANGE
- **G.** based on the look of a rose garden in spring
- **H.** based upon a rose garden in spring
- **J.** based on a rose garden in spring

17. Which of the following sentences is the most logically organized?
- **A.** NO CHANGE
- **B.** Although she warned that she hadn't tried her hand at baking sweets for some time, I knew the cookies would be perfect for certain, just like everything else about her was perfect.
- **C.** Despite the fact that she warned that she hadn't tried her hand at baking sweets for some time, I knew that like everything else about this woman, the cookies for certain would be perfect like her.
- **D.** Although she warned that she hadn't tried her hand at baking sweets for some time, I was certain that like everything else about her, the cookies would be perfect.

[18] She talked; I listened. She said that I must always be intolerant of ignorance but understanding of <u>illiteracy; that</u>[19] some people, unable to go to school, were more educated and even more intelligent than college professors. She encouraged me to listen carefully to what country people called mother wit. [20] That in those homely sayings was couched the collective wisdom of generations. She told me to raise my future children in the nurture

18. The writer is considering adding the following sentence at this point in the paragraph:

> As I ate, she began the first of what we later called my "lessons in living."

Should it be added?

- **F.** No, because the sentence adds misleading information that could be misconstrued.
- **G.** No, because the current first sentence already explains what is about to occur in the paragraph succinctly, and since it doesn't add any new information, it would be redundant.
- **H.** Yes, provided the current first sentence is removed because the new sentence provides a clear introduction to the paragraph and hints at the further relationship of the women better than the current first sentence.
- **J.** Yes, because the paragraph needs it to maintain logical order and cohesiveness.

19.

- **A.** NO CHANGE
- **B.** illiteracy, and that
- **C.** illiteracy. That
- **D.** illiteracy, that

20. Which choice would be the most consistent with the language provided previously in the paragraph?

- **F.** NO CHANGE
- **G.** That the country slang was filled with wisdom passed down from one generation to the next.
- **H.** Those sayings held wisdom from generations past.
- **J.** She told me that the country folks' wit was chock full of wisdom that I may never understand.

and admonition of the Lord from wee babes to full-grown adults.[21] To never raise my hand to them. To never raise my voice.

21.
A. NO CHANGE
B. from babies to adults
C. from small infants to grown men and women
D. Omit the underlined portion

When I finished the cookies, she brushed off the table, brought a thick, small book from the bookcase, and she settled herself quietly in a chair.[22] I had read *A Tale of Two Cities* and found it up to my standards as a romantic novel. She opened the first page and I heard poetry for the first time in my life.

22.
F. NO CHANGE
G. she brushed off the table, brought a thick, small book from the bookcase, and she settled herself quietly in a chair.
H. she brushed off the table, brought a thick, small book from the bookcase, and settled quietly in a chair.
J. she brushed off the table, brought a thick, small book from the bookcase, and quietly settled herself in a chair.

"It was the best of times and the worst of times . . . "

As her voice slid[23] in and curved down through and over the words. She nearly[24] was singing. I wanted to look at the pages. Were they the same that I had read? Or were there notes, music, lines on the pages, as in a hymn book? I wanted to see the words, the sounds, and even more, the music.[25] Her sounds began cascading gently. I knew from listening to a thousand preachers that she was nearing the end of her reading, and I hadn't really heard, heard to understand, a single word.

"How do you like that?"

23.
A. NO CHANGE
B. While her voice slid
C. When her voice slid
D. Her voice slid

24. The best place for the underlined word would be
F. where it is now
G. before the word *She*, capitalized and followed by a comma
H. after the word *was*
J. after the word *singing*

25.
A. NO CHANGE
B. the music, mostly.
C. most of all, the music.
D. the music the most.

GO ON TO THE NEXT PAGE.

It occurred to me that <u>she expects a response</u>. The sweet vanilla flavor was still on
₂₆

my <u>tongue—her reading</u> was a wonder in my
₂₇
ears. I had to speak.

<u>I said, "Yes ma'am." It was the least I could do, but it was the most also.</u>
₂₈

"There's one more thing. Take this book of

poems and memorize one for me. 29 When you next visits me, you is gonna recite something."

Maya Angelou, from I Know Why the Caged Bird Sings, *copyright 1969 by Maya Angelou, New York, New York: Bantam Books, Feb., 1980.*

26.
 F. NO CHANGE
 G. she expected a response
 H. she had expected a response
 J. she was expecting

27.
 A. NO CHANGE
 B. tongue and her reading
 C. tongue: her reading
 D. tongue; and her reading

28.
 F. NO CHANGE
 G. I said, "Yes ma'am" It was the least I could do, but it was the most also.
 H. I said, "Yes ma'am," It was the least I could do, but it was the most also.
 J. I said, "Yes ma'am;" because it was the least I could do, but it was the most also.

29. Which of the following sentences best reflects the tone of the passage?
 A. NO CHANGE
 B. Next time you pay me a visit, I want you to recite.
 C. During your next visit, I'll look forward to your recitation.
 D. The next time you come to visit, Marguerite, I would like you to recite.

The following question relates to the passage as a whole. (Starts on page 299.)

30. Which choice would best summarize the main point of the excerpt?

- **F.** Often, the smallest, most seemingly insignificant instances in life can have the most impact if a person just takes the time to pay attention.
- **G.** Anyone can teach, just as anyone can learn. True knowledge is imparted when the right teacher finds the right student.
- **H.** Wisdom comes most often when a person quiets the mind and listens to what the universe has to say.
- **J.** Soaking in wisdom from elders in personal communities is better than any formal education one can achieve.

Passage III

More Than Light Itself

On hot and humid summer evenings, almost everyone has witnessed fireflies, also called lightning bugs, flitting around your yard or landing on a windowsill [31] and occasionally

31.

- **A.** NO CHANGE
- **B.** their yard or landing on a windowsill
- **C.** his or her yard or landing on a windowsill *correct*
- **D.** your yard or landing on a windowsill

emitting a soft glow. [32] Flashing on and off like flashlights or twinkling holiday lights, a firefly is just one of the many organisms that can produce it's[33] own light. This feature[34], known

32. The writer is considering deleting the first part of the preceding sentence, so that it would read:

> Almost everyone has witnessed fireflies, also called lightning bugs, flitting around your yard or landing on a windowsill and occasionally emitting a soft glow.

If the writer were to make this change, the paragraph would primarily lose:

F. an indication of the tone that will be used in the rest of the passage.
G. details that emphasize the time of year bioluminescence occurs.
H. an example of the kinds of weather imperative for bioluminescence to occur.
J. nothing, because it is irrelevant to the paragraph.

33.
A. NO CHANGE
B. its
C. its'
D. their

34. Which of the following is NOT an acceptable alternative for the underlined portion?
F. light, this feature
G. light; this feature
H. light, and this feature
J. light. This dramatic feature

as bioluminescence or cold light, actually appears in nature quite often. more often than you might think. [35]

All forms of light occur through a similar process. To understand this process, you must first know a little bit about atoms. Atoms are the smaller [36] part of an element, such as iron or sodium, which have the same chemical properties as the element. [37] The center of an atom is called the nucleus and is composed of particles called protons and neutrons. Other particles, called electrons, orbit the nucleus of an atom; just like [38] the earth orbits the sun. The electrons' orbit does not change unless the electrons are excited or energized in some way.

35. The writer would like to indicate here the surprising frequency of bioluminescence. Which choice does this most effectively while maintaining the tone of the passage?

- **A.** appears in nature at a higher frequency than one might come to expect.
- **B.** appears in nature more often than you might think.
- **C.** actually appears in nature more often than not.
- **D.** actually appears in nature more than you could ever believe it.

36.

- **F.** NO CHANGE
- **G.** most small
- **H.** smallest
- **J.** more small

37.

- **A.** NO CHANGE
- **B.** despite having the same chemical properties as the element
- **C.** that have the same chemical properties as the element
- **D.** and have the same chemical properties as the element

38.

- **F.** NO CHANGE
- **G.** atom just like
- **H.** atom, just like
- **J.** atom: just like

[39] Then, when they fall back to their normal energy level, they fall back to a lower orbit and release packets of energy called photons, which produce light. Light from [40] a lamp or streetlight is produced when electrons are excited by heat from electricity.

In bioluminescent organisms, electrons are excited by a chemical reaction, not heat, which is why the phenomenon is often referred to as cold light. The chemicals that various organisms use to create light are luciferin and luciferase. Luciferin is the substance that produces light luciferase [41] is the enzyme that causes the chemical reaction to begin. In the simplest terms, luciferase makes luciferin react with oxygen, which produces light.

[42] [1] Many organisms, from bacteria and mushrooms to certain sea creatures, insects, and others are [43] capable of producing their own light. [2] Certain fungi, such as the jack-o'-lantern mushroom, can also create light. [3] The orange jack-o'-lantern mushrooms are often found growing on trees in the fall. [4] Among the terrestrial creatures are fireflies, glowworms,

39. Given that all the choices are true, which choice provides the most effective transition from the preceding sentence to this one?

A. When electrons absorb energy, they move to a higher orbit.
B. When electrons take in energy, they resume their normal energy level and move to the highest orbit.
C. After they are energized, they move into a lower orbit.
D. After they are energized, they resume their normal energy level.

40. Which of the following is NOT an acceptable alternative to the underlined portion?

F. which produce light; light from
G. which produce light. Light such as that from
H. that produce light. Light from
J. that produce light from

41.

A. NO CHANGE
B. light. Luciferase
C. light, but luciferase
D. light; and luciferase

42. Which of the following sentence orders makes the paragraph the most logical?

F. NO CHANGE
G. 1, 4, 6, 5, 2, 3
H. 1, 4, 2, 6, 5, 3
J. 1, 4, 2, 3, 6, 5

43.

A. NO CHANGE
B. from bacteria and mushrooms to certain sea creatures, insects, and others is
C. from bacteria and mushrooms to certain sea creatures and insects are
D. from bacteria, mushrooms, and certain sea creatures are

and some centipedes and millipedes. [5] Foxfire is another type of glowing fungus, usually found growing on dead or decaying trees. [6] At night, the gills of the mushroom, found beneath the cap and partway down the stalk, emit a greenish light.

Questions 44 and 45 relate to the passage as a whole.

44. The writer is considering adding a statement to the beginning of the passage, clarifying the purpose for writing. Which statement LEAST emphasizes the writer's purpose?

F. Reading this passage will inform you of instances of bioluminescence in nature and the science behind this phenomenon.

G. Although the primary cause of bioluminescence is unclear, after reading this passage, you'll know a little more about the science surrounding this magical feature of nature, a few examples of it in the wild, and the chemical reactions that cause it to occur.

H. After you finish reading this passage, you'll be able to explain scientific data about bioluminescence and provide a few examples of this wonder in the natural world around us.

J. When you've finished reading this information about bioluminescence, you'll be persuaded to study the complexities of the science behind this phenomenon, and the different forms of nature preserving themselves with a bioluminescent feature.

45. The writer would like to add a paragraph to the end of the passage challenging readers to donate money to fund research on bioluminescence in habitats around the world. Should this paragraph be added?

A. Yes, because the passage is left without a conclusion, and adding a challenge to the end of this piece is a great way to create a conclusion without repeating too much information.

B. Yes, because it would tie the whole point of the passage together while offering a way for readers to connect to the scientific data presented.

C. No, because although the passage is left without an appropriate conclusion, adding a paragraph about donating money changes the purpose of the essay.

D. No, because the paragraph that is currently at the end sums up the passage enough for the reader to be left with information about bioluminescence that he or she didn't know prior to reading.

Passage IV

Mabel's Churchyard

[1]

She had suffered badly[46] through the period of poverty. Nothing, however, could shake the curious, sullen, animal pride that dominated each member of the family. Now, for Mabel, the end had come.[47] Still she would not cast

46.

F. NO CHANGE

G. more badly

H. worse

J. the worst

47.

A. NO CHANGE

B. Now for Mabel; the end had come.

C. Now for Mabel: the end had come.

D. Despite the end coming for Mabel.

about her. She would follow her own way just the same she would[48] always hold the keys'[49] of her own situation. Mindless and persistent, she endured from day to day. [50] Why should she think? Why should she answer to anybody?

48.
F. NO CHANGE
G. just the same. She would
H. just the same or she would
J. just the same: she would

49.
A. NO CHANGE
B. hold the key's
C. hold the keys
D. hold its keys

50. The writer is considering deleting the following clause from the preceding sentence (revising the capitalization accordingly):

Mindless and persistent

Should this clause be kept or deleted?

F. Kept, because it clarifies Mabel's mental state of being, which is crucial to understanding her actions later on.
G. Kept, because it shows Mabel's character, which helps the reader relate to the protagonist.
H. Deleted, because it contradicts the essay's revelations about Mabel, which show her as a concerned woman caring for her deceased mother.
J. Deleted, because it misleads readers into believing Mabel is an uneducated woman, and that fact goes against the author's point of view.

She need not demean herself any more, going into the shops and buying the cheapest food. [51] She thought of nobody, not even of herself.

[2]

In the afternoon, she took a little bag, with shears and sponge and a small scrubbing-brush, and went out. <u>It was a gray, wintry day, with saddened</u> [52] dark green fields and an atmosphere blackened by the smoke of foundries not far off.

[3]

There, she always <u>feels</u> [53] secure, as if no one could see her, although as a matter of fact, she was exposed to the stare of everyone who

51. After reading the previous sentence, the writer decides to compose a different one to replace it that includes more vivid, descriptive language while maintaining the style and tone. Given that all the choices are true, which sentence accomplishes the writer's goal?

A. NO CHANGE
B. She need not demean herself any more, going into the grocers to buy old turnips and wilted cabbage.
C. She need not demean herself any more, going around to all the shops and buying the cheapest food they had to offer.
D. She didn't need to put herself down any more by going into grocery stores to buy old turnips, wilted cabbage, and stale bread.

52.

F. NO CHANGE
G. It was a gray wintry day with saddened
H. It was a gray wintry day, with saddened
J. It was a gray, wintry day with saddened

53.

A. NO CHANGE
B. felt
C. had felt
D. is feeling

passed along under the churchyard wall. [54]

Nevertheless, once beneath the eaves of the great church's structured walls [55], among the

54. At this point in the story, the writer is considering adding this sentence:

> She was exposed to the stares of the townspeople—the ones who could see her stoically going about her mission.

Should it be added?

F. Yes, because it adds details to the story that help explain how cruel the townspeople were to Mabel and her family.

G. Yes, because it changes the reader's perception of Mabel, by demonstrating the strength it must have taken to keep working despite the stares.

H. No, because it provides no pertinent information to the passage, basically repeating the sentence preceding it.

J. No, because it adds bulk to an already wordy story.

55. The writer would like to indicate at this point the vast size of the church. Given that all the choices are true, which one best accomplishes the writer's goal?

A. NO CHANGE

B. beside the great church's fearsome brick facade

C. under the shadow of the great looming church

D. adjacent to the stony, secure walls of the great church

graves, she felt immune to the world, and more reserved within the thick churchyard wall than being in another country. [56]

56.

F. NO CHANGE

G. felt immune to the world, reserved like being in another country within the thick churchyard.

H. felt immune to the world, and very reserved within the thick churchyard wall as in another country.

J. felt immune to the world, reserved within the thick churchyard wall as in another country.

[4]

[57] [1] Carefully, she took the pinky-white, small chrysanthemums from her pocket, clipped the weedy growth from the grave, and arranged them in the tin cross. [2] When this was done, she took an empty jar from a neighboring grave, brought water, and fully, most scrupulously sponged the marble headstone and coping-stone. [3] It gave her sincere satisfaction to do this, for in so doing these menial tasks, she gave what couldn't be given in life to someone else.

57. Which choice provides the most logical arrangement of the parts of this sentence?

A. NO CHANGE

B. Carefully, she took the pinky-white, small chrysanthemums from her pocket, arranged them in the tin cross, and she clipped the weedy growth from the grave.

C. Carefully, she clipped the weedy growth from the grave, and took the pinky-white, small chrysanthemums from her pocket and arranged them in the tin cross.

D. Carefully, she arranged the flowers in the tin cross after taking the pinky-white, small chrysanthemums from her pocket and clipping the weedy growth from the grave.

[4] She took minute pains, she went [58] through the park in a state bordering on pure happiness, as if in performing this task she came into a subtle, intimate connection with her mother. [5] For the life she followed here in this world was

58.

F. NO CHANGE

G. minute pains; and she went

H. minute pains, and so she went

J. minute pains. She went

far less real than the world of death she inherited from her mother. [59] [60]

From "The Horse Dealer's Daughter" by D. H. Lawrence.

59. The writer is considering adding the following sentence to the end of one of the paragraphs to transition to the next paragraph.

> She went quickly, darkly along the causeway, heeding nobody, through the town to the churchyard.

To which paragraph should it be added?

A. Paragraph 1
B. Paragraph 2
C. Paragraph 3
D. Paragraph 4

60. If the writer were to divide the preceding paragraph into two shorter paragraphs in order to differentiate between Mabel's actions and the effects of her actions, the new paragraph should begin with Sentence:

F. 2
G. 3
H. 4
J. 5

Passage V

Tony Hawk: Master Skateboarder

[1]

In 1983, Tony Hawk—a fifteen-year-old from <u>San Diego, California, won</u> (61) his first professional skateboarding contest. Two years later, he landed the first "720," a 720-degree spin,

61.
A. NO CHANGE
B. San Diego, California won
C. San Diego, California: won
D. San Diego, California—won

or two full revolutions. Considered a pioneer in the world of extreme sports, Tony Hawk's determination and drive [62] helped transform his hobby of skateboarding into a profitable business, yet [63] a way in which to make a positive difference in the world.

[2]

In his childhood, Tony had lofty ambitions and a lot of energy, but he was hard on himself when he did not succeed at the gamut of things he attempted. Although [64] his mom describes young Tony as "challenging," because he had so much liveliness but no outlet for it.

[65] However, when Tony was just nine years old, his older brother finally found something that Tony could devote his attention to: a skateboard.

[3]

Frank Hawk, Tony's father, contributed to his son's success by being supportive of his interest. While everyone else in the family was too busy to drive Tony to competitions, Frank

62.
- **F.** NO CHANGE
- **G.** Tony Hawk along with his determination and drive
- **H.** Tony Hawk
- **J.** Tony Hawk's extreme ability to use his determination and drive

63.
- **A.** NO CHANGE
- **B.** , but
- **C.** , and as such
- **D.** , and

64.
- **F.** NO CHANGE
- **G.** Because
- **H.** Since
- **J.** OMIT the underlined word

65. Which of the following true statements, if added here, would best emphasize Tony Hawk's need for an individual, active sport?
- **A.** She put Tony in basketball, baseball, and soccer, but these group sports seemed to deflate rather than inspire this active child of hers.
- **B.** She enrolled him in all sorts of group sports, but he never picked up on anything.
- **C.** When group sports like basketball and baseball failed, she decided to let his older brother choose something that would work for Tony.
- **D.** When basketball, soccer, and baseball seemed to crush Tony's spirit, she decided that she'd finally allow him to choose whichever sport he wanted.

made himself more available than he or she was[66], and drove him across California to participate. In the family's backyard, he built skate ramps, half pipes, and areas for Tony to refine his talent. Disappointed with the privation of skateboarding gatherings for his young son,[67] Frank founded both the California Amateur Skateboard League and the national Skateboard Association. He was so involved, that some skateboarding officials commented that it was increasingly difficult to determine[68] who had the most zeal[69] for the sport: Tony or his father.

66.
F. NO CHANGE
G. more available than them
H. available
J. more available than him or her

67.
A. NO CHANGE
B. Dissatisfied with the skateboarding groups available to his son,
C. Annoyed with the ridiculous lack of skateboarding groups for his talented son,
D. Disheartened by his attempts to find appropriate skateboarding groups for his kid,

68. Which choice provides the most specific and precise information without altering the meaning of the text?
F. NO CHANGE
G. said it was tough to determine
H. were quoted as saying it was hard to figure out
J. wondered

69.
A. NO CHANGE
B. who had more zeal
C. who had the most zeal of all
D. whom had the most zeal

[4]

[1] At the 1999 X Games, Tony landed a "900": a two-and a half[70] rotation midair flip above the lip of a vertical ramp. [2] Not long after the X Games, with many victories to his name, he retired from competitive skateboarding. [3] He had been practicing the trick for

70.
F. NO CHANGE
G. "900:" a two-and a half
H. "900"; a two-and a half
J. "900" a two-and a half

a decade during his attempts to master it, time after time he fell horribly, suffering four injuries that included broken ribs and compressed vertebrae. [4] Although he no longer competes, Tony still performs on his board in front of large audiences. [73]

71.
A. NO CHANGE
B. decade, during
C. decade; during,
D. decade. During

72. The place for the underlined phrase is
F. where it is
G. after the word *he*
H. after the word *fell*
J. after the word *horribly*

73. For the sake of the logic and coherence of this paragraph, sentence 2 should be placed:
A. where it is now
B. before Sentence 1
C. after Sentence 3
D. after Sentence 4

Questions 74 and 75 ask about the preceding passage as a whole. (Starts on page 313.)

74. The writer is considering deleting the last sentence of paragraph 2. If the writer were to make the deletion, the essay would primarily lose:
F. a statement that explains how Tony Hawk was first introduced to the sport of skateboarding
G. an indication of where Tony Hawk's talent came from.
H. a revelation about Tony Hawk's rise to fame and how he uses his talents to this day.
J. excessive detail that distracts the reader from the point of the essay.

75. Suppose the writer's goal had been to write a brief explanatory biography of Tony Hawk's skateboarding career. Would this essay fulfill that goal?

A. No, because a biography is supposed to include information about all aspects of a person's life, not just one facet.

B. No, because although it mentions many aspects of Tony Hawk's skateboarding life, it fails to name many of his skateboarding competitions, fiercest competitors, and major accomplishments.

C. Yes, because the essay explains how he started skateboarding, became successful, and continued growing professionally and personally.

D. Yes, because the essay gives a detailed account of the skateboarding legend Tony became after his amazing start.

END OF TEST 1
STOP! DO NOT TURN THE PAGE UNTIL TOLD TO DO SO.

Practice Test
Mathematics

TIME: 60 minutes
60 questions

DIRECTIONS: Solve each problem, choose the correct answer, and then fill in the corresponding oval on your answer document.

Do not linger over problems that take too much time. Solve as many as you can, then return to the others in the time you have left for this test.

You are permitted to use a calculator on this test. You may use your calculator for any problems you choose, but some of the problems may best be done without a calculator.

Note: Unless otherwise noted, all of the following should be assumed.

1. Illustrative figures are NOT necessarily drawn to scale.
2. Geometric figures lie in a plane.
3. The word *line* indicates a straight line.
4. The word *average* indicates arithmetic mean.

DO YOUR FIGURING HERE

1. $\dfrac{\frac{2}{3}+\frac{5}{9} - \frac{8}{9}-\frac{2}{3}}{\frac{1}{2}+\frac{1}{4}} = ?$

A. $\frac{3}{4}$

B. $\frac{4}{3}$

C. $\frac{1}{2}$

D. $\frac{2}{3}$

E. 2

DO YOUR FIGURING HERE

2. If $x = 2$ and $y = -5$, then $3y^2 + 2y - x = ?$

F. –42

G. 18

H. 63

J. 213

K. 238

3. What is the difference between the mean and the median in the set {4, 7, 9, 12}?

A. 0

B. 1

C. 2

D. 8

E. 32

4. Certain video games at a department store are discounted by 15%. Marissa wants to buy one of those games originally priced at $40. Assuming there will be no sales tax, what will she have to pay for the game?

F. $6

G. $15

H. $25

J. $34

K. $60

5. A solution to the equation $x^2 + 3x - 40 = 0$ is

A. –8

B. –5

C. 8

D. 40

E. No real solution

DO YOUR FIGURING HERE

6. In a pet store, the ratio of dogs to cats is 5:4. If there are a total of 27 dogs and cats in the store, how many dogs are there?

F. 9
G. 12
H. 15
J. 18
K. 21

7. An ice cream store offers three different sauce toppings and seven different mix-ins. There is a special sundae offer where you can pick one sauce, two mix-ins (including doubles), and one flavor of ice cream (there are four for this offer). How many ways are there to order a sundae with this offer?

A. 4
B. 21
C. 84
D. 147
E. 588

8. If an apple weighs 5.25 ounces and an orange weighs 10 ounces, then what is the weight in ounces of x apples and y oranges?

F. $15.25xy$
G. $15.25(x + y)$
H. $5.25xy + 10yx$
J. $x + y + 15.25$
K. $5.25x + 10y$

9. Dimitri is skipping stones on a lake. After three tosses, he has skipped stones two, seven, and five times. If he is going to throw one more stone, how many times does it have to skip for him to have an average of five skips?

A. 3
B. 4
C. 5
D. 6
E. 7

DO YOUR FIGURING HERE

10. $3a^2b^4 \times 2b \times 4a^4b^2 = ?$

F. $24a^6b^7$
G. $9b^8$
H. $24b^8$
J. $9a^2b^{-2}$
K. $24a^8b^8$

11. Lines *IL*, *JM*, and *KN* all pass through central point O. If $\angle KOL = 40°$ and $\angle NOJ = 100°$, what is the measure of $\angle MOI$?

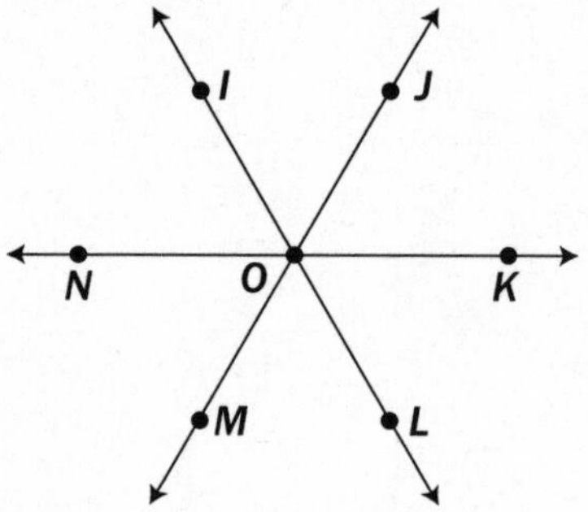

A. 80°
B. 100°
C. 120°
D. 140°
E. 160°

12. A bird can eat 5 pounds of bird seed in 3 days. At this rate, how many pounds of bird seed does the bird eat in 3 + *d* days?

F. $\frac{5}{3} + d$
G. $\frac{5}{3} + \frac{d}{3}$
H. $\frac{5}{3} + \frac{5}{3d}$
J. $5 + \frac{d}{3}$
K. $5 + \frac{5d}{3}$

DO YOUR FIGURING HERE

13. $(3-4)^2 + 2 - \frac{15}{3} = ?$

A. -2
B. -1
C. 0
D. 1
E. 2

14. Fill in the missing relation:
$|-3+1| \ ? \ |-3-1|$

F. $<$
G. $>$
H. $\geq$
J. $=$
K. Not enough information

15. Which of the following is equivalent to $\sqrt{40}$?

A. $\sqrt{10}$
B. $\sqrt{20}$
C. $2\sqrt{10}$
D. $2\sqrt{20}$
E. $2+\sqrt{20}$

16. Lines *l* and *m*, pictured below, are parallel with a transversal line going through them. Which of the following statements about the angles created is *not* necessarily true?

DO YOUR FIGURING HERE

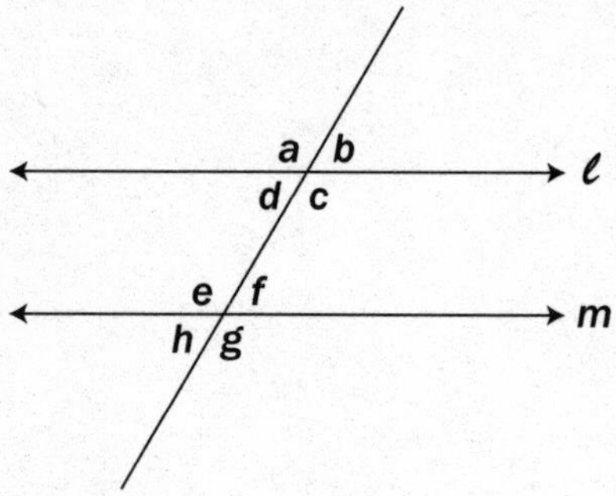

F. $\angle a = \angle g$

G. $\angle a + \angle f = 180°$

H. $\angle f = \angle h$

J. $\angle a = \angle h$

K. $\angle g + \angle h = 180°$

17. If $3(x + 2) - 4 = -2x + 7$, what is the value of x?

A. –2

B. –1

C. 0

D. 1

E. 2

18. If a certain function $f(x)$ is translated to make a new function $g(x)$ where $g(x)$ is a reflection of $f(x)$ across the x-axis and is translated right three units, which of the following equations represents $g(x)$?

F. $g(x) = -f(x - 3)$

G. $g(x) = -f(x + 3)$

H. $g(x) = -f(x) + 3$

J. $g(x) = -f(x) - 3$

K. $g(x) = f(x) - 3$

DO YOUR FIGURING HERE

19. Two rectangles are inscribed in a square. What is the combined area of the shaded regions in the figure below?

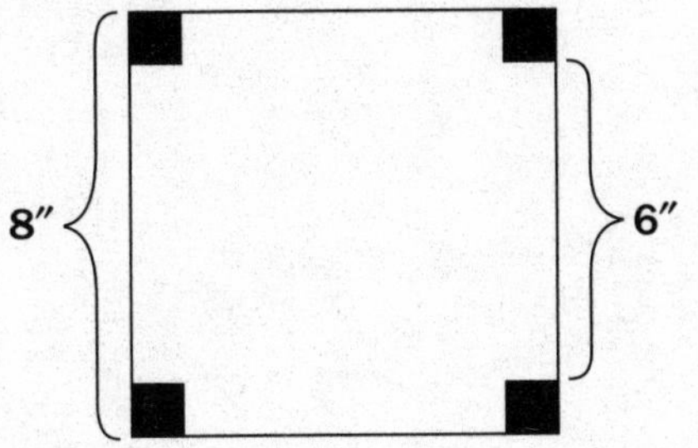

A. 1
B. 2
C. 2.5
D. 3
E. 4

20. If $|2x + 6| - x = 12$, then $x = ?$
F. –4, 6
G. –5, 5
H. –6, 6
J. –5, 6
K. –3, 5

21. How many distinct prime factors does the number 56 have?
A. 1
B. 2
C. 3
D. 4
E. 5

22. What is the length in inches, rounded off to the nearest tenth, of the missing side in the trapezoid pictured below?

DO YOUR FIGURING HERE

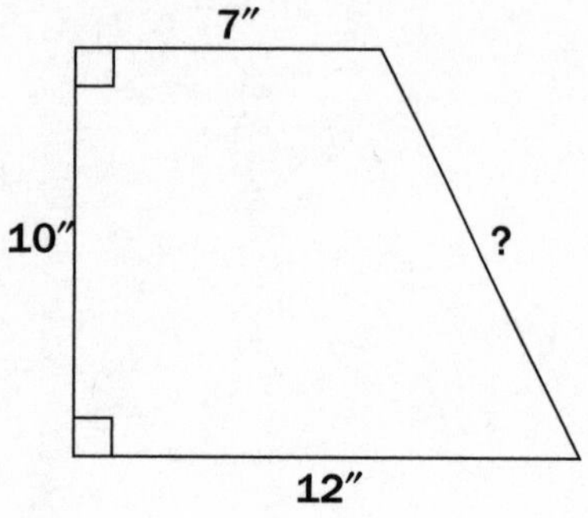

F. 10.8
G. 11.2
H. 11.8
J. 12.2
K. 12.8

23. Simplify $\frac{32x^2y^4z^6}{4x^6y^4z^2}$:

A. $\frac{8z^4}{x^4}$

B. $\frac{8x^4}{z^4}$

C. $\frac{z^4y}{8x^4}$

D. $\frac{x^4}{8z^4}$

E. $8x^4z^4$

DO YOUR FIGURING HERE

24. In the figure shown below, the measure of $\angle BAC$ is $(x + 30)°$ and the measure of $\angle BAD$ is 90°. What is the measure of $\angle CAD$?

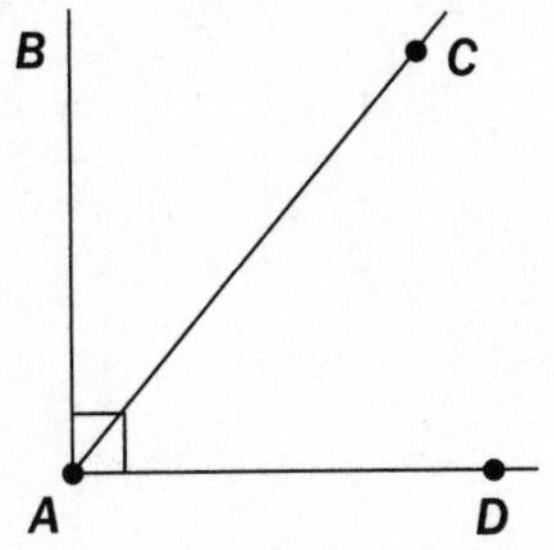

F. $(x - 60)°$
G. $(60 - x)°$
H. $(60 + x)°$
J. $(150 - x)°$
K. $(150 + x)°$

25. Circle P has radius r and circumference $2\pi r$. If the radius of circle Q is $\frac{3}{4}$ the length of r, what is the circumference of circle Q in terms of r?

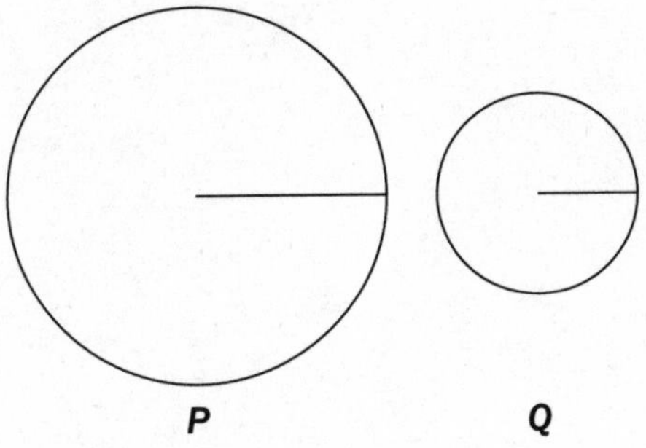

A. $\frac{3}{4}r$
B. $\frac{3}{4}\neq r$
C. $2\pi r$
D. $\frac{3}{2}\neq$
E. $\frac{3}{2}\neq r$

DO YOUR FIGURING HERE

26. Which whole number is closest to the solution of $\frac{\sqrt{106}}{\sqrt{27}}$?

F. 1
G. 2
H. 3
J. 4
K. 5

27. If $2x+3y=26$ and $x-2y=-1$, then $x+y=$?

A. 7
B. 9
C. 11
D. 13
E. 15

28. Max's current hourly wage for working at Grace's Grocery is $14.00. Max was told that at the beginning of next month, his new hourly wage will increase by 8% of his current hourly wage. What will be Max's new hourly wage?

F. $14.08
G. $14.80
H. $15.12
J. $22.00
K. $23.40

29. Which number below makes the following conversion equivalent?

$$15{,}200{,}000 = 1.52 \times 10^{?}$$

A. 7
B. 8
C. 9
D. 10
E. 11

DO YOUR FIGURING HERE

30. What is the equation of a circle which contains the point (0, –3) and has center (4, –3)?

F. $x^2 + (y + 3)^2 = 4$
G. $(x + 4)^2 + (y - 3)^2 = 4$
H. $(x + 4)^2 + (y - 3)^2 = 16$
J. $(x - 4)^2 + (y + 3)^2 = 16$
K. $x^2 + (y + 3)^2 = 16$

31. What percent of 5800 is 2088?

A. 36%
B. 37.12%
C. 42%
D. 58%
E. 277%

32. The length of a rectangle with an area of 56 square meters is 8 meters. What is the perimeter of the rectangle, in meters?

F. 7
G. 14
H. 15
J. 28
K. 30

33. $\sqrt{6} \cdot \sqrt{24}$ is equivalent to:

A. 4
B. $\sqrt{30}$
C. 10
D. 12
E. 36

34. The polynomial function $f(x) = a_4x^4 + a_3x^3 + a_2x^2 + a_1x + a_0$ has at most how many real roots?

F. 2
G. 3
H. 4
J. 5
K. Infinitely many

DO YOUR FIGURING HERE

35. Given that a graph of a function has exactly 2 values for x that make $f(x) = 0$, which could be an equation of the function?

A. $f(x) = 2x + 5$
B. $f(x) = 3(x - 7)^2 - 10$
C. $f(x) = \log(x + 4)$
D. $f(x) = 2^x + 3$
E. $f(x) = 8$

36. There are 32 adults and 20 children in a restaurant. Which ratio describes the numbers of adults to children in the restaurant?

F. 7:4
G. 3:2
H. 8:5
J. 10:3
K. 6:5

DO YOUR FIGURING HERE

37. Which system of inequalities represents the graph below?

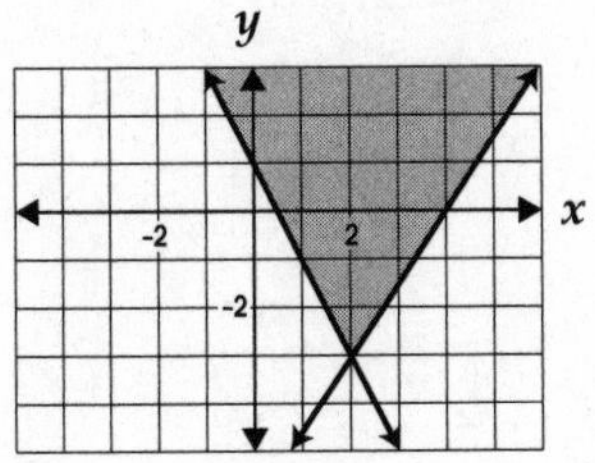

A. $y \le -2x + 1$

$y \ge \frac{3}{2}x - 6$

B. $y \ge -2x + 1$

$y \le \frac{3}{2}x - 6$

C. $y \ge -2x + 1$

$y \ge \frac{3}{2}x - 6$

D. $y \le -2x + 1$

$y \le \frac{3}{2}x - 6$

E. $y = -2x + 1$

$y \ge \frac{3}{2}x - 6$

38. Jane is drawing cards out of 4 bags for a grand prize on a game show. Each bag has 3 cards and only one card in each bag has a dollar sign on it. If she independently and randomly draws a card from each bag, and she needs 4 dollar signs to win, what is the probability of her winning?

DO YOUR FIGURING HERE

F. $\frac{27}{81}$

G. $\frac{12}{81}$

H. $\frac{4}{81}$

J. $\frac{3}{81}$

K. $\frac{1}{81}$

39. The radius of the base of the cylinder pictured below is 4 and the height is 7. Using $V = \pi r^2 h$, what is the volume of the cylinder?

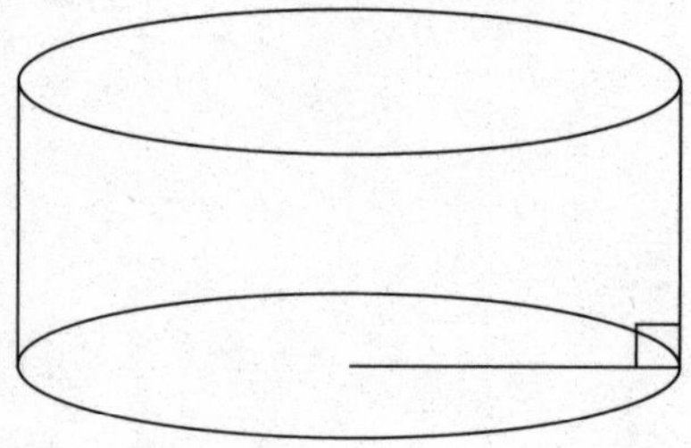

A. 28π

B. 49π

C. 56π

D. 98π

E. 112π

DO YOUR FIGURING HERE

40. Simplify $(3 + 2i) \times (3 - 2i)$

F. 6

G. 9

H. 11

J. 13

K. 15

41. What fraction lies exactly halfway between $\frac{1}{3}$ and $\frac{1}{2}$?

A. $\frac{2}{5}$

B. $\frac{3}{5}$

C. $\frac{2}{6}$

D. $\frac{5}{6}$

E. $\frac{5}{12}$

42. Sydney has been studying population growth of cells and noticed that for each minute, the population followed an exponential model: $P = 1.2^t$ where P is the total population and t represents minutes. About how many cells should she expect in the population after 20 minutes?

F. 6

G. 24

H. 36

J. 38

K. 144

DO YOUR FIGURING HERE

43. Order these numbers from lowest value to highest value: $0.5, \sqrt{14}, -3, -\sqrt{2}+10$

A. $0.5, \sqrt{14}, -3, -\sqrt{2}+10$

B. $-3, 0.5, \sqrt{14}, -\sqrt{2}+10$

C. $-3, \sqrt{14}, 0.5, -\sqrt{2}+10$

D. $-3, -\sqrt{2}+10, 0.5, \sqrt{14}$

E. $-3, 0.5, -\sqrt{2}+10, \sqrt{14}$

44. If $3x - y = 9$, then $2\sqrt{3x-y} = ?$

F. 3
G. 6
H. 9
J. 12
K. 18

45. 40% of eligible Americans have said they have received a letter in the mail stating that they are to serve jury duty. Past records show that 80% of all people who show up for jury duty are selected to serve. Based on these figures, how many Americans in a random group of 1,000 who are eligible to participate in jury duty would you expect to serve?

A. 200
B. 320
C. 400
D. 650
E. 800

DO YOUR FIGURING HERE

46. If $x{:}y = 4{:}9$ and $y{:}z = 2{:}9$, what is the ratio of $x{:}z$?

F. 2:1
G. 2:4
H. 4:2
J. 6:18
K. 8:81

47. Two points *P* and *Q* are connected by line segment *PQ*. If *P* is located at (2, 8) and the midpoint of *PQ* is (–4, 10), what are the coordinates of *Q*?

A. (–2, 18)
B. (10, –12)
C. (2, –18)
D. (–10,12)
E. (18, –2)

48. Where does the function $y = a + bx$ intersect the *x*-axis?

F. a
G. b
H. $-\frac{a}{b}$
J. $-\frac{b}{a}$
K. $a - b$

49. Parallelogram *ABCD* has $\angle ABC = 130°$. What is the measure of $\angle BCD$?

A. 30°
B. 50°
C. 60°
D. 90°
E. 130°

GO ON TO THE NEXT PAGE.

DO YOUR FIGURING HERE

50. What is the inverse of the function $y = x^2 - 8x + 16$?

F. $y = \dfrac{1}{x^2 - 8x + 16}$

G. $y = \dfrac{1}{x^2} - \dfrac{1}{8x} + \dfrac{1}{16}$

H. $y = x^2 + 8x + 16$

J. $y = -x^2 + 8x - 16$

K. $y = 4 \pm \sqrt{x}$

51. What is the length of the missing side in figure below?

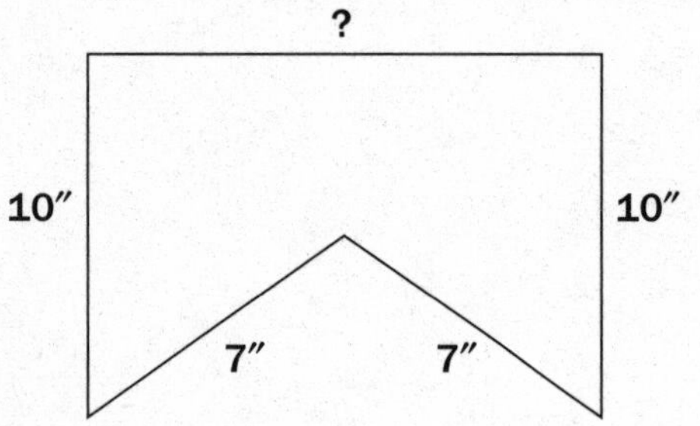

A. 12

B. 13

C. 14

D. 15

E. Cannot be determined

52. Which of the following equations represents the graph below?

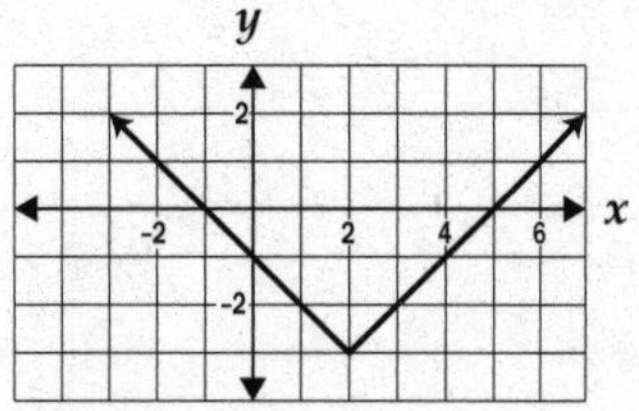

F. $y = (x - 2)^2 - 3$

G. $y = \sqrt{x - 2} - 3$

H. $y = (x - 2)^3 - 3$

J. $y = |x - 2| - 3$

K. $y = \log(x - 2) - 3$

DO YOUR FIGURING HERE

53. The table below shows the number of dollhouses Bev sold each month last year. What is the median of the data in the table?

Month	Number of dollhouses sold
January	14
February	24
March	20
April	21
May	12
June	17
July	18
August	26
September	27
October	28
November	28
December	30

A. 14
B. 18
C. 21
D. 21.5
E. 22.5

54. If $x^2 - 4 < 0$, which of the following describes the solution?

F. $x < 2$
G. $x > -2$
H. $-2 < x < 2$
J. $x < -2$ or $x > 2$
K. $x \neq 3$ and $x \neq 4$

55. One taxi drives 2 blocks south and then 3 blocks west. Another taxi, starting at the same spot, drives 7 blocks north and then 2 blocks east. If each block is 50 feet, what is the distance in feet between the two taxis?

A. $\sqrt{26}$

B. $50\sqrt{26}$

C. $50\sqrt{50}$

D. $\sqrt{106}$

E. $50\sqrt{106}$

DO YOUR FIGURING HERE

56. To attract more customers, a small candy store made 5 extra candy bars that had a special giveaway in the wrapper. If they added the 5 extra bars randomly to the other 1,250 bars, and you were to go to that candy store, what is the probability that the special giveaway would be in 1 of the extra bars?

F. $\frac{1}{5}$

G. $\frac{1}{1{,}255}$

H. $\frac{1}{1{,}250}$

J. $\frac{5}{1{,}255}$

K. $\frac{5}{1{,}250}$

DO YOUR FIGURING HERE

57. The monthly fees for apartments in a certain complex are \$410, \$440, \$450, \$500, and \$470, respectively. What is the mean of these monthly fees?

A. \$410
B. \$450
C. \$454
D. \$460
E. \$500

58. Steven is going to measure the height, h, of a kite he is flying. To do so, he measures the length of the string b feet and measures the angle of elevation to be θ as shown in the figure below. Which of the following relates h and b?

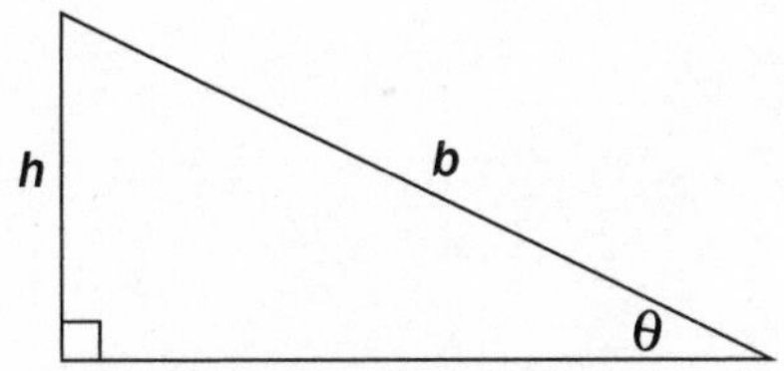

F. $\sin\theta = \frac{h}{b}$

G. $\sin\theta = \frac{b}{h}$

H. $\sin\theta = \frac{b}{\sqrt{b^2 + h^2}}$

J. $\sin\theta = \frac{h}{\sqrt{b^2 + h^2}}$

K. $\sin\theta = \frac{\sqrt{b^2 + h^2}}{b}$

DO YOUR FIGURING HERE

59. Jan polled her class and found that of her 24 classmates, 17 are involved in athletics and 12 are involved in the school play. At least how many students must be involved in both?

A. 0

B. 1

C. 3

D. 5

E. 24

60. Let $|2x - 5| + 6 < -5$. Which expression best describes the solution?

F. $x > 8$ or $x < -3$

G. $-3 < x < 8$

H. $x > -3$ or $x < 8$

J. No real solution

K. All real numbers

END OF TEST 2
STOP! DO NOT TURN THE PAGE UNTIL TOLD TO DO SO.
DO NOT RETURN TO A PREVIOUS TEST.

Practice Test
Reading

TIME: 35 minutes
40 questions

DIRECTIONS: There are four passages in this test. Each passage is followed by several questions. After reading a passage, choose the best answer to each question and fill in the corresponding oval on your answer document. You may refer to the passages as often as necessary.

Passage I

PROSE FICTION: This passage is adapted from the novel *Bread Givers* by Anzia Yezierska (© Anzia Yezierska 1925).

I had just begun to peel the potatoes for dinner when my oldest sister Bessie came in, her eyes far away and very tired. She dropped on the bench by the sink and turned her head to the wall. One look at her, and I knew she had not yet found work. I went on peeling the potatoes, but I no more knew what my hands were doing. I felt only the dark hurt of her weary eyes. I was about ten years old then. But from always it was heavy on my heart the worries for the house as if I was mother. I knew that the landlord came that morning hollering for the rent. And the whole family was hanging on Bessie's neck for her wages. Unless she got work soon, we'd be thrown in the street to shame and to laughter for the whole world.

I already saw all our things kicked out on the sidewalk like a pile of junk. A plate of pennies like a beggar's hand reaching out of our bunch of rags. Each sigh of pity from the passers-by, each penny thrown into the plate was another stab into our burning shame.

Laughter and light footsteps broke in upon my dark thoughts. I heard the door open.

"Give a look only on these roses for my hat," cried Mashah, running over to the looking glass over the sink.

With excited fingers she pinned pink paper roses under the brim. Then, putting on her hat again, she stood herself before the cracked, flystained mirror and turned her head first on this side and then on the other side, laughing to herself with the pleasure of how grand her hat was. "Like a lady from Fifth Avenue I look, and for only ten cents, from a pushcart on Hester Street."

Again the door opened, and with dragging feet my third sister Fania came in. Bessie roused herself from the bench and asked, "Nu, Any luck with you?"

"Half the shops are closed," replied Fania.

"They say the work can't start till they got a new president. And in one place, in a shirt factory, where they had a sign, 'Girls Wanted,' there was such a crowd of us tearing the clothes from our bodies and scratching out each other's eyes in the mad pushings to get in first, that they had to call two fat policemen with thick clubs to make them stand still on a line for their turn. And after we waited for hours and hours, only two girls were taken."

Mashah looked up from the mirror.

"Didn't I tell you not to be such a yok and kill yourself pushing on a line a mile long, when the shop itself couldn't hold those that were already on the doorstep? All the time that you were wasting yourself waiting to get in, I walked myself through the stores, to look for a trimming for my hat."

"You heartless thing!" cried Bessie. "No wonder Father named you 'Empty Head.' Here you go to look for work, and you come back with pink roses for your doll face."

Undisturbed by the bitter words, Mashah finished the last stitch and then hung up her hat carefully over the door.

"I'm going to hear the free music in the park tonight," she laughed to herself, with the pleasure before her, "and these pink roses on my hat to match out my pink calico will make me look just like the picture on the magazine cover."

Bessie rushed over to Mashah's fancy pink hat as if to tear it to pieces, but instead, she tore her own old hat from her head, flung it on the floor, and kicked it under the stove.

Mashah pushed up her shoulders and turned back to the mirror, taking the hairpins carefully from her long golden hair and fixing it in different ways.

"It ain't my fault if the shops are closed. If I take my lunch money for something pretty that I got to have, it don't hurt you none."

Worry or care of any kind could never get itself into Mashah's empty head. Although she lived in the same dirt and trouble with us, nothing ever bothered her.

Everywhere Mashah went men followed her with melting looks. And these melting looks in men's eyes were like something to eat and something to drink to her, so that she could go without her lunch money to buy pretty things for herself, and not starve like the rest of us.

1. Based on the information in lines 8–16, it could be suggested that the narrator believes their situation to be:
   A. bleak, but survivable
   B. hopeful only because of Mashah's laughter
   C. dire and disgraceful
   D. grim, but honorable

2. It can be reasonably inferred from the passage that Bessies' most fervent goal is to:
   F. find suitable work to support her family
   G. provide a safe place for her sisters to live
   H. shelter Mashah and the narrator from harm
   J. enlist the help of her sisters in searching for provisions for the family

3. As it is used in line 92, the word *melting* most nearly means:
   A. smitten
   B. suspending
   C. dissolving
   D. admiring

4. According to the passage, one of the things Mashah had NOT done that day was:
   F. visit a pushcart on Hester street
   G. wait in line to find work
   H. walk around stores looking for hat trimmings
   J. fix her golden hair in the mirror

5. The narrator most likely believes that Fania is:
   A. arrogant for assuming she can get a job
   B. using her time in a courageous, but useless way
   C. wasting an entire day
   D. doing exactly what she needs to be doing to help the family by searching for a job

6. The author most likely includes the information in lines 87–97 in order to:
   F. identify the reasons Mashah didn't believe she needed to work
   G. critique Mashah's work ethic
   H. contrast the difference between Mashah's values and the narrator's values
   J. demonstrate that although Mashah wasn't contributing to the family, she wasn't hurting it, either

7. Which of the following best describes the structure of the passage?
   A. a dialogue explaining the differences in values between four sisters
   B. a narration detailing the events of one family's struggle to survive
   C. a character sketch of Mashah and her three sisters
   D. a personal essay outlining a family's monetary struggles

8. Based on the information in paragraphs 1 and 2, the best description of Bessie would be:
   F. apologetic
   G. exhausted
   H. irate
   J. hopeful

GO ON TO THE NEXT PAGE.

9. All of the following phrases are used in the passage to display the family's *current* dire financial status EXCEPT:
   A. "I knew that the landlord came that morning hollering for the rent."
   B. ". . . so that she could go without her lunch money to buy pretty things for herself, and not starve like the rest of us."
   C. "And the whole family was hanging on Bessie's neck for her wages."
   D. "Each sigh of pity from the passers-by, each penny thrown into the plate was another stab into our burning shame."

10. The author most likely includes the information in lines 44–52 in order to:
   F. demonstrate the work ethic of the entire city
   G. compare the finances of this family to others in the area
   H. intensify the bleakness of the family's financial situation by showing the city in crisis
   J. suggest an answer to the city's fiscal predicament

Passage II: Social Science

Passage A

Elizabeth Cady Stanton had always believed that women should be treated equally to men, but didn't begin her steady championing for equal rights until 1840, after getting turned away from the World Anti-Slavery Convention in London, because female delegates, she was told, were unwelcome.

This injustice convinced Stanton that women needed to pursue equality for themselves before they could seek it for others. In the summer of 1848, she—along with the abolitionist and temperance activist Lucretia Mott and a handful of other reformers—organized the first women's-rights convention in Seneca Falls, New York. Some 240 men and women gathered to discuss what Stanton and Mott called "the social, civil, and religious condition and rights of women." One hundred of the delegates—68 women and 32 men—signed a Declaration of Sentiments, modeled on the Declaration of Independence, declaring that women were citizens equal to men with "an inalienable right to the elective franchise." The Seneca Falls Convention marked the beginning of the campaign for woman suffrage.

Like Susan B. Anthony, Stanton was a committed abolitionist; however, she too refused to compromise on the principle of universal suffrage. As a result, she campaigned against the ratification of the 15th Amendment to the Constitution, which guaranteed black men the right to vote but denied it to women.

After the fight over the 14th and 15th Amendments, Stanton continued to push for women's political equality—but she believed in a much broader vision of women's rights. She advocated for the reform of marriage and divorce laws, the expansion of educational opportunities for girls and even the adoption of less confining clothing (such as the pants-and-tunic ensemble popularized by the activist Amelia Bloomer) so that women could be more active. She also campaigned against the oppression of women in the name of religion—"From the inauguration of the movement for woman's emancipation," she wrote, "the Bible has been used to hold her in the 'divinely ordained sphere'"—and in 1895 published the first volume of a more egalitarian Woman's Bible.

Passage B

Adapted from Elizabeth Cady Stanton's Seneca Falls Keynote Address delivered July 19, 1848, Seneca Falls, New York.

We have met here today to discuss our rights and wrongs, civil and political, and not, as some have supposed, to go into the detail of social life alone. We do not propose to petition the legislature to make our husbands just, generous, and courteous, to seat every man at the head of a cradle, and to clothe every woman in male attire.

But we are assembled to protest against a form of government existing without the consent of the governed—to declare our right to be free as man is free, to be represented in the government which we are taxed to support, to have such disgraceful laws as give man the power to chastise and imprison his wife, to take the wages which she earns,

GO ON TO THE NEXT PAGE.

the property which she inherits, and, in case of separation, the children of her love; laws which make her the mere dependent on his bounty. It is to protest against such unjust laws as these that we are assembled today, and to have them, if possible, forever erased from our statute books, deeming them a shame and a disgrace to a Christian republic in the nineteenth century. And, strange as it may seem to many, we now demand our right to vote according to the declaration of the government under which we live.

This right no one pretends to deny. We need not prove ourselves equal to Daniel Webster to enjoy this privilege, for the ignorant man digging in the ditch has all the civil rights he has. We need not prove our muscular power equal to this same man in the ditch to enjoy this privilege, for the most tiny, weak, ill-shaped stripling of twenty-one has all the civil rights of this man.

The right is ours. The question now is: how shall we get possession of what rightfully belongs to us? We should not feel so sorely grieved if no man who had not attained the full stature of a Webster, Clay, Van Buren, or Gerrit Smith could claim the right of the elective franchise. But to have drunkards, idiots, horse-racing, rum-selling rowdies, ignorant and silly boys fully recognized, while we ourselves are thrust out from all the rights that belong to citizens, it is too grossly insulting to the dignity of woman to be longer quietly submitted to.

Questions 11–13 ask about Passage A.

11. Which of the following best expresses the main idea of the passage?

A. In the 19th century, Elizabeth Cady Stanton was one of the first women to fight to secure a woman's right to vote.

B. Elizabeth Cady Stanton, an activist and philosopher of the 19th century, held steadfast in her beliefs despite immense pressure for her to quit.

C. In the 19th century, Elizabeth Cady Stanton fought bravely to ensure equal rights for all races and genders.

D. Elizabeth Cady Stanton was one of the foremost women's rights activists of the 19th century.

12. According to paragraph 4, Stanton believed that since the women's movement first began, protesters had used religion to:

F. keep women in their Biblically-ordained place.

G. hold women to a higher standard than others.

H. contain the women's movement to one small area.

J. squelch further uprisings from the movement.

13. The author mentions the information about the ratification of the 15th Amendment in order to:

A. show that Stanton was equally committed to the cause of abolition as she was to women's suffrage.

B. demonstrate both Stanton and Anthony's commitment to abolition.

C. explain that both Stanton and Anthony valued women's suffrage above all else.

D. demonstrate that while Stanton was more committed to women's suffrage than abolition, she fought valiantly for the ratification of the 15th Amendment.

Questions 14–17 ask about Passage B.

14. Stanton uses the sentence starting with "We do not propose to petition the legislature. . ." in paragraph 1 in order to:

F. suggest that escalating tension between men and the women of the movement can be reversed if they tried to understand where each other was coming from.

G. criticize the crowd for telling the women's movement that they should go back to wearing skirts instead of "men's attire" and go back to caring for their children.

H. illustrate the idiocy of the current voting regulations and demand a change in favor of women's suffrage.

J. show the crowd that the women's movement is not trying to reverse the roles women and men played in the 19th century.

15. Based on the information presented in the passage, which of the following activities would Elizabeth Cady Stanton most likely disapprove of a woman doing?

A. peacefully protesting an anti-woman rally

B. choosing not to vote

C. getting married when she didn't want to

D. enlisting in the army

16. The last paragraph, which ends with Stanton's phrase in line 48, "it is too grossly insulting to the dignity of woman to be longer quietly submitted to," indicates that:

F. she is outraged that low-esteemed men have the right to vote when women do not and indicates that she will no longer remain silent about the issue.

G. she will no longer remain quiet about the unfair treatment of women by men who have unscrupulous morals.

H. she is insulted by the lack of concern great men like Webster and Clay have given to the cause while men of low esteem have rallied behind her.

J. she is finished with silence after witnessing men with low morals exercising their right to vote even though men like Webster and Clay have championed her cause.

GO ON TO THE NEXT PAGE.

17. Based on the information in paragraphs 3 and 4 in Passage B, it can be reasonably inferred that Stanton believes Daniel Webster to be:

A. pretentious
B. charitable
C. intelligent
D. responsive

Questions 18–20 ask about both passages.

18. Which details from Passage B most strongly support the author of Passage A's premise that Stanton believed in a much broader vision of women's rights than just the right to vote?

F. Canton asks legislature to consider women as strong as men, if not physically, then certainly in mind and in spirit.
G. Canton explains her grievance that even men who have not attained the full stature of a Webster, Clay, Van Buren, or Gerrit Smith can claim the right of the elective franchise.
H. Canton petitions the legislature to urge men to take up the familial burdens left behind when a woman earns her own wages.
J. Canton renounces men's ability to imprison his wife, take her earned wages, take her inherited property, and keep the children if they should separate.

19. Which of the following statements provides the most accurate comparison of the tone of each passage?

A. Passage A is dismissive in tone, whereas Passage B is arrogant.
B. Passage A is restrained in tone, whereas Passage B is fervent.
C. Passage A is reflective in tone, whereas Passage B is enthusiastic.
D. Passage A is diplomatic in tone, whereas Passage B is cautionary.

20. Both Passage A and Passage B characterize Elizabeth Cady Stanton as:

F. a committed, independent revolutionary
G. a calm, determined negotiator
H. a negligible, disturbing agitator
J. a contradictory, polarizing alarmist

Passage III

HUMANITIES: This passage is adapted from the memoir *The Immigrant's Daughter* by Mary Terzian. ©2005 by Booklocker.com, Inc.

I reach the threshold of my teens without displaying any signs of normalcy defined by the image that Father imported from his native provincial town in Historic Armenia, now Eastern Turkey. That image has been frozen in his memory for forty years and at this time I have to live up to it as a young girl in Cairo—a bustling, Westernized, modern city. The generation gap, in our case, is an abyss. Is it any wonder that whenever we meet, we collide?

The presence of the British Army creates another cultural imbalance. Local young girls, as well as young men, are recruited as civilian workers. The soldiers date the girls. Father cannot accept such changes in lifestyle.

"How shameful. In our time, we didn't see a girl until our wedding day"!

Is he going to use the same methods on me? I shudder at the thought of being given away to a man I have never met. I certainly would like to measure his ability to think and feel before saying "yes." I am like a mouse trying to hang a bell on a cat; all protests and no solution.

Father expects me to be an accomplished housewife like Mama; sew quilts, cook *dolma*, make preserves, and raise children, even though this is a gross underrating of her qualities. I have no interest in such homely occupations in Cairo, which offers more options than domesticity. I want to go to school and read to my heart's content.

"What do girls need an education for?" Father repeats often. "Once a woman earns money, you can't control her."

"Control" irks me to no end. It is demeaning to be controlled like an inane person. I wish Mama were alive to defend me. She is probably turning over in her grave now. What happened to the promise to Mama to educate me?

"You should learn how to keep house," Stepmother rubs in. "How will you ever be ready for marriage?"

Sure, I think. *It suits you fine.*

I already provide mundane daily services and, whenever we have an occasional maid, train her to Stepmother's directives.

"Do you see what I have become?" I confide in Kev, "I'm no better than a maid!"

"What do you think I do?" he replies, "I have to be in Papa's shop during all my free hours! He uses me as a delivery boy."

"Why can't she do some of the work?" I complain. "She's supposed to be our Mama!"

"She'd drown in a cup of water!" Kev remarks with disdain, and adds, with a sour note, "Papa pays his help weekly. I work there for free."

His and my concepts on lifestyle differ distinctly from our parents'. Kev occasionally escapes to the Armenian Fine Arts Club where he enjoys playing ping-pong or socializing with friends. I love reading and bury myself in books, anything I can lay hands on; novels, non-fiction books, anthologies, and dictionaries. Even the labels on Quaker Oats tins that come in several languages are not immune to my voracious appetite for the printed word. I read books secretly, for a long time after I go to bed, in the shadow of the hall light, by moonlight, or by the light of the street lamps shedding pale beams through the window. I slide them underneath my notebooks at my desk whenever I hear footsteps. I read them walking to school, in the classrooms, at recess, in the restroom. It is an addiction all right. My parents cannot tolerate this abnormal attraction to the printed word.

"Those books are raping your mind!" Father yells with exasperation. *I'm not going to give them up whatever you say*! I determine.

Without a real mother, whose advice I can trust, books are my guiding light and my fantasy world. They provide excitement, exhilaration, dreams and a bridge to the outside world. They teach me high aspirations like the ethnic poem "Rise and raise others with you," or excerpts like,

"Always target the summit
In trying to reach your goal.
Even if you don't reach it,
The effort prevents your fall . . ."

I am fascinated by new words. I entertain myself for hours looking up synonyms. One summer, I decide to learn the whole French dictionary by heart.

21. The passage establishes all of the following about the narrator EXCEPT:

A. She is determined to live her life the way in which she prefers.

B. She refuses to be controlled by anyone, including her father.

C. She values the insight of her brother, Kev.

D. She struggles against her feelings of wanting to savor the traditions of her heritage.

22. Based on the narrator's account, what is the primary reason she continues to read despite her father's protests?

F. She wants to prove to her father that girls are equal to boys.

G. Books help guide her since her mother passed away.

H. Books allow her to get away from her stepmother for a few hours.

J. She wants to show Kev that she's not just a maid.

23. As it is used in line 29, the word *gross* most nearly means:

A. crass.

B. vulgar.

C. blatant.

D. whole.

24. The author most likely includes the information in paragraph 1 in order to:

F. identify one of the causes of friction between the narrator and her father.

G. contrast the image of a "normal" Turkish teen with that of a modern girl in Cairo.

H. describe the circumstances in which the narrator grew up.

J. compare Historic Armenia with modern Cairo.

25. By his statement in line 57, "She'd drown in a cup of water!" Kev believes his stepmother to be:

A. disqualified.

B. fragile.

C. overbearing.

D. incompetent.

26. Which of the following words best describes the narrator's craving for the printed word?

F. Insatiable

G. Abnormal

H. Illicit

J. Insurmountable

27. The narrator compares herself to a "mouse trying to hang a bell on a cat" in line 23–24 order to illustrate:

A. her attempts at gaining the favor of her father.

B. the uselessness of trying to change her father's beliefs about marriage.

C. her feelings about being stuck in a city where she has no voice.

D. the bravery she shows in trying to change her family's long-standing beliefs.

28. Which one of the following statements is NOT used in the passage to illustrate the father's outdated point of view?

F. "Father expects me to be an accomplished housewife like Mama."

G. "Those books are raping your mind!"

H. "What do girls need an education for?"

J. "You should learn how to keep house. How will you ever be ready for marriage?"

29. The author most likely includes the information in lines 97–99 in order to demonstrate:

A. the narrator's keen intelligence.

B. the narrator's flagrant bragging.

C. the narrator's ability to craft stories.

D. the narrator's desire to escape.

30. The author uses the information in lines 71–79 in order to demonstrate that in order for the narrator to continue to read, she must:

F. avoid reading in her bedroom.

G. keep her true aspirations away from her family.

H. hide it from her parents.

J. only read books at school.

Passage IV

NATURAL SCIENCE: This passage is adapted from an essay entitled "Internet Governance: Privatized Control Vs. Governmental Control" by Kay Caslmon (© Kay Caslmon 2003).

People can argue this thing all day long: should a private company or the government regulate the Internet? Here's the right answer—because the Internet exists in a world that is already regulated by policies and laws, government officials, the makers and upholders of these current laws, should be the people responsible for the overall regulation of the Internet.

With this responsibility comes the enormous task of managing the protection of First Amendment rights in the United States, and honoring social and public interests across the world. Despite the fact that governmental agencies should have official control, ultimate responsibility is still in the hands of the Internet users who vote; they, along with the officials elected to serve them, make up the global community. Voters have the ability to stay informed and elect responsible individuals to the appropriate governmental posts, and the elected officials have the responsibility to act on the will of the people.

Many people would argue that a private organization, with no governmental interference, should regulate the Internet. This is a potentially hazardous idea for two reasons: first, there are few checks and balances within private corporations to keep public interests from getting trampled and to keep them from becoming too powerful, and second, the public does not get a voice in who runs the operations in a private company. Top-level management of companies is never elected.

One such private company whom the government signed an almost eight-year contract with was called Network Solutions, Inc. (NSI). In the early '90's, the government gave them complete control over domain-name registration. NSI, with no competition, turned the public Internet into a lucrative business by charging fees for domain name registration. They were granted control of a precious resource in cyberspace and turned it into a moneymaking venture instead of the public service it should have been. There were few checks to control NSI's profiteering, and the government ended its contract with the company. Now, the same complaints are being made about the Internet Corporation for Assigned Names and Numbers (ICANN), another private company.

ICANN promises to be a "global, consensus-driven, non-profit organization," but has come under attack for having private meetings and administering unauthorized fees like its predecessor. The public was never given a say in much of the Internet policies they provide and its interests are not being put first. Imagine what this or another private organization could do if it had *complete* control over Internet regulation. The public could be charged exorbitant prices to even get on-line, let alone exercise their First Amendment rights and publish in cyberspace.

Government regulation of the Internet would be much better than regulation by a private company for both international and national Internet users. In order to best serve the interests of the global community, an international organization like the World Intellectual Property Organization (WIPO) could be established where agents of each member country could represent the interests, culturally and politically, of their respective countries. This WIPO-like establishment could work to institute proactive, rather than reactive, flexible laws and rights for Internet users like the rights guaranteed U.S. citizens in the Constitution. One of the established laws would have to guarantee every person free access to domain names, thereby ensuring that DN registration is not used to make money. Since everyone would have that right, people who would choose to disregard their countries' or the international Internet policies could be subject to fines, revocation of domain names, or even prison sentences. For example, in the U.S., this may help deter those people who commit libel, publish obscenity, or spread hate speech.

U.S. citizens would gain from this type of governmental regulation as well. Through their representatives, adaptations to existing copyright and commerce laws could be made suitable for the Internet, thereby protecting businesspeople, artists, and trades people from Internet users bent on crime. Also, the First Amendment right of free speech could be better protected.

Governmental regulation of the Internet would help the global community far better than privatized management would because it would represent the will of more Internet users across the globe, granting rights and privileges a private company could not, and would create a stable environment where every type of communication is imaginable.

31. Which of the following lists of evidence does the author use to support her claim that private organizations should not regulate the Internet?

A. Private organizations would protect businesspeople, artists, and trades people from Internet users bent on crime.

B. Private organizations would keep their own interests in mind, would have too much power, and the public would not have a voice in the running of the business.

C. Private organizations would institute reactive, inflexible laws, would provide unrecompensed access to domain names, and would require registration for users.

D. Private organizations would fail to protect First Amendment rights, would discredit organizations like WIPO and NSI, and would make changes to existing copyrights.

32. The author makes the argument that a WIPO-like organization designed to regulate the Internet would best serve the public by doing all of the following EXCEPT:

F. representing the cultural interests of each member's country

G. representing the political interests of each member's country

H. instituting steadfast, reactive laws to protect citizens

J. instituting flexible, proactive laws to protect citizens

33. It can be reasonably inferred from the passage that the author believes that domain name registration should be:

A. heavily controlled by the government
B. free
C. privatized
D. revised to adhere to existing copyright laws.

34. The author most likely includes the information in lines 95–103 in order to suggest:

F. specific ways U.S. citizens can conform to the government's regulations
G. the benefits to citizens of the United States of moving to a governmental regulatory agency
H. the flaws in adapting a new set of regulations from a privatized company
J. the increased awareness of U.S. citizens regarding the government's Internet regulations.

35. Which of the following statements best expresses the main idea of the passage?

A. The government, not a private company, should regulate the Internet.
B. A private company, not the government, should regulate the Internet.
C. The people, instead of the government, should regulate the Internet.
D. Internet regulation should not occur in any way, so as not to inhibit the First Amendment.

36. According to the passage, which privatized company used domain name registration as a way to profit?

F. WIPO
G. ICANN
H. NSI
J. DN

37. The main function of the sixth paragraph (lines 69–94) is to:

A. contrast the differences between WIPO and a private company's Internet regulations.
B. list the credits of a governmental organization that currently helps regulate the Internet
C. identify a strategy for the implementation of governmental regulation
D. compare the different regulatory functions of WIPO to other governmental agencies

38. Based on details in the passage, how could one describe the author's stance about privatized management of Internet regulation?

F. She is firmly against it.
G. She is against it, but only slightly.
H. She is for it with adaptations.
J. She is in favor of it.

39. According to the passage, the author compares ICANN's regulatory style to NSI's because:

A. ICANN has refused to publish reports of Internet fees.

B. ICANN is not allowing the public to have a say in Internet policy.

C. ICANN is having private meetings and administering unauthorized fees and regulations.

D. ICANN is dodging governmental checks and balances.

40. As it is used in line 28, the word *hazardous* most nearly means:

F. unpredictable

G. crucial

H. unsafe

J. risky

END OF TEST 3
STOP! DO NOT TURN THE PAGE UNTIL TOLD TO DO SO.
DO NOT RETURN TO A PREVIOUS TEST.

Practice Test
Science Reasoning

TIME: 35 minutes
40 questions

DIRECTIONS: There are several passages in this test. Each passage is followed by several questions. After reading a passage, choose the best answer to each question and fill in the corresponding oval on your answer document. You may refer to the passages as often as necessary.

You are NOT permitted to use a calculator on this test.

Passage I

The owners of a greenhouse wish to optimize the light and watering schedules for their plants to achieve maximum growth. They have a choice of three light bulbs, which emit different intensities at different wavelengths as shown in Figure 1. The blue-green light (A) has the highest intensity. The blue-red light (B) has the next highest intensity. The red-yellow light (C) has the least high intensity. They examine the growth of four plants with each of these lights; the results are shown in Figure 2.

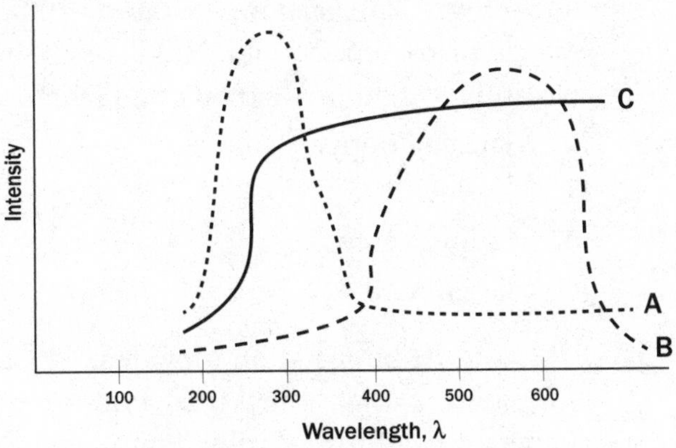

Figure 1

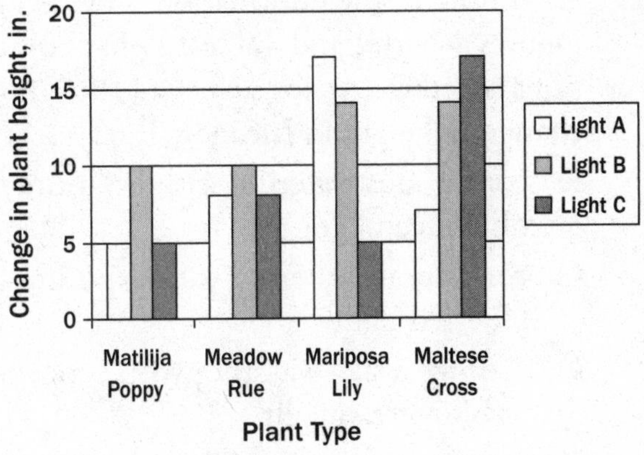

Figure 2

After being subjected to different lighting conditions, the plants are subjected to differing watering schedules to determine the changes that occur. Plant characteristics are shown in Table 1.

Table 1

Plant	Water Schedule	Change in Height	Number of New Branches	Number of New Blooms	Number of New Leaves
Matilija Poppy	Continuous	1.8	8	32	85
	Once a day	—	35	79	159
	Twice a day	3.8	25	68	136
	4 times a day	2.5	14	55	112
Meadow Rue	Continuous	6.4	45	95	176
	Once a day	—	10	22	95
	Twice a day	5.2	14	65	114
	4 times a day	5.7	26	76	121

1. Based on the information provided in Figures 1 and 2, the bulb the greenhouse owners should select to achieve the highest growth from all four plants has a high intensity in the range:

A. 250–325

B. 250–600

C. 300–450

D. 450–650

2. According to the information provided in Figures 1 and 2 and Table 1, what conditions are the best for achieving the most change in height in Meadow Rue?

F. continuous watering with exposure to blue-green light

G. continuous watering with exposure to blue-red light

H. 4 times a day watering with exposure to blue-green light

J. 4 times a day watering with exposure to blue-red light

3. The greenhouse owners lost the information in Table 1 for the change in height according to watering once a day. Which figure is most likely to be correct for Matilija Poppy?

A. < 3.8

B. > 3.8

C. ≤ 1.8

D. ≥ 1.8

4. Sunlight produces visible light over a wide range of wavelengths, from ~350λ to ~700λ. Which plant type would NOT reach its maximum height if it had only sunlight?

F. Matilija Poppy

G. Meadow Rue

H. Mariposa Lily

J. Maltese Cross

5. Based on the information provided, which two lights caused the same amount of change in height in Matilija Poppy?

A. blue-green and red-yellow

B. blue-green and blue-red

C. blue-red and red-yellow

D. red-yellow and blue-green

Passage II

A chemist is performing a series of experiments to determine the best use for a new protein molecule called *immunoglobin*. He believes it may prevent the binding of either the HIV-1 or HIV-2 virus's *protein coat* (outer shell of the virus) to the CD3 receptor on *T cells* (types of white blood cell affected by the HIV virus). The scientist has already determined that this new protein molecule thrives the best inside the *intracellular* (internal) fluid of a cell, but must then pass through the plasma membrane of the cell and be excreted into the *extracellular* (external) fluid where it can interact with the HIV virus. Here, the scientist believes that immunoglobin will bind to the protein coat of the HIV virus, causing it to lose its capacity to bind to the CD3 receptors. Thus, neither strain of HIV could infect the T cells in the body.

Experiment 1

The intracellular fluid of twelve different samples of cells containing immunoglobin was extracted and concentrated. Each of the twelve concentrated samples was placed into a petri dish in differing amounts. Cultured T cells and the HIV-1 strain, which is the most common and most easily transmittable strain, were added to petri dishes 1–6. Cultured T cells and the HIV-2 strain, which is less easily transmittable and less easily affected by intracellular factors, were added to petri dishes marked 7–12. The scientist wanted to determine if, based on the microliters of intracellular fluid present, the immunoglobin attached to the protein coat of both strains of HIV virus. He also wanted to determine if the virus attached to the CD3 receptor on the T-cells. The results are displayed in Table 1.

Table 1

Petri Dishes	Intracellular Fluid (microliters/ul)	Did Bonding Occur Between Immunoglobin and the HIV Strain?	Did Bonding Occur Between the HIV Strain and T Cells?
1	50	No	Yes
2	100	No	Yes
3	250	No	Yes
4	500	Yes	No
5	750	Yes	No
6	1000	Yes	No
7	50	Yes	Yes
8	100	No	No
9	250	No	No
10	500	Yes	No
11	750	Yes	No
12	1000	Yes	No

Experiment 2

The scientist wanted to determine if adding an amount of a sodium ion solution into the intracellular fluid affected the bonding between immunoglobin and the strains of HIV. He extracted 6 new samples of intracellular fluid (250 ul) and added various amounts of sodium ions to the fluid. He then added HIV-1 and the cultured T cells to petri dishes 13–15 and HIV-2 and cultured T-cells to the petri dishes 16–18. The results are displayed in Table 2.

Table 2

Petri Dishes	Sodium Ion Solution (microliters/ul)	Did Bonding Occur Between Immunoglobin and the HIV Strain?	Did Bonding Occur Between the HIV Strain and T Cells?
13	0.00001	No	Yes
14	0.0001	No	Yes
15	0.001	Yes	No
16	0.00001	No	No
17	0.0001	No	No
18	0.001	No	No

6. According to the Scientist's data in Experiment 2, did the amount of sodium ion solution in the intracellular fluid affect the immunoglobin's binding to the HIV-1 strain?

F. Yes, because when 0.001 of the solution was added to the 250 ul of intracellular fluid, the immunoglobin bonded with HIV-1, but didn't when 250 ul was used without the addition of the sodium.

G. Yes, because when 0.0001 of the solution was added to the 250 ul of intracellular fluid, the immunoglobin bonded with HIV-1, but didn't when 250 ul was used without the addition of the sodium.

H. No, because when 0.001 of the solution was added to the 250 ul of intracellular fluid, the immunoglobin did not bond with HIV-1, but bonded when 250 ul was used without the addition of the sodium.

J. No, because when 0.0001 of the solution was added to the 250 ul of intracellular fluid, the immunoglobin did not bond with HIV-1, but bonded when 250 ul was used without the addition of the sodium.

7. In Experiment 1, the least amount of concentrated intracellular fluid containing immunoglobin that prevents the spread of the HIV-1 virus is:
   A. 50 ul
   B. 100 ul
   C. 500 ul
   D. 750 ul

8. Which one of the following best depicts immunoglobin's process to bond with the HIV virus?
   F. Immunoglobin inside intracellular fluid → Immunoglobin moves through plasma membrane → Immunoglobin excreted into extracellular fluid → Immunoglobin binds to protein coat of HIV virus
   G. Immunoglobin inside extracellular fluid → Immunoglobin moves through plasma membrane → Immunoglobin binds to protein coat of HIV virus → Immunoglobin binds to CD3 receptors on T cells
   H. Immunoglobin binds to CD3 receptors on T cells → Immunoglobin moves through plasma membrane → Immunoglobin excreted to extracellular fluid → Immunoglobin binds to protein coat of HIV virus
   J. Immunoglobin inside intracellular fluid → Immunoglobin excreted to extracellular fluid → Immunoglobin binds to CD3 receptors on T cells → Immunoglobin binds to protein coat of HIV virus

9. Based on the information in Experiment 1, which amount of intracellular fluid failed to prevent HIV infection despite immunoglobin's bonding with the virus?
   A. 1000 ul
   B. 750 ul
   C. 250 ul
   D. 50 ul

10. Is immunoglobin more effective at preventing the HIV bond with the T cells after the addition of the sodium solution in 250 ul?
   F. Yes for HIV-1 and Yes for HIV-2
   G. Yes for HIV-1 and No for HIV-2
   H. No for HIV-1 and Yes for HIV-2
   J. No for HIV-1 and No for HIV-2

11. Based on the information in Experiments 1 and 2, in which of the following petri dishes did an infection of the HIV virus NOT occur?
   A. 2
   B. 7
   C. 14
   D. 15

Passage III

The term *GM* foods or *GMOs* (genetically-modified organisms) is most commonly used to refer to crop plants created for consumption using the latest molecular biology techniques. The precursor to this was conventional plant breeding, where plants with a desired characteristic were bred with other plants in hopes of developing offspring plants with the desired characteristic. Scientists created GM plants by isolating genes responsible for a desired trait and inserting that gene into a different plant. The new genetically-modified plant will have the desired trait as well.

Here, two theorists debate the benefits and risks of these genetically modified foods.

Theory 1

Genetically modified foods are a viable, healthy option for consumers. The enhancement of desired traits has traditionally been undertaken through breeding, but conventional plant breeding methods can be very time consuming and are often inaccurate. Genetic engineering, on the other hand, can create plants with the exact desired trait very rapidly and with great accuracy.

Not only can genes be transferred from one plant to another, they can also be transferred from non-plant organisms to plants, making the modification options almost limitless. The best-known example is the use of the bacterium B.t. (*Bacillus thuringiensis)* genes in corn. When B.t.'s crystal proteins that are lethal to insect larvae are transferred into corn, they enable the corn to produce its own pesticides against insects such as the European corn borer.

The world population is predicted to double in the next 50 years. Ensuring an adequate food supply is going to be a major challenge. GM foods meet this need by providing pest and disease resistance along with herbicide, cold and drought tolerance, as well.

Theory 2

Genetically modified foods are not a viable, healthy option for consumers, because of their tendency toward environmental hazards and human health risks. Last year a laboratory study was published showing that B.t. toxins kill many species of insect larvae indiscriminately; it is not possible to design a B.t. toxin that would only kill crop-damaging pests and remain harmless to all other insects. In addition, although creating herbicide tolerant plants is beneficial to crops, the problem lies in discrimination; through pollination, the crops crossbreed with other nearby plants, creating herbicide tolerant weeds. Weedkillers that used to be effective against those encroaching weeds are therefore no longer effective, causing GM weeds to inhibit food production.

Introducing foreign genes into food plants also has an unexpected and negative impact on human health. Inserting a foreign gene into a food can create a new allergen thereby causing allergic reactions in susceptible individuals. Conventional breeding techniques are proven to work, and have made great advancements in more recent years and would continue to do so if more capital were poured into the research instead of into the development of risky GM foods.

12. With which of the following statements would both theorists agree? Herbicide tolerance:

F. is theoretically a great way to reduce the number of weeds overtaking plants used for food.

G. is beneficial whether it's created in plants used for food by breeding or by creating genetically modified foods.

H. works against itself because when herbicide tolerant plants breed with nearby weeds, the new weeds are herbicide resistant.

J. is a dangerous way to modify plants used for food because of the risks of cross-pollinating with nearby weeds.

13. According to the passage, a similarity between conventional breeding techniques and genetic engineering of plants is:

A. they are both ways of producing plants with desired characteristics.

B. they are both time-consuming ways to produce plants with desired characteristics.

C. they are both costly ways to produce plants with desired characteristics.

D. they are both negligent ways of producing plants with desired characteristics.

14. Which of the following best describes each theorist's points about conventional plant breeding in plants used for food?

	Theory 1	Theory 2
F.	wasteful of resources	contingent on too many factors
G.	time-consuming	too risky
H.	too costly	proven
J.	often inaccurate	would continue to advance with more money

15. Assume Theory 2's assertions about genetically modified foods are correct. Based on this assumption and the information provided, which of the following is most likely to occur when a herbicide resistant gene is inserted into a plant used for food?

A. The plant will become herbicide resistant, will cross breed with a nearby weed, and thus create a weed resistant to herbicides.

B. The plant will become herbicide resistant, which will cause the weeds nearby to be killed off by the herbicides and the plant used for food to thrive.

C. The plant will become herbicide resistant, will breed with other plants used for food, spreading the herbicide resistance to other plant life.

D. The plant will become herbicide resistant, creating a new allergen that will cause allergic reactions in susceptible individuals.

16. The scientist in favor of Theory 2 implies that Theory 1 is *weakened* by which of the following statements?

F. B.t. toxins kill insect larvae of the European corn borer.

G. B.t. toxins kill insect larvae without regard to the nature of the insect.

H. B.t. toxins create new allergens in plants used for food.

J. B.t. toxins create herbicide tolerance in plants used for food.

17. Which one of the following statements is NOT an argument made in Theory 1 in support for genetically modified foods as viable and healthy choices for consumers?

A. GM foods can be created using genes from other organisms besides plants, making the options for modification far-reaching.

B. Foods can be modified to be resistant to cold.

C. GM foods can be created to be resistant to certain allergens.

D. With the growing population, GM foods are necessary to meet the provisional needs of humanity.

18. Suppose a researcher genetically modified a soybean that was herbicide tolerant, drought tolerant, and easily produced. After consumption, it created an allergic reaction in 3% of the population who didn't have an allergic reaction before. This creation would significantly strengthen which argument?

F. This strengthens Theory 1, because 3% of the population is a small number of people, and the herbicide and drought tolerance is vitally important.

G. This strengthens Theory 1, because although 3% of the population is a large number of people, the benefits outweigh the risks.

H. This strengthens Theory 2, because creating a new allergic reaction has dangerous implications if the plant were to cross breed with other plants.

J. This strengthens Theory 2, because it produced a new allergen, one that could be avoided with conventional breeding techniques.

Passage IV

Figure 1 shows a *Fenn-Winterstein Respirometer*. Living bacterial cells are sealed in Flask B, along with a strip of paper soaked in *potassium hydroxide* (KOH), which changes color depending on the cells inside the flask. As the cells inside Flask B consume oxygen, the kerosene drop moves inside the capillary tubing. If the diameter of the capillary tubing is known, the amount of oxygen consumed can be determined.

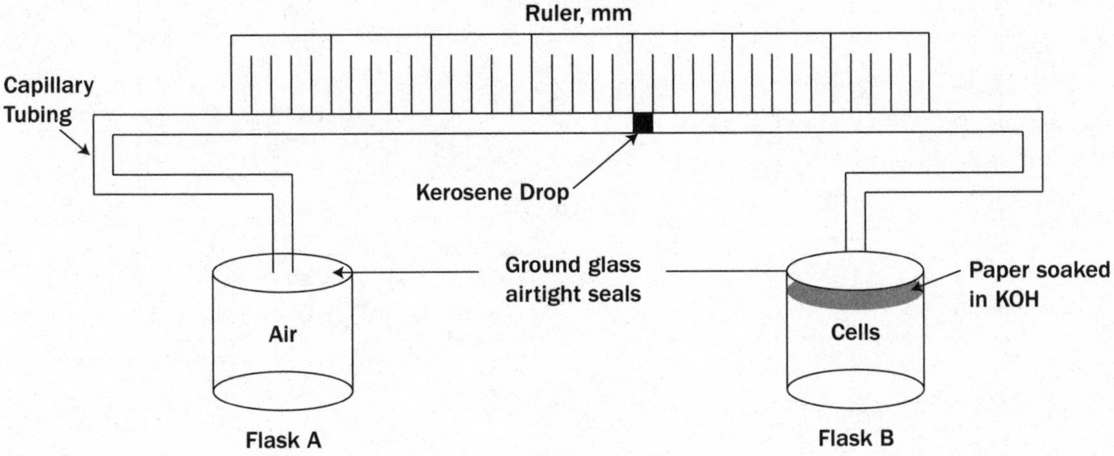

Figure 1

Table 1 shows five different types of bacterial cells, the time it took them to begin respiration, and the amount of oxygen consumed after respiration had begun.

Table 1

Cell Type	# Cells/ml	Initial Onset of Respiration (min.)	Oxygen Consumed (ml/h)	Kerosene Drop Moved in .5 hours (mm)	Kerosene Drop Moved in 2 hours (mm)	Color of KOH strip
E. coli	1×10^6	21.34	.32	4.1	9.3	green
Dillococcus	1×10^6	13.22	.9	6	11.2	red
Rhodospirillum	1×10^6	16.11	.52	5.7	10.8	brown
Lactobacillus spp	1×10^7	58.54	.1	0	7	beige
Lactobacillus spp	1×10^6	48.22	.16	0	8.7	beige

Table 2 shows the KOH strip results after four separate trials were completed on various bacterial cells in Flask B.

Table 2

Trial	Oxygen Consumed (l/h)	Color of KOH strip
1	1.42	red brown
2	1.22	green red
3	.16	beige
4	.48	beige green

19. Based on the information in Tables 1 and 2, one could conclude that Sample 4 contained which bacterial cells?

A. *Dillococcus* and *Lactobacillus spp* 1×10^7

B. *E. coli* and *Lactobacillus spp* 1×10^7

C. *Dillococcus* and *Lactobacillus spp* 1×10^6

D. *E. coli* and *Lactobacillus spp* 1×10^6

20. Table 1 best supports which of the following hypotheses about the onset of initial respiration and the amount of oxygen consumed in Flask B?

F. The slower the initial onset of respiration, the more oxygen is consumed.

G. The faster the initial onset of respiration, the more oxygen is consumed.

H. The initial onset of respiration has no bearing on the amount of oxygen consumed.

J. The initial onset of respiration only affects the amount of oxygen consumed for *E. coli.*

21. Suppose the ground glass airtight seals for Flask A and Flask B in Figure 1 were replaced with cotton. Based on the information provided, what reaction is most likely to take place?
   A. The kerosene drop would move to the left when bacterial cells began respiration.
   B. The kerosene drop would move to the right when bacterial cells began respiration.
   C. The kerosene drop would not move when bacterial cells began respiration.
   D. The bacterial cells would not begin respiration.

22. According to the information provided in Tables 1 and 2, which two trials contained the bacterial cells that made the kerosene drop move the farthest?
   F. Trials 1 and 2
   G. Trials 3 and 4
   H. Trials 2 and 4
   J. Trials 1 and 3

23. Based on the information provided in Table 1, the best explanation for *Lactobacillus spp* not moving the kerosene drop in .5 hours is:
   A. Since *Lactobacillus spp's* KOH strip was always beige, the amount of oxygen consumed was always less than the other three types of bacterial cells, causing the kerosene drop not to move.
   B. Since *Lactobacillus spp* had two different trials with two varying amounts (1×10^6 and 1×10^7), the results were distorted.
   C. Since both amounts of *Lactobacillus spp* moved the kerosene drop fewer mm than the other bacterial cells in two hours, the amount of oxygen consumed was less, causing the kerosene drop not to move at all in .5 hours.
   D. Since *Lactobacillus spp's* earliest onset of initial respiration didn't occur until 48.22 minutes after the trial began, the kerosene drop couldn't have moved because the cells weren't consuming oxygen yet.

Passage V

Students performed the following experiments to measure the effect of the enzymes in a potato with the substrate *catechol.*

Experiment 1

The students set up three beakers and added solutions of 200 ml of catechol in equal concentrations to each beaker. They either heated or cooled the beakers to three different temperatures. Then, they created a potato mixture by homogenizing 75 grams of potatoes and 500 ml of water. They placed three drops of this potato mixture into each of the three beakers and noted the color changes if any were present. A color would indicate that a reaction had occurred with darker shades indicating the greatest reactions. The results of the experiment are noted in Table 1.

Table 1

Beaker	Temp. °C	Color after 5 min.	Color after 30 min.
1	0°	Light yellow	Yellow
2	25°	Yellow	Dark Yellow
3	100°	Clear	Clear

Experiment 2

The students set up three new beakers and added solutions of 200 ml of catechol in equal concentrations to each beaker. Then, they adjusted the pH values of each beaker to differing values, noting that a pH value greater than 7 would be basic, a value at 7 would be neutral and a pH value less than 7 would be acidic. They placed three drops of the potato mixture into each of the three beakers and noted the color changes if any were present. The results of this experiment are noted in Table 2.

Table 2

Beaker	pH Value	Color after 5 min.	Color after 30 min.
4	4	Dark Yellow	Light Brown
5	7	Light Yellow	Yellow
6	10	Clear	Clear

Experiment 3

In a third experiment, the students set up four beakers with 200 ml of the catechol solution. They then added a new substance, *phenylthiourea* (PTC) to each beaker in various amounts. The potato mixture was added incrementally, with color changes noted after each addition. After 5 minutes and again at 30 minutes, the students recorded the color of the solution in each beaker. The results are displayed in Table 3.

Table 3

Beaker	Drops of PTC	Drops of Potato Mixture	Color after 5 min.	Color after 30 min.
7	0	1	Clear	Clear
		3	Clear	Clear
		5	Clear	Clear
8	1	1	Clear	Very Light Yellow
		3	Very Light Yellow	Light Yellow
		5	Light Yellow	Yellow
9	10	1	Very Light Yellow	Light Yellow
		3	Light Yellow	Yellow
		5	Yellow	Dark Yellow
10	20	1	Light Yellow	Yellow
		3	Dark Yellow	Dark Yellow
		5	Dark Yellow	Light Brown

GO ON TO THE NEXT PAGE.

24. In which 3 beakers did NO reaction take place between the catechol solution and potato mixture after 30 minutes?
   F. Beakers 1, 5, and 8
   G. Beakers 2, 5, and 10
   H. Beakers 3, 6, and 7
   I. Beakers 3, 7, and 9

25. According to Experiment 3, in which situation would the catechol solution NOT turn light yellow?
   A. 20 drops of PTC and 1 drop of the potato mixture in 5 minutes
   B. 10 drops of PTC and 3 drops of the potato mixture in 5 minutes
   C. 10 drops of PTC and 5 drops of the potato mixture in 5 minutes
   D. 1 drop of PTC and 3 drops of the potato mixture in 5 minutes

26. During Experiment 1, a student claimed that the warmer the temperature, the greater the reaction of the potato mixture and the catechol solution. Was she correct?
   F. No, because although a slight temperature increase increased the reaction, when the solution boiled, the solution stayed clear, indicating no reaction had taken place.
   G. No, because although a reaction occurred at each of the three temperature settings, the reaction at the boiling point was much less than that at the two cooler temperatures.
   H. Yes, because as the temperature increased, the color of the solution became lighter and lighter, indicating that a greater reaction was occurring.
   J. Yes, because although the color of the solution was clear at the boiling point, a reaction had to have taken place because it had taken place at 25 degrees, and that reaction must have been greater since the temperature had risen by 75 degrees.

27. Suppose the students wanted to determine the fastest way to achieve the darkest shade of yellow in the catechol solution and potato mixture with the least amount of additional substances. Based on the results of Experiments 1, 2 and 3, which conditions should the students replicate?
   A. Add 10 drops of *phenylthiourea* to the catechol solution and add 3 drops of the potato mixture
   B. Set the catechol solution to a pH of 7 and add 3 drops of the potato mixture
   C. Add 20 drops of *phenylthiourea* to the catechol solution and add 3 drops of the potato mixture
   D. Set the catechol solution to a pH of 4 and add 3 drops of the potato mixture

28. Based on the results of Experiment 3, the students could conclude that:
   F. The more drops of *phenylthiourea* added to the catechol solution and potato mixture, the greater the reaction
   G. The more drops of *phenylthiourea* added to the catechol solution and potato mixture, the greater the reaction, but only when combined with increasing drops of the potato mixture
   H. The fewer drops of *phenylthiourea* added to the catechol solution and potato mixture, the greater the reaction
   J. The fewer drops of *phenylthiourea* added to the catechol solution and potato mixture, the greater the reaction, but only when combined with decreasing drops of the potato mixture.

29. Based on the results of Experiment 2, which pH value resulted in a clear solution?
   A. an acidic pH
   B. a basic pH
   C. a neutral pH
   D. a pH of 4

Passage VI

To test the validity of global warming, scientists have investigated the average temperature and rainfall over the 100 years between 1900 and 2000. They wanted to determine if there were any climate changes, and if so, if those climate changes resulted from natural phenomena or human interference.

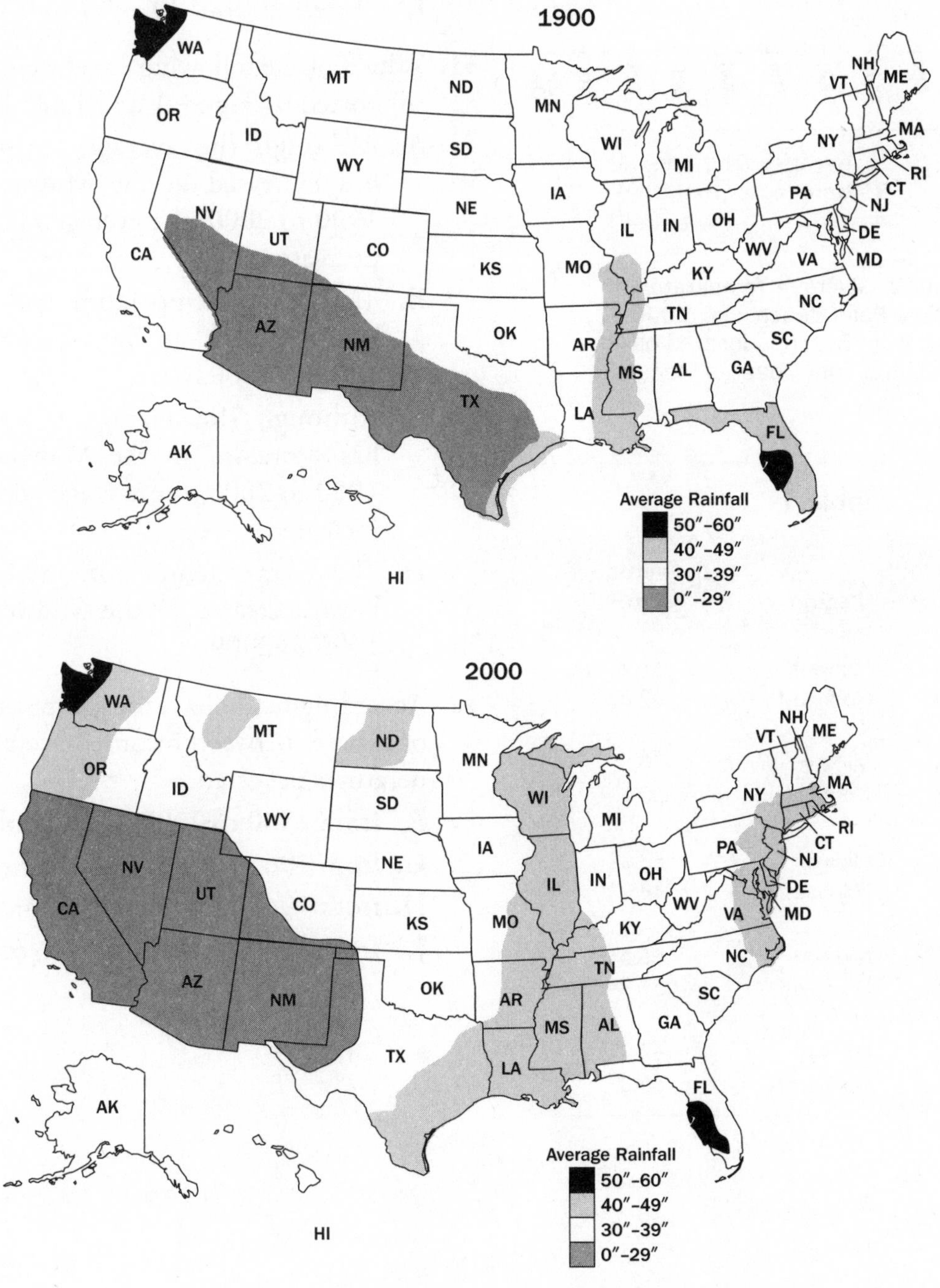

Figure 1 Average Rainfall: 1900 and 2000 Comparison

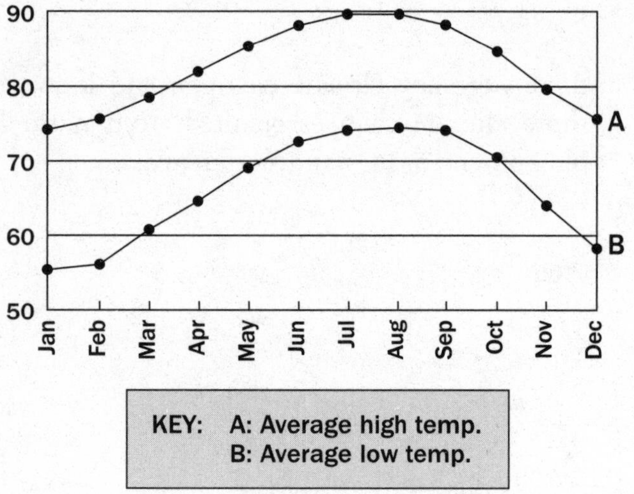

Figure 2 Average Temperature in West Palm Beach, Fla., 2000
West Palm Beach is located on the Central East Coast of Florida

Table 1

Year	Region	Average Temp. °F
1900	Midwest Northeast	61.2° 52.5°
1940	Midwest Northeast	60.3° 50.4°
1960	Midwest Northeast	63.4° 48.2°
1980	Midwest Northeast	65.5° 51.3°
2000	Midwest Northeast	67.2° 55.3°

30. Based on the information provided in Figure 1, we can conclude that the rainfall in California from 1900 to 2000:

F. increased from 0″–29″ to 30″–39″
G. increased from 30″–39″ to 40″–49″
H. decreased from 40″–49″ to 30″–39″
J. decreased from 30″–39″ to 0″–29″

31. Which of the following conclusions is best supported by Figure 1 and Table 1?

A. Although the average temperature has increased in the Midwest from 1900 to 2000, the average rainfall has decreased
B. The average temperature and rainfall have increased in the Midwest from 1900 to 2000.
C. Although the average temperature has decreased in the Midwest from 1900 to 2000, the average rainfall has increased.
D. The average temperature and rainfall have decreased in the Midwest from 1900 to 2000.

32. According to Table 1, the greatest number of degrees between recorded average temperatures occurred:

F. from 1900 to 2000 in the Midwest
G. from 1960 to 2000 in the Northeast
H. from 1940 to 2000 in the Midwest
J. from 1940 to 2000 in the Northeast

33. Suppose a person was living in West Palm Beach, Florida in the year 2000. What temperature and rainfall could they expect to NOT experience in August?

A. rainfall of 32″ and a low average temperature of approximately 74 degrees

B. rainfall of 30″ and a low average temperature of approximately 75 degrees

C. rainfall of 31″ and a high average temperature of approximately 85 degrees

D. rainfall of 39″ and a high average temperature of approximately 90 degrees

34. Based on the information provided, could scientists determine whether any possible climate changes resulted from natural phenomenon or human interference?

F. No, because there is no information provided that determines what impact humans have had on rainfall or temperature shifts.

G. No, because although the temperature has been proven to steadily increase in the Southwest from 1900 to 2000, there is no information provided that determines what impact humans have had on those temperature shifts.

H. No, because although the rainfall has been proven to steadily decrease in the Midwest and Northeast from 1900 to 2000, there is no information provided that determines what impact humans have had on this rainfall.

J. Yes, because although there is no information provided that determines what impact humans have had on rainfall or temperature shifts, scientists can still accurately deduce human influence.

Passage VII

To determine how nuclear energy released during thermonuclear fusion in stars can fully be utilized, researchers study two chain reactions that lead to the creation of helium nuclei (^4_2He). These chain reactions are expressed in nuclear equations where the elements that start the reaction (reactants) are placed to the left of the arrow and the elements produced (reaction products) are placed to the right. *Neutrino particles* (ν), subatomic *particles* similar to electrons and *gamma ray photons* (γ), packets of electromagnetic energy, are also released and noted in the nuclear equations.

Study 1: Proton-Proton Chain

In this study, researchers observed how hydrogen (H) protons interact to form helium in a 3-step chain reaction. The three-step branch in Table 1 indicates the primary branch used by stars with core temperatures less than about 15 million Kelvin. Researchers noted that since the third step of the chain results in the creation of one He nuclei, the first and second steps must have each happened twice. The chain reaction ends with the release of the helium produced and the hydrogen that started the reaction, thus allowing the reaction to take place again to produce more energy.

Table 1

Step	Reaction	Energy Released	Time Scale
1	$^1_1H + ^1_1H \rightarrow ^2_1D + e^+ + \nu$	1.441 MeV	14 billion years
2	$^2_1D + ^1_1H \rightarrow ^3_2He + \gamma$	5.494 MeV	6 seconds
3	$^3_2He + ^3_2He \rightarrow ^4_2He + ^1_1H + ^1_1H$	12.859 MeV	1 million years

Study 2: The Carbon Cycle

In stars where the core temperature is greater than about 15 million Kelvin, the carbon cycle chain is used to create energy. Here, hydrogen is converted into helium through a cycle involving carbon, nitrogen, and oxygen. Like the proton-proton chain, the carbon cycle allows the thermonuclear reaction to be repeated because as the last step indicates, helium is formed and released, and the carbon nuclei is left to interact with hydrogen and start the process again.

Table 2

Step	Reaction	Energy Released	Time Scale
1	${}^{12}_{6}C + {}_{1}H \rightarrow {}^{13}_{7}N + \gamma$	1.943 MeV	13 million years
2	${}^{13}_{7}N \rightarrow {}^{13}_{6}C + e^{+} + \gamma$	2.221 MeV	7 minutes
3	${}^{13}_{6}C + {}^{1}_{1}H \rightarrow {}^{14}_{7}N + \gamma$	7.551 MeV	2.7 million years
4	${}^{14}_{7}N + {}^{1}_{1}H \rightarrow {}^{15}_{8}O + \gamma$	7.297 MeV	320 million years
5	${}^{15}_{8}O \rightarrow {}^{15}_{7}N + {}^{12}_{6}e^{+} + {}^{4}_{2}H$	2.753 MeV	82 seconds
6	${}^{15}_{7}N + {}^{1}_{1}H \rightarrow {}^{12}_{6}C + {}^{4}_{2}H$	4.966 MeV	110,000 years

35. According to the information presented in Table 1, how many hydrogen nuclei must be present to initiate a reaction to produce the helium nuclei in the third step?

A. two

B. three

C. four

D. six

36. Based on the information provided in both studies, it can be concluded that:

F. stars with the highest core temperatures produce the most energy in the final reaction.

G. stars with the lowest core temperatures produce the most energy in the final reaction.

H. stars with the highest core temperature produce energy in the fewest steps.

J. stars with the lowest core temperatures produce energy in the most steps.

37. According to Table 2, when 13 6 carbon reacts with hydrogen, which two reaction products are produced?

A. 14 7 Nitrogen and gamma ray photons

B. 13 7 Nitrogen and gamma ray photons

C. 14 7 Nitrogen and neutrinos

D. 14 7 Nitrogen and neutrinos

38. In a single step, hydrogen produces the most energy when it reacts with which element?

F. Carbon

G. Oxygen

H. Nitrogen

J. Hydrogen

39. The total energy produced by the method used by stars with core temperatures less than 15 million Kelvin is approximately:

A. 20 MeV

B. 27 MeV

C. 25 MeV

D. 23 MeV

40. The researchers are trying to determine if the release of neutrinos affects the time scale of the reaction following its release. Based on the information presented, can the researchers make a determination?

F. No, because although the neutrino was released in the first step of the proton-proton chain and the reaction time in step 2 increased, there is not enough data to show that the neutrino caused it. The e^+ could have caused the increase in reaction time.

G. No, because although the neutrino was released in the first four steps of the carbon cycle, the e^+ seems to be the reason the reaction time increased.

H. Yes, because when the neutrino was released in the first step of the proton-proton chain, the time scale of step 2 was only 6 seconds, which indicates that the neutrinos caused the reaction time to increase.

J. Yes, but only when the neutrino is paired with the e^+ as is evidenced by the increasing of the reaction times in the carbon cycle.

END OF TEST 4
STOP! DO NOT TURN THE PAGE UNTIL TOLD TO DO SO.
DO NOT RETURN TO A PREVIOUS TEST.

Practice Test
Enhanced ACT Writing

DIRECTIONS: This is a test of your writing skills. You will have forty (40) minutes to read the prompt, plan your response, and write an essay in English. Before you begin working, read all material in the test booklet carefully to understand exactly what you are being asked to do.

During the actual ACT test, you will write your essay on the lined pages in the **answer document** provided. Your writing on those pages will be scored. You may use the unlined pages and the back cover in the test booklet to plan your essay. Your work on these pages will not be scored.

Your essay will be evaluated based on the evidence it provides of your ability to:

- Analyze and evaluate multiple perspectives on a complex issue
- State and develop your own perspective on the issue
- Explain and support your ideas with logical reasoning and detailed examples
- Clearly and logically organize your ideas in an essay
- Effectively communicate your ideas in standard written English

Lay your pencil down immediately when time is called.

ACT Writing Practice Prompt

Genetic engineering of food is the process of changing the DNA of plants or animals. It is an old agricultural practice carried on by farmers since early historical times, but recently it has been improved by technology. Many foods consumed today are either genetically modified (GM) whole foods, or contain ingredients derived from gene modification technology. Despite the potential benefits of genetically engineered foods such as fighting disease, enhancing flavor, resisting pests, and improving nutrition, the technology is surrounded by controversy. Organic farmers, environmentalists, concerned scientists, and food advocacy groups criticize the practice, fearing decreased nutritional quality, potential toxicity, and possible antibiotic resistance from these foods. As the usage of genetic modification increases, it is worth examining the potential consequences and rewards of changing DNA.

GO ON TO THE NEXT PAGE.

Perspective One

Genetic engineering will negatively impact humanity, because this kind of technology cannot be controlled. Crops and livestock are currently modified, but in the future, no one will be able to stop scientists from using this technology to modify human beings.

Perspective Two

Genetic engineering is an answer to a worldwide food crisis. The population of the earth continues to multiply and there is simply too much starvation to criticize the means to feed hungry people. If GM foods can provide nutrition to millions who would do without otherwise, it's important to use them.

Perspective Three

Genetically modified foods may curb short-term hunger, but have unknown lasting side effects on humans. Since DNA from GM plants can be transferred into humans who eat these foods, the actual DNA of humanity can be altered moving forward and that is a terrifying prospect.

Essay Task

Write a unified, coherent essay in which you evaluate multiple perspectives on the question of weighing the potential benefits versus consequences of genetic modification. In your essay, be sure to:

- Analyze and evaluate the perspectives given
- State and develop your own perspective on the issue
- Explain the relationship between the perspective and those given

Your perspective may be in full agreement with any of the others, in partial agreement, or wholly different. Whatever the case, support your ideas with logical reasoning and detailed, persuasive examples.

Planning Your Essay

Your work on the prewriting pages will not be scored.

Use the space below to generate ideas and plan your essay. You may wish to consider the following as you think critically about the task:

Strengths and weaknesses of the three given perspectives

- What insights do they offer, and what do they fail to consider?
- Why might they be persuasive to others, or why might they fail to persuade?

Your own knowledge, experience, and values

- What is your perspective on the issue, and what are its strengths and weaknesses?
- How will you support your perspective in your essay?

END OF TEST
STOP! DO NOT TURN THE PAGE.
DO NOT RETURN TO A PREVIOUS TEST.

Practice Test Answer Keys and Explanations

English Answer Key

#	Answer	English Skills Tested
1	B	**Grammar:** Misplaced modifiers
2	F	**Punctuation:** Commas
3	C	**Punctuation:** Colons
4	H	**Strategy:** Relevance
5	A	**Organization:** Transitions
6	J	**Style:** Redundancy
7	C	**Sentence Structure:** Parallelism
8	G	**Style:** Ambiguity
9	A	**Strategy:** Relevance
10	G	**Sentence Structure:** Comma splices
11	D	**Sentence Structure:** Fragments
12	H	**Grammar:** SV agreement
13	B	**Sentence Structure:** Run-ons
14	F	**Organization:** Passage
15	C	**Organization:** Paragraphs
16	J	**Grammar:** Idiomatic usage
17	D	**Organization:** Sentence
18	H	**Strategy:** Relevance
19	B	**Punctuation:** Semicolon
20	F	**Style:** Consistency
21	D	**Style:** Redundancy
22	H	**Sentence Structure:** Parallelism
23	D	**Sentence Structure:** Fragments
24	H	**Organization:** Misplaced modifiers

#	Answer	English Skills Tested
25	C	**Grammar:** Superlative adverbs
26	G	**Grammar:** Verb tense
27	B	**Punctuation:** Dashes
28	F	**Sentence Structure:** Correct
29	B	**Style:** Tone
30	G	**Strategy:** Main Idea
31	C	**Strategy:** Deleting elements
32	F	**Grammar:** PA agreement
33	B	**Punctuation:** Apostrophes
34	F	**Sentence Structure:** Comma splice
35	B	**Style:** Tone
36	H	**Grammar:** Comparative adjectives
37	D	**Style:** Ambiguity
38	H	**Punctuation:** Semicolons
39	A	**Organization:** Transitions
40	J	**Sentence Structure:** Run-ons
41	B	**Sentence Structure:** Run-ons
42	J	**Organization:** Paragraph
43	C	**Sentence Structure:** Parallelism
44	J	**Strategy:** Author's Purpose
45	C	**Strategy:** Adding elements
46	F	**Grammar:** Adverb usage
47	A	**Sentence Structure:** Correct in passage
48	G	**Sentence Structure:** Run-ons
49	C	**Punctuation:** Apostrophes
50	F	**Strategy:** Deleting elements

#	Answer	English Skills Tested
51	B	**Style:** Vivid Language
52	J	**Punctuation:** Commas
53	B	**Grammar:** Verb Tense
54	H	**Strategy:** Adding elements
55	C	**Style:** Word Choice
56	J	**Sentence Structure:** Parallelism
57	C	**Style:** Ambiguity
58	J	**Sentence Structure:** Comma splices
59	B	**Organization:** Passage
60	G	**Organization:** Paragraph
61	D	**Punctuation:** Dashes
62	H	**Style:** Modifiers
63	D	**Organization:** Transitions
64	J	**Sentence Structure:** Fragments
65	A	**Strategy:** Adding Elements
66	H	**Grammar:** PA Agreement
67	B	**Style:** Tone
68	G	**Style:** Wordiness
69	B	**Grammar:** Comparative Adjectives
70	F	**Punctuation:** Colons
71	D	**Sentence Structure:** Run-Ons
72	J	**Grammar:** Misplaced Modifiers
73	C	**Organization:** Paragraphs
74	F	**Strategy:** Deleting Elements
75	C	**Strategy:** Author's Purpose

English Practice Test
Detailed Explanations of Answers

Passage I: Vincent van Gogh: Mad, Genius, or Both?

1. **B** The adverb *almost* is modifying the adjective *exactly*, and since modifiers must stalk their victims, it's currently too far away. Keeping the word where it is makes the sentence ludicrous; moving it after the words *exactly* or *years* makes the sentence awkward.

2. **F** The only other tempting choice was H, if you do the Comma Pause test. The name *Theo* can be yanked right out of the sentence, though, so it needs commas around it to tell the reader that it's extra information.

3. **C** Remember, colons must separate equal ideas and the statement in front must be able to stand alone. Choice B creates a semicolon error; Choice D creates a comma splice sentence; Choice A makes a fatal colon error.

4. **H** This should definitely stay in because it demonstrates how he was able to get help. Putting it anywhere else makes the paragraph illogical.

5. **A** Because the sentence makes a comparison between his works and questions, it needs to be clearly organized. B and C cause new errors with the verb, and Choice D is clunky.

6. **J** The underlined portion repeats the same information, so it needs to be removed altogether.

7. **C** The choice that makes each item in the series balanced the most is Choice C.

8. **G** All three choices besides G put an ambiguous pronoun reference in the second part of the sentence: *who*. We don't know who the *who* is referring to in those choices.

9. **A** Choices B, C, and D are all incorrect because the statements are false.

10. **G** As is, the sentence is a comma splice. To fix it, you can either change the sentence to a conjunction with a comma like Choice G, or add a semicolon or end mark in its place. Choice J is incorrect because it uses a semicolon with a coordinating conjunction, which is a semicolon no-no.

11. **D** Choices A, B, and C are all sentence fragments.

12. **H** The subject *crop* is singular, so the singular verb *has* must be used. Choice J is incorrect because it creates a comma error.

13. **B** This is a run-on in the text. Choice B fixes it with a semicolon, Choice D creates a comma splice, and Choice C incorrectly uses a semicolon.

14. **F** A sentence that joins the conclusion to the introduction must address info from both paragraphs. Choice F fails to talk about his impairments mentioned in the conclusion.

15. **C** The first sentences in paragraphs 2 and 3 offer the clues for placement. Paragraph 3 starts with a sentence about van Gogh's death, which naturally follows info from paragraph 1. Paragraph 2 starts with a sentence about van Gogh's works, which naturally follows info from paragraph 3. If you switch the paragraphs, the passage is more logical.

Passage II: Getting Educated

16. **J** The correct idiom is *based on*. Choice G adds unnecessary words, so that just leaves Choice J.

17. **D** The other choices make inappropriate usage of the prepositional phrase, *for certain,* rendering the sentences unclear.

18. **H** Both Choices F and G are not true, and Choice J offers a function that the sentence doesn't serve. Choice H is the best answer.

19. **B** Remember that semicolons must be placed between two independent clauses, so it's incorrect in context. Choice C forms a fragment and Choice D forms a comma splice.

20. **F** Here, you must pay close attention to the writer's phrasing—the tone. Of all of the choices, the sentence in context most closely resembles the sentences in the rest of the paragraph.

21. **D** Choices A, B, and C are redundant. The sentence already provides accurate and clear information, so any of these additions is unnecessary.

22. **H** If you played the "Name That Part of Speech" game show, you'd realize that Choice H is the only one that follows the pattern: a past-tense verb comes first. She brushed, brought, and settled.

23. **D** Choices A, B, and C are all fragments. Only Choice D fixes the fragment by getting rid of the adverb at the front.

24. **H** Keeping the *nearly* where it is insults the woman. Putting it anywhere else makes the sentence sound strange. Remember that modifiers need to be next to the word they are modifying. Here, *nearly* is modifying *singing.*

25. **C** The word *more* is only used when two things are being compared. Here, she wants to see music *the most* out of three things. Choice C is correct. Choosing another letter reduces the clarity of the sentence.

26. **G** Verbs have to agree in tense, meaning that when a past tense verb is used at the beginning, it more than likely will be repeated at the end. Here, the other choices offer different verb tenses, and for clarity and parallelism, the same tense should be used.

27. **B** When used alone, dashes have the same function as a colon—the words behind the dash need to be equal to the words in front of the dash, and the words in front of the dash need to be able to stand alone. Choice C repeats the error of inequality, and Choice D adds a new error: a misuse of a semicolon.

28. **F** It's correct in context. Choice G is a run-on, Choice H is a comma splice, and Choice J improperly uses the semicolon.

29. **B** Here, your ears are your best guide. The woman's language in the text is not as improper as the sentence in question. So Choice A is out. Choices C and D are too formal, whereas Choice B hits just the right mix of education and informality.

30. **G** Pay close attention to what the other choices are saying. If they add meaning to the text that isn't there, they are incorrect. All three offer ideas that are either too general or too specific to the text. Choices F and H are too general, and Choice J offers an opinion not expressed in the text.

Passage III: More Than Light Itself

31. **C** Here, the antecedent is *everyone*, which is singular. It requires the singular *his or her*, although we can all agree that you'd probably use the word *their* in spoken English.

32. **F** Although this phrase mentions weather, the rest of the essay never indicates that bioluminescence has anything to do with the weather, which gets rid of Choices G and H. If you completed this question second as part of the "tough" questions, you'd know that! J is obviously incorrect.

33. **B** Here, we need the possessive pronoun for firefly, so *its* is appropriate. *It's* is a contraction of *it is*. *Its'* is not a word, and *their*, Choice D, changes the pronoun to plural when it must be singular.

34. **F** This one is tricky, because you have to figure out which one is *not* acceptable. Choice F creates a comma splice sentence, but every other choice is structurally sound.

35. **B** Choice A is too formal, Choice C is inaccurate, and Choice D is too informal. Choice B maintains the casual tone the best.

36. **H** Here, the superlative form should have been used, which would make it *smallest,* which rules out Choice F. Choices G and J are never appropriate.

37. **D** This is a matter of an ambiguous pronoun reference. We're not sure if the pronoun *which* is referring back to atoms or the elements. To fix it, you could just avoid it altogether by putting in the word *and* to indicate that the interrupting material isn't being referred to at all.

38. **H** Remember that a semicolon must follow the same rules as an end mark, by joining independent clauses. Here, the second clause is not independent, so a better usage is a comma and the conjunction.

39. **A** This sentence must join the previous and following sentences together. Since the following sentence mentions the lower orbit in the comparative sense, we have to assume that *higher* is what it's being compared to.

40. **J** This is one of those NOT questions, which means you simply have to cross off the stuff that *does* work. Here, you're looking to form a correct sentence, so check each one by plugging in. Choice J changes the meaning of the sentences altogether, so it doesn't work.

41. **B** In the passage, the sentence is a run-on. So, Choice A is out. Choice C creates faulty meaning, and Choice D uses the semicolon improperly.

42. **J** The easiest way to figure this out is by underlining the topic of each sentence, and paying close attention to transitions. That way, you'll logically figure out which should come next.

43. **C** Choice B creates another error: subject verb agreement. Choice D leaves out some information (insects), so it has to go. Choice A is wrong because the sentence isn't parallel in context.

44. **J** Here, you'll greatly benefit from having read the entire passage. If you skimmed, you'll miss out on what the author was clearly trying to do, which is to inform you about something. Since Choice J says the author was trying to persuade you, it is wrong.

45. **C** Although Choices A and B indicate that the essay is missing a conclusion and it is, the reason for adding it is incorrect. That kind of a conclusion would neither tie anything together, nor would it keep the tone of the piece. Choice C indicates this.

Passage IV: Mabel's Churchyard

46. **F** This is one of those tricky adverbs. To turn the word *bad* into an adverb when you're not comparing it to anything, you need to use the word *badly.*

47. **A** Choices B and C improperly use the semicolon and colon. Choice D creates a sentence fragment, so the sentence is correct as written.

48. **G** It's a run-on in context, so Choice F is out. Choice H creates an unintended meaning, and Choice J uses a colon incorrectly.

49. **C** Even though the word *keys* has an "s" at the end, it is not possessive in this sentence. Choices A and B are out. Choice D changes the meaning of the sentence by adding a neutral pronoun.

50. **F** Choice G is half right, which makes it all the way wrong. Choices H and J are false, so that leaves F.

51. **B** As the sentence stands in context, it is not as vivid as some of the other choices, so it's out. Choice C is also not vivid, so it's out. Choice B maintains the tone better than Choice D, so it is correct.

52. **J** A comma rule: Put commas between two adjectives that you can switch the order of "It was a gray, wintry day = The day was gray and wintry." That gets rid of Choices G and H. Choice J is better than F because you don't need the comma in front of the prepositional phrase.

53. **B** The story is written in the past tense, so that needs to be maintained. The past tense of the word *feels* is *felt.*

54. **H** This sentence doesn't change our perceptions of Mabel or add any new information about the townspeople; this info was already stated in the previous sentence. Therefore, it's redundant. Choice H is correct.

55. **C** Choices A and D make the church sound more secure. Choice B makes the church sound scary. Choice C best indicates the size of the church by placing her in its shadow and having it *loom* above her.

56. **J** Here, you'll need to rely on the Name That Part of Speech Game Show. If you did, you'd see that the clauses in question call for a past tense verb followed by a prepositional phrase. Choice J keeps it parallel: *immune to the world, reserved within.* Choice H adds the word *very* in front of the prepositional phrase and Choice G adds a preposition followed by a gerund phrase.

57. **C** The problem is that pronoun *them* in the last part of the sentence. What did she put in the tin cross? Weeds? Surely not, but the reference is ambiguous. Choice C is the only one that clarifies this, and keeps the sentence the least bulky.

58. **J** In the passage, the sentence is a comma splice. Choice G uses a semicolon incorrectly, and Choice H changes the intended meaning.

59. **B** Because the sentence indicates where she's going—the churchyard—it should naturally go at the end of paragraph 2, because paragraph 3 discusses the churchyard.

60. **G** Here, deciding the spot to break apart the paragraphs is easy: we have to put her actions in the first paragraph, and the effects in the second. Sentence 3 provides a clear topic sentence for the effects, so the answer is G.

Passage V: Tony Hawk: Master Skateboarder

61. **D** Whenever there is one dash used to set off interruptive material, there has to be another. The only choice that even offers two is Choice D.

62. **H** The question here is, "Who was considered a pioneer in extreme sports?" Tony Hawk was, not Tony Hawk's determination. The answer is H.

63. **D** The words *but* and *yet* indicate something contradictory following, and the words *and as such* indicate an effect following a cause. The statement following is equal in weight, so Choice D is correct—*, and.*

64. **J** Although this is testing your transition knowledge, it is also testing your sentence structure knowledge. If you keep any of the transitions, your sentence is a fragment. Therefore, you need to OMIT those words to make it able to stand alone. Choice J is correct.

65. **A** Choice B makes Tony sound lazy. Choice C repeats information stated in the following sentence, and Choice D negates information in the following sentence. Choice A is the only one that meets all the criteria of the question.

66. **H** In the text, the antecedent (everyone) is plural, and the pronoun replacing it is singular (he or she). Wrong! However, answer Choice G offers a plural pronoun in the wrong case (objective rather than subjective) and Choice J offers a different case of the singular form. Choice H is perfect—it gets rid of the problem altogether and reduces the wordiness, too.

67. **B** The phrase in the text is too formal compared to the rest of the passage. Choice C is way too informal. Between Choice B and D, Choice B is slightly more appropriate, since the word *son* is used as opposed to the word *kid.*

68. **G** Although Choice J is succinct (i.e., not wordy), it changes the meaning of the text. The officials didn't just wonder; they talked about it. Choice G reflects that while reducing the wordiness.

69. **B** Only two people are compared: Tony and his father. Therefore, the word *more* should be used. Choice A is out. Choice C repeats the error and creates another one by adding unnecessary words. Choice D changes the pronoun, making it disagree with the antecedent, so Choice B is correct.

70. **F** The colon usage is correct in the text. You never put a colon or semicolon inside quotation marks, which gets rid of Choice G. Choice H and J create new errors: improper semicolon usage and leaving out a comma.

71. **D** This is a run-on in the text—two complete sentences are smooshed together with no punctuation. You could fix it with a semicolon, a period and capitalization, or a coordinating conjunction with a comma. The only appropriate fix is Choice D.

72. **J** Leaving the phrase where it is or putting it after the word *he* makes the sentence sound awkward. Adding it after the word *fell* makes the sentence clunky, too. Choice J is the best bet.

73. **C** Sentence 4 provides us with the best clue: "Although he no longer competes . . . " starts the sentence. Sentence 2 ends with him giving up competition, so it needs to be placed after sentence 3 to make the most sense.

74. **F** This sentence says nothing about talent, his rise to fame, nor does it distract us in any way. It's a pivotal sentence about how he got his start. Choice F is correct.

75. **C** Choice A is incorrect because it's not true. Choice B is incorrect because that would require a longer explanation, and the question asked that it be "brief." Choice D is incorrect because the passage never gives detailed info about Tony Hawk's legendary status, so Choice C is the clear answer.

Mathematics Answer Key

#	Answer	Math Skills Tested
1	B	Fraction Operations
2	H	Algebraic Substitution
3	A	Distinguishing Mean and Median
4	J	Finding a Discounted Price
5	A	Solving a Quadratic Equation
6	H	Using a Ratio
7	E	Probability
8	K	Variable Expressions
9	D	Computing Averages
10	F	Exponent Properties
11	C	Vertical Angles and Angle Properties
12	K	Algebraic Ratios
13	A	Basic Operations with Integers
14	F	Absolute Value
15	C	Square Root Operations
16	J	Transversal Angles
17	D	Linear Equations in One Variable
18	F	Function Transformation
19	E	Area of a Figure
20	H	Absolute Value Equation

#	Answer	Math Skills Tested
21	B	Finding Factors
22	G	Trapezoid Properties
23	A	Exponent Properties
24	G	Complimentary Angles
25	E	Circle Properties
26	G	Square Root Approximation
27	C	Systems of Equations
28	H	Percent Increase
29	A	Scientific Notation
30	J	Circles
31	A	Computing Percent
32	K	Area and Perimeter
33	D	Square Root Properties
34	H	Roots of Polynomials
35	B	Graphs of Functions
36	H	Finding Ratio
37	C	Systems of Inequalities
38	K	Probability and Independence
39	E	Volume of a Cylinder
40	J	Complex Numbers
41	E	Rational Number Sense
42	J	Exponential Growth

(continued)

#	Answer	Math Skills Tested
43	B	Ordering Numbers by Value
44	G	Algebraic Substitution
45	B	Probabilities and Percent
46	H	Ratios
47	D	Midpoint
48	H	Zeros of a Linear Function
49	B	Parallelogram Properties
50	K	Inverse Functions
51	E	Perimeter of a Figure
52	J	Recognizing an Absolute Value Function
53	E	Finding the Median
54	H	Quadratic Inequalities
55	E	Distance
56	J	Probability
57	C	Finding Mean
58	F	Applying Sine
59	D	The Addition Rule
60	J	Absolute Value Inequalities

Mathematics Practice Test
Detailed Explanations of Answers

1. **B** First, rewrite so that each fraction of the numerator and denominator of this complex fraction has a lowest common denominator. For the numerator, rewrite it so that each fraction is represented in ninths and remove the parentheses. Then $\frac{2}{3}+\frac{5}{9} - \frac{8}{9}-\frac{2}{3} = \frac{6}{9}+\frac{5}{9}-\frac{8}{9}+\frac{6}{9}=\frac{9}{9}=1$. For the denominator, $\frac{1}{2}+\frac{1}{4}=\frac{2}{4}+\frac{1}{4}=\frac{3}{4}$.
Finally, $1\div\frac{3}{4}=\frac{1}{1}\times\frac{4}{3}=\frac{4}{3}$.

2. **H** Substitute two and negative five in for x and y, respectively. Then you get the expression $3(-5)^2 + 2(-5) - 2 = 3\,(25) - 10 - 2 = 75 - 10 - 2 = 63$.

3. **A** The median is between 7 and 9 which is 8. The mean is also 8. So the difference between the two is $8 - 8 = 0$.

4. **J** Marissa's game is 15% off of the original price. So to find the amount of the discount, it will be $40 \times 0.15 = 6$. Then the discounted price is $40 - 6 = 34$

5. **A** This trinomial is factorable, so start with that: $x^2 + 3x - 40 = (x + 8)(x - 5)$. Setting each factor equal to zero, you get $x = -8, 5$. The only answer of those provided is -8.

6. **H** If the ratio of dogs to cats is 5:4, then there are 5 dogs for every 9 cats and dogs. Now set up a fraction and let the total number of dogs be x: $\frac{5}{9}=\frac{x}{27} \rightarrow 5\times\frac{27}{9}=x \rightarrow 15=x$.

7. **E** With these kind of probabilities, you just multiply the amount of ways together. So you need sauce × mix-in × mix-in × ice cream flavor. That's $3 \times 7 \times 7 \times 4 = 588$.

8. **K** If x is your amount of apples, and y is your amount of oranges, then you need to multiply the respective weight and amount together and then add them up to get the total weight. So the weight of an apple times the amount of apples plus the weight of an orange times the amount of oranges is $5.25x + 10y$.

9. **D** To find the number of skips, set up the average like you already know the answer, just using x for the last skip. Then you get $\frac{2+7+5+x}{4} = 5 \rightarrow 2 + 7 + 5 + x = 20 \rightarrow 14 + x = 20 \rightarrow x = 6$. So he has to skip the rock 6 times to give him an average of 5.

10. **F** The whole numbers get multiplied while the exponents get added (as long as they are attached to a respective base). So $3 \times 4 \times 2 = 24$, and adding up the exponents on the *a*'s and *b*'s separately, you get $24a^6b^7$.

11. **C** We are looking for the measure of angle *MOI*, which can be split up into *MON* and *NOI*. Angle *NOI* is equal to *KOL* since they are vertical angles, so $NOI = 40°$. Note that the angles *MON* and *NOJ* are supplementary. So $NOJ + MON = 180°$; therefore, $100° + MON = 180°$ and $MON = 80°$. So $MOI = MON + NOI = 80° + 40° = 120°$

12. **K** We can solve this one by setting up a ratio and isolating *x*. $\frac{5}{3} = \frac{x}{3+d} \rightarrow x = \frac{15+5d}{2} = 5 + \frac{5d}{3}$.

13. **A** You just have to remember PEMDAS to be successful here.

$$(3-4)^2 + 2 - \frac{15}{3} = (-1)^2 + 2 - \frac{15}{3} = 1 + 2 - \frac{15}{3} = 1 + 2 - 5 = -2.$$

14. **F** $|-3+1| = |-2| = 2$ and $|-3-1| = |-4| = 4$. Then $2 < 4$.

15. **C** With square roots, just remember to factor, then circle and pull out one of any two repeating numbers. $\sqrt{40} = \sqrt{2\times2\times2\times5} = 2\sqrt{2\times5} = 2\sqrt{10}$

16. **J** Using the transversal rule, $a = c = e = g$ and $b = d = f = h$. One choice has $a = h$ which is not true, and is our answer. Note that the sum of any two nonequal angles must be 180°, when two parallel lines are intersected by a transverse.

17. **D** For this problem, use algebraic properties to isolate *x*.

$$3(x+2) - 4 = -2x + 7 \rightarrow 3x + 6 - 4 = -2x + 7 \rightarrow 3x + 2 = -2x + 7 \rightarrow 5x = 5 \rightarrow x = 1.$$

18. **F** The secret to function translation is in knowing what is translated outside the function is your vertical movement and always does what you expect. What is translated within the function is your horizontal movement and does the opposite of what you expect. Also, to reflect over the *x*-axis, the function will be negative. So eliminating K, then we know it's moving to the right which means it's a horizontal movement, and therefore will be inside the function. That eliminates H and J. Now you have to remember that it doesn't behave as you expect. For that reason, you are looking for subtraction within the function to move right. Our choice is clear—F.

19. **E** The two rectangles cut the square into four equal shaded smaller squares. So all you have to do is find the length of one side, then square it and multiply it by four. The length of the large square is 8 and the side of the rectangle that cuts the square is 6, so $8 - 6 = 2$. Since there are two sides on either side of the rectangle, you need to divide it in half,

so $\frac{2}{2} = 1$. 1 is the length of the small shaded square. Now just square it and multiply it by 4: $4(1)^2 = 4(1) = 4$.

20. **H** First isolate the absolute value sign: $|2x + 6| - x = 12 \rightarrow |2x + 6| = 12 + x$. Now split it into two equations without the absolute value and making one of the equations the opposite of $12 + x$, which is $-12 - x$.

$$2x + 6 = 12 + x \rightarrow x = 6$$

$$2x + 6 = -12 - x \rightarrow 3x = -18 \rightarrow x = -6.$$

Finally, check both answers and since both work, your answer is –6, 6.

21. **B** $56 = 2 \times 2 \times 2 \times 7$. There are two prime numbers represented in this factorization: 2 and 7.

22. **G** To find the missing side length, just create a right triangle by subtracting the length of the bottom by the length of the top: $12 - 7 = 5$. Now use the height and the Pythagorean theorem to solve for the missing side: $5^2 + 10^2 = c^2 \rightarrow 125 = c^2 \rightarrow 11.2 \approx c$

23. **A** $\frac{32}{4} = 8$ in the numerator. Now remember that the division of exponents means you have to subtract them. So, you end up with $8x^{-4}y^0z^4 = \frac{8z^4}{x^4}$.

24. **G** Since the two smaller angles add to make the larger angle and the larger angle is 90°, then we can set up an equation.

$$\angle BAC + \angle BAD = 90° \rightarrow (x + 20)° + \angle BAD = 90° \rightarrow \angle BAD = (70 - x)°$$

25. **E** To solve, just replace r with $\frac{3r}{4}$ in the circumference expression. Then you get $2\pi \times \frac{3r}{4} = \frac{3}{2} \times \pi \times r$.

26. **G** $\sqrt{106}$ is about 10 and $\sqrt{27}$ is about 5. So $\frac{10}{5} = 2$.

27. **C** Multiply the bottom equation by –2 and add it to the top equation:

$$[-2x + 4y = 2] + [2x + 3y = 26] \rightarrow 7y = 28 \rightarrow y = 4.$$

Now substitute y and solve for x.

$$2x + 3(4) = 26 \rightarrow 2x + 12 = 26 \rightarrow 2x = 14 \rightarrow x = 7.$$

Now find $x + y$.

$$4 + 7 = 11.$$

28. **H** To find the increase, we need to multiply the percent times his current wage. $\$14.00 \times 0.08 = \$1.12$. Since that's his increase, now we need to add that to his current wage, so $\$14.00 + \$1.12 = \$15.12$.

29. **A** To convert from regular notation to scientific notation, you need to count how many times you need to move the decimal place to get to the first non-zero number to the left. In this case, you need to move the decimal 7 times. (And remember if no decimal is given, assume it is at the end of the number.)

30. **J** To write the equation of a circle, you need 3 things: the x coordinate of the center, the y coordinate of the center, and the radius length. We are given two of the three pieces, so now we just need to use a little logic to find the third. If the center of the circle is at (4, –3) and a point on the circle lies at (0, –3), then the radius is 4 units long. We know this because the y coordinate did not change, so we can just subtract the x-coordinate and we get 4. Now to put it in equation form, just remember to flip the sign of your center coordinates and to square your radius: $(x - 4)^2 + (y + 3)^2 = 16$.

31. **A** Part = Whole times Percent. So $2088 = 5800 \times x \rightarrow x = 0.36$ or 36%.

32. **K** Since the area of a rectangle is length times width, $x \times 9 = 54$, so $x = 6$. To find the perimeter, we have to add up all four sides of the rectangle. Since we know the sides now, it's a matter of doubling them and adding them up: $6 \times 2 + 9 \times 2 = 12 + 18 = 30$.

33. **D** Here, just use the square root rules of multiplication to simplify.

$$\sqrt{6} \cdot \sqrt{24} = \sqrt{6 \cdot 24} = \sqrt{144} = 12$$

34. **H** According to the fundamental theorem of algebra, the number of possible real roots is equal to the degree of the polynomial. This polynomial has degree 4, so there are 4 possible real roots.

35. **B** For the function to have two values for x that make $f(x) = 0$, the function would have to intersect the x-axis twice. There are 4 different types of functions represented here, (linear, quadratic, logarithmic, and exponential), and only one of them can cross the x-axis more than once, the quadratic function. B is our only one.

36. **H** Ratios are basically interchangeable with fractions, so to find the correct ratio, just divide out the GCF. The GCF of 32 and 20 is 4, so dividing both numbers by four gives us 32:20 = 8:5.

37. **C** The answer to a system is the region which makes both inequalities true. You could try plugging in points, but that would take a long time. If you look at each line, and the

shaded region, you will notice that the consistent feature of that region is that it is above both lines. So both equations would need a "greater than or equal to" sign and there is only one choice with that sign in both equations.

38. **K** Since we are told the draws are independent and random, the chances of her winning is the product of the probabilities of each draw. So $\frac{1}{3} \times \frac{1}{3} \times \frac{1}{3} \times \frac{1}{3} = \frac{1}{81}$. The probability of her winning is 1 in 81.

39. **E** All you have to do is plug your variables into the correct place. The radius is 4 and the height is 7. So $V = \pi 4^2(7) = 112\pi$

40. **J** Multiply the binomials just like you would if i was a regular variable.

$$(3 + 2i)\ (3 - 2i) = 9 - 6i + 6i - 4i^2 = 9 - 4i^2.$$

Now use the fact that $i^2 = -1$. Then $9 - 4(-1) = 9 + 4 = 13$.

41. **E** To find any number exactly between two numbers, we add them and divide by 2. So $\frac{1}{3} + \frac{1}{2} = \frac{2}{6} \times \frac{3}{6} = \frac{5}{6}$ and $\frac{5}{6} \div 2 = \frac{5}{12}$.

42. **J** To find the population after 20 minutes, just plug 20 in for t. Then $P = 1.2^{20} \approx 38$.

43. **B** The best thing to do is turn all numbers into decimals. Arrange them and then find the solution: $-3, 0.5, \sqrt{14}, -\sqrt{2}+10$.

44. **G** Since $3x - y = 9$, we can plug 9 in for $3x - y$ in the second expression. $2\sqrt{9} = 2 \times 3 = 6$

45. **B** Starting at 1,000 people, only 40% actually get letters, so 40% of 1,000 is 400 people who get letters. Then of those 400 people, only 80% serve, so 80% of 400 is 320. That means out of 1,000 people, based on the percentages given, an expected 320 people will serve jury duty.

46. **H** Through the transitive property, if $x{:}y$ is as $y{:}z$, then $x{:}z = \frac{x{:}y}{y{:}z} = \frac{\frac{4}{9}}{\frac{2}{9}} = \frac{4}{2}$.

47. **D** Here we need to use the midpoint formula and plug in everything we know. We know our (x_1, y_1) and our midpoint, but not our (x_2, y_2). So $\frac{2+x_2}{2} = -4 \rightarrow 2 + x_2 = -8 \rightarrow x_2 = -10$. There is only one solution with $x_2 = -10$. Note that $y_2 = 12$ because $\frac{8+12}{2} = 10$.

48. **H** A function intersects the x-axis where $y = 0$. So $0 = a + bx \rightarrow -a = bx \rightarrow x = -\frac{a}{b}$.

49. **B** Since the two angles are adjacent to each other, in a parallelogram, they are supplementary. So, $130° + \angle BCD = 180° \rightarrow \angle BCD = 50°$.

50. **K** In an inverse function, you switch the *x*'s and *y*'s and solve for *y*. So $x = y^2 - 8y + 16 \rightarrow x = (y-4)^2 \rightarrow \pm\sqrt{x} = y - 4 \rightarrow y = 4 \pm \sqrt{x}$.

51. **E** Since we do not know the length of the triangle made by $10 - x$ where x is the vertical length not included in the potential right triangles with hypotenuse 7, we cannot determine the length of the top side of the figure.

52. **J** Absolute value functions have the parent function $y = |x|$. Any function whose graph looks like a V (right-side up or upside down) will be absolute value. Check that Choice J is accurate. Two of the points that satisfy the graph are (–1, 0) and (2, –3). By substitution, we note that $0 = |-1-2| - 3$ and that $-3 = |2-2| - 3$.

53. **E** The median is the data point directly in the middle of any data. Since this is an even number of data, you have to find the average between the two middle data which are 21 and 24. The midpoint of those two data is 22.5, so our answer is E.

54. **H** This quadratic inequality is "less than" so it is associated with a bounded compound inequality. $x^2 - 4 < 0 \rightarrow x^2 < 4 \rightarrow x < 2$ and $x > -2$. This inequality can be simplified to $-2 < x < 2$.

55. **E** First use the distance formula to find out how many blocks apart the two taxis will be.

$$\sqrt{(-2-7)^2 + (-3-2)^2} = \sqrt{81+25} = \sqrt{106}$$

Now, if each block is 50 feet, then the total distance is $50\sqrt{106}$ feet.

56. **J** Since there are 5 extra candy bars, and any one of those 5 will make you a winner, the probability is $\frac{\text{favorable outcomes}}{\text{total sample space}} = \frac{\text{winning candy bars}}{\text{all candy bars}} = \frac{5}{1{,}255}$.

57. **C** The mean is found by adding up all of the values and dividing by the number of values. So $\frac{410 + 440 + 450 + 500 + 470}{5} = \frac{2270}{5} = 454$.

58. **F** Sine is always the opposite over the hypotenuse and in this problem, that's exactly what the problem gives you. So $\sin\theta = \frac{h}{b}$.

59. **D** Since 17 are involved in athletics and 12 are involved in the play, we can't be exactly sure how many cross over. But we know there are 24 in the class, so there aren't any more students than that. If we add 17 and 12, we get 29 which is more students than there are in the class. So at least 5 students have to be involved in both activities.

60. **J** First isolate the absolute value. Now $|2x - 5| < -11$. Now recognize that no value for x will make the absolute value less than -11. Therefore, there are no real solutions.

Reading Answer Key

Passage I: Prose Fiction

#	Answer	Reading Skills Tested
1	C	Finding Supporting Details
2	F	Inference
3	A	Vocabulary in Context
4	G	Finding Supporting Details
5	D	Finding Supporting Details
6	H	Author's Purpose
7	B	Author's Purpose
8	G	Finding Supporting Details
9	D	Vocabulary in Context
10	H	Author's Purpose

Passage II: Social Science

#	Answer	Reading Skills Tested
11	D	Main Idea
12	F	Finding Supporting Details
13	C	Finding Supporting Details
14	J	Author's Purpose
15	C	Drawing Conclusions
16	F	Author's Purpose
17	C	Inference
18	J	Finding Supporting Details
19	B	Author's Tone
20	F	Inference

Passage III: Humanities

#	Answer	Reading Skills Tested
21	D	Inference
22	G	Finding Supporting Details
23	C	Vocabulary in Context
24	F	Author's Purpose
25	D	Inference
26	F	Inference
27	B	Narrator's Purpose
28	J	Finding Supporting Details
29	A	Author's Purpose
30	H	Finding Supporting Details

Passage IV: Natural Science

#	Answer	Reading Skills Tested
31	B	Main Idea
32	H	Finding Supporting Details
33	B	Inference
34	G	Author's Purpose
35	A	Finding Supporting Details
36	H	Author's Tone
37	C	Inference
38	F	Finding Supporting Details
39	C	Finding Supporting Details
40	J	Finding Supporting Details

Reading Practice Test

Detailed Explanations of Answers

Passage I: Prose Fiction

1. **C** The narrator, the 10-year-old little girl, believes that the situation is *dire*, or dreadful, which gets rid of Choice B. She has little faith in her sisters' abilities to get work and imagines how disgraceful it would be if they were tossed out of their home to beg on the streets. So, Choice C is the best answer here.

2. **F** Bessie's sisters already have a safe place to live, so Choice G is out. She is irritated with Mashah, which automatically tosses out Choice H. When left between Choice J and F, you have to ask yourself, "Which is her NUMBER ONE goal?" If her most important goal was enlisting the help of her sisters, she'd be begging them to join her on the hunt for work vs. spending the entire day searching herself. Choice F is the best answer.

3. **A** Since we are told that Mashah is beautiful, we can assume that the answer is either A or D. Melting seems to insinuate a slightly more intense feeling than just *admiring*, which is Choice D, so Choice A, *smitten*, which means "lovestruck," is the best choice.

4. **G** This is one of those Skip, Clock it and Search questions. Skip it and answer every other question. Then, clock your time; if you have less than a minute to go, move on to another passage and answer easier questions. If you have more, then look for the things she did in the day. Here, Mashah had done everything in the story except for wait in line to find work. Choice G is correct.

5. **D** Here, we're asked to infer the beliefs of the narrator, the 10-year-old girl who is worried about being tossed on the street. Most likely, she agrees that Fania is doing the right thing because she believes Bessie is doing the right thing. Choice D is most accurate.

6. **H** Here, Choice F is incorrect, because those lines never say anything about Mashah not believing she needs to work. The narrator is also not criticizing Mashah in any way here, so Choice G is out. Although Choice J may be accurate, these lines aren't demonstrating that notion, so Choice H is correct. The narrator values food like the other sisters, whereas Mashah values the compliments of men.

7. **B** Since dialogue is used, but not exclusively, Choice A is incorrect. Choice C is wrong because the passage doesn't focus on Mashah. Choice D is also incorrect because an essay doesn't typically involve dialogue, so Choice B is the best because it acknowledges the usage of a narrator and the story is definitely about a family's struggle to survive.

8. **G** In paragraphs 1 and 2, we are given details that show how *exhausted* Bessie is. In paragraph 1, her eyes are "far away and very tired." She then "dropped on the bench." In paragraph 2, the narrator feels the "dark hurt of her weary eyes." So, the best answer choice is Choice G.

9. **D** Every other answer choice addresses the family's current monetary status but D, which addresses the narrator's fears of what could happen in the future.

10. **H** Because these lines show girls scratching at each other's eyes and pushing and shoving until they have to be broken apart by police officers, the best choice is H—the bleakness of the family's situation is intensified by these lines.

Passage II: Social Science

11. **D** Choice A is too narrow—it only references part of Canton's mission. Choice B is too general; it could be a description of anything because it does not give specifics. Choice C is incorrect because she campaigned against the ratification of the 15th Amendment, which gave the vote to black men.

12. **F** The last paragraph says that the Bible had been used to hold her in the "divinely ordained sphere," or a metaphorical bubble that would keep her in her place.

13. **C** The author wanted to ensure that the reader understood that while Stanton and Anthony were both abolitionists, they would eschew that belief if it came into conflict with women's suffrage.

14. **J** Stanton's point was to demonstrate that she wasn't trying to reverse the common roles held by men (wearing men's clothes) and women (sitting at the head of a cradle).

15. **C** Here, you have to infer based on the evidence and your own experience. Most likely, Stanton would disapprove of a woman doing anything she didn't want to do because she fought so hard for women to have choices. She would likely respect a woman choosing not to vote, merely because it was her choice, but we can infer that she'd LEAST likely approve of a woman getting married if she didn't want to.

16. **F** Choice G is incorrect because the men she didn't call out the men in that section as having mistreated her personally. Choice H is incorrect because she spoke highly of both Webster and Clay in that passage and Choice J is incorrect because although the first half of the sentence is correct, she does not give any evidence that either Webster or Clay championed her cause.

17. **C** Stanton contrasts Webster with an "ignorant man digging in a ditch" in order to say that even the most ignorant of men have the right to vote, so why can't women? So we can safely assume that she believes him to be intelligent.

18. **J** Paragraph 2 from Canton's speech shows her protesting the social fate many women experience, and Choice J gives those examples listed in that paragraph.

19. **B** Passage A is a factual encounter of Stanton's life, which knocks out Choices C and A. It is neither dismissive of Stanton nor reflective, thinking back while musing. Choice D could possibly fit the tone, but the last half of the sentence does not describe Passage B, because it is not cautionary. Rather, Passage B is fervent—you can feel Stanton's passion and zeal in those words!

20. **F** In the passages, Stanton does not negotiate anything with anyone, so Choice G is out. Choice H is out because Stanton is anything but negligible since she helped to change American history. Choice J is also incorrect because she wasn't contradictory in her message. Hence, Choice F is the best answer.

Passage III: Humanities

21. **D** The first part of the passage indicates that she wants to break away from traditions. Paragraph 1 demonstrates the chasm that lies between the narrator, as a modern young woman, and her father, someone rooted in the past. Hence, Choice D is correct. She never wants to savor the traditions of her heritage, so she doesn't have to struggle against those feelings.

22. **G** Lines 85–87 sums this up quite nicely. Since the narrator's mother had passed away, she substituted books for her mother's guidance, since she didn't completely trust her father and stepmother.

23. **C** Out of context, people use the word *gross* as something disgusting, crass or vulgar. In this context, however, it doesn't make sense, so Choices A and B are out. The word *gross* can

also mean the *whole* of something, but again, not in this context, so Choice C—*blatant or obvious*—is right.

24. **F** No details are really used to contrast a "normal" girl with a modern one, so Choice G is out. The narrator's early years aren't really described, so that gets rid of Choice H. Choice J is completely incorrect because those two places are mentioned, but not compared, so that leaves Choice F, which is true. One source of friction for the narrator and her father is the grating of her modern beliefs against his traditional beliefs.

25. **D** It's obvious that Kev criticizes his stepmother, but since she is not shown to be fragile, Choice B is out. Choice A doesn't make sense with his insult, and Choice C, although accurate, doesn't fit the insult either. Choice F is correct. Someone would have to be incompetent or unskilled—to drown in a cup of water.

26. **F** Although her parents thought it was abnormal, she and the rest of the world would not think so, so Choice G is out. Although her actions were illicit or illegal, her *craving* was not, so Choice H is incorrect. Her craving was obviously not insurmountable or unachievable because she read as much as was possible, so the only answer that fits is F: insatiable or unable to be satisfied.

27. **B** If you imagine what a mouse would look like trying to hang a bell on a cat, you'd realize that its attempts would be useless or futile, which fits with Choice B.

28. **J** Choice F is spoken by the narrator in line 26. Choice G is a line not easily forgotten—line 82. Choice H is spoken in line 34, again by the narrator's father. Choice J is spoken by her stepmother in lines 43–45, so it's correct.

29. **A** Since learning an entire French dictionary by heart would have to take keen intelligence, and the narrator is not known as a braggart or liar, Choice A is correct. Choice D is possible, but it isn't the most likely reason the author included that information.

30. **H** Lines 71–79 review all of the places she must read in secret, Choice H is correct. If you chose Choice G, you were misled by the word "family." The narrator doesn't have to keep her aspirations a secret from her brother.

Passage IV: Natural Science

31. **B** Choice A says the opposite of what the author states. Choice B, the correct answer, is clearly explained in paragraph three. Choice C, which is the best distractor, says that privatized companies would access "unrecompensed" (or free) access to users, which negates the point of the question. Choice D just pulls information from the article that has nothing to do with private company control.

32. **H** The sixth paragraph, which contains the info about a WIPO-like organization, clearly explains that the cultural and political interests would be served if such were implemented, which gets rid of Choices F and G. Likewise, Choice J indicates that flexible *proactive* laws be instituted. *Reactive* laws are considered bad, which is why Choice H is NOT one of the ways this type of organization would best serve the public.

33. **B** The author indicates in lines 42–48 that NSI's usage of domain name registration should have been a public service, which tells you that the author believes it should have been free of charge. Choice A is wrong because the author doesn't believe the Internet should be *heavily* controlled by anyone. Choice C is wrong because the whole passage indicates that privatization is not smart, and Choice D doesn't even make sense.

34. **G** The entire essay demonstrates the benefits that a governmental regulatory agency would have on U.S. citizens like the protection of users against crime and the protection of the First Amendment.

35. **A** Here, the main idea is stated time and again throughout the essay. In the first paragraph, the author comes right out and says that "Government officials . . . should be the people responsible for the overall regulation of the Internet."

36. **H** NSI is the company that used domain-name registration as a "money-making venture." WIPO (Choice F) is the organization upon which an Internet regulation company could be based. ICANN (Choice G) is the group that took over control of some Internet regulation policy and DN (Choice J) stands for domain name.

37. **C** Choice C is correct because the paragraph shows how government regulation could work through a WIPO-like organization. Choice A is incorrect because WIPO is not being contrasted with a private company. Choice B is incorrect because WIPO does not currently regulate the Internet, and Choice D is incorrect because no other governmental agencies are mentioned in the paragraph.

38. **F** Throughout the essay, we can see that the author is firmly against privatized control. She states how NSI and ICANN are corrupt and offers a strategy for the government to safely and accurately regulate the Internet.

39. **C** Lines 55–63 shows that ICANN is acting of its own accord, just like NSI had, who was ICANN's predecessor. Choice A is incorrect because publishing records of fees is never mentioned. Choice B is partly correct, but fails to mention the private meetings. Choice D is never mentioned in the passage.

40. **J** *Risky* is the best choice! Choice F, *unpredictable*, is inaccurate—*hazardous* predicts a bad outcome. Choice G is off. *Crucial* means "important" or "necessary." Choice H is incorrect because although *hazardous* can be synonymous with *unsafe*, in this situation *risky* is a better choice because safety generally refers to a person's physical well-being. *Risky* is broader and includes more of what the author was referencing.

Science Reasoning Answer Key

Passage I: Data Representation

#	Answer
1	D
2	G
3	B
4	H
5	A

Passage II: Research Summaries

#	Answer
6	F
7	C
8	F
9	D
10	G
11	D

Passage III: Conflicting Viewpoints

#	Answer
12	F
13	A
14	G
15	A
16	J
17	C
18	H

No Subscores Given

Passage IV: Data Representation

#	Answer
19	D
20	G
21	C
22	F
23	D

Passage V: Research Summaries

#	Answer
24	H
25	C
26	F
27	D
28	F
29	B

Passage VI: Data Representation

#	Answer
30	J
31	B
32	G
33	C
34	F

Passage VII: Research Summaries

#	Answer
35	D
36	G
37	A
38	F
39	B
40	F

No Subscores Given

Science Reasoning Practice Test
Detailed Explanations of Answers

Passage I: Data Representation

1. **D** First, we look at Figure 2. The best possible height growth for each plant type is with Light B. A and C provide higher growth rates for two of the plants, but overall B is the better choice for all four. Figure 1 shows us that Light B achieves a high intensity in the 450–650 range.

2. **G** Looking at Table 1, we see that the highest change in height is achieved with continuous watering, so that knocks out Choices H and J. To figure out the lights, we have to look at the intro paragraph. A blue-green light has the highest intensity, which would be Light Bulb A. The blue-red light has the medium intensity, which would be Light Bulb B. Since we know that according to Figure 2, Meadow Rue gains the most height with Light Bulb B, our answer is the blue-red light, Choice G.

3. **B** According to the data in Table 1, it seems like the less you water Matilija Poppy, the more it grows, so Choice B, greater than 3.8, which is the change in height at twice a day, is the most reasonable guess.

4. **H** If we look at Figure 1, we see that Light Bulb A achieves the maximum intensity at 200 to about 350. According to Figure 2, Mariposa Lily grows best under Light Bulb A, which doesn't go near 350–700 wavelengths, so this is our answer.

5. **A** Looking at Figure 2, we see that Matilija Poppy's height changed the same amount of inches with Light Bulbs A and C. If we look at Figure 1, we see that Light Bulb A has the highest intensity and Light Bulb C has the lowest intensity. In the introduction, the blue-green light has the highest intensity, making Light A blue-green, and red-yellow has the least highest intensity, making Light C, red-yellow. Choice A is correct.

Passage II: Research Summaries

6. **F** When 0.001 of the solution was added to the 250 ul of intracellular fluid, the immunoglobin bonded to the HIV-1 strain. This did not happen in the other samples used in the experiment. Choice F is the correct answer.

7. **C** We know that if bonding occurred between the immunoglobin and HIV-1 (petri dishes 1–6), then HIV-1 infection was prevented because the HIV virus didn't bond with the T-cells. In Table 1, 500, 750 and 1000 uls of the intracellular fluid caused a bonding between the immunoglobin and HIV-1, so the infection was prevented. Since 500 is the least amount, it's the correct answer.

8. **F** The answer here lies in the introduction to the passage.

9. **D** In petri dish 7, we see that despite immunoglobin bonding with the HIV-2 strain, the HIV strain was still passed along at 50 ul, because bonding occurred between the HIV strain and the T cells. Logic tells us that this may have been an error in the records, since the results do not match the rest of the experiment.

10. **G** Petri dishes 13, 14, and 15 contain HIV-1, and 16, 17, and 18 contain HIV-2. Since we see that in dish 15 the addition of the sodium ion solution caused the immunoglobin to bond in the HIV-1 virus, but in no cases did it cause the immunoglobin to bond in HIV-2, the answer is G.

11. **D** Here, you simply have to look at the petri dishes listed to see if bonding occurred between the HIV strain and the T cells. The only one in the list where an HIV infection did NOT occur is petri dish 15.

Passage III: Conflicting Viewpoints

12. **F** Both of the theorists would agree that herbicide tolerance is a good thing. Theorist 1 believes that it's such a good thing, that foods should be genetically modified to achieve it. Theorist 2 believes it's a good thing, but only if weeds are not also made herbicide tolerant due to cross-breeding with herbicide tolerant plants used for food.

13. **A** We can get rid of C right away—the passage doesn't mention cost in relation to either method. Choice D is just silly. Obviously neither theorist believes that conventional breeding is negligent. Theorist 1 would dispute Choice B, because he mentions that genetic engineering is quick. That leaves Choice A.

14. **G** If the B.t. toxins kill larvae without regard to the nature of the insect this definitely weakens Theory 1, because it would mean that genes injected into GM foods are not controllable.

15. **A** Theory 2 states that since modifications to foods are hard to control, it would cross breed with nearby weeds and create weeds resistant to herbicides. Choice A is right!

16. **J** The easiest way to attack this question is by eliminating anything negative under Theory 2, because Theory 2 is in favor of conventional breeding. That gets rid of Choices F and G. Since Theory 1 never mentions that breeding is too costly, we're left with Choice J.

17. **C** Theory 2 talks about allergens, but Theory 1 does not.

18. **H** Choice F is ridiculous. Who gets to decide that 3% is a small percentage of the population? Again, Choice G runs into moral questions, and they are not talked about in the passage. Choice J is incorrect because the passage never talks about conventional breeding being able to avoid allergen creation, so Choice H is the best answer.

Passage IV: Data Representation

19. **D** Here, we have to look at both the color of the KOH strip and the oxygen consumed. Since the colors are beige and green in Table 2, we can look at Table 1 to see that *E coli* has to be one of the choices and either *Lactobacillus spp* 1×10^7 or 1×10^6 has to be the other. That helps us eliminate Choices A and C. If we subtract .32 (*E. coli*'s oxygen consumed) from .48 (total oxygen consumed in Trial 4) we're left with .16, which is the oxygen consumed by *Lactobacillus spp* 1×10^6.

20. **G** We can eliminate every choice besides G right away, because it's easy to see that the cells with the fastest onsets of respiration consumed the most oxygen when we look at Table 1.

21. **C** If the glass were to remain in place, we'd know that the kerosene drop would move to the right if oxygen were consumed, because the oxygen making its way into Flask B would pull it along. However, if Flask B had an alternate oxygen supply, which it would if a porous material such as cotton replaced the glass, we could expect the kerosene not to move at all.

22. **F** To figure this one out, we need to look at which cells caused the kerosene to move the farthest in Table 1. In 2 hours, *Dillococcus* moved the kerosene drop 11.2 mm, which was the most. Since Trials 1 and 2 contained red KOH strips which indicated the presence of *Dillococcus*, Choice F is the correct answer.

23. **D** Since initial respiration has to occur before the kerosene drop can move, it makes sense that the drop didn't move in .5 hours since respiration didn't begin until 48.22 seconds had gone by.

Passage V: Research Summaries

24. **H** Here, we simply need to find which beakers had a clear solution after 30 minutes. If we go through all three experiments, beakers 3, 6, and 7 remained clear after 30 minutes, indicating that no reaction had taken place.

25. **C** The only way to get to this answer is by a process of elimination. Go through each answer choice until you figure out which choice does not end up with a light yellow reaction.

26. **F** The student was not correct because when the solution boiled, the solution stayed clear showing that no reaction occurred. Choice F is the correct answer.

27. **D** Basically, this question is asking you to locate the darkest color in the tables and see which factors created this reaction. If you do another process of elimination, you'll see it's Choice D.

28. **F** Since the introduction tells us that the darker the color the greater the reaction, and the more drops of PTC (phenylthiourea) creates a darker solution, we know that Choice F must be correct.

29. **B** Experiment 2 reminds us of the pH values for acids and bases. Since Beaker 6 resulted in a clear solution, and the pH value was a 10, we know that was a basic pH.

Passage VI: Data Representation

30. **J** This one's easy! All we have to do is look at Figure 1. Since CA is white in 1900, we know that it had between 30–39″ of rain. Since it's the dark gray in 2000, we know it had between 0–29″ of rain, which means as the years went on, the amount of rain decreased, which is Choice J.

31. **B** If we look at Table 1 first, we'll see that overall, the temperature has increased from 1900 to 2000, which eliminates Choices C and D. Choice A is incorrect because it says that the rainfall decreased, but Figure 1 clearly shows an increase in rainfall. Choice B is right!

32. **G** We'll do a tiny bit of math here. We simply have to check out the numbers and figure out which was the most. Choice F only gives us an increase of 6.2°. Choice H gives us 6.9°. Choice J only gives us 4.9°, and the correct answer is Choice G with 7.1°.

33. **C** Here, we need to figure out which weather conditions the person would NOT experience. We need Figure 1 and Figure 2 for this question. Figure 1 tells us that we'll have rainfall somewhere in the 30's range, which fits with each choice. Choices A and B tell us that lows will be in the mid-70s, which fits with Figure 2. Choice D tells us that the high will be around 90, which also fits with Figure 2. That means Choice C's conditions won't be experienced, making it the correct choice.

34. **F** The explanation is given in the answer choice.

Passage VII: Research Summaries

35. **D** The key to answering this question is to remember that Steps 1 and 2 in Table 1 had to be completed TWICE according to the paragraph. So, when you count the Hydrogen (H) nuclei, you'll see that there are three present in Steps 1 and 2. Double those numbers to see how many are really needed, and you get Choice D—six.

36. **G** First, we have to figure out which stars have the lowest core temperatures. If we check out the paragraphs, we see that those that use the proton-proton chain have temps less than about 15 million Kelvin. The carbon cycle chain is greater than 15 million. Then, look at the tables. The last reaction in the proton-proton chain (Table 1) produced 12.859 MeV, and the last step produced 4.966 MeV in the carbon cycle, which means that stars with the lowest core temperatures produce more energy in the last step. Choice G.

37. **A** This just requires looking at the table and remembering what the symbols stand for. If you chose C or D, you got neutrinos and gamma ray photons mixed up.

38. **F** The best way to get at the right answer here is by circling the steps where hydrogen reacts with any element and narrowing down the choices. The highest energy produced when H reacted with another element was in step 3 of the carbon cycle, when it reacted with Carbon. Choice F is correct.

39. **B** This is a tricky question, because again, you have to remember that steps 1 and 2 were completed twice. Then, simply add up all the energy released and round to the nearest whole number. Choice B is correct.

40. **F** Although an increased time scale followed the release of a neutrino, we have no idea if it was causational. So, Choice F must be correct.

Writing Practice Test

Detailed Explanation of Answer Scoring

Sample Essay — Score of 6

The word "advancement" makes people think of growth. Positive change. Bright futures. But not all advancement is progressive. Technological advancement has been known to have unintentional negative consequences. People use their cell phones to connect with others in distant places, yet, while using this advancement, ignore the ones they love right in front of them. Technological advancements in food production have led to overcrowded, horrific living conditions for animals. And genetic modification of food is just such an advancement that has numerous, if unintentional, negative consequences for humanity and should be stopped immediately.

The terrible impact on human bodies alone should be enough to dissuade those in favor of genetically engineering plants and animals from these modifications. Since genetic engineering of plants and animals has begun, the nutritional content of modified food has actually decreased, which defeats the purpose of food creation in the first place. Even more disturbing, since DNA from genetically modified plants can be transferred into humans who eat these foods, the actual DNA of humanity can be altered, causing irreparable changes. Modifying the building blocks of people at a fundamental level can destroy the very thing people are trying to save. And the effects on human bodies is just the start.

Scientists who advocate for genetic modification of food have not considered the thorough and disturbing changes to the human psyche that can evolve from such a powerful tool, as well. Changing DNA in animals means that changing DNA in humans is not far behind. If this kind of modification becomes mainstream, any trait deemed unsatisfactory — hair color, eye color, skin color, intelligence level — could be altered, and that kind of power should never be given to humanity. Not only does it devalue people's differences at a very personal level, it gives scientists and geneticists risky, life-altering power. This could lead to an extreme paradigm shift from a world that tries to create conversations about acceptance to a world that promotes only certain traits as valuable. This technological "advancement" would take the human psyche backward in time instead of propelling it forward.

Human rights groups and farmers who grow these modified crops or raise these modified animals, state that the detriment to humanity notwithstanding, there is too much starvation in the world to ignore a readily available food source. And while it is true that people need to eat to thrive, proponents of genetic engineering are risking short-term gains for long-term losses. For example, since some of these genetically modified foods are pest-resistant, bees, who are vital to the food chain, are being killed off. The very act meant to feed people is actually risking a world-wide starvation epidemic. There is a simpler, healthier answer to the food crisis. The government, instead of supporting companies like Monsanto who profit from GM foods, could subsidize organic farmers so food production that comes without the risk of toxicity and allergy creation, is less costly and more efficient.

Advancements are usually desirable. People want advancements in school, in their future careers, and in their health. But sometimes, advancements come with inadvertently hefty price tags as in the case of genetically modified foods. These foods that have been changed on a molecular level create serious problems for the human body and the human psyche, issues that are too disturbing to ignore. If human rights activists and concerned citizens around the world are truly interested in saving others from starvation, they should consider utilizing a healthy approach like organic farming, one that minimizes unintentional negative consequences.

Scoring Explanation

Ideas, Analysis, Development, and Support

The issue along with the three perspectives on the given issue are critically analyzed. In body paragraph one, Perspective Three is agreed with and further explained, showing the discrepancy between what advocates for GM foods are trying to accomplish and what they actually achieve. In body paragraph two, Perspective One is thoughtfully expanded upon. The argument moves from just mentioning that people wouldn't be able to control this type of technology by claiming it would impact the actual psyche of those in power. In body paragraph three, Perspective Two is used as a counterpoint and is effectively dismissed. A better option is also introduced. The value of human life, starvation, and the costs associated with GM are discussed at length.

Organization

The essay is organized into a 5-paragraph Point-Point-Counterpoint (PPC) outline. The thesis of "genetic modification of food is just such an advancement that has numerous, if unintentional, negative consequences for humanity and should be stopped immediately" is supported throughout. The ideas progress from damage to the human body to damage to the human psyche, which increases the argument's success. Transitional use strengthens the ideas between and inside of paragraphs.

Language Use

Word choice is skillful and precise. Sentence structures are varied and clear. Tone is strategically formal to enhance the argument. No errors in grammar or usage are present, so the meaning of the essay is clear.

NOTES

NOTES

NOTES

NOTES

NOTES